The Golden Way

*The Hebrew Sonnet during
the Renaissance and the Baroque*

Medieval and Renaissance
Texts and Studies

Volume 304

The Golden Way

*The Hebrew Sonnet during
the Renaissance and the Baroque*

by
Dvora Bregman

Translated by
Ann Brener

ACMRS
(Arizona Center for Medieval and Renaissance Studies)
Tempe, Arizona
2006

© Copyright 2006
Arizona Board of Regents for Arizona State University

Library of Congress Cataloging-in-Publication Data

Bregman, Dvora.
 [Shevil ha-zahav. English]
 The golden way : the Hebrew sonnet during the Renaissance and the Baroque / Dvora Bregman ; translated by Ann Brener.
   p. cm. -- (Medieval and Renaissance texts and studies ; v. 304)
 Includes bibliographical references and index.
 ISBN-13: 978-0-86698-348-8 (alk. paper)
 ISBN-10: 0-86698-348-1 (alk. paper)
  1. Sonnets, Hebrew--History and criticism. I. Title. II. Series: Medieval & Renaissance Texts & Studies (Series) ; v. 304.

PJ5025.S55B7513 2006
892.4'104209--dc22

2005035248

∞
This book is made to last.
It is set in Adobe Caslon Pro,
smyth-sewn and printed on acid-free paper
to library specifications.
Printed in the United States of America

Contents

Preface	*vii*
Introduction	1

PART ONE
THE ANCIENT HEBREW SONNET

I. Forming the Corpus of Hebrew Sonnets	9
II. General Structure and Rhyme-Scheme	19
III. Meter	31
IV. Rhyme	43
V. Structures of Syntax and Rhetoric	51
VI. Developing the Subject	57
VII. Theme, Attitude, and Mood	69

PART TWO
THE REVIVED HEBREW SONNET

VIII. The Flowering of the Italian Sonnet	85
IX. The Revival of the Hebrew Sonnet: The Corpus	97
X. General Structure and Rhyme Scheme	119
XI. Meter	133
XII. Rhyme	147
XIII. Structures of Syntax and Rhetoric	161
XIV. Developing the Subject	169
XV. Subjects, Approaches, and Attitudes	193
XVI. Sonnet Sequences	249
XVII. The Hebrew Sonnet: Continuity and Change	267
Appendix: Table of Quantitative-Syllabic Meters	275
Bibliography	277
Index of Names	287
General Index	294

About the Cover:
Wedding Contract, Venice 1642,
courtesy of the Jewish National and University Library, Jerusalem.
The contract was witnessed by Leone da Modena,
one of the most important Hebrew sonneteers of the period.

Preface

The Golden Way is the translation of my Hebrew book *Shevil ha-Zahav: Ha-Sonet ha-ʿIvri bi-Tequfat ha-Renasans ve-ha-Baroq* (Jerusalem and Beer Sheva, 1985), which deals with the evolution of the Hebrew sonnet during the Renaissance and Baroque. *Shevil ha-Zahav* was followed by *Tzror Zehuvim: Sonetim ʿIvri'im bi-Tequfat ha-Renasans ve-ha-Baroq* (Jerusalem and Beer Sheva, 1997), an anthology of 423 Hebrew sonnets from the Renaissance and Baroque, gathered from a variety of sources including manuscripts and hard-to-find books in print. These sonnets form the corpus upon which the theory of *The Golden Way* is based.

In general, *The Golden Way* seeks to be a faithful translation of *Shevil ha-Zahav*. However, the two versions are not wholly identical. Some paragraphs that in the original contain details of a linguistic nature were abridged or summarized in the English edition. The same is true for the many quotations from sonnets, but in some cases when a sonnet was only mentioned in the original, the English version supplies the sonnet itself, in part or in full. The English version of course includes an updated bibliography, which required changes in the footnotes. Among these are references to *Tzror Zehuvim*, which replaces references to manuscripts, old printed books, and earlier editions that often present partial or incorrect texts, and to which *Shevil ha-Zahav* had necessarily to refer, as *Tzror Zehuvim* did not exist at the time of its writing. Also new to the English version are the references to my *Sharsheret ha-Zahav* (Tel Aviv, 2000) which deals with the Hebrew sonnet up to the present day, and did not exist when *Shevil ha-Zahav* was published. This book enables the English reader to gain a contemporary perspective of the Hebrew sonnets from the Renaissance and Baroque.

I would like to convey my gratitude to all those who helped with this edition. First of all is the translator, Dr. Ann Brener of Ben Gurion University, whose talent, knowledge, and patience are no doubt evident to any sensitive reader. Many thanks to the members of the Arizona State University Press: Prof. Robert Bjork, who accepted the book for publication; Mr. Roy Rukkila, Managing Editor; and Mr. Todd Halvorsen, Manager of Design and Production.

I wish also to thank all the libraries that permitted me to use their various collections: the Jewish Theological Seminary of Budapest, the Cambridge University Library, the Ferrara Jewish Community, the British Library, the Montefiore Collection in London, the New York Theological Seminary, and the Bodleian Library of Oxford.

I am grateful to to The Lucius N. Littauer Foundation for their generous support of the translation, Ben Gurion University of the Negev for its generous help with the typesetting, and lastly, Mr. Eran Tzelgov for his expertise in preparing and editing the final text for publication.

Introduction

1. A Discontinuous History?

> Thou art dear to me, how dear to me, sonetta, O golden poem
> Preserved since the Renaissance since days gone by
> Thy echoing melody was loved by Immanuel of Rome
> The noble few tended thee in Italy, thou didst not die

With these lines penned in the second decade of the twentieth century, poet Saul Tchernikhowsky begins his sonnet-on-the-sonnet in Hebrew.[1] Using the form of the poem he celebrates, Tchernikhowsky surveys the fascinating history of the Hebrew sonnet up to his own day. He begins with the thirty-eight poems composed by Immanuel of Rome before 1300, not long after the form was invented in Italian, and some two hundred years before it was absorbed into other languages. But, as Tchernikhowsky goes on to say, this impressive beginning of the Hebrew sonnet was followed not by general acclaim and further development, but by a period of stagnation that threatened its very existence.

Tchernikhowsky published his sonnet in 1920 at a time when there was little knowledge of Hebrew poetry in Italy. The "noble few" to whom Tchernikhowsky refers are the Hebrew poets who rescued the Hebrew sonnet from oblivion, in the seventeenth century at the earliest.[2] This "rescue" date was pushed back when M. D. Cassuto and H. Schirmann published several sonnets by Moses ben Joab Rieti and Joseph Tzarfati, which were apparently composed shortly after 1500. It also turns out that the "rescuers" were more numerous than Tchernikhowsky had realized. During the course of my research on the Hebrew sonnet, I found some eighty Hebrew sonnets from the sixteenth century, and more than three hundred from the seventeenth century; altogether the work of more than eighty different poets.[3] Undoubtedly, the extent of this corpus must have been even greater than that which has come down to our own time. But as things stand now, the only Hebrew sonnets from before 1500 are the thirty-eight sonnets of Immanuel of Rome. Thus in one important respect Tchernikhowsky's description still holds true today.

---

[1] S. Tchernikhowsky, *Maḥberet ha-Sonetot* (Berlin, 1923), 96.
[2] Tchernikhowsky, *Maḥberet ha-Sonetot*, 22–25.
[3] D. Bregman, "Ha-Sonet ha-ʿIvri ba-Meot Tet-Zayin – Yud-Zayin" (Ph.D diss., Hebrew University, 1986) and now eadem, *Shevil ha-Zahav: Ha-Sonet ha-ʿIvri bi-Tequfat ha-Renasans ve-ha-Baroq* (Jerusalem and Beer Sheva, 1995).

This situation raises questions about the real beginning of the sonnet in Hebrew.[4] The fact that we cannot trace a continuous line from the early corpus of Hebrew sonnets to the later corpus makes it necessary to question whether there was, in fact, any relationship between them. Perhaps there were two different attempts to absorb the sonnet form in Hebrew poetry: the first, which failed, and the second, which succeeded. If this be the case, Immanuel's sonnets were merely a passing fad in the history of Hebrew poetry. The real beginning of the Hebrew sonnet would then be not around 1300, but some two hundred years later. This would ostensibly make the history of the Hebrew sonnet similar to that of the Spanish. Sonnets were written in Spanish during the fifteenth century, but they remained in manuscript and did not inspire any followers. Because of this, their author, the Marques de Santillana, is not considered the father of the Spanish sonnet. Instead, credit goes to Juan Boscán and Garcilaso de la Vega, whose joint volume of sonnets was published posthumously in 1543, thereby ushering in the *Siglo de Oro*, the "Golden Age" of Spanish poetry.[5]

On the face of things, it seems reasonable to assume that the Hebrew sonnet originated around 1500, since it was during the sixteenth century that other languages began to absorb the form: in Spanish, as described above; in Portuguese by Luis de Camões; in French by Clément Marot, Mellin de Saint-Gelais, and others; in English by Thomas Wyatt and Henry, Earl of Surrey; in Dutch by Jan van der Noot; in German by Martin Opitz. Furthermore, it would also seem highly reasonable to assume that the Hebrew sonneteers of the sixteenth century had no need of the old Hebrew model. In all the other languages poets simply adopted the form from the Italian; why would Hebrew poets, who were actually living amongst the Italians and speaking their language, not do the same? Hebrew poets in Italy were familiar with Italian poetry. They composed poems and sonnets in Italian, translated Italian poems into Hebrew, and created a new body of Hebrew poetry and drama based on Italian models. The Hebrew sonnet had been neglected for two hundred years, and in the meantime the Italian sonnet underwent a number of changes and variations. In the sixteenth century the literary world was busy celebrating Petrarch, and poets by the score sought to imitate his sonnets. Why dredge up an old Hebrew model whose time had passed?

In order to clarify the apparently discontinuous history of the Hebrew sonnet, I devoted several years of research to this topic. I pored through the not inconsiderable corpus of Hebrew sonnets from the sixteenth and seventeenth centuries that gradually revealed itself to me, comparing it to the sonnets of Immanuel of Rome and other poems in Hebrew, as well as non-Hebrew poetry

---

[4] On this question, see D. Bregman, "The Emergence of the Hebrew Sonnet," *Prooftexts* 11 (1991): 231–39.

[5] See T. Navarro, *Mètrica Española* (Syracuse, 1956), 286; G. Brenan, *The Literature of the Spanish People from Roman Times to the Present* (New York, 1957), 94, 147–48.

from that period.[6] My investigations revealed a marvelous tapestry of closely-woven threads that begin with Immanuel's *Maḥbarot* and end with the Hebrew sonnet of the sixteenth and seventeenth centuries. It became clear to me that the early sonnets by Immanuel influenced not only Hebrew sonnets of the sixteenth and seventeenth centuries, but indeed the entire range of Hebrew poetry during this period, and, in some ways, even various schools of poetry up to our own day.

In the wake of these investigations, there can no longer be any doubt that the beginnings of the Hebrew sonnet indeed go back to Immanuel's day, and that the story of the Hebrew sonnet can be told in chronological fashion from his time on. It is a story which continues up to our own time and is still being written. The Hebrew sonnet is alive and well, undergoing perpetual change and renewal. But the most decisive phases in its formation came to an end towards the close of the seventeenth century. These phases are the topic of the present book.

2. The State of Research

The sonnet has been the subject of countless studies and discussions, from early treatises composed during the fourteenth century to various readings, surveys, and analyses written during our own time in various languages. The fifteen-page bibliography which Walter Mönch compiled in 1955[7] is constantly being updated and expanded.[8] This abundance, which makes it hard to pick and choose, has been of tremendous help to me. Hebrew poetry in Italy did not exist in a vacuum. During the centuries in question it closely adhered to its Italian counterpart in a number of ways, and developed an affinity with Spanish and Portuguese poetry, each of which was enjoying a "Golden Age" of its own and also influencing, and being influenced by, Italian poetry. The sonnet was often the link in this chain of mutual influences. For this reason, research on the Hebrew sonnet also depends on the study of its non-Hebrew counterpart and of non-Hebrew poetry during this period, especially Italian and Spanish.

The Hebrew sonnet also won admiration and attracted considerable attention in early Hebrew literary criticism and theory. But it has yet to be the subject of new and comprehensive research. The majority of the sonnets remained buried in manuscript and scattered in dusty old tomes until the appearance of Tzror

---

[6] Cf., for example, Bregman, "The Emergence of the Hebrew Sonnet"; "Le-Parashat ha-Hitqablut shel ha-Sonet ha-ʿIvri," *Tarbiz* 56 (1987): 109–23 and "Shitat Immanuel u-Meqomah be-Toldot ha-Metriqa ha-ʿIvrit," *Tarbiz* 58 (1989): 413–52.

[7] W. Mönch, *Das Sonet, Gestalt und Geschichte* (Heidelberg, 1955), 311–25.

[8] For a more updated bibliography, see J. Fuller, *The Sonnet* (London, 1972); A. Ruschioni, *Il sonetto italiano*, 2 vols. (Milan, 1985); and S. L. Berman, *The Sonnet over Time* (Chapel Hill and London, 1988).

Zehuvim.[9] A minority, published in more or less recent editions, was often printed with errors, without commentary, and sometimes even without vocalization. Under these circumstances it is hardly surprising that the story of the Hebrew sonnet remained largely unknown even to Hebrew speakers, not to mention those unfamiliar with the language. Mönch, who surveyed the history of the verse-form in world literature, has only five words for the Hebrew sonnet, which he mentions during his discussion of the Turkish parallel, noting that "Modern Hebrew also has sonnets." In a footnote he adds, "by Tchernikhowsky."

The breeding grounds for the Hebrew sonnet — Hebrew poetry in Italy and elsewhere during the Renaissance and Baroque — have attracted more than a few scholars and even famous poets, among them: Moshe David Cassuto, Hayyim (Jefim) Schirmann, Cecil Roth, Avigdor Shulvass, Mordechai Hak, Dov Jarden, Dan Pagis, Yonah David, Benjamin Hrushowsky, Shimon Zandbank, Hayyim Nachman Bialik, Saul Tchernikhowsky, Jacob Fichman, Leah Goldberg and Nathan Alterman. Their work has been enormously helpful. But this broad topic has yet to receive systematic research. Whole segments of Hebrew poetry in Italy remain unknown, while other fields necessary to the study of the Hebrew sonnet — such as Hebrew poetry in Holland, Turkey, the Balkans, and North Africa — are basically foreign territory.[10] In order to clarify various issues I had, then, to examine the relevant sources themselves, which I did to the extent that they were available. This book, therefore, more than it feeds on an extant body of scholarly literature, in everything related to its literary background, may hopefully nourish investigation into this background.

The claim heard from time to time, that to study the sonnet is essentially to study the period in which it flowered, is of course an exaggeration. But it is not altogether incorrect, especially concerning the period under discussion, in which the sonnet figured conspicuously in poetry and in society. These facts, which are a given in the study of the non-Hebrew sonnet, are just as true of the Hebrew sonnet of the fourteenth century and of the sixteenth and seventeenth centuries. The same can be said for the eighteenth and nineteenth centuries in Italy, and even for the fifteenth, from which not a single Hebrew sonnet has come down to us: the rejection of the sonnet tells us a good deal both about those who rejected the form, and those who chose to accept it.

---

[9] D. Bregman, *Tzror Zehuvim: Sonetim ʿIvri'im mi-Tequfat ha-Renasans ve-ha-Baroq* (Jerusalem and Beer Sheva, 1997).

[10] It is worthwhile to mention two volumes that have recently been published: B. Bar Tikvah, *Piyyutei Rabbi Yitzhaq ha-Seniri* (Ramat-Gan, 1998), on liturgical Hebrew poetry in Provence; and E. Hazan, *Tehilla le-David* (Ramat-Gan, 1999), on the same in Morocco.

Part One:

The Ancient Hebrew Sonnet

I. Forming the Corpus of Hebrew Sonnets

1. The Emergence of the Italian Sonnet

The sonnet-form was born in Italy. It first appeared in the third decade of the thirteenth century, when Italian poetry was still in its infancy. Writing in the "vulgar" (spoken) tongue came late to Italy, apparently because of the Italians' special bond with Latin, the language of their forefathers. The first sonnets were written in a combination of Italian and Provençal. They were composed after the initial flowering of poetry in the local dialect, during the course of a concerted effort led by King Frederick II of Sicily to encourage poetry in the vernacular. Between 1220–1250 the king, who was a poet in his own right, cultivated the poetic arts among the various jurists and officials who made up his court. In the surveys of Italian literature, these poets are known as the "Sicilians," since Sicily was the site of the royal capital, Palermo. But the royal court was in fact constantly on the move throughout Italy, and dialect aside, there is nothing particularly Sicilian about these poets.

The royal effort achieved its goal. In their leisure hours, these non-professional poets composed an impressive body of Italian poetry. Their poems — mostly love lyrics — were inspired by the Provençal troubadours, the French trouvères, and the German minnesingers in everything from metrics to metaphors and development of theme. Like their European counterparts they praised the beloved lady, submitted to her "tyranny," and despaired of her cruel indifference. They rehearsed tired clichés, but also showed signs of independence and innovation. Their most important innovation was the invention of the sonnet.

While there are different opinions concerning the origins of the sonnet-form, there does seem to be a scholarly consensus that basic elements of this form, which was created entirely on Italian soil, existed already in Provençal poetry. The first sonnets — nineteen in number — are attributed to Giacomo da Lentino, "the notary," the most prominent of the Sicilian poets.[1]

The Sicilian court dispersed with the death of the king in 1250. After this, poetic creativity in Italy centered primarily in Tuscany, where a large group of

---

[1] So called by Dante, *Purgatorio* xxiv, 55. On the Sicilian School, see for instance J. Usher in the *Cambridge History of Italian Literature*, ed. P. Brand and L. Pertile (Cambridge, MA, 1999), 9–17. Concerning the earliest Italian sonnets, see E.F. Langley, ed., *The Early Poetry of Giacomo Da Lentino* (Cambridge, 1915); E. H. Wilkins, *The Invention of the Sonnet* (Rome, 1959).

poets led by Guittone d'Arezzo created a new trend of poetry, hermetic and highly stylized, that combined formal elegance with linguistic and rhetorical virtuosity. The sonnet was the form most commonly used by poets of this new school. They developed increasingly sophisticated patterns for their sonnets, and filled them with the sounds and scenes of bustling urban life, newly flourishing with the active economic and social life of the Italian city-states.

The sonnet attained greater importance towards the end of the century when it became central to a third trend of poetry that revolted against Guittone and his friends to cultivate a "sweet new style" (*il dolce stil nuovo*). Among its poets we find a number of famous names: Guido Cavalcanti, Guido Guinizzelli, Cino da Pistoia (Petrarch's teacher),[2] and of course Dante Alighieri, in whose hands Italian poetry reached its apogee.[3] These poets learned from the "Sicilians" a poetic idiom that went back to the Provençal troubadours, but then "sweetened" it with motifs taken from Italian religious poetry; hence the name of this school.

Dante left a considerable corpus of sonnets, though in his *De Vulgari Eloquentia* it is the *canzone* which he exalts as the "most noble of forms."[4] The sonnet was apparently considered rather common, a well-loved simple poem. In fact, the word "sonetto" means "a small poem," and during this early period the name appears to have been applied rather indiscriminately to poems of different forms.[5] Indeed, the sonnet was not restricted to the more aristocratic spheres of poetry, for it penetrated popular and burlesque poetry as well. The poets who wrote this kind of poetry — Rustico di Filippo, Cecco Angiolieri, Folgore da San Gemignano, and many others — also composed sonnets.[6] During the course of the thirteenth century approximately one thousand sonnets were written in Italian.

2. The Earliest Hebrew Sonnets

Hebrew poetry absorbed the sonnet form towards the end of the thirteenth century in Italy. By this time Hebrew-Italian poetry could already boast of a long and glorious tradition that marked the beginning of Hebrew literature in

---

[2] See, for instance, *The Cambridge History of Italian Literature*, ed. Brand and Pertile, 19–27.

[3] See, for instance, *The Cambridge History of Italian Literature*, ed. Brand and Pertile, 39–69.

[4] *De Vulgari Eloquentia*, ed. and trans. S. Botterill (Cambridge, 1996), 184, para. 3, l. 25.

[5] L. Biadene, *Morfologia del sonetto nei secoli XIII-XIV* (Florence, 1997), 220–24.

[6] See M. Marti, *Cultura e stile nei poeti giocosi del tempo di* Dante Pisa, 1953, passim. See also the various entries in P. Bondanella and C. J. Bondanella, *Dictionary of Italian Literature* (Westport, 1979).

Europe, and was deeply embedded in Jewish traditions going back to the Bible. It was also already acquainted with the conventions of Hebrew poetics from Spain, thanks to Abraham ibn Ezra and his *Sefer Tzaḥut*, or "Book of Linguistic Purity" (Mantua, 1145). During this period we find a long list of amateur Hebrew poets in Italy: cantors, physicians, teachers, and so forth. Judging from the remains that have come down to us, these poets did not shy away from secular topics. Benjamin ben Abraham Min H'anavim of Rome satirized the flamboyant lifestyle of Jews in his own day in *Masa Gei Ḥizzayon* or "Valley of Vision."[7] He also wrote a didactic poem: *Sha'arei 'Etz Ḥayyim* or "The Gates to the Tree of Life."[8] Ahitub ben Isaac of Palermo composed a philosophical allegory called *Maḥberet ha-Tenne* or "The Book of the Basket."[9] Kalonymos ben Kalonymos of Provence, who lived at the beginning of the thirteenth century in Rome, composed, in addition to an ethical treatise, *Even Boḥan* or "Touchstone," a daring parody on the Talmud and its commentators, *Masekhet Purim*.[10] All of this is secular poetry. But most of these writers' poetry deals with liturgical subjects and themes,[11] and because of this Immanuel of Rome stands out in conspicuous fashion. It is in his *Maḥbarot* ("Notebooks"), and only there, that Hebrew sonnets from that period have survived down to our own day. As a professional poet Immanuel depended on the generosity of patrons, and his *Maḥbarot* are, for the most part, unabashedly secular in character. They display an exuberant variety of topics and literary forms, including highly erotic love poems and stories.

The influence of Italian literature is evident at every level of language, form, and content. This would seem to explain why, of all the Hebrew poets of his day, Immanuel was the only one who wrote sonnets. The writing of Hebrew sonnets required a high level of professional expertise. Though not restricted to a particular subject, the sonnet was a favored vehicle for love poetry from the beginning, and no such poetry has come down to us from the hands of Immanuel's fellow poets. In order for Hebrew to absorb the sonnet it required a rich soil of secular poetry open to outside influences. And apparently, this was available only in the work of Immanuel of Rome.

---

[7] First printed in Riva di Trento in 1560. This was reprinted by U. Nahon (Jerusalem, 1967) with an introduction in English.

[8] See *Qovetz 'al-Yad* 1–2 (1885) 71–74.

[9] See J. Schirmann, "Zur Geschichte der Hebräischen Poesie in Apulien und Sizilien," *Mitteilungen des Forschungsinstituts für Hebräische Dichtung* 1, Berlin (1933): 132–47.

[10] See I. Davidson, *Parody in Jewish Literature* (New York, 1966), chap. 2.

[11] See J. Schirmann, *Mivḥar ha-Shirah ha-'Ivrit be-Italia*, (Berlin, 1934), 85–182; S. Bernstein, *Mi-Shirei Yisrael be-Italia* (Jerusalem, 1939), Introduction; A. M. Habermann, *Toldot ha-Piyyut ve-ha-Shirah* (Ramat-Gan, 1972), 2: 31–42.

But Immanuel did not work in a vacuum. The *Maḥbarot* reveal a world of intense and secular poetic activity that went far beyond the fragments which have come down to us today. According to the *Maḥbarot*, Immanuel corresponded extensively with other Hebrew men of letters, and indeed conducted lively *tenzones*, "literary duels," from the Provençal word *tensó*, through an exchange of epistolary verse. In these *tenzones*, a poet issued a poetic "challenge" that would then be met and answered in the same rhyme and meter as the original poem. Immanuel describes one such "duel" in his *Maḥbarot*, after he is provoked by a young man acting as a messenger for another poet:

> Why stand there astonished? / Write the same way and your verse will be varnished / . . . Judah Siciliano sends the poem that you see / if it isn't enough, he'll send more to thee / Then the poems will show / who's the best poet: soon we will know![12]

Immanuel then explains that various troubles forced him to wait nearly two years before replying to his friend in due form, and adds that the delay brought him considerable shame. But another poetic challenge finds him on the offensive:

> Are you not afraid, you asleep in the bath / of the sword of my pen and my poetry's wrath? / Soon you will hear my poems' arrows hiss / Though my target's a hair, my poems never miss!

On this occasion he claims a decisive victory:

> And when I came towards him with my poems all arrayed / He gaped and stood still, staring amazed / And as I said to him: Let's have it out and see who's better / Write a poem in the form of this letter / He ran and took flight / and stayed out of sight . . .[13]

This *tenzone* continues for several more rounds.

Stories like these testify to the natural subject matter of the tenzone: friendship, praise, rebuke, boasting, and so on. Who were the poets composing these poems? Immanuel tells us about a few of them, sometimes indirectly. In this particular case, Immanuel notes that he initiated a poetic correspondence with the renowned Kalonymos ben Kalonymos during the latter's stay in Italy, and that the two then became friends. Kalonymos showed Immanuel some of his work ("though nothing with meters"), and Immanuel wrote a poem in his praise.[14] We

---

[12] Immanuel of Rome, *Maḥbarot Immanuel ha-Romi*, ed. D. Yarden (Jerusalem, 1957), 233–34.

[13] Immanuel, *Maḥbarot*, ed. Yarden, 153, 159.

[14] Immanuel, *Maḥbarot*, ed. Yarden, 424.

can assume that Immanuel was not the only one to take note of the distinguished translator during his sojourn in Italy, and that other poets also wrote panegyrics in his honor. Immanuel devoted an entire chapter to the praise of Judah Siciliano, informing us that he was a professional poet who "stayed with us for years, plying his pen for a fee / selling for cash his rhymes and poetry." Immanuel further notes that Siciliano wrote laments "capable of rousing the Leviathan."[15] Modesty is never one of Immanuel's strong points, but he does take his hat off to Siciliano. Towards another poet, however, Joseph ha-Nahtom, Immanuel expresses only contempt, snidely remarking that the latter had rarely "tasted the nectar of verse or its honey."[16] The same goes for Joab, "Prince of Hosts," who initiated a *tenzone* with Immanuel — and almost certainly lived to regret it:

> You showed me your pleasant rhymes / and thought them sublime . . . / In our eyes they're only tedious chimes / Were they not written in the letters of the Holy Tongue / We would have used them to wipe our dung.

After insults Immanuel turns to literary criticism. According to him, Joab's poetry is as weak as "the voice of the turtle dove," and it is no "virgin" — nothing fresh about it. Joab's grammar is deemed faulty and his rhymes deplorable: *tza-mid-tamid-ʿolamit* ("bracelet-always-forever"). Immanuel quotes expressions of modesty in Joab's poem, and then takes these apart, too. This is not the only case of astute literary criticism in the *Maḥbarot*. Indeed, it seems to have been the norm amongst a wide and discriminating audience of poetry lovers.

The story of Joab testifies to a generation of young poets (in which he figured prominently) as well as a circle of more mature poets (to which Immanuel sought to bar access): "You gave a thrashing to kids your own age / stop pretending to be so sage." Immanuel's threat is particularly interesting: "I'll erase you from the membership book I compiled for the group [*ḥavruta*]." This line seems to hint at the existence of a literary group rather like the academies that sprang up in Italy during later periods.[17]

We learn from the *Maḥbarot* that teachers were sometimes hired to instruct pupils in the art of poetry. Concerning Siciliano Immanuel notes: "The reason he writes his verse so fast / is that he spends all his time teaching children in class / This was his only occupation and task."[18] The long-suffering Joab mentioned above calls Immanuel his teacher, but this is an honor that Immanuel willingly foregoes, "lest people say 'like master like pupil'." He does not deny, however, that he instructed others in the art of poetry.[19]

---

[15] Immanuel, *Maḥbarot*, ed. Yarden, 241.
[16] Immanuel, *Maḥbarot*, ed. Yarden, 201.
[17] Immanuel, *Maḥbarot*, ed. Yarden, 154–57; 159–60.
[18] Immanuel, *Maḥbarot*, ed. Yarden, 241.
[19] Immanuel, *Maḥbarot*, ed. Yarden, 156.

Nor was Immanuel the only Hebrew poet to deal with erotic subjects, in the manner of Italian poetry. By his own account he had at least one colleague who kept pace with, or even outdid him. This was the poet Menahem, possibly Menahem Bozecco.[20] Menahem penned his rhymes on the back of a tablecloth, accompanied by appropriate illustrations:

> In a garden of Eden plump with delights / under the shade of a myrtle, a lady and knight / A river with ladies flowed across the green dell / each of them a lovely gazelle / and around that river the valiant young men / throw nets round the girls and then haul them in / And you too, O fawn, like the knights on the grass / toss in your net and bring up a lass![21]

This little vignette describes the ideal background for a meeting with Italian society and the creation of love poetry.

Immanuel's letters to Menahem include several realistic touches and expressions of deep friendship: "O poem, what will you tell him? / That I am sick with love for him." As young men, Immanuel further informs us, they had often written poetry together, and then adds: "We outdid all who came before us in song." Just what the nature of this poetry was we learn from the disapproving reaction of the rabbis:

> They both transgress the Jewish religion / They are both without light and utterly pagan / Both learned from the Greeks / and took a branch from their tree, / Both are clever and adept in the Law / Yet the actions of both are disgraceful and flawed![22]

We can assume, therefore, that Immanuel's contemporaries created a genuine corpus of secular poetry influenced by the Italian poetry of their own day and age. Unfortunately, though, this poetry has not come down to us. This loss occurred already in Immanuel's day, as may be assumed from his relating the loss — as "evil fate would have it" — of the much-admired poems by Judah Siciliano.[23] Immanuel seems to have possessed a keen sense of history. The introduction to his *Maḥbarot* finds him worrying over the fate of his poems, which he feared would be scattered over time. To hear Immanuel, he wrote the *Maḥbarot* only in order to keep his formerly composed poems together and to save them from oblivion.[24] His fellow poets did not make collections of their poetry, and as a

---

[20] Immanuel, *Maḥbarot*, ed. Yarden, 139.
[21] Immanuel, *Maḥbarot*, ed. Yarden, 142.
[22] Immanuel, *Maḥbarot*, ed. Yarden, 139, 143, 152.
[23] Immanuel, *Maḥbarot*, ed. Yarden, 235.
[24] Immanuel, *Maḥbarot*, ed. Yarden, 4–6.

result most of these poems have been lost. But they did exist during the thirteenth century, providing the background necessary for the absorption of the sonnet in Hebrew.

3. The Author of the First Hebrew Sonnet

Immanuel was a man of wide learning. He was familiar with the Hebrew poets of Spain and learned a great deal from them. According to him, he modeled his *Maḥbarot* on the *maqamas* ("rhymed-prose stories") of Judah Alharizi; and indeed Alharizi's influence, like that of other Hebrew poets from Spain, is well-evident in Immanuel's work. Immanuel was knowledgeable in medieval philosophy and apparently familiar with the writings of Plato and pseudo-Plato in their Hebrew translations. He read medical literature and mystical lore, and was an expert in Hebrew grammar. As a commentator on substantial parts of the Bible, Immanuel had a complete mastery of the biblical tongue and the language of preachers, rabbis, and philosophers. Immanuel was also in contact with such well-known Italian poets as Bosone da Gubbio and Cino da Pistoia, and probably others as well.[25] Though we have no proof that he was personally acquainted with Dante, as M. D. Cassuto has shown,[26] he clearly knew the *Divine Comedy* and wrote the final chapter of his *Maḥbarot* ("Heaven and Hell") under the influence of that masterpiece. Immanuel also composed poems in Italian, including sonnets. These poems reveal a poetic persona characterized by an uninhibited lust for life and a striking receptivity to the surrounding culture.[27]

For all these reasons, it seems only right that Immanuel should be the first writer of Hebrew sonnets, and indeed it is in this capacity that he has always been known. In the seventeenth century Immanuel Frances noted that "it was Rabbi Immanuel, the son of Solomon, who first brought the *sonetto* into the Holy Tongue."[28] Yet, while this is still the general opinion today, it now appears that there are reasons to doubt it.

For one thing, Immanuel does not claim to have invented the Hebrew sonnet. In fact he never calls attention to that verse-form at all, but simply weaves

---

[25] See Immanuel, *Maḥbarot*, ed. Yarden, 13, 16, 561.

[26] M. D. Cassuto, *Dante ve-Imanuel ha-Romi*, ed. M. Dorman (Jerusalem, 1966).

[27] Much has been written about Immanuel. See the copious bibliography (up through the year 1956) provided by Dov Yarden in his edition of the *Maḥbarot* (578–87); D. Pagis, *Ḥiddush u-Masoret be-Shirat ha-Ḥol ha-ʿIvrit* (Jerusalem, 1976), 247–355. In English see W. J. van Bekkum, "What is Hebrew in the Hebrew Sonnet?", *Frankfurter Judaistische Beiträge* 27 (2000): 95–107; and D. Bregman, "Hebrew Literature and Language," in *Encyclopedia of the Renaissance*, 6 vols. (New York, 1999), 3: 121–25.

[28] Immanuel Frances, *Meteq Sefatayim*, ed. H. Brody (Cracow, 1892), 48.

it into his narratives in the most matter-of-fact way. This is a strange oversight indeed, considering his sensitivity to poetic forms and their relationship to questions of theoretical and ethno-historical importance. In the introduction to his *Maḥbarot* Immanuel discusses the evolution of the *maqama*, the editing of poetic anthologies, and the attribution of poems to their rightful authors. He explains the link between Alharizi and his own work, comparing the stages in their respective development and hinting that his enterprise was much more challenging. Throughout the *Maḥbarot* Immanuel demonstrates pride in the traditions of Hebrew poetry and its manifold riches.[29] In light of all this, it is hard to believe that he simply forgot to take credit for the Hebrew sonnet. He certainly did not hesitate to claim a pioneering role in another Italian genre. In the preface to his *sirventese*, Immanuel dwells on the challenge of writing a Hebrew poem in this genre, and quotes the patron who commissioned it:

> I saw amongst the Christians a poem / the likes of which in Hebrew there's none. / All the trades of the world are mentioned within / every kingdom and land / every tongue and wisdom. / This single poem leaves nothing unsung / so I wanted one like it in the Hebrew tongue.[30]

Immanuel sounds a similar note of "ethnic pride" in explaining his decision to compose the poem, through a witty use of Exodus 1:19: "So that you will know / that the poems of Israel are not like those of Egypt — they are lively." Yet Immanuel wrote only one *sirventese*. Could he possibly have valued this one poem more than his thirty-eight sonnets?

Given the sonnet's roots in Provençal, and perhaps even in Arabic poetry, there is a possibility, albeit remote, that Immanuel simply did not regard the sonnet as being all that innovative. Strophic forms of one sort or another had been common in Hebrew poetry in Provence for over a hundred years, and remained in use in his own day.[31] It might be suggested, then, that Immanuel regarded the sonnet as just another variation of the strophic form. Yet this suggestion would clearly be incorrect. As we shall see below, Immanuel did not view the sonnet as just another vehicle for rhyming, but as a poem that is unique in every respect. Adopting the form into Hebrew clearly took a great deal of effort, and had Immanuel been the inventor of the Hebrew sonnet it is hard to believe that he would fail to take credit for this with his usual bravado. Thus it seems more likely that Immanuel was not, in fact, the inventor of the Hebrew sonnet, scholarly consensus notwithstanding. As we have seen, poets of his generation did

---

[29] See, for example, Immanuel, *Maḥbarot* ed. Yarden, 4–5.

[30] Immanuel, *Maḥbarot*, ed. Yarden, 174.

[31] For example, in the poems of Todros Abulafia in northern Spain. See Pagis, *Ḥiddush u-Masoret*, 180–82.

compose secular poetry, but these have not come down to us for the most part. Could the missing first sonnet belong to this lost body of work? There is no reason to rule out the possibility.

This theory finds support in two of Immanuel's epistolary sonnets. The first of these, *Ḥusha, meshiaḥ el ʿaseh saraf* ("Hurry, anointed of God, make a snake-charm"), is a panegyric for Judah Romano, Immanuel's relative and a well-known scholar and translator to whom Immanuel devoted his entire twelfth chapter.[32] This sonnet, together with two other poems, was composed at the request of three "men of renown / nobles who wear wisdom's crown."[33] All three poems were warmly received by both the person who commissioned the poem and the addressee, and — it is important to note — no one appears at all surprised by the sonnet included therein. Apparently they had already seen poems of this kind. Nor is it impossible that the sonnet elicited a response in the same form from Judah Romano, as was the custom between men of letters. The second sonnet is *At bein ʿatzei yaʿar*[34] ("You are amongst the trees of the forest"). It is included in the letter in which Immanuel chastised the unfortunate Joab, as mentioned above. Immanuel's letter, let us recall, came in response to Joab's poem, and since the response is in the form of a sonnet, this may well be true of the challenge-poem as well. These hypothetical sonnets by Romano and Joab would not have been quoted in the *Maḥbarot*, since this work only preserves the writing of Immanuel himself (as indeed Immanuel takes pains to note, informing the reader that all the poems uttered by various personages in his dialogues were his own creation).[35] But this does not mean that the poems never existed at all.

There is nothing, therefore, to keep us from thinking that among the lost poems of Siciliano, Menahem, Joab, and Romano, there might have been Hebrew sonnets, some of them earlier than the ones written by Immanuel. But since these have not come down to us, and since they were most likely not available to the poets who revived the Hebrew sonnet in the sixteenth and seventeenth centuries, we have no choice but to accept Immanuel's sonnets as the first poems of their kind in Hebrew, and as the sonnets that served as a model for those who came afterwards. Moreover, it is still quite possible that Immanuel was the first to compose a significant body of Hebrew sonnets. As we shall see, his work with the sonnet testifies to the sensibilities of a master artist anxious to instruct fledgling poets in the basic principles of the genre and its essential form. And in this, without doubt, Immanuel of Rome is indeed unrivaled.

---

[32] Immanuel, *Maḥbarot*, ed. Yarden, 228; also printed in *Tzror Zehuvim*, ed. Bregman, sonnet 36.
[33] Immanuel, *Maḥbarot*, ed. Yarden, 378.
[34] Printed in *Tzror Zehuvim*, ed. Bregman, sonnet 20.
[35] Immanuel, *Maḥbarot*, ed. Yarden, 5.

II. General Structure and Rhyme-Scheme

"Immanuel loved your echoing melody"
Saul Tchernikhowsky

1. The Sonnet's Charm

The sonnet-form has a special charm. From its invention in the early thirteenth century down to our own day, poets the world over have never ceased to compose sonnets. In Italian poetry the sonnet became the form of poetry *par excellence*, and in the western world in general it has enjoyed popularity almost without precedence during various periods of its long life.

The sonnet-form arouses interest and emotion. Tchernikhowsky's sonnet about the Hebrew sonnet, with its emotional appeal to the "*sonetta*, O golden poem," is only one in a long line of sonnets-about-sonnets in various languages from the thirteenth century down to this day.[1] In Hebrew literature since the beginning of the sixteenth century, the sonnet has been called by various affectionate nicknames alluding to its prestige or to its structure, and linking it to the Bible or other sacred texts. Thus it is variously called a "golden poem," a "well-loved golden poem," a "poem on thirds and fourths," and so on. The seventeenth-century poet Immanuel Frances, author of the Hebrew *ars poetica* known as *Meteq Sefatayim* or "The Lips' Sweetness," to which we will be referring throughout this book, described the sonnet as "an important poem that no one unfamiliar with Christian poetry could successfully write."[2] Jacob Burckhardt, the eminent historian of the Renaissance, claimed that "the sonnet became for Italian literature a condenser of thoughts and emotions such as was possessed by the poetry of no other modern people."[3]

No less unique are the feelings of distaste or criticism which the sonnet has inspired over the centuries. It has been called "that Procrustean bed"[4] and derided

---

[1] See L. E. Kastner, "Concerning the Sonnet of the Sonnet," *Modern Language Review* 11 (1916): 205–11.
[2] Frances, *Meteq Sefatayim*, ed. Brody, 48.
[3] J. Burckhardt, *The Civilization of the Renaissance in Italy* (New York, 1958), 186.
[4] J. Burckhardt, *The Civilization of the Renaissance*, 187.

even by such eminent writers of sonnets as Du Bellay and Shakespeare.[5] Even Bialik's "Sonnet not like Gordon" seems to have a trace of disdain.[6]

What is the secret of the sonnet's charm? Why has this genre been preserved from the thirteenth century down to our own times? Why have poets of all generations been attracted to this form, and why have they occupied themselves with it so incessantly?

These and similar questions have been discussed at length in the research.[7] We will not present here the range of opinions, formulas and definitions that have accumulated over the centuries in the attempt to unravel the secret of the sonnet's charm. But we will try to separate the wheat from the chaff and to present the major points of the argument. To do so, it is necessary to refute a fundamental misconception regarding the sonnet that goes back to two Italian critics from the fourteenth century (and whose words may possibly have been misinterpreted).[8] In Hebrew, it was Tchernikhowsky who first gave voice to this misconception:

> The sonetta — in Hebrew a "golden poem" — is a poem of fourteen lines, divided into four strophes [. . .] the ideas in the last two strophes are a kind of crisis in relation to the ideas in the first ones.[9]

The weak point in this description comes at the end. Though there are many sonnets that agree with Tchernikhowsky's definition, there are many others that do not, among them sonnets written by some of the greatest sonneteers of all time. Let us take in example one of Petrarch's most famous sonnets (rhyme-scheme, in the Italian text: ABBA ABBA CDC DCD):[10]

---

[5] See L. Forster, *The Icy Fire: Five Studies in European Petrarchism* (London, 1969), 24, 56, 172–73; and see C. Kleinhenz, *The Early Italian Sonnet* (Lecce, 1986), 8, and esp. note 3.

[6] Hayyim Nachman Bialik, *Shirim*, ed. D. Miron (Tel Aviv, 1983), 299.

[7] See for example, Tchernikhowsky, *Maḥberet ha-Sonetot*, 18–21; C. Tomlinson, *The Sonnet: Its Origin and Place in Poetry* (London, 1874, repr. 1970), 1–50; M. Praz, "Sonetto," in *Enciclopedia Italiana* (Rome, 1936), 32: 141–43; Mönch, *Das Sonett*, 39–41; Fuller, *The Sonnet*, 1–2; Pagis, *Ḥiddush u-Masoret*, 315–29; Ruschioni, *Il sonetto italiano*, 11–14; Berman, *The Sonnet Over Time*, 1–15.

[8] See D. Bregman, "Ha-Sonet ha-Klassi: Immanuel ha-Romi u-Petrarcha," in *Divrei ha-Qongres ha-ʿOlami ha-ʿAsiri le Madaʿei ha-Yahadut*, ed. D. Assaf, 2 vols. (Jerusalem, 1990), 1: 298–302.

[9] S. Tchernikhowsky, *Immanuel ha-Romi* (Berlin, 1925), 136–37. A similar opinion is found, for example, in Tomlinson, *The Sonnet*, 28. On the subject of Tchernikhowsky's own sonnets and their place in Hebrew literature, see D. Bregman, *Sharsheret ha-Zahav* (Tel Aviv, 2000), 108–16.

[10] Petrarch, *Rime*, ed. G. Bezzola (Milan, 1976), 179: *Benedetto sia 'l giorno*. English translation from C. B. Cayley, *The Sonnets and Other Poems of Petrarch* (London, 1879), 82.

> Blessed be the day, the month, the year,
> The season, hour, and smallest part of it,
> And place, and pleasant land where I was smit
> By two fair eyes, my shackles' fasteners dear.
>
> Blessed be my delectable first tear,
> That I felt flow, when I to love was knit;
> And both the weapons, wherewith I was hit,
> And all my wounds, which to my heart flew sheer.
>
> Blessed be every word which, on the name
> Of my sweet lady calling, I have strown;
> Blessed my sighs, my tears, and my desire;
>
> And blessed be the pages whereby fame,
> That from no woman springs but her alone,
> For my own thoughts and self I do acquire.

The poem is unified by a single theme, a single idea, and a single feeling. The anaphora stresses the sense of unity, and there is no "crisis" of the kind mentioned by Tchernikhowsky.

The misconception comes from confusing the verbal content of the poem with its form. If we wish to understand the properties of the sonnet as a genre, and not the traits of any one sonnet in particular, it is necessary to look at the abstract form and to understand it on its own terms as a musical model distinct from any specific wording, for better or worse. As a scholar Tchernikhowsky erred, but as a poet he got it exactly right: "Immanuel loved your echoing melody." The term *sonetto*, a diminutive derived from the Latin term *sonitus*, is primarily a musical term, meaning "a small sound." The charm of the sonnet comes from the orchestration of its sounds.

The characteristic musicality of the Italian sonnet expresses itself to a great extent through the prosody of its classic form: ABBA ABBA CDE CDE. The pattern represents fourteen lines subdivided into two parts, one of eight lines and one of six — octave and sestet — and then further divided into two quatrains and two tercets. This pattern embodies various combinations of harmony and tension, agreement and opposition.

In terms of size, rhyme, and symmetry, the quatrains are identical to each other, just as the tercets are also identical to each other. But the quatrains and tercets differ from each other in every respect. They have different rhymes, and different numbers of rhymes. The quatrains have paired symmetry; the tercets three-part symmetry. The rhymes of each quatrain are completed within the quatrain itself. But in the sestet every rhyme is distributed between the two tercets and is completed only after a tense pause. There are only two rhymes in the octave: these are spread across eight lines, so that every rhyme is heard four times. There are three rhymes in the sestet: these are crowded into six lines, and every rhyme is heard only twice. It might be said that the octave is pleasant, simple and relatively poor in musical information, whereas the sestet is complex, fraught with tension, and packed with musical information.

The octave acquaints us with the musical pattern of the first quatrain and then repeats and consolidates it in the second quatrain, creating a pleasant sense of familiarity. This is disrupted in the transition to the sestet, which is orchestrated in a different manner and is altogether new, condensed, and difficult to grasp.

Thus we see that the transition from the octave to the sestet is indeed a "crisis," as Tchernikhowsky said, but a crisis in the music of the poem and not in its ideas. While the crisis can also be reflected in the wording of the poem, this is not always the case. Indeed, just the opposite is true. The various combinations of harmony and tension in the basic musical pattern give the poet a wide range of options; disrupting the idea in the transition from octave to sestet (parallel to the musical disruption) is only one of these options. There are more than ten different patterns of thematic development in the Hebrew sonnet of the sixteenth and seventeenth centuries, with some of these arranging various elements of the sonnets in harmony with the sound orchestration, and others in opposition to it. In the above-quoted sonnet by Petrarch, the unchanging tone of the words gains a striking effect from its musical accompaniment that shifts from the easy and familiar to the sudden and complex.

The musical pattern of the sonnet verse-form is unique. Static forms, such as those used in the mono-rhymed classic Spanish poem, and repeating forms of various kinds, such as the strophes used in liturgical Hebrew poetry or the various kinds of octaves and sestinas, all lack the inner tension and sharp contrasts of the sonnet. Nor can the forms which do have an element of tension, such as the *terza rima*, the *canzone*, and the madrigal, be compared to the sonnet, since these lack the unequal distribution into two parts. And finally, the fourteen-line pattern, unique to the sonnet, is not only a good basis for the unequal distribution (8 + 6) which characterizes it, but also a good size: not too small to stand on its own as an independent poem or to contain the traits we just mentioned, and not too big to contain them with suitable concentration and compactness. The charge that the sonnet is a short poem that necessarily cramps the poet's style is obviously unfounded: the sonnet is larger than many of the common Italian forms. The term *sonetto* was not coined in order to indicate the sonnet's size in relation to the other forms, for it came into being even before most of these arrived on the scene.

2. The Development of the Classical Model of the Italian Sonnet

The Sicilian sonnet from which the Italian sonnet evolved consists of fourteen lines of equal meter. Its usual rhyme-scheme is ABABABAB CDE CDE. In a few cases it ends in a different rhyme-pattern, of which the most common variation is CDC DCD. Leaving aside this secondary pattern for the time being, we immediately see that the Sicilian sonnet is not that different from the classic sonnet described above. Like the classic model, the Sicilian sonnet has fourteen lines divided into two parts, with the second part composed of two tercets connected by all three rhymes but separated on the page by the visual layout of the text. Only the first part of the Sicilian sonnet is different: its octave is not divided into two closed quatrains either through rhyme or even through visual layout.[11]

The blurring of the quatrains makes for a smoother, more harmonious poem. It prevents the kind of dichotomy and imbalance characteristic to the classic sonnet. And if we look now at the secondary patterns of the Sicilian sonnet, we can see that the most frequent of these patterns makes it possible to divide the entire poem into couplets: AB AB AB AB CD CD CD. Divided in this fashion, the poem obviously loses much of its typical sharpness.

On the face of things, the road from the Sicillian pattern to the classic form should have been relatively short and simple. It was only necessary to consolidate the quatrains; that is, to go from the pattern of AB AB AB AB[12] to that of ABBA ABBA. But in actual fact, this took over a hundred years to achieve.

By the middle of the thirteenth century, the path carved out by the first sonneteers split into a number of different directions. In Tuscan poetry, which was no longer composed by a small and tightly-knit group but by a number of independent poets, sonnets became increasingly complicated and varied. While the large corpus created in Tuscany testifies to a great enthusiasm for the sonnet-form, it also indicates a certain dissatisfaction with it. These sonnets experiment with every element of the sonnet-form: length, rhyme, division of strophes, meter. Here, for example, are the rhyme-schemes for three Tuscan sonnets (the capital letters indicate lines of longer meter; the small letters lines of short meter):

ABABABABAB CDC DCD
AaBAaB AaBAaB CDDC CDDC
AaBAaB AaBAaB CcDdCcDD

---

[11] See Wilkins, *The Invention of the Sonnet*, 18–19.
[12] Below, the ABABABAB octave will be called an "open octave." In early Italian theory a sonnet with this octave was known as a *sonetto dimidiato*.

These and similar poems[13] were still considered sonnets, and were not at all uncommon. Dante included two of them in his *Vita Nuova*.[14]

The closed octave (ABBA ABBA) was invented during the course of these experiments, thus giving the sonnet all that it needed to attain the classic form. But its inventor, Guittone d'Arezzo, who has already been mentioned above, also composed dozens of "monster" sonnets of the kind described, including one sonnet of twenty-seven lines.[15] Only two of his sonnets have a closed octave. It seems that he regarded this pattern as only one of many possibilities, and of no particular significance. Nevertheless, the new octave took root, and by the beginning of the fourteenth century was even fairly common. By then, however, poets preferred the sestet CDC DCD over the old Sicilian sestet of CDE CDE. Thus the sonnet edged its way closer to the classic pattern in the octave, but away from it in the sestet.

At some point in this process sonnets in the classic pattern appeared here and there, but they got lost in the heap and failed to arouse any particular interest. From this period we find only two theoreticians who discuss the sonnet-form: Francesco da Barberino in 1316, and Antonio da Tempo in 1332.[16] Both of these still describe the octave as having eight lines *(pedes)* or four pairs of lines *(copulae)*; Da Tempo counts sixteen kinds of sonnets, among them long poems of different meters, all of them equally legitimate in his eyes.[17]

The Italian sonnet suffered from this embarrassment of riches until Petrarch came "and fixed them permanently."[18] His *Canzoniere* of Italian poems includes three hundred and seventeen sonnets. Every one of these has fourteen lines in a single meter, and most of them have a rhyme-scheme of ABBA ABBA CDE CDE. In the sestet, the variation of preference is CDC DCD.

Petrarch was not the first to create the classic sonnet, but he purified the form of all its superfluities. He was the first to rule out any form which deviated from the boundary of fourteen lines and a single meter, and he gave clear preference to the desired form in a large body of work. Petrarch restored the sonnet to its former simplicity, and added the finishing touches to the old model.

---

[13] See Biadene, *Morfologia del sonetto*, 26–82; W. T. Elwert, *Versificazione italiana* (Florence, 1973), 130–32.

[14] See Dante, *Vita Nuova*, trans. D. S. Cervigni and E. Vasta (London and Notre Dame, 1995), 54 and 58.

[15] V. Moleta, *The Early Poetry of Guittone d'Arezzo* (London, 1976), 8.

[16] The latter's *Summa artis rithimici* is the more important.

[17] See Mönch, *Das Sonett*, 23–27.

[18] Burckhardt, *Civilization of the Renaissance*, 186.

3. The Model of Immanuel of Rome

In view of the slow development of the Italian sonnet, the Hebrew sonnets of Immanuel of Rome come as an impressive surprise: every one of his sonnets has fourteen lines in a single meter, and the great majority is rhymed ABBA ABBA CDE CDE. Without doubt, this is the classic model of the sonnet in Hebrew guise. Immanuel completed his *Maḥbarot* no later than 1328.[19] Petrarch began writing his *Canzoniere* in 1336 and did not finish editing it until 1374.[20] In establishing the classic sonnet, Immanuel thus preceded Petrarch by more than forty years.

The depth of Immanuel's poetic perception is amazing. This poet, who so brilliantly composed Hebrew poetry in the traditions of medieval Spain, was able to liberate himself from the old, if not sacred conventions of this rich tradition to penetrate the very heart of Italian poetry, and to precede the Italians themselves in establishing the classic model of the most common and basic form in their poetry.

The model which Immanuel created is actually purer in form than that of Petrarch. In order to examine this matter, let us take a closer look first at the octave. Petrarch did not renounce the traditional open octave. A number of his sonnets have an octave that rhymes ABAB ABAB.[21] The sonnets of Immanuel, on the other hand, all have octaves rhyming ABBA ABBA, without exception. Let us take a look now at the sestet. Both Petrarch and Immanuel preferred the CDE CDE pattern in their sestets,[22] but also used a secondary rhyme-scheme of CDC DCD. As we have already noted, this two-rhyme pattern weakens the difference between the octave and the sestet by emphasizing their common paired element. This common element is particularly conspicuous in sonnets with an open octave. The combination of an open octave with a sestet of two rhymes creates a form that can easily be seen as a string of couplets, as we have seen. This undesirable combination does occur in Petrarch's work, since he sometimes used an open octave. It never appears in the *Maḥbarot,* because Immanuel never used anything but a closed octave. The two-rhyme sestet is "weaker" than the three-rhyme sestet in yet another way. Its two tercets are not bound together by three rhymes, each of them divided by the pause among the tercets, but rather by one rhyme alone: D. The rhyme C is completed in the first tercet and only repeated in the second. The tension created by the "turn" of the sestet in the CDE-CDE pattern is obviously lost here. And obviously, this sestet is not as dense as its

---

[19] Immanuel, *Maḥbarot*, ed. Yarden, 17–18.
[20] Petrarca, *Rime*, ed. G. Bezzola (Milan, 1976), 19–20.
[21] A few sonnets also have ABAB BABA.
[22] Concerning Petrarch, cf. Mönch, *Das Sonett*, 17 with Fuller, *The Sonnet*, 4.

three-rhyme counterpart since it has only two rhymes. In Immanuel's sonnet this weakness is compensated for. Since there is only one kind of octave, variations in the sestet reinforce the octave's unity. This creates an additional element in the delicate balance between the harmony and tension traditional to the form: the octave is always the same, and therefore always anticipated; the sestet takes many guises and is therefore always unexpected, and always surprising.

These "improvements" in the Hebrew model can be explained by the very fact that it was new. Petrarch filtered his options through the light of the Sicilian tradition, and his loyalty to this tradition, or his own attraction to it, caused him to accept its limitations. But things were different for Immanuel, who was not bound by this tradition and may even have been unaware of its existence. He was free to choose his options according to his own judgment.

4. Immanuel's Adherence to the Model He Created

The classic model of the sonnet required the poet to refrain from using the various options, however inviting those might be. Such "asceticism" was completely foreign to Immanuel's poetic temperament, with its wealth of expressive language and marked talent for improvisation. This is especially true in regard to Immanuel's prodigious rhyming abilities, a talent in which he openly takes pride.

These limitations must have weighed more heavily on Immanuel than on the younger Petrarch. In Immanuel's day, poets composed sonnets with a free hand and a minimum of rules. It was only later in the fourteenth century that the customary freedom began to decline. And because Immanuel came earlier than Petrarch, he had less chance of encountering stray models of the classic pattern, which, once invented, naturally became more common as time went by. Even so, Immanuel never once deviated from his chosen course.

Immanuel was eminently aware of the merits of his choice. In order to highlight the distinction between the quatrains he sometimes adopted the rather extreme measure of making slight changes in the rhymes. Thus in some sonnets we find:

> in the first quatrain: nefesh-refesh, and in the second *ḥofesh-nofesh*;
>
> in the first: *torah-korah*, and in the second *seraḥ-teraḥ*,
>
> in the first: *tofet-nofet*, and in the second *zefet-yalefet*.[23]

---

[23] See *Tzror Zehuvim*, ed. Bregman, sonnets 38, 33, and 25.

Rhymes such as *nefesh-nofesh* or *toraḥ-teraḥ* were considered perfect rhymes in the Hebrew-Spanish tradition, but not in Italian poetry. And indeed, these "imperfect" rhymes drew criticism in the following generations, as we shall see below.[24]

In order to achieve a closed octave, Immanuel was willing to make certain poetic sacrifices. This we can see, for example, in the octave of the following sonnet jeering at the poet Joab (*At bein ʿatzei yaʿar*):[25]

> You are amongst the trees of the forest of Lebanon: a thistle
> Amongst the princes of the land and its nobles: a pigmy
> Amongst the holy places: like a cow-shed and chicken coop
> Amongst the prophets: Manoaḥ
>
> Amongst the kingdoms of Sihon and ʿOg: Zanoaḥ
> All human beings are the cause, and you: the effect
> Amongst those who creep along the ground: a snail
> Amongst the flowing rivers: the Silwan.

By switching line 6 with line 5, Immanuel could have opened the second quatrain with the subject of the poem ("you") as in the first quatrain, continued the string of anaphoras in the second quatrain, and created a neat parallel between the two halves of the octave.[26] Only that would have spoiled the desired ABBA ABBA pattern.

Immanuel's loyalty to the classic model is well evident in the sestet. While in principle he allowed variations here, in actual fact he made minimum use of secondary rhyme-schemes. Thus he rhymed twenty-two of his sestets CDE CDE, eleven CDC DCD, four CDD CDD, only one CDC CDC, and another ACD ACD. This last variant is used in a sonnet whose rhymemes consist of complete words — the Hebrew version of the Italian *sonetto continuo*:[27] *Mi he'emin ʿofera* ("Who would believe, O gazelle").[28] It seems that he could make do with one or two secondary patterns, but used more just to demonstrate that all variations are permitted in the sestet. Immanuel's strict method in the sestet is (again) highly striking when compared with Petrarch. Petrarch plays with the order of rhymes in the sestet, whether this consists of two rhymes (such as CDD DDC; CDC CDC) or three (such as CDE EDC). Immanuel never changes the order of the rhymes in the three-rhyme pattern. Thus the classic model is always retained, and is only too obvious in the early Hebrew corpus.

---

[24] As we shall see below, Chap. 12, Part 1.

[25] *Tzror Zehuvim*, ed. Bregman, sonnet 20.

[26] Similarly in sonnet 30, he preferred the order 6, 7, 8, 5.

[27] On the subject of the *sonetto continuo*, see Biadene, *Morfologia del sonetto*, 80–82. Here, the words are *ʿeynaykh-panaykh* ("your eyes - your face").

[28] *Tzror Zehuvim*, ed. Bregman, sonnet 24.

5. The Source of Inspiration

How can we explain this amazing similarity between Immanuel and Petrarch? Obviously, there can be no question of any actual relationship between two poets who composed in different times and even in different places, since Petrarch lived for many years outside Italy, in Avignon. We can also dismiss the possibility that Immanuel unwittingly continued some Hebrew tradition which just happened to match the one developed by Petrarch later on. The rhyme-schemes in which Immanuel composed his sonnets were new to Hebrew poetry. In fact, the rhyme-schemes that he rejected for his sonnets were precisely the ones that would have matched the traditional rhyme of Hebrew poetry in Spain. Had he chosen the open octave and the two-rhyme sestet (AB AB AB AB CD CD CD), his sonnets would have looked like a combination of two poems in the classic Hebrew mold; one of four distichs (with the running rhyme B) and the second of three (with the running rhyme D). It appears, therefore, that Immanuel did not seek to continue the formal Hebrew tradition in his sonnets, and may even have intentionally cut himself off from it. Having eliminated these possibilities, the only way left to explain the fascinating similarity between Immanuel and Petrarch is to suggest that both poets shared an Italian source of inspiration. If so, it appears that this source can be none other than Dante Alighieri.

Some fifty sonnets can definitely be attributed to Dante, but it is thought that he may also be the author of *Il Fiore*, a work which consists of two hundred and thirty-two sonnets and was written in the thirteenth century by one Durante.[29] *Il Fiore* is the Italian version of the famous allegory of love, *Le Roman de la Rose*, composed during the thirteenth century by two French poets: Guillaume de Lorris, who began the poem, and Jean de Meun, who completed it.[30] It contains some 22,000 lines of poetry in rhymed couplets. *Il Fiore* is a delightful work. Its author consolidated the plot, which was marred in the original by numerous digressions and a wearying profusion of detail. He balanced the composition — adding here, removing there — and transformed it from a cumbersome tale of chivalry into a tightly-knit love story of great charm. The sonnet proved to be an effective instrument for the enterprise.[31] The name "Durante," the time in which the *Fiore* was written and the talent of its creator all lend credence to the theory that Dante was indeed its author.

---

[29] On the basis of this reasonable assumption, *Il Fiore* was included in a modern edition of his poems; see G. Contini, ed., *Poeti del Duocento* (Milan, 1960).

[30] See A. Lanly, trans., *Le Roman de la Rose: traduction en francais moderne* (Paris, 1971–1976); Eng. trans. Charles Dahlberg (Hanover and London, 1986); and F. Castes, ed., *Il fiore* (Paris, 1881).

[31] See L. F. Benedetto, *Il Roman de la Rose e la letteratura italiana* (Halle, 1910), 101–7.

The sonnets in the *Fiore* have a uniform pattern. They all have closed octaves and sestets composed of two rhymes. This was also the pattern Dante preferred in the rest of his sonnets, which come in a great variety of forms, including the longer ones mentioned above. However, in the midst of this variety we also find twelve sonnets in the pattern ABBA ABBA CDE CDE. These "classic sonnets" are not conspicuous in Dante, who varied his patterns according to the traditions of the late thirteenth century and obviously preferred a different pattern. But in light of Petrarch's work, they assume a special significance as an important step towards the ultimate goal.

Both Immanuel and Petrarch were well-acquainted with Dante's poetry. They learned from it and used it as a model for their own writing. It has already been shown that Petrarch wrote his *Canzoniere* (consisting largely of sonnets) according to the example provided by Dante's *Vita Nuova*,[32] while the influence of *Il Fiore* on Petrarch has also been demonstrated in detail.[33] Immanuel wrote his *Maḥberet Ha-Tofet ve-ha-ʿEden* ("Hell and Heaven") in the wake of Dante's *Divine Comedy*. Dante's influence on his work is apparent in several places in the *Maḥbarot*, and especially in the sonnets.[34] Moreover, some of his Italian poems were obviously influenced by *Il Fiore*.[35] We can therefore assume that Immanuel and Petrarch were careful readers of Dante's sonnets, which in fact represent all the various stages that went into the making of the classic Italian sonnet. Both of them pored over Dante's writings, considered the various options, and ultimately chose those same twelve sonnets as the pattern worthy of emulation.

This is the amazing point of convergence between Rabbi Immanuel ben Solomon and *Ser* Francesco Petrarca; one that goes beyond the boundaries of time and space, religion and language. It was a meeting that never could have taken place had not each of these poets, each in his own time and place, been graced with so penetrating an understanding of the sonnet-form, or devoted to it the better part of his poetic energy.

---

[32] See R. M. Durling, ed. and trans., *Petrarch's Lyric Poems* (Cambridge, MA and London, 1976), 10–11.

[33] See Benedetto, *Il Roman de la Rose*, 164–71.

[34] As shown by Cassuto. See his *Dante ve-Immanuel*; and idem, "L'elemento italiano nelle 'Mechaberoth' di Immanuele Romano," *Rivista Israelitica* 2 (1905); 3 (1906).

[35] As M. Marti showed in his study of poets who wrote for entertainment in Dante's time: *Cultura e stile nei poeti giocosi del tempo di Dante* (Pisa, 1953), 175–76. This scholar marvels at the ease, uniqueness, and audacity of Immanuel of Rome. Together with this, he does find some of Immanuel's ideas and motifs in *Il Fiore*, and, indeed, precisely those that stand out for their daring, such as the poet's claim that all religions are equal in his eyes.

III. Meter

1. The Phonetic Syllable

In the last chapter we discussed the importance of the musical dimension in the sonnet form. The original musicality of the sonnet was of course Italian. To take this form and transfer it into another language without that characteristic Italian ring just did not seem possible. And since it was meter which created it, a suitable meter parallel to that of the Italian was the necessary prerequisite in any language that adopted it. The earlier a language absorbed a parallel meter, the earlier it absorbed the sonnet.[1] Hebrew was the first language after Italian to absorb the sonnet, thanks to the meter invented by Immanuel of Rome, which allowed him to create a Hebrew poem that still had that special Italian ring to it.

Italian poetry uses syllabic meters. Such meters are characterized by the relationship between the number of syllables in a line and the kind of stress in which they end. The syllabic meter of the sonnet is known as the *endecasillabo*, and it has eleven syllables. This is the regular *endecasillabo*, the *endecasillabo piano*, but there is also a short version of the meter, the *endecasillabo tronco*, which has only ten syllables. In both of these the final stress falls on the tenth syllable.[2] This stress gives the regular *endecasillabo*, the one with eleven syllables, a feminine ending, and the short *endecasillabo* of ten syllables — a masculine ending.

It was up to Immanuel, therefore, to create a Hebrew *endecasillabo*, and this he accomplished. The major difficulty was linguistic. In Italian the syllables are considered equal; there are no short or long syllables. Hebrew, however, distinguishes between a short syllable (*ma, gam, dod*) and a composite syllable (*kemo, beli*). It is therefore difficult to translate a syllabic meter from Italian to Hebrew. Then there was also the question of tradition, which presented Immanuel with an additional problem: secular Hebrew poetry during Immanuel's day, and some of the liturgical poetry as well, was scanned in the quantitative meters hallowed by the classical Hebrew poets of Spain, and brought over to Italy by Abraham ibn Ezra in the twelfth century. From a psychological point of view, therefore, it was hard to simply give up these meters.

Immanuel overcame these problems with the help of the Italian Hebrew accent, which tended to pronounce consonants with both the mobile *shewa* and

---

[1] See Forster, *The Icy Fire*, 35–36; Bregman, "Shitat Immanuel."
[2] The same is true of a third *endecasillabo*: the twelve-syllable meter which does not interest us here.

ḥataf as full syllables (i.e. *kemo*, *beli*).³ On the basis of this accent Immanuel created a fundamental new concept in Hebrew poetry: the phonetic syllable. Into this category he put the mobile *shewa* and *ḥataf*, regarding them as full syllables even though they are not considered as such according to the rules of Hebrew grammar. Thus, the word *beli* ("without") contains two phonetic syllables; the word *le'ekhol* ("to eat") contains three, and so on. In Immanuel's system, the poet counts the number of phonetic syllables in the line.

With the help of the phonetic syllable, terms used in quantitative meters took on syllabic equivalents. Thus every *yated* or "peg" which consists of a mobile Sehwa, a consonant and a vowel counts as two phonetic syllables; every *tenuaʿ* or "cord" which consists of a consonant and a vowel counts as one phonetic syllable. These equivalents make it possible to create meters that fulfill the obligations of two different metrical systems at one and the same time: the mobile *shewa* or *ḥataf* functions both as a beginning of a *yated* and as a phonetic syllable, and the regular *tenuaʿ* as both a quantitative vowel and a phonetic syllable. We thus stand before a new Hebrew meter, the quantitative-syllabic meter in which Immanuel composed his sonnets, and from which we can extrapolate its principles. Let us, then, take a closer look at both sides of this quantitative-syllabic meter: first as a syllabic system, and afterwards as a quantitative system. This will serve to clarify Immanuel's new metrical system as a whole.

2. Syllabic Models

Immanuel required two new lines for his sonnets: one to parallel the eleven-syllable feminine line (*endecasillabo piano*), and the second to parallel the ten-syllable masculine line (*endecasillabo tronco*). In creating the first of these, Immanuel adopted the metrical scheme of the Italian sonnet: eleven phonetic syllables, with the accent on the tenth syllable:

Im	ha	ge	ze	ra	yo	re	da	mi	má	ʿal
1	2	3	4	5	6	7	8	9	10	11

This feminine line can be called the Hebrew *endecasillabo piano* (Scheme 1 in the Table of Metrical Schemes).

To create an equivalent for the masculine line, Immanuel deviated from Italian practice. He did not leave off the final phonetic syllable in the eleven-syllable feminine line, nor did he leave the stress on the tenth phonetic syllable in the

---

³ A. S. Ḥartom, "Mivta ha-ʿIvrit etzel Yehudei Italia," *Leshonenu* 15 (1947): 52–61.

line. Instead, he added an extra phonetic syllable at the end of the line, and gave this syllable the stress:

hu	sha	me	shi	ah	el	ve	la	ma	ta	ʿa	mód
1	2	3	4	5	6	7	8	9	10	11	12

This masculine line we can call the Hebrew *endecasillabo tronco* (Scheme 2 in the Table of Metrical Schemes). Below it will become clear why Immanuel created a masculine line of twelve syllables rather than ten, as was customary in Italian poetry. At any rate, this line created a striking hallmark of the early Hebrew sonnet, and endowed it with its typical cadence.

Immanuel was careful to match the length of the poetic line to the kind of stress at its end, apart from one single exception, which can be explained.[4]

3. Quantitative Models

As already mentioned, the two lines quoted above are quantitative as well as syllabic. Both of them use one traditional meter, *ha-shalem (b)*,[5] but the distich is split into two lines. The first part of this distich (in Hebrew the *delet*) serves as the line with the masculine rhyme, while the second part (in Hebrew the *soger*) serves as the feminine line (Schemes 1 and 2 in the Table of Metrical Schemes):

−	−	ᴗ	−	−	−	ᴗ	−	−	−	ᴗ	´
1	2	3	4	5	6	7	8	9	10	11	12

−	−	ᴗ	−	−	−	ᴗ	−	−	´	−
1	2	3	4	5	6	7	8	9	10	11

Of Immanuel's thirty-eight sonnets, fifteen are composed in feminine lines of eleven syllables, that is, using only the *soger* of *ha-shalem (b)*; ten sonnets are composed in masculine lines of twelve syllables and scanned, therefore, according to

---

[4] In the sonnet *Naflah ʿateret ha-zeman* (in *Tzror Zehuvim*, ed. Bregman, sonnet 9), line 9 has twelve syllables and ends in the penultimate-stressed word *ha-mavtah*. Because this is a unique case, and in light of the fact that the line rhymes with a masculine line of twelve syllables, it seems that Immanuel pronounced the word *ha-mavtah* with the stress on the last syllable. He was in effect forced to do so because of the practice in Italy of pronouncing a mobile *shewa* as a *tzere*. Apparently he stressed two syllables in this long word: *ha-ma-ve-tah*.

[5] J. Schirmann, *Ha-Shirah ha-ʿIvrit bi-Sefarad u-bi-Provans*, 4 vols. (Jerusalem and Tel Aviv, 1971), 4: 722.

the *delet* of this same meter. In the rest of the sonnets feminine lines of eleven syllables alternate with masculine lines of twelve syllables; these, therefore, have both the *delet* and the *soger* of *ha-shalem (b)*, but not necessarily one after the other, as in the classic Hebrew poetry of Spain. We can thus say that in Immanuel's sonnets the quantitative meter splits into two parts, with each part becoming an independent meter in its own right.

Why, of all the quantitative meters, was it *ha-shalem (b)* that Immanuel chose for his sonnets? There were historic roots behind his choice. Although the Hebrew-Spanish quantitative system allowed masculine and feminine lines to rhyme together, Hebrew poets did in fact sometimes distinguish between the two. In doing so they used *ha-shalem (b)*, just as Immanuel was later to do when composing his sonnets.

This meter was preferred by Hebrew poets in Christian domains in both Spain and Provence.[6] Immanuel himself also composed poems in the classical mold of Spain using this same pattern. But in his sonnets he completed the process of absorbing the syllabic norm. He divided the classic distich (the *bayit*) which was too long for this norm,[7] and discarded the traditional running rhyme, which was foreign to it. He did, to be sure, leave one superfluous element — the *yetedot* — but these were not really apparent to the ear, since they were pronounced as regular syllables.

In creating a Hebrew *endecasillabo*, *ha-shalem (b)* seemed made to order. The properties of this traditional quantitative pattern had reasonable equivalents in the Italian meter: a unit of eleven phonetic syllables in the traditional feminine ending, together with a masculine unit distinguished from the former by one syllable. No other classic quantitative meter possessed both of these options.

Ostensibly, Immanuel should have been able to renounce the classic Spanish meter and create a new quantitative pattern suitable to strophic poetry, just as Hebrew poets had done for the strophic "girdle" poem in Spain.[8] Indeed, Immanuel did not include girdle poems in his *Mahbarot*, and may not even have been acquainted with these forms.

The classic quantitative distich often joins its two parts through one word, and because of this enjambement is common in Immanuel's sonnets. Enjambement from line to line is found in Italian sonnets, especially in the ones composed during the first few centuries of the form's existence. We find a striking example of this in the first sonnet of Petrarch's *Canzoniere*.[9] Immanuel sometimes uses one word to link two successive lines, with the first half of a word ending the first line,

---

[6] See, for example, Schirmann, *Ha-Shirah ha-ᶜIvrit*, 1: 187.

[7] On this matter cf. A. Coen, *Sefer Ruah Hadashah* (Reggio, 1822), 3.

[8] See Pagis, *Hiddush u-Masoret*, 263.

[9] Elwert, *Versificazione italiana*, 40–41.

and the second half beginning the one after it.[10] This phenomenon was also common in Italian *rima rotta* ("broken rhyme").[11] In Immanuel's sonnets enjambement occurs only between lines that connect like the distich (*delet* and *soger*) of the classical Spanish line: 1-2, 3-4, 5-6, 13-14. They never occur in lines that would not constitute a *delet* and *soger*, such as 2-3 or 4-5.[12] This prosodic outlook found a perfect match in the textual layout of the early Hebrew sonnet, as we see in examples from early manuscripts of the *Maḥḥarot*:

MS. 1386 of the Jewish Theological Seminary of New York, ca. sixteenth century

This graphic scheme was preserved by tradition throughout the sixteenth century even after enjambements had become rare.

Choosing *ha-shalem (b)* and it alone had its price. It forced Immanuel to swerve from normal Italian practice and to create a masculine line of twelve syllables rather than ten. But we should note that in Immanuel's day it was not obligatory to stress the tenth syllable in the line even in Italian poetry. Thus we find lines of twelve syllables with the stress on the eleventh syllable in Dante, and even in Petrarch after him.[13] The deviation therefore was not so great. Nevertheless, since the twelve-syllable line is the only masculine line in Immanuel's sonnets, it is a hallmark of Immanuel's style, and unique to the Hebrew sonnet.

---

[10] *Tzror Zehuvim*, ed. Bregman, sonnets 14, 34, 23, and 24.

[11] Biadene, *Morfologia del sonetto*, 138.

[12] Concerning Moses Luzzato's reliance on this, see his *Sefer Leshon Limmudim*, ed. A. M. Habermann (Jerusalem, 1945), 56.

[13] M. Casella, "Endecasillabi di dodici sillabe?", *Studi Danteschi* 24 (1939): 79–109. See also L. Goldberg, "Petrarca, Hayyav vi-Yetzirato," in *Mi-Dor u-Meᶜever*, ed. A. Krauss and S. Penini (Tel Aviv, 1977), 123–99.

4. Internal Rhythm

The Caesura

Another element in the syllabic Italian line is the caesura. The Italian *endecasillabo* is divided by the caesura into two or even three unequal parts. It usually falls after a word that ends on a strong stress, due to a logical pause in the syntax. There are really no strict guidelines for the caesura. In practice it usually appears after the sixth syllable, less frequently after the eighth or the fourth. One way or the other, it wanders from place to place, and is likely to change place from line to line within the same poem itself. The kind of stress that occurs before the caesura is also not fixed, and can be either feminine or masculine. In eleven-syllable lines the caesura is considered a secondary element, and may be dispensed with altogether.

These traits make the Italian *endecasillabo* different from the lines of poetry in other languages, which distinguish between short and long syllables. In those languages the caesura falls after a given stressed syllable whether it comes at the end of a word or in the middle of it. Fixing the caesura in the middle of a word obviously contradicts the syntax, but it does provide it with a fixed position in the poetic line.[14] Below, in order to distinguish between the two different caesuras, we will call the first one "syntactical," and the second "musical."

Given all the above, it follows that Immanuel had three different options from which to choose. The first option was simply to ignore the question of caesura, since the *endecasillabo* did not actually require one. The second was to create a syntactical caesura corresponding to the syllabic nature of Immanuel's meters. And the third option was to create a "musical" caesura corresponding to the quantitative nature of these meters and in agreement with Hebrew grammar, which distinguishes between short and long syllables.

A study of Immanuel's sonnets shows that his lines are divisible by caesuras. He thus rejected the first option. In one case, we can even see that Immanuel made a special effort to create a caesura, even though it meant reversing the usual word-order:

> To abhor the Eden garden and to desire Hell
> What good is the Eden garden when there is no lover?[15]

---

[14] Elwert, *Versificazione italiana*, 54–57.

[15] From the sonnet *Nafshi be-qirbi* (*Tzror Zehuvim*, sonnet 25). The order ʿ*eden-gan* also appears in the Bible (Ezekiel 28: 13), but there it is necessary because of the construct *gan-elohim*.

The usual "Garden of Eden" (*gan-ʿeden*) is here written as "the Eden garden (*ʿeden-gan*); a change in the standard word-order that sounds just as forced in Hebrew as it does in English. Perhaps Immanuel inverted the word-order in order to make the caesura more prominent. By inverting the word-order, he was able to position the caesura at the optimal place: at the end of a syntactical unit, at the end of the sixth syllable, and also after the stress.

Did Immanuel use a syntactical caesura, or was it the musical kind? It turns out that a number of Immanuel's lines read equally well using either caesura, as we can see in the example below. Using the syntactical caesura we read:

Alas my soul	how greatly I do fear!
If I am summoned	to the King's judgment
My tears will then flow like dew	and my spirit flee
Then my soul	for death will long.[16]

Using the syntactic system the caesura wanders from line to line: in the first line it falls after the fourth phonetic syllable; in the second line after the fifth; in the third line after the seventh; and in the fourth line after the third. A musical caesura divides these same lines in a different way:

Alas my soul, how great-	ly I do fear!
If I am summoned to	the King's judgement
My tears will then flow like	dew and my spirit flee
Then my soul for its death	will long

In this reading, the caesura always falls after the sixth syllable, which is stressed.

Sometimes the division is identical using both kinds of caesura, as we see in the continuation of the same sonnet in Hebrew. However, some lines in Immanuel's sonnets cannot be neatly divided using the musical caesura and require the syntactical caesura alone.[17]

We must conclude, therefore, that Immanuel preferred the syllabic syntactical caesura over the quantitative musical caesura, and it seems that things were also interpreted this way in the sixteenth century.[18] Immanuel thus preferred the practices of Italian syllabic poetry over those of quantitative Hebrew poetry. Even so, he created a form that was unique to him and to Hebrew poetry. As already

---

[16] *Tzror Zehuvim*, ed. Bregman, sonnet 13.

[17] E.g. *Tzror Zehuvim*, ed. Bregman, Vsonnet 18.

[18] Concerning Samuel Archivolti's thoughts about the caesura, see below, Chap. 11, Part 2. Pagis dealt with the question of the Hebrew caesura in Italy and concluded that "undoubtedly, such a caesura was found already in the seventeenth century." It turns out that the phenomenon goes back much further See D. Pagis, "Hamtza'at ha-Iambus ha-ʿIvri u-Temurot ba-Metriqa ha-ʿIvrit be'Italia," *Ha-Sifrut* 4 (1973): 651–712 [repr. in Idem , *Ha-Shir Davur ʿal ʿOfanav*, ed. E. Fleischer (Jerusalem, 1993): 166–255].

noted, the caesura divides the Italian line into unequal parts, and this is also true of Immanuel's eleven-syllable feminine line. But in his twelve-syllable masculine lines the caesura that typically falls after the sixth syllable divides them into two equal parts. This division is customary in metrical systems that distinguish between long and short syllables, and is a signal feature in the Hebrew sonnet.[19]

Tonal Elements

The *endecasillabo* can embody an orderly rhythm of stress in either ascending (iambic, anapaestic) or descending (trochaic, dactylic) patterns.[20] Immanuel's Hebrew sonnets do not have a similar flexibility since their internal rhythm was restricted from the beginning by the various rules of his double system. According to the quantitative pattern in Immanuel's sonnets, odd-numbered phonetic syllables — the third, the seventh, the eleventh — could not be stressed, since each of those is either a mobile *shewa* or a *ḥataf*. In his syllabic pattern the stress had to fall on either the tenth or twelfth syllable. All this conspired to create an internal iambic rhythm. The "iambic effect" was noticed in later Italian Hebrew poetry, and as a result some scholars mistakenly concluded that Hebrew poetry in Italy was scanned in tonal meters.[21] Later scholars (Hak, Hrushowsky, and Pagis)[22] straightened out this misconception, but they did not get to the root of the "iambic effect": the sonnets of Immanuel of Rome.

5. Symmetrical Alternating Stress

When one of Immanuel's sonnets combines both feminine and masculine lines, they unite by force of meter and form into a symmetrical arrangement of alternating stress. Immanuel varied these by using an impressive wealth of patterns. All in all, Immanuel created twelve symmetrical arrangements of stress, which can be divided into seven groups, as follows: (For the sake of brevity we will denote the feminine line as 11, and the masculine line as 12, based on their number of syllables).

---

[19] Elwert, *Versificazione italiana*, 40–41.
[20] Elwert, *Versificazione italiana*, 60–63.
[21] See Y. Fichmann, *Anshei Besorah* (Tel Aviv, 1938), 19; M. Hak, "Nitzanei ha-Mishqal ha-Toni ba-Shirah ha-ʿIvrit," *Tarbiz* 11 (1940): 91–109.
[22] See B. Hrushowsky, "Prosody, Hebrew," in *Encyclopedia Judaica*, 16 vols. Jerusalem, 1972), 13: 1195–1240; Pagis, "Hamtza'at ha-Iambus," 657–76 (in *Ha-Shir Davur*, 174–211). Neither of them realized that the twelfth syllable had to be stressed.

A. The entire sonnet is rhymed using one stress:
    I. Every line is 11 (15 sonnets. Example: Im ha-gezera yoreda)[23]
    II. Every line is 12 (10 sonnets. Example: Ereh ani haman)[24]
B. The octave has one stress; the sestet another:
    III. The octave is 11; the sestet 12[25]
C. The octave has one stress; the sestet repeats one pattern:
    IV. The octave is 11; the sestet: (12, 12, 11) x 2[26]
    V. The octave is 11; the sestet: (11, 12, 11) x 2[27]
    VI. The octave is 12; the sestet: (11, 12, 11) x 2[28]
D. The octave has one stress; the sestet two different patterns:
    VII. The octave is 11; the sestet: 12, 11, 12; 11, 12, 11[29]
E. The octave has a repeating pattern; the sestet one stress:
    VIII. The octave is (11, 12, 12, 11) x 2; the sestet 12[30]
    IX. The octave is (11, 12, 12, 11) x 2; the sestet 11[31]
    X. The octave is (12, 11, 11, 12) x 2; the sestet (12, 11, 10) x 2[32]
    XI. The octave is (12, 11, 11, 12) x 2; the sestet (12, 12, 11) x 2[33]
F. The octave has a repeating pattern; the sestet two different patterns:
    XII. The octave: (12, 11, 12) x 2; the sestet 11, 12, 11; 12, 11, 12[34]

The unique musicality that is so charming in Immanuel's sonnets owes much to this wealth of stress-patterns. It imbues his sonnets with symmetry over and above the symmetry inherent in the sonnet form and stamps them with another unique hallmark of the Hebrew sonnet.

Let us now examine the relationship of the stress-schemes to the rhyme-patterns:

---

[23] *Tzror Zehuvim*, ed. Bregman, sonnet 1.
[24] *Tzror Zehuvim*, ed. Bregman, sonnet 32.
[25] *Tzror Zehuvim*, ed. Bregman, sonnet 13: *Oyah le-nafshi*.
[26] *Tzror Zehuvim*, ed. Bregman, sonnet 7.
[27] *Tzror Zehuvim*, ed. Bregman, sonnet 24.
[28] *Tzror Zehuvim*, ed. Bregman, sonnet 15.
[29] *Tzror Zehuvim*, ed. Bregman, sonnet 37: *Husha levavi*.
[30] *Tzror Zehuvim*, ed. Bregman, sonnet 20: *At bein ʿatzei yaʿar*.
[31] *Tzror Zehuvim*, ed. Bregman, sonnets 3 and 16: *Dodai she'ealuni; Devar shamativ*.
[32] *Tzror Zehuvim*, ed. Bregman, sonnet 14: *Tzivu yetzirotai*.
[33] *Tzror Zehuvim*, ed. Bregman, sonnets 31, 17, and 6: *An tahanot libakh; Sikel zeman yadav; Yomru shehaqim*.
[34] *Tzror Zehuvim*, ed. Bregman, sonnet 19: *Yom ererah ʿofra*.

A parallel structure is created in the octaves: ABBA ABBA goes with 11 12 12 11, 11 12 12 11 or with 12 11 11 12, 12 11 11 12. It may also occur in the sestet, as in the sonnet *Ḥusha levavi*:[35]

C D C D C D
12 11 12 11 12 11

Similarly in the sonnet *Yom ererah ʿofra*:[36]

C D C D C D
11 12 11 12 11 12

But when the sestet has three rhymes, the two patterns clash in a variety of ways, as in *Mi he'emin ʿofra*:[37]

C D E C D E
11 12 11 11 12 11

or *Tzuvu yetzirotai*:[38]

C D E C D E
12 11 11 12 11 11

or *An taḥanot libakh*:[39]

C D E C D E
12 12 11 12 12 11

Once again we have a harmonious, fixed, and anticipated octave versus a sestet of many possibilities, the distinction having been made in a way that is typical of the Hebrew corpus.

The twelve stress-patterns that Immanuel created in the sonnets of mixed stress do not exhaust the possibilities or the theoretical combinations. In the wake of Immanuel, some poets added new combinations in their sonnets, largely using his method. But none of them could even begin to rival the richness of his patterns.

---

[35] *Tzror Zehuvim*, ed. Bregman, sonnet 37.
[36] *Tzror Zehuvim*, ed. Bregman, sonnet 19.
[37] *Tzror Zehuvim*, ed. Bregman, sonnet 24.
[38] *Tzror Zehuvim*, ed. Bregman, sonnet 14.
[39] *Tzror Zehuvim*, ed. Bregman, sonnet 31.

Despite the considerable significance of the stress patterns in the Hebrew sonnet, it has not received notice in the editions of Immanuel's *Maḥḥarot* due to the editor's unawareness of his dual metrical system. No editor has found it necessary to indicate the places where meters change, either alongside the poem or in the notes, marking only the quantitative pattern. Frequently only one quantitative meter is noted (the first or second hemistich in the *ha-shalem*, even in sonnets which have both meters), and worse than that, not only in Immanuel's sonnets, but also in the sonnets of many poets who came after him and used his methods. The delicate patterns of sound have even been corrupted by incorrect vocalization.[40]

However, not only modern editors but even some of his ardent adherents failed to understand Immanuel's poetics. In the sixteenth century his mixed stress-patterns gained followers, only to be later rejected and even branded as "heavy". Due to the increased influence of Italian poetry, which favored poems of unified stress, changes in rhythm and sound were perceived as interruptions in the smooth, pleasant flow. But in our time, with the revival of spoken Hebrew, Immanuel's methods of changing stress have enjoyed something of a renaissance.[41]

---

[40] See for example the sonnet by Moses ben Joab in Schirmann, *Mivḥar*, 238, where we find *nifTAḥu* instead of *nifteHU* ("opened"), and *aSAfu* instead of *asFU* ("gathered"). For a corrected text see *Tzror Zehuvim*, ed. Bregman, sonnet 44.

[41] Bregman, *Sharsheret ha-Zahav*, 77–78.

IV. Rhyme

1. Homogenous Rhyme

The Italians did not rhyme the two different kinds of *endecasillabo* together, but each with its own kind. That is, a masculine line was rhymed with a masculine rhyme (*piano* with *piano*) and a feminine line with a feminine line (*tronco* with *tronco*). In this way they created homogenous rhymes: feminine or masculine.

Like the Italians, Immanuel rhymed his sonnets using homogenous rhymes: eleven-syllable lines with eleven-syllable lines, and twelve-syllable lines with twelve-syllable lines. He never deviated from this rule.[1] Homogenous rhyme was a complete innovation in Hebrew poetry, where ultimate and penultimate stressed words had always been allowed to rhyme freely together.

2. Stressed Rhyme

Immanuel made yet another, even more fundamental innovation in the definition of the rhyme itself, and here too he followed the Italians. Unlike the terminal rhyme in the classic Hebrew poems of Spain, which is formed from the final syllable of the line (like the French *consonne d'appui*), the Italian rhyme is formed by all the sounds from the final stress in the end of the line. Rhymes such as *revaʿ-rovaʿ* or *orekh-ʿerekh* in Hebrew create terminal but not Italian rhymes, since they do not involve all of the sounds in the word after the stress. If an Italian sonnet has an octave rhymed *determinare-avere-diletare-savere*,[2] its rhyme-scheme is ABAB and not AAAA, since the rhyme is *are* and not *re*.[3] Similarly, when Immanuel rhymed a sestet using *shiviti-ʿavarti-shakhaḥti / kiviti-tzarti-hipaḥti*, the rhymes were created by *viti, varti, aḥti* (CDE CDE) and not simply *ti*.[4]

A Hebrew rhyme that depends on the position of its stress can be called a "stressed rhyme,"[5] to distinguish it from the old, terminal rhyme which does

---

[1] One "deviation" in Yarden's edition is nothing but an editorial mistake (in the sonnet *Shadai nekhonim*, line 10).

[2] For an example see E. F. Langley, ed., *The Early Poetry of Giacomo Da Lentino*, (Cambridge, 1915), 59, sonnet 1.

[3] On the normative Italian rhyme, see Elwert, *Versificazione italiana*, 83.

[4] See *Tzror Zehuvim*, ed. Bregman, sonnet 2.

[5] Hrushowsky, "Prosody, Hebrew," 1222.

not depend on it. Immanuel accepted the rigors of the new norm. According to Yarden's edition, he deviates several times from the obligation of including all the sounds after the final stress, but these deviations can be explained. One of them is due to an editorial mistake;[6] another apparently to earlier scribal errors;[7] others to the particular concept of the sonnet.[8] The only exception is the combination *Camerino-arinu*,[9] in which it is actually the last vowel that does not rhyme. This can be attributed to the fact that the Jews of Italy did not always clearly distinguish between *o* and *u* in non-Hebrew proper names.[10]

3. Rich Rhyme

The system of stressed rhyme creates a distinction between masculine and feminine rhymemes. The former is shorter than the second and involves fewer sounds. In Italian poetry the feminine rhymeme is prevalent, and the rhymes are naturally rich. The Hebrew language is largely masculine and thus confronts the Hebrew poet with a problem: feminine rhymemes enrich the rhyme but risk being hackneyed; masculine rhymes do not risk being hackneyed, but impoverish the rhymeme. The poet must ostensibly choose between a poor rhymeme and a hackneyed rhyme.[11]

As the first, or almost the first Hebrew sonneteer, Immanuel of Rome could have made extensive use of feminine rhymes without the risk of being hackneyed, since feminine rhymes had never yet figured prominently in Hebrew poetry. And indeed, compared to the rest of his poems or to his rhymed prose, Immanuel's sonnets show a profuse, though not exclusive use of feminine rhymes. As noted, ten of his sonnets use masculine rhyme exclusively; fifteen use feminine rhymes exclusively, and the rest use both.

Immanuel endeavored to enrich his rhymemes to the maximum. In order to enrich the masculine rhymeme, that is poor by its very nature, he included the stressed consonant in the rhymeme: *mi-zevul-yevul-levul-ha-gevul; qetzar-maʿatzar-neʿetzar-va-tzar*.[12] Thus he took upon himself an obligation not required in Italian poetry, but typical to traditional Hebrew-Spanish poetry which prohibited

---

[6] See above, note 1.

[7] For details see Bregman, *Shevil ha-Zahav*, 42, note 7.

[8] As noted above, Chap. 2, Part 4, and as we shall see below, Chap. 12, Part 1.

[9] *Tzror Zehuvim*, ed. Bregman, sonnet 31.

[10] See Solomon Almoli, *Sheqel ha-Qodesh* (Constantinople, 1506), 65r; Hartom, "Mivta ha-ʿIvrit," 58–59.

[11] See Hrushowsky, "Prosody, Hebrew," 1222–23, 1227.

[12] *Tzror Zehuvim*, ed. Bregman, sonnets 9 and 14.

rhyming *shor* ("ox") with *ḥamor* ("ass"), a poetic rule humorously based on the biblical injunction "Thou shalt not plow with an ox (*shor*) and an ass (*ḥamor*) together" (Deuteronomy 22:10). *Shor* and *ḥamor* sound like perfect rhymes, and indeed are usually regarded as such except in the Hebrew tradition.[13]

That Immanuel consciously accepted this extra obligation can be deduced from the fact that when using feminine rhyme, which is naturally rich, he allowed himself to dispense with the stressed consonant in the rhymeme: *tovu-yahshovu*; *binoti-shaloti-baroti-rivoti*.[14] But his craving for musical richness would not let him stop here, and he sometimes applied his rhyme-enriching technique to the feminine rhymeme as well, by including the stressed consonant: *lanu-higlanu*; *ḥasdekha-nodekha*; *ʿomer-omer-Cedarlaʿomer*.[15]

Nor was this all. More than once Immanuel expanded his rhymeme (whether feminine or masculine) to include sounds even before the stressed consonant: *da'avon-raʿavon*; *na'avah-ta'avah-ga'avah*.[16] Expanding the rhymeme to include sounds before the stress can sometimes come at the expense of consonants within the basic rhymeme and create a discontinuous rhyme: *yaʿapilu-yavhilu*; *nikhtevu-nitzvu*.[17] And sometimes the rhyme is composed of entire words distinguished from each other only by their meaning: *shaḥaq-shaḥaq* ("heaven-dust"); *maʿal-maʿal* ("above-deceit"); *yahalom-yahalom* ("diamond-will pound").[18]

With this it would seem that Immanuel had exhausted all the options for enriching his rhyme. Only he did not restrict the rhymeme to the rhyme-word, and sometimes started it even before this.[19] Expanding the rhymeme in this fashion creates a rich (and sometimes discontinuous) rhyme that is characteristic of Immanuel: *el-ʿever-el qever* ("towards-to the grave"); *asher hekhanti-asher he'emanti* ("which I prepared-which I believed"); and so on.[20]

The rule, no doubt, seems to be that no rhyme can be too rich!

---

[13] This is the origin of the phenomenon described by Hrushowsky, concerning Hebrew rhyme in Italy. See Hrushowsky, "Prosody, Hebrew," 1222–23.
[14] *Tzror Zehuvim*, ed. Bregman, sonnet 7.
[15] *Tzror Zehuvim*, ed. Bregman, sonnets 6, 8, and 37.
[16] *Tzror Zehuvim*, ed. Bregman, sonnets 18 and 3.
[17] *Tzror Zehuvim*, ed. Bregman, sonnets 10 and 15.
[18] *Tzror Zehuvim*, ed. Bregman, sonnets 4, 28, and 34.
[19] For examples, see *Tzror Zehuvim*, ed. Bregman, sonnets 15, 19, and 37.
[20] *Tzror Zehuvim*, ed. Bregman, sonnet 12; see also sonnets 6 and 3.

4. Alternating Rhymes

The alternation of masculine and feminine lines in Immanuel's sonnets naturally creates alternating rhymes. These are extremely varied, as already noted, and the rhymes fall therefore in various kinds of patterns, such as:

> feminine-masculine-masculine-feminine in the quartets, and masculine alone in the sestets;[21]

> masculine-feminine-feminine-masculine in the quartets, and masculine-masculine-feminine in the sestets;[22]

> feminine rhymes only in the quartets, and in the sestets masculine-feminine-masculine.[23]

In his Hebrew-language article about Hebrew rhyme, Hrushowsky wrote:[24]

> The revolution that occurred in the poetry of Bialik was two-fold. First of all, the reign of the feminine rhyme came to an end, and there arose the desire for alternating rhymes (masculine-feminine-masculine-feminine etc.) as in Russian poetry. Of course, such alternating rhyme was achieved only in Israeli spoken Hebrew . . . ; second, and most important, the entire range of the Hebrew language was made available for the purposes of rhyme, in keeping with the poet's pronunciation — the Ashkenazi pronunciation of whatever dialect.

The dimensions of the "revolution" dwindle considerably in view of Immanuel's sonnets, and in view of the fact, to be explained below, that alternating rhyme continued in Hebrew poetry in Italy until the end of the long days of the school.

5. Rhymed Biblical Phrases

The rhymes in Immanuel's sonnets are virtuoso in every respect: their patterns are sophisticated, their symmetries intricate and varied, their rhymemes rich and refreshing. There is a clear mixture of Italian and Hebrew elements in all these, as noted above. However, Immanuel stressed the Jewish-Hebrew element in his

---

[21] *Tzror Zehuvim*, ed. Bregman, sonnet 13.
[22] *Tzror Zehuvim*, ed. Bregman, sonnet 31.
[23] *Tzror Zehuvim*, ed. Bregman, sonnet 37.
[24] B. Hrushowsky, "Ha-Shitot ha-Rashiot shel he-Ḥaruz ha-ʿIvri min ha-Piyyut ʿad Yameinu," *Ha-Sifrut* 2 (1969): 744.

sonnets through yet one other technique. This involved rhyming the Bible into his sonnets.[25]

Hebrew poets have studded their poems with quotations from sacred Jewish texts since antiquity. Such quotations linked the poem to a sacred tradition, infusing it with some of the majesty of the source and depths of association. The poetic advantage of this custom was clear, and the ability to weave biblical phrases into a poem much admired.[26] These quotations could be either subject to the same demands of prosody as the other elements of the poem, or exempt from them.[27] When Immanuel embedded biblical phrases into his sonnets, he made sure that they conformed with the meter of the poem, the rules for rhyming, the poem's rhyme-scheme, and the rhymemes.

Quotations from the Bible and other sacred Hebrew texts are woven into the sonnets in a variety of ways. Sometimes a quotation takes up the entire line, but contributes only one of the rhyme members:

o laʿasot yanshof ve-kof yazamta ("or to make an owl and an ape you schemed")
ma he-ḥalom ha-zeh asher ḥalamta ("What is this dream you dreamed?": Genesis 37:10)[28]

qatzti be-maḥmadav u-vo nivashti ("I was sick of his quirks and ashamed of him")
el maḥanot ha-el asher pagashti ("These camps that I have met": Genesis 33:8).[29]

Some quotations take up only part of the line but contribute both rhyme members:

asher lo karuʿ la-baʿal ("who did not bow down to Baal": 1 Kings 19:18)

[lahem mekora'] beit ḥalutz ha-naʿal ("[Those will be named] the house of him that had his shoe loosed": Deuteronomy 25:10)[30]

---

[25] See D. Bregman, "Ha-Shibbutz ha-Mitharez," *Mehqarei Yerushalayim be-Sifrut ʿIvrit* 13 (1992): 103–18.

[26] See below for a quotation from Moses ibn Ezra. David ben Bilia, who lived in the thirteenth-fourteenth centuries, notes that "the best poets" often used quotations from the Bible. Ben Bilia's treatise on the techniques of Hebrew rhyme, *Derekh Lacasot Haruzim*, was published by N. Allony in *Qovetz al-ʿYad* n.s. 6/16 (1966): 225–46.

[27] See Moses ibn Ezra, *Sefer Shirat Yisrael*, ed. B. Z. Halper (Leipzig 1924): 205–6; and in recent research see A. Mirsky, *Maḥtzavatan shel Tzurot ha-Piyyut* (Jerusalem and Tel Aviv, 1969); E. Fleischer, "Mivnim Strof'im Meʿayn Ezori'im ba-Piyyut ha-Qadum," *Ha-Sifrut* 2 (1970): 194–240; Y. Yahalom, "Reshita shel ha-Sheqila ha-Meduyeqet be-Shira ha-ʿIvrit," *Leshonenu* 47 (1983): 25–61.

[28] *Tzror Zehuvim*, ed. Bregman, sonnet 5.

[29] *Tzror Zehuvim*, ed. Bregman, sonnet 30.

[30] *Tzror Zehuvim*, ed. Bregman, sonnet 1.

And sometimes the quotations contribute both rhyme members, with one quotation taking up an entire line, and the other, only part of the line:

be-rov ḥasdeikha ("in your great loving-kindness": Psalm 5:8)

miqdash adonai konenu yadeikha ("Thy hands established the Lord's sanctuary": Exodus 15:17)[31]

Occasionally, Immanuel even managed to get three rhymes out of quotations from the sacred texts. This could sometimes require a slight change in the original for metrical reasons:

ʿal yedei hadaḥaq ("in a big rush": BT Shabbat 100b)

kemo mar mi-deli u-kheshaḥaq ("like a drop in the bucket and like dust": Isaiah 40:15)

ʿal maḥaq ("used writing-paper": BT Baba Batra 163b)[32]

And in the following example, Immanuel gets all four rhyme members for the octave from the Bible (once again incorporating slight changes in each one for metrical reasons):

names levavi az ve-haya mayim ("my heart melted then and became water": Isaiah 7:5)

. . . habat Yerushalayim ("My daughter, Jerusalem": Lamentations 2:13 and elsewhere)

nata ke-doq shamayim ("He hung the heavens like a curtain": Isaiah 40:22)

li-zevuv asher bi-qtzeh yeʾor Mitzrayim ("to the fly at the farthest end of the Egyptian Nile": Isaiah 7:19)[33]

In poems that are not sonnets, Immanuel sometimes used rhyming quotations from the sacred writings in order to end a poem with a flourish. Just how conscious Immanuel was of this function of the rhymed phrases we can see in the commission which he puts in the mouth of his patron:

---

[31] *Tzror Zehuvim*, ed. Bregman, sonnet 8.
[32] *Tzror Zehuvim*, ed. Bregman, sonnet 4.
[33] *Tzror Zehuvim*, ed. Bregman, sonnet 19.

> Compose two poems for me to say / I'll put them where I study and pray / one of them will complete "Know before whom you stand" / and the second will rhyme with "Know before whom you are destined to render an account."[34]

The rhyming of phrases from the Bible and other sacred Hebrew sources links the innovative stressed rhyme to the Hebrew traditions of antiquity, and also endows the Hebrew sonnet with yet another unique trait.

---

[34] *Maḥbarot*, ed. Yarden, 213. The first phrase comes from *Berakhot* 28b, the second from *Pirkei Avot* 3:1.

V. Structures of Syntax and Rhetoric

1. Syntax

Syntactic Distribution

Immanuel of Rome's Hebrew sonnet is, as we have seen, a two-part musical system: harmonious in the first part, complex and tense in the second. This system is reinforced by means of syntax.

The basic foundation is the fourteen lines divided into two parts: the octave and the sestet. This division is unfailingly supported by the syntax in Immanuel's sonnets: each and every octave ends with a final punctuation mark.

Quatrains are clearly outlined through syntax as well. The end of the first quatrain is also the end of a sentence. Only in two sonnets does a sentence that has begun in the first quatrain conclude at the end of line five, and not at the end of line four.[1] But because here too the octave is clearly divided into two parts, we can probably attribute the "overflow" to a poetic blunder and not to the expression of a different trend.[2] We thus have before us a well-coordinated system in which syntax works together with rhyme to separate the octave from the sestet and divide it into two quatrains. This cooperation presents us with a harmonious, simple, and uniform octave: harmonious, because it co-ordinates the division of strophe and rhyme; simple, because it clearly divides the octave in two; and uniform, because it remains permanent throughout the corpus of Immanuel's sonnets.

Syntax is no less important to the sestet. Because of the conflict between rhyme and strophic division, syntax is crucial to interpretation. In most sonnets the sestet is divided into two tercets with a final punctuation mark that creates a clear pause between them:

> Garlic is the beauty of the land; the flower of every crop,
> Grace gave birth to it, and splendor embroidered it,
> Orion and her progeny used it to strike a covenant with God!

---

[1] *Tzror Zehuvim*, ed. Bregman, sonnets 17 and 20. A "sentence" here refers to words with a subject-object relationship. This syntactical division is sometimes blurred in *Tzror Zehuvim*, since syntax is not the only factor determining punctuation there.

[2] See below, Chap. 13, Part 2.

> Bulbs of onions are like balls of sop,
> Wheels within wheels, and the stalk of it
> Is like Elisha's wonder-worker of a rod.[3]

The syntax in this sestet supports the strophic division, unlike the rhyme which links the sestet into a single unit.

In a few sonnets, the first strophe does not end with a final punctuation mark, so that the sestet tends to sound like a sextain. For example:

> How wise were the heavenly hosts up in the skies,
> If it was they who encouraged You to place
> The beauty of their form, wherein we dwell,
>
> Only through her can we attain their glory: we'll rise
> To see the glory on high and the crown of grace —
> The day our eyes gaze upon the gazelle![4]

Here the syntax determines in favor of rhyme against strophic division.

Sometimes the sestet divides syntactically into three pairs of lines (with a final punctuation mark at the end of each pair); into a quatrain and a pair (by means of a final punctuation mark at the end of each); into a pair and a quatrain; or into single lines. Here, for example, we have three pairs of lines:

> And I set my heart to thinking: is it because of my sin
> The sorrows of Time weigh on me today?
> I see my conscience and upright action
>
> Mourning my loss of good sense every day.
> I rage over youth itself, and fling my shoe again and again
> at my youthful vigor, which drove my good sense away.[5]

These divisions contradict both the strophic divisions and the rhymes.

One way or the other, syntax creates a tense, varied, and flexible sestet: tense, because of the contradictions it creates or reinforces between the different elements of poetry; varied, because of the different syntactical options; and flexible, because of the lack of conformity or of rules guiding the syntactic division of the sestet. This sestet stands in opposition to the harmonious octave, where the syntax is simple and unified. Thus the dichotomy inherent in the prosodic structures invades the verbal structures of logic.

---

[3] *Tzror Zehuvim*, ed. Bregman, sonnet 32. The reference to Elisha comes from 2 Kings. 4:29.

[4] *Tzror Zehuvim*, ed. Bregman, sonnet 8. Similarly, see sonnets 1, 18, and 20.

[5] *Tzror Zehuvim*, ed. Bregman, sonnet 29. Similarly, see sonnets 11 and 36.

Syntactic Symmetry

Syntactic division is often emphasized through symmetrical syntax. This symmetry can result from having the same number of sentences in each of the quatrains, with each quatrain containing one,[6] two,[7] or three sentences.[8] The same is true for the tercets and other syntactic divisions in the sestet, whether pairs of lines, four lines and a pair, or a pair and four lines. These can be identical to each other through having the same number of sentences, as we can see in the examples cited above.

Symmetry can also be created through the parallel syntax of strophes. This can take the form of: (a) an octave in which every quatrain has a short beginning followed by a long sentence unified by punctuation; (b) a first quatrain with a long sentence followed by a brief one, and vice versa in the second quatrain; or (c) two quatrains composed of a sentence in indirect speech, followed by a sentence in direct speech.[9] In the following example, each quatrain has three sentences and is the mirror image of its parallel:

> The crown of Time has fallen this morn / For from her throne in heaven this bright star did fall.
> Our flowers are withered, the crops are gall.
> The blossom of the land is wilted, forlorn.
>
> The skies are gloomy and the world does mourn.
> Alas for Spring that has turned to Fall.
> Sighs without number burst through one and all / For this heavenly star, from our very midst torn.[10]

Sometimes the symmetry between the first (I) and the second quatrain (II) is created through identical syntax in parallel lines:

> I. How can I regain my strength when great is the sadness / Of my heart, and there is nothing . . .
>
> II. For my husband does not have enough to fill the hunger / Of my house, and does not . . . [11]

---

[6] *Tzror Zehuvim*, ed. Bregman, sonnets 3 and 11.
[7] *Tzror Zehuvim*, ed. Bregman, sonnets 1, 16, 18, 24, 28.
[8] *Tzror Zehuvim*, ed. Bregman, sonnet 9.
[9] *Tzror Zehuvim*, ed. Bregman, sonnets 19, 34, and 35.
[10] *Tzror Zehuvim*, ed. Bregman, sonnet 9.
[11] *Tzror Zehuvim*, ed. Bregman, sonnet 18.

I. You are amongst the trees of the forest of Lebanon: a thistle /
   Amongst the princes of the land and its nobles: a pigmy

II. Amongst the kingdoms of Siḥon and ʿOg: Zanoaḥ / All human
    beings are the cause, and you: the effect[12]

The same is true for the syntactic units in the sestet. Here, for example, are two tercets with the same syntax:

> Dawn awakened me, and my spirit pounded
> From the beauty of the sun's face, whose light
> Hid the beauty of the graceful gazelle and her figure of diamond.
>
> The world's face grew light, and my soul darkened
> From seeing that it was only a vision of the night
> And thus, upon wakening, it saddened.[13]

Sometimes the quatrains are parallel through constructions of logic:

I. If the girl would walk upright, /
   So that angels upon her light could gaze —

II. Or, if she walked bent over, her sight /
    Would make people rush amazed.[14]

The sestet may also have parallel logic in keeping with the syntactic division. Here is an example in two tercets:

> I will not call the girl's body mere clay /
> For . . .
>
> I will sing a new song and say /
> For . . . [15]

Generally, the same symmetrical structure does not reoccur in both the octave and the sestet, and the symmetrical structures of syntax create two separate entities in the poem as a whole.

---

[12] *Tzror Zehuvim*, ed. Bregman, sonnet 20.
[13] *Tzror Zehuvim*, ed. Bregman, sonnet 34; and see, for example, sonnet 33.
[14] *Tzror Zehuvim*, ed. Bregman, sonnet 23, and see also sonnets 2, 4, and 24.
[15] *Tzror Zehuvim*, ed. Bregman, sonnet 4.

2. Rhetorical Patterns

Immanuel's rhetoric divides his sonnets in complete harmony with syntax. Together they create an opening line that divides the sonnet in two and begins the sestet on a dramatic note, as in the openings below from four different sonnets:

> Alas, my soul! Alas, generosity! On your life, my friend! Awake, O Messiah![16]

The separation between the octave (I) and the sestet (II) is emphasized by means of similar opening lines:

> I. Hurry, O anointed of God . . .
> II. Awake, O pride of Jacob[17]
>
> I. The heavens say to you . . .
> II. I hear Orion, the Pleiades and the Great Bear say[18]

The division of the octave into quatrains also receives a boost from the rhetoric, which separates the first quatrain (I) from the second quatrain (II) by giving the latter a dramatic opening line. This function of the opening line becomes abundantly clear when the words that open the second quatrain are more dramatic than those at the beginning of the octave:

> I. I heard something, expressed from day to day
> II. What do we have in common, O my evil urge . . . ?[19]
>
> I. It's been two years since I married / a husband
> II. Death did I cry for, day after day . . . ![20]
>
> I. My soul within me would consider
> II. What is there for me in Eden . . . ?[21]

Sometimes the second quatrain repeats information that is already known, and can be justified only by its stylized rhetoric and dramatic opening line:

---

[16] *Tzror Zehuvim*, ed. Bregman, sonnets 13, 2, 33, and 22.
[17] *Tzror Zehuvim*, ed. Bregman, sonnet 36.
[18] *Tzror Zehuvim*, ed. Bregman, sonnet 6.
[19] *Tzror Zehuvim*, ed. Bregman, sonnet 16.
[20] *Tzror Zehuvim*, ed. Bregman, sonnet 27.
[21] *Tzror Zehuvim*, ed. Bregman, sonnet 25.

I. They did not know that from the lusty I moved away
II. I sifted the criminals from the general sway[22]

I. A messenger from old age has already arrived . . . and the hands of death have prepared the kill.
II. Time will rise like a murderer still.[23]

Things are similar in the sestet. When the syntax divides the sestet into two tercets (as in the example cited above), the rhetoric emphasizes the division between the third (III) and fourth strophe (IV) by means of dramatic opening lines that often parallel each other:

III. Alas is me, O Time . . .
IV. Woe is me, O youth . . . [24]

III. I shall reproach the graceful girls . . .
IV. I shall say to the graceful gazelles . . . [25]

A sestet divided by syntax is likely to have as many rhetorical openings as it does sections. For example, the sestet below is divided by syntax into a pair of lines and four single lines:

Where is the wealth, and where are the provisions I made
For the pitfalls of death over which I must leap?
Where are the commandments that I obeyed?

Where is the Covenant of God that I must keep?
Where are the good deeds which I pre-paid?
Who has sown them for me to reap?[26]

Opening lines help divide the sonnet into different sections and strophes, but too many of them can turn the sonnet into a string of opening lines that blurs these divisions by their similarity. They also give the sonnet a jarring quality that interrupts the flow of the message, both linguistically and musically. This flaw has ramifications for the development of the subject, a topic which we will discuss in the next chapter.

---

[22] *Tzror Zehuvim*, ed. Bregman, sonnet 7.
[23] *Tzror Zehuvim*, ed. Bregman, sonnet 10.
[24] *Tzror Zehuvim*, ed. Bregman, sonnet 10.
[25] *Tzror Zehuvim*, ed. Bregman, sonnet 7.
[26] *Tzror Zehuvim*, ed. Bregman, sonnet 12.

VI. Developing the Subject

1. A Bipartite Structure

The subject, matter, or argument treated in Immanuel's sonnet also develops in structures that reflect his concept of form, and here too Immanuel composed in a fairly uniform way. Basically, he separated the content of the poem into two kinds of messages and organized each kind in an established place and order. As an example, let us take a look at the sonnet *Kol ya'alot:*

> All the gazelles were created from grime,
> At sunset, in great haste,
> Thus, like a drop in the bucket and like waste
> They came forth from the netherworld of Time.
>
> But the actions of the doe ascend and climb
> With all the Heavenly Host and celestial greats;
> She is a letter from God, not to be erased;
> Thus, the gazelle is indeed sublime.
>
> I will not call the girl's body mere clay,
> For not like the clay of the common gazelles,
> Is it, except in name: it bears an exalted soul.
>
> I will sing a new song and firmly say
> That she bursts all bounds and excels,
> That her great worth is hidden from one and all.[1]

The poem is divided into two sections, each composed according to a different approach to the subject. The first, which makes up the octave, presents the situation and all of the relevant information. This is the dynamic part of the poem; it progresses and develops. The second part, which makes up the sestet, does not add new information to the situation itself, but rather responds to it. This is a reflective part. It gazes backwards rather than forward, and looks at matters already discussed from a fresh point of view.

In addition to these basic differences between the two parts of this sonnet, we also find other kinds of differences: the situation is reported in the third person,

---

[1] *Tzror Zehuvim*, ed. Bregman, sonnet 4.

while the reflection is in the first person and has a personal tone. The situation is conveyed from up close by an omniscient speaker, while the reflection is conveyed from a different point of view. Here the poet presents himself in the persona of the speaker. His words are preceded by verbs of speech, as in the sonnet above where he says "I will not call" in line 9, and "I will sing" in line 12.

The entire sonnet deals with a single subject and situation. However, the situational part introduces them by their realistic components, while the reflective part detaches them from the level of actuality and speaks of them in the abstract. There is an epic quality in the situational part; it narrates and formulates narrative in the past tense. The reflective part, on the other hand, is introspective: it describes a state of mind and lacks the epic quality.

The situational part presents a state of reality, the cast of characters, the problematics of the situation or its conflict, the solution and the result. The reflective part relates to all these as matters already established, and seeks to assess them. Once the situational part of the sonnet turns to reflection, there is a narrowing of focus. The reflective part isolates one element out of all those included in the preceding part (in this case "the girl's body"), and confronts it alone.

Other sonnets by Immanuel of Rome allow us to suggest additional differences:

The situation (*) can be reported in direct or indirect speech; the reflection (**) passes into direct speech and dialogue:

* Time will rise like a murderer still. / . . . ah, my Time will be the winner.
** Alas is me, O Time . . . Woe is me, O youth.[2]

* My soul within me thinks it swell / to despise Paradise and desire Hell.
** What do we have in common, Paradise! . . . Hell! In my eyes you are great in grace and splendor.[3]

The introspective nature of the reflection takes the form of a dialogue between the speaker and his own self:

— And I set my heart to thinking: is it because of my sin / The sorrows of Time sink upon me today?
— Why moan, my soul, and why be cast down?
— O my hard-hearted soul, are you not ashamed?[4]

---

[2] *Tzror Zehuvim*, ed. Bregman, sonnet 10.
[3] *Tzror Zehuvim*, ed. Bregman, sonnet 25, and see also sonnet 9.
[4] *Tzror Zehuvim*, ed. Bregman, sonnets 29, 31 and 14.

In the sestet, various features respond verbally to elements in the situation, as in *Kol ya'alot*. The responses often take the form of an indirect quotation, and come after a few words of preface:

— Princes also sat and discussed me: / any woman who dies a virgin will be cut off.
— I will hear Orion, the Pleiades and the Great Bear say: / "May the day come . . ."[5]

Of course, not every sonnet uses all these techniques to create the different sections of the poem. But apart from one single exception,[6] all of Immanuel's sonnets are constructed in two parts formed through a substantial difference; they all put the situational part before the reflection; and most of them begin the reflection precisely in line 9, as in *Kol ya'alot*. Thus the system for developing the subject is linked to the system of prosody, and works with it to establish the sonnet as a two-part poem.

2. A Diffused Octave

Because Immanuel's sonnets confine the reflection to the end of the poem and the situational information to the first part, we might have expected a dense and dynamic octave, but Immanuel's octaves are not like this. Instead, the content in the quatrains is diffused in an elegant and stylized way through the impressive coordination between the prosodic, syntactic, and rhetorical structures. As the situation unfolds, the quatrains progress at a gentle pace. Often they parallel each other in verbal content and symmetry. So, for example, in *Kol ya'alot* the first quatrain declares that all the "gazelles" — the girls, that is — are made of "grime"; the second parallels this with the lovely, immortal "doe." In this octave and in others like it,[7] most of the information is contained in the second quatrain. The only purpose of the first quatrain is to provide a rhetorical flourish and to introduce the situation in a ceremonious way.

The second quatrain sometimes repeats the information from the first quatrain almost without change:

---

[5] *Tzror Zehuvim*, ed. Bregman, sonnets 26 and 6, and see also sonnet 3.
[6] *Tzror Zehuvim*, ed. Bregman, sonnet 34. The dominant motif in this sonnet is found in Italian poetry from this period, and Immanuel may have borrowed it from some Italian sonnet or other, together with its way of unfolding.
[7] Such as sonnets 3, 12, and 13 in *Tzror Zehuvim*, ed. Bregman.

> If man's fate from heaven doth descend —
> If indeed for nought people act on the level;
> Time will increase the bad and the very devil
> For every thug on high will ascend.
>
> Indeed, those who before Baal do not bend,
> Time like earthen jars will make them level
> In its eyes they are like the priests of Jezebel
> Called: "the house of the person whose shoe is loosened."[8]

Even when the situation grows complicated, it tends to exhaust itself in the first quatrain:

> Your daughter, charming buck, is a pain to me /
> I thought she was Esther, but lo, she's Zeresh. /
> By the covenant! Instead of Memuhan — Teresh /
> And instead of Aaron — it's Koraḥ you see![9]

Immanuel's tendency to present the situation early on sometimes causes the central idea to play itself out already in the opening lines:

> — My soul within me thinks it swell / to despise Paradise and desire Hell.
> — Woe is me, for I knew the worth of the soul / over the worth of the body — and feared it not.
> — It's been two years since I married / a husband, but he still lives, and I get no variety.[10]

The second quatrain often seems to struggle after the one before it, a fact occasionally emphasized by the unnecessary presence of conjunctions in the opening line: "indeed," "also," and so on. Sometimes it seems that the situation, often far from routine in itself, could have been limited to the first quatrain, and that it was stretched out only to keep the second one going. Thus, the quatrains so clearly outlined through prosody, syntax, and rhetoric are not over-stuffed with information. They unroll gently before the reader, like a finely-worked carpet.

---

[8] *Tzror Zehuvim*, ed. Bregman, sonnet 1. Line 5 uses a pun on the two meanings of the word "Baʿal" ("husband," lit. "lord") and the Babylonian deity of antiquity. Line 8 includes a quotation from Deuteronomy 25:10. For sonnets with structures similar to this example, see 21, 29, 33, and others.

[9] *Tzror Zehuvim*, ed. Bregman, sonnet 33; see also sonnets 3 and 21. The references to the lines translated here are to Haman's wife in Esther 5–6 and to a royal chamberlain in the same book, as well as to the story of Aaron's opponents in Numbers 16.

[10] *Tzror Zehuvim*, ed. Bregman, sonnets 25, 38, and 27.

3. Straggling Sestets

Immanuel's system of development limits the sestet in terms of content. It was supposed to be limited to reflections of an introspective, logical or emotional nature, preferably the second of these. Describing emotions in a state of flux is a difficult task, and Immanuel thus consigned the sestet from the beginning to a kind of static rhetoric that risked being monotonous.

Sometimes Immanuel was able to overcome these problems, and to create a reflective part that develops and adds something new. Especially successful in this respect is the sonnet *Ḥusha meshiaḥ-el ve-lama taʿamod* [11] ("Hurry, Messiah of God: why do you tarry?"). Its octave presents a common situation: the suffering Jews await the coming of the Messiah. The reflection also appears banal enough at first. It begins with a routine plea to the Messiah ("Rise, O Messiah, and ride forth today!"), but then suddenly turns the tables against him:

> If you mean to ride on an ass, my lord, go back and lie down!
> I urge you, O prince and Messiah, with a heart that is pure:
> Stop the redemption and leave the future obscure.[12]

This is an audacious reflection, surprising and dynamic. It crams its three lines to the bursting point and brings the second tercet to life. The sharpness of the warning is reinforced by the rhymed couplet of the last two lines, which is an unusual rhyme-scheme for Immanuel and brings the sonnet to a definitive conclusion. A similarly impressive development occurs in the sonnets *Yom erera ʿofra* ("The day the gazelle cursed") and *Amru u-ma isha* ("They said: and what is a woman?").[13] But most of his sonnets do not escape the dangers mentioned above, and the sestet often suffers from monotony and a surplus of space.[14]

The lines of the sestet often repeat themselves, as in the sonnet *Ilu anashim yelkhu el ʿever la-yam* ("If people were to go across the sea"):[15]

> Line 9: Where is the wealth, and where are the provisions . . . ?
> Line 11: Where are the commandments that I obeyed?
> Line 12: Where is the Covenant of God that I must keep?[16]

---

[11] *Tzror Zehuvim*, ed. Bregman, sonnet 22.
[12] *Tzror Zehuvim*, ed. Bregman, sonnet 22.
[13] *Tzror Zehuvim*, ed. Bregman, sonnets 19 and 28.
[14] As noted by Pagis in a few of his sonnets. See, for example, *Ḥiddush u-Masoret*, 319–20.
[15] *Tzror Zehuvim*, ed. Bregman, sonnet 12.
[16] *Tzror Zehuvim*, ed. Bregman, sonnet 12, and see also 29 and 37.

Only rarely is the internal distribution of the sestet, which is established by syntax, accompanied by sharp transitions. The static quality is especially striking in sestets that rehash topics already treated in the octave, with only a change of formulation (as required in the reflective part of the poem). So, for example, in

Oyah le-nafshi ("Alas, my soul")[17] the octave speaks about Judgment Day and the sestet about the "refining crucible." In *Haged, keruv mimshaḥ* ("Say, O divine cherub")[18] the octave speaks about the Temple of God, the sestet about the holy crown, and so forth.

Sometimes even the verbal differences vanish, and ideas from the first strophes (I–II) are repeated in the later ones (III–IV) almost verbatim:

II. There is neither wealth nor provisions nor sustenance for me
III. Where is the wealth, and where are the provisions I made?[19]

I. ... your eyes / would go up in a storm to the skies / for I see them in Heaven
III. ... your eyes / are the stars of the skies; / at night they go up to Heaven.[20]

In extreme cases, a sestet that repeats either itself or the octave is linked to an octave that repeats itself too. So, for example, the chain of repetitions in *Im ha-zeman ʿiver* ("If Time is blind")[21] begins already in the second line of the octave. The sestet is left with nothing to say.

Generally speaking, the octave in Immanuel's sonnet is identified with the situation, the sestet with the reflective part of the poem. Such is the case with *Kol yaʿalot*, translated above as an example. But sometimes one section is drawn out at the expense of the other. In a very few sonnets, such as *Amru u-ma isha* and *Yom erera ʿofra*, already singled out above, the situation overflows into the sestet, relegating the reflection to the very end of the poem. In such cases the expanded situation has a favorable effect on the poem; these are sonnets without a single superfluous word. Then again, there are also sonnets in which the reflection begins early, and the opening line typical of this section appears already in the octave:

---

[17] *Tzror Zehuvim*, ed. Bregman, sonnet 13.
[18] *Tzror Zehuvim*, ed. Bregman, sonnet 8.
[19] *Tzror Zehuvim*, ed. Bregman, sonnet 12.
[20] *Tzror Zehuvim*, ed. Bregman, sonnet 24.
[21] *Tzror Zehuvim*, ed. Bregman, sonnet 2.

Line 6: "What more can I say?"[22]
Line 4: "What does Paradise have for me?"[23]
Line 4: "How can I burst through the fence?"[24]

A reflection that begins before the usual ninth line generally has a greater number of rhetorical repetitions, so that the sonnet appears to be spinning its wheels.

In a sonnet-on-the-sonnet, the English poet Christopher Pilling writes:

This sonnet's nucleus
Leaps from octet to sestet and does not know
There are less lines to go than have been unreeled.[25]

To be sure, few of Immanuel's sonnets create such a "dashing" impression. Nevertheless, even his slowest sonnets do not weary their listeners. The effects of prosody and syntax are not lost. They give the poem freshness and variety, and infuse it with content and tension. The reader remains attentive from the beginning of the poem till the end. Of course, such attentiveness derives from other factors as well, which we will describe in detail below.

4. Affinity to the Italian Sonnet

Immanuel's system for developing the subject relies, like his prosodic system, on the poetic norms of his time and place. Italian poets often established the heart of the poem in the first part of the sonnet, or even at the very beginning. This is the case, for example, in Dante's *Negli occhi porta la mia donna amore* ("In her eyes, my lady bears love"), Cecco Angiolieri's *S'i' fosse foco arderei 'l mondo* ("If I were fire I would burn the world"), and Cino da Pistoia's *Tutto ch'altrui aggrada a me disgrada* ("Every thing that pleases others, displeases me").

With openings like these, it was hard to avoid anti-climax. And indeed, Italian poets of the period were charged with just such failures. The above-noted sonnets of Cecco Angiolieri and Cino da Pistoia were brought as examples of poems that went into decline after the opening line.[26] Petrarch also wrote some sonnets of the same kind. Charles Tomlinson, who regarded Petrarch as the greatest sonneteer of all time (and the English sonnet as having failed in its duty

---

[22] *Tzror Zehuvim*, ed. Bregman, sonnet 30.
[23] *Tzror Zehuvim*, ed. Bregman, sonnet 25.
[24] *Tzror Zehuvim*, ed. Bregman, sonnet 14.
[25] Fuller, *The Sonnet*, 3.
[26] Praz, "Sonetto."

to Petrarch), nevertheless points out the straggling sestet in some of the Italian masters less successful sonnets, such as *La vita fugge* ("My Life flees").[27]

While some may dispute the validity of this criticism in relation to Petrarch, it certainly holds true for many of Immanuel's sonnets, as we have already seen. But if we can justify this phenomenon in Italian sonnets on the grounds that these tended to put the primary part of the message already at the beginning of the poem, then Immanuel can be justified several times over. Not only did he begin his sonnets with the primary message, but he also took it upon himself to divide the message in two and establish the reflex at the end of the second part. All this positively forced him to create a straggling sestet.

Why did Immanuel limit his poetic options? Local influence can explain the reason for establishing the situation at the beginning of the poem. His desire to stress the dichotomous nature of the sonnet explains his reason for dividing the sonnet in two. Other elements in his system can be explained by examining Immanuel's sonnets in context, that is, by seeing them as poems embedded in a *maqama*.

5. Context-Dependent Development

Immanuel's sonnets are distributed among thirteen of the twenty-eight *maqamas* in his *Maḥbarot*. As a rule, they are not fully integrated into their immediate context. Various signs of Western-Italian influence distinguish his sonnets from his rhymed prose, which is distinctly Eastern in nature. Immanuel was not alone in his time in creating stylistic differences between his poems and the prose in which they are embedded. This kind of difference was also prominent in Dante's *Vita Nuova*. Apparently no one saw anything wrong with this. In fact, neither Dante nor Immanuel ever pretended that their poems were written at the same time as the surrounding prose. Both poets openly acknowledge that the poems were written first, and embedded into the surrounding prose only at a later date.[28] In the introduction to his *Maḥbarot* Immanuel even stresses that he composed the prose part of the work only to provide a setting for his poems, and thereby save them from the ravages of time, plagiarists, and ignorant anthology-makers.[29] But if we examine the sonnets in context, we realize that Immanuel is shading the truth when he claims to have written all of the poems before embarking on the *Maḥbarot*. Most of his sonnets fit neatly into their prose context, and some are so dependent on it that they cannot be fully understood without it.

---

[27] Tomlinson, *The Sonnet*, 36–37: "Those that are inferior have an awkward straggling distribution of the tercets."

[28] *Maḥbarot*, ed. Yarden, 4–5; Dante, *Vita Nuova*, trans. Cervigni and Vasta, 47, 49.

[29] *Maḥbarot*, ed. Yarden, 4–5.

The sonnets are also linked to poems and sonnets in the surrounding text, despite the barrier of prose separating one poem from the other. There was a precedent in Italian poetry for such links between poems. From the very emergence of the genre, Italian poets composed sonnet *tenzones* in which the challenge-sonnet was linked to the answering sonnet through subject matter and prosody.[30] They also composed sonnets in given combinations: *serie* and *corone di sonetti*.[31] Guittone d'Arezzo, for example, composed two cycles of sonnets: one on the months of the year, and another on the weeks.[32] Fazio degli Uberti composed a series of seven sonnets about the Seven Deadly Sins, and "Durante" — whom we presume to be Dante — composed his *Fiore* entirely in this manner. Italian poets also wrote jousting sonnets known as *contrasti* — a kind of dialogue between literary figures, generally a suitor and his lady-love. *Contrasti* are mostly sonnets with an earthy, popular appeal.[33] The early Italian sequences were usually linked to each other not through rhyme-words, but through subject matter, development of theme, and, sometimes, rhyme-schemes. But already in Petrarch's *Canzoniere* we can distinguish a series of sonnets (nos. 26–28) linked through a common rhyme. Over the course of time, poets created even stronger prosodic links.[34]

The affinity of Immanuel's sonnets to the prose surrounding them, and to the poems and sonnets near them, varies.

In the first *maqama* of the *Maḥbarot*, two sonnets complaining about fate appear one after the other: *Im ha-gezeira yorda* ("If fate descends") and *Im ha-zeman ʿiver* ("If Time is blind").[35] The second of these is a continuation of the first, and that which serves the first sonnet as a reflection becomes the situation in the second sonnet, which then receives a new reflection in turn. A third sonnet, *Dodai she'eluni* ("My friends asked me"),[36] provides a counterweight to the first two sonnets, for here the speaker delights in the wife granted him by fate.

The two sonnets in the second *maqama* act like sibling rivals: one praises the beautiful woman, and the other disparages the ugly woman.[37] The entire *maqama* is united around this subject, with the sonnets as their focal point. The link between

---

[30] See Biadene, *Morfologia del sonetto*, 94–114.
[31] See Elwert, *Versificazione italiana*, 133–34; Biadene, *Morfologia del sonetto*, 121–34; Mönch, *Das Sonett*, 28–29.
[32] Immanuel of Rome also wrote poems about the months of the year, as did Alharizi before him. See *Maḥbarot*, ed. Yarden, 167–71; Judah Alharizi, *Taḥqemoni*, ed. Y. Toporowsky (Tel Aviv, 1952), 59–73.
[33] Biadene, *Morfologia del sonetto*, 114–21.
[34] Mönch, *Das Sonett*, 31–32.
[35] *Tzror Zehuvim*, ed. Bregman, sonnets 1 and 2.
[36] *Tzror Zehuvim*, ed. Bregman, sonnet 3.
[37] *Tzror Zehuvim*, ed. Bregman, sonnets 4 and 5.

the two sonnets is stressed in brief poetic introductions that are identical in structure but opposite in content: "See the gazelle . . . " versus "See the hand maiden . . . ". The prose explains that the poems were composed in a contest between poets, and in this way links them together in a unified framework that invites the reader to compare their values and poetic merits.

The third *maqama* ("The Scroll of Desire") is a tightly-woven story in which the protagonists take on distinct personalities as the plot unfolds and the tone becomes more refined.[38] It gradually changes from an amusing *maqama* of the kind that Hebrew poets wrote in Spain, to a tragic Italian *novella*. Four sonnets[39] are woven seamlessly into this structure: the first three sonnets cap various episodes, and the fourth and last sonnet brings the entire story to a dramatic conclusion. The first two sonnets are striking examples of *contrasti*: one is a wooing poem, the other a flat-out rejection. They even imitate the circumstances of a non-literary *tenzone*: the suitor and his beloved are both poets, and the sonnets they exchange are appended to letters. This sophisticated touch fits in beautifully with the overall perfection of the story as a whole. The two sonnets are tightly linked to each other; indeed, the second one cannot be understood without the first.

The *Maḥbarot's* fourth *maqama*, which deals with the onset of old age, has seven sonnets.[40] These fit well into the general structure. The first is a lament for lost youth; the others are poems of religious rebuke. While the sonnets can all stand on their own, they are also reinforced by the context and by the cumulative effect of the poems as a whole. Each sonnet serves as a link in a sequence of poems that culminates at the end of the *maqama* in a poem (in running rhyme) about the thirteen principles of Jewish faith.

Three burlesque sonnets[41] in *Maqama* Seven are nourished by a racy love story, and contribute to its satirical flavor.

The eighth *maqama* has one sonnet, *At bein ʿatzei yaʿar* ("You are amongst the trees of the forest"),[42] and it is a caustic one, as we have seen. Only through the prose which comes before the sonnet do we learn that its taunts are directed at a poet (Joab), and that it deals with poetic criticism. Though it can be understood on its own, the context illuminates it in a concrete way.

The ninth *maqama* has two sonnets: *Bi baʿalat ha-ov* ("Please, necromancer!") and *Ḥusha meshiaḥ-el ve-lama taʿamod* ("Hurry, Messiah of God: why do

---

[38] See Pagis, *Ḥiddush u-Masoret*, 265–68.
[39] *Tzror Zehuvim*, ed. Bregman, sonnets 6, 7, 8, and 9.
[40] *Tzror Zehuvim*, ed. Bregman, sonnets 10, 11, 12, 13, 14, 15, and 16.
[41] *Tzror Zehuvim*, ed. Bregman, sonnets 17, 18 and 19.
[42] *Tzror Zehuvim*, ed. Bregman, sonnet 20.
[43] *Tzror Zehuvim*, ed. Bregman, sonnets 21 and 22.

you tarry?").⁴³ While there is no relation between these sonnets in themselves, the prose presents both of them as boasts — something that only the first sonnet makes clear — and thus links them together.

Maqamas Sixteen and Seventeen share the same plot and have six love sonnets between them.⁴⁴ The sonnets are in harmony with the tone and subject matter of the surrounding prose, and linked to each other in subject matter. The first of these is eminently dependent on context: the prose before it relates that the young woman "does not walk upright"; the sonnet gives the reason for this without explaining the problem all over again.

Maqama Eighteen relates the adventures of a wanderer and has four sonnets.⁴⁵ Two of these give a poetic touch to some otherwise philosophical moments, while the other two combine popular motifs with good cheer to thrash out the comparative virtues of onion and garlic. The sonnet *Ha-sho'alim eykh ohali ʿazavti* ("Those who ask how I abandoned my tent")⁴⁶ is dependent on context: it tells about known "camps," which are mentioned only in the prose that comes before it.

Maqama Twenty deals with a variety of topics and has four sonnets.⁴⁷ They are unrelated to each other, and the surrounding prose provides them with a rather artificial framework.

The single sonnet in *Maqama* Twenty-Three, *Ḥusha levavi, kaḥ lekha tzintzenet* ("Hurry, my heart, get yourself a jar"),⁴⁸ relates to the preceding poem (in running rhyme) as the reflection of a situation: the first poem describes the speaker's illness, while the sonnet grumbles about doctors. The relationship between the two poems is emphasized by the use of identical rhyme-words. Both poems are rather unconnected to the surrounding prose, eloquent testimony to the fact that they were composed independently.

Another sonnet with a weak affinity to context is *Tzar li be-yodʿi* ("It grieves me to know"), the only sonnet in *Maqama* Twenty-Seven.⁴⁹

Weak or strong, the relationship between the sonnets and the surrounding prose and poems sheds light on Immanuel's system of subject development. Since the poems in the *maqama* are not required to advance the plot but rather to provide it with a poetic interlude, Immanuel's sonnets are likely to hinge on a situation already developed in the prose before them and thus be exempt from the need to advance it themselves. Even if they do refer back to the situation,

---

[44] *Tzror Zehuvim*, ed. Bregman, sonnets 23, 24, 25, 26, 27, and 28.
[45] *Tzror Zehuvim*, ed. Bregman, sonnets 29, 30, 31 and 32.
[46] *Tzror Zehuvim*, ed. Bregman, sonnet 30.
[47] *Tzror Zehuvim*, ed. Bregman, sonnets 33, 34, 35 and 36.
[48] *Tzror Zehuvim*, ed. Bregman, sonnet 37.
[49] *Tzror Zehuvim*, ed. Bregman, sonnet 38.

they obviously cannot provide much suspense, since the situation has already been discussed and resolved. The role of the sonnets in the *Maḥbarot* is lively and varied, but for the most part reflective in nature. Because the reflective element is crucial in them, we can understand why Immanuel expanded the reflective section in some of his sonnets. We can also understand why he invariably established the situation in the first part of the sonnet, for this was directly linked to a plot previously developed in the prose part of the *Maḥbarot*.

After saying all this, we can add yet another way for telling whether a given sonnet was composed independently, perhaps before the surrounding rhymed prose of the *maqama*. Up till now, we have examined the linkage between the sonnets and their context, pointing out context-dependent sonnets and noting that they could not have been composed prior to the composition of the surrounding story. Now we can also suggest that sonnets in which the situational part is developed at the expense of the reflexive part were likely composed independently and possibly before the *maqama* itself.

VII. Theme, Attitude, and Mood

1. The Thematic Approach

During the first hundred years of its existence the Italian sonnet greatly expanded its range of subjects, approaches, and attitudes. Unlike the Sicilians, who devoted the sonnet mostly to the subject of love, the Tuscan poets cultivated a number of new themes: religious and philosophical thought (based on the principles of Aristotelian scholasticism or mystical Neo-Platonism), ethics (largely allegorical), social issues, politics, and others. Guittone d'Arezzo, who, as already mentioned, greatly contributed to the diversity of the prosody, was also instrumental in expanding the sonnets' range of themes.

With the development of new styles, the thematic expansion of the sonnet, and of poetry in general, again became an important question. The poets of the *dolce stil nuovo* saw poetry as something sublime, deserving of only the most exalted subjects. Dante in his essay *De Vulgari Eloquentia* limited these subjects to three: arms, love, and virtue.[1] For the sonnet, this limitation would seem to recommend a return to the limited thematic choice of the Sicilian poets. And indeed, Dante and his circle wrote poetry largely on the subject of love, though they broadened its significance in various ways. The "realistici", on the other hand — Cecco Angiolieri, Rustico di Filippo, and others — demonstrated a totally different approach. These poets saw poetry as a vehicle for rich expression in all areas of human life, and provocatively wrote about every topic under the sun, "trivial" as it might be. Between these two conflicting trends the corpus of sonnets split in two. The first trend created an "exalted" sonnet — limited in subject matter, Platonic, religious, serious and refined — while the latter created a "low" sonnet varied in subject matter, realistic, vulgar, filled with humor and a kind of street-smart cynicism. The attitude towards subject-matter was a fundamental element in the different styles and a clear expression of the poet's world-view.

This, then, was the situation in which Immanuel found himself when it came time to choose his own poetic path. He could either reject both of the Italian styles or, like Italian poets, choose one over the other, or negotiate a compromise between them. Against this background, Immanuel's sonnets are unique indeed. They deal with every subject, high and low: love, religious rebuke, complaint, praise, ridicule and boasts. In this he is reminiscent of the "realistici", who adopted a popular approach to their poetry. And indeed, in more than a few

---

[1] Dante Alighieri, *De Vulgari Eloquentia*, ed. and trans. Botterill, 53.

sonnets Immanuel does adopt stylistic traits characteristic of this trend. But this does not mean that he avoided the usages of the dolce stil nuovo, as we shall see below.[2]

Once again, we are witness to Immanuel's independent course, this time well suited to his natural tendency towards poetic diversity. The colorful thematic range of his sonnets made up for their modest choice of structures, but must have posed no small challenge to him either, as we shall see. What did Immanuel take from Italian poets, and to what extent? How did he negotiate the different styles? To what extent did he remain faithful to the traditional approaches of Hebrew poetry? Did he manage to blend the new with the old? Were his Italianized sonnets accepted by the Jewish community? These are the questions which we shall now try to answer. In the discussion below, Immanuel's sonnets are grouped according to subject matter. Because this sort of categorization is not always clear-cut, a sonnet examined from one angle may sometimes be reexamined from another. Let us begin with the love sonnet, which makes up the largest part of Immanuel's corpus.

2. The Love Sonnet

Love as Grace

Love is the highest value in the *dolce stil nuovo*, and its major characteristic is that of love as divine grace. This kind of love is devoid of all sensuality and physical desire; its true fulfillment can be attained only in a world that lies outside of our own reality. In this style the beloved lady is presented as a celestial being, not far removed from the Virgin Mary. For her there is no contradiction between love for God and love for man. She sheds divine grace on her beloved and causes him to draw closer to God. Dante's *Vita Nuova*, which describes his beloved Beatrice during her lifetime and after her death, is a preface to *The Divine Comedy*, where she leads him to the very throne of God.[3]

The beloved of the *dolce stil nuovo* is a noble lady, and in this she is reminiscent of the lady in troubadour poetry. She rarely speaks, and there is no real attempt to penetrate her inner life or to describe her thoughts. But unlike her courtly predecessors, her elevation is spiritual and has none of their cruelty and arrogance. It is her modesty, good heart, and courtesy that attract her lover, and only through his basic spiritual fitness, which grows in proportion to his love

---

[2] Motifs of this kind have already been discussed by Cassuto: i.e. *Dante ve-Immanuel*, 36–42; and "L'elemento italiano."

[3] See Dante, *Vita Nuova*, trans. Cervigni and Vasta, 145.

for her, can he get to know her. The lovers, who represented the feudal nobility in the Middle Ages, represent in the *dolce stil nuovo* a spiritual level — a refined spirit and noble heart.

The lady of the *dolce stil nuovo* is seen, so to speak, at the center of an aristocratic, enlightened circle, and whoever enters it becomes ennobled by its atmosphere and exalted in spirit, in a veritable foretaste of Paradise. When Dante sees Beatrice, her "miraculous greeting" leaves him unable to feel hate towards any one,[4] and indeed, there is not a single negative figure or attitude in the whole book. Even death is not particularly bad, for it separates the lovers for only a limited space of time. Yet the *dolce stil nuovo* is not over-sweet. There is a fragile tension in the encounter between that which is good, and that which is even better: "In her eyes my lady brings Love / whereby is ennobled whatever she looks upon . . . and whoever she greets trembles at heart / . . . / and for each fault one then sighs."[5]

In keeping with these qualities of his beloved, Dante, both as narrator and fictional persona, uses a modest and delicately nuanced language. The *dolce stil nuovo* is pervaded by a deep tension rooted in the concept of love as divine grace. The beloved lady, who represents this grace, is unobtainable not through her stubbornness, but because of the very nature of her being, in a way that is outside of the human experience. This tragic understanding clashes with feelings of joy and fulfillment: in the elevated spheres of the *dolce stil nuovo* the lover is satisfied with a single glance from his lady, whom he sees as an angel of God. The optimistic trends in the *dolce stil nuovo* are emphasized by Dante, whereas Guinizzelli emphasizes the tragic, but the tension between the two extremes is present in both.

Writing a Hebrew poem in the *dolce stil nuovo* was a difficult, almost impossible, task. To perceive love for a woman as an instrument of divine grace and to identify her with the salvation of the soul is something essentially Christian in nature and must have been perceived as completely foreign by any believing Jew, whether poet or reader. This was especially true for the Jews of Italy, who were familiar with Christian culture from close quarters and capable of sensing its presence, no matter how concealed. But this was not the only problem confronting a Hebrew poet eager to compose in the *dolce stil nuovo*. Its unassuming style was a far cry from the traditional poetics of Hebrew poetry in Spain, with its bold, colorful expressions and tendencies towards the dramatic and marvelous. Immanuel was well-versed in every technique of this tradition: verbal and intellectual fireworks fill every page of his *Maḥbarot,* a fact in which the author takes pride time and time again. Absorbing the "sweet style" in Hebrew meant

---

[4] Dante, *Vita Nuova*, trans. Cervigni and Vasta, 63.
[5] Dante, *Vita Nuova*, trans. Cervigni and Vasta, 89.

freeing himself from the claims of this weighty heritage. This was true whether it was just a matter of appreciating the charm and beauty of the *dolce stil nuovo*, or devising suitable Hebrew equivalents for its concepts and ideas.

Immanuel was able to overcome this artistic obstacle. His familiarity with contemporary Italian poetry, his aesthetic sense, and his complete mastery of the Hebrew language served him well in this case and allowed him to transfer all the highly-nuanced characteristics of the *dolce stil nuovo* to the Hebrew poem. But he did not blur its philosophical platform, or entirely alienate it from its source. Some of Immanuel's sonnets in the "sweet style" sound to the sensitive reader like Italian poems translated into Hebrew.

The sonnets which Immanuel composed in the spirit of the *dolce stil nuovo* vary in the degree to which they adhere to this style. Some were composed in all its purity, while others are flavored with elements quite foreign to it. But no matter how many extraneous elements we find in a poem, nothing can remove it from the domain of the *dolce stil nuovo* so long as it is ruled by the concept of love as divine grace.

The poem *Meh ʿarvah shenah* ("How sweet was sleep")[6] was composed in all the purity of the "sweet new style." The lover's feelings have not changed with time, or perhaps even with death. "I have not seen her, after all, / for twelve years," the lover says of his lady, who appears to him in a dream; whether she is dead or alive is not clear. In keeping with this deliberate blurring of the boundaries, the lady appears in a vision like "an image in a dream", or a celestial being: "When I saw her in the vision / my soul rejoiced. / There opened before me the gates / of Heaven." The lady is surrounded by "streams of light, angels of heaven." Like a divine apparition she banishes darkness and makes a powerful impression on her beholder, filling his soul with sublime wonder: "my soul soared . . . my spirit weakened." Her presence gives life, her absence death: "No sooner did she leave than my soul nearly died."

The same goes for the sonnet *Haged keruv mimshaḥ* ("Tell me, O anointed cherub").[7] To be sure, the maiden in this poem is compared to the Holy Ark and the Temple — Hebrew substitutes for the Christian theological elements in the style — but these are not the metaphors for feminine beauty so exciting to the old Hebrew love poets. Here the beloved is a divine entity who ennobles the spirit of the platonic lover: "We shall rise / to see the divine majesty and its heights / the day our eyes gaze upon the gazelle."

Naflah ʿateret ha-zeman ("The crown of Time has fallen")[8] shows how creation is blighted after the death of the beloved, thus expressing the central image

---

[6] *Tzror Zehuvim*, ed. Bregman, sonnet 34.
[7] *Tzror Zehuvim*, ed. Bregman, sonnet 8.
[8] *Tzror Zehuvim*, ed. Bregman, sonnet 8.

of the *dolce stil nuovo* through its absence: love as the source of abundance and grace. Particularly characteristic is the claim in this sonnet that bitter death, into whose realm the beloved has passed, is made sweet by her sweetness. This is love in the "sweet new style," where the beloved is the incarnation of God's grace both in life and in death. Death does not end, but rather magnifies her attractions.[9]

The opening line of *Yomru shehakim lakh* ("The heavens say to you")[10] expresses a commonplace of the "sweet style" by describing the eyes of the beloved and comparing them to stars. On the other hand, in *Kol ya'alot* ("All gazelles")[11] a foreign element invades the "sweet style." All of the maidens — apart from the lover's sublime lady — are here portrayed as "spittle and dust," in total contrast to the refined, lovely ladies surrounding Beatrice or Dante in various scenes of the *Vita Nuova*. Here Immanuel did not stand the test, and, yielding to the conventions of Hebrew poetry from Spain, used strong contrasts with burlesque overtones to magnify the image of the beloved. Nevertheless, he remained faithful to the sublime image of the beloved lady, making her one of "the heavenly host" and transforming her from a mere mortal into an eternal being: "A letter from God is she, on unwritten parchment."

In *Mi he'emin 'ofra* ("Who would believe, O gazelle")[12] the face of the beloved is termed "the vaults of Heaven"; her eyes "the stars of the sky" that "go up like a storm to the firmaments." That these metaphors have religious implications is clear from the rhymed prose accompanying the poem: "When she dies, she will dwell in heavenly paradise."[13] True, a few hints of realism do invade the description: "the hail of your teeth" and "the earring of your earlobe" are added to "the stars of your dawn." To magnify her charms the poet enlists the sorcerers of Egypt and other girls that are like "a drop in the bucket and dust" compared to her. The accompanying prose is strongly flavored with a mix of both styles: "And where will the noble hearts encamp / if not on [the girl's] hills and mountains?" Here we find one of the fundamental concepts of the "sweet new style" — the "noble heart" — only now it is surrounded by motifs that are both realistic and sensual. Still, none of this blurs the fundamental concept of love as divine grace, though it does perhaps detract from its purity of expression.

The conventions of the *dolce stil nuovo* are exploited to particular effect in the sonnet *Dodai she'eluni* ("My friends asked me").[14] In keeping with convention, the

---

[9] Cassuto (*Dante ve-Immanuel*, 41) saw clear similarities between this sonnet and Dante's sonnet about the death of Beatrice.
[10] *Tzror Zehuvim*, ed. Bregman, sonnet 6.
[11] *Tzror Zehuvim*, ed. Bregman, sonnet 4.
[12] *Tzror Zehuvim*, ed. Bregman, sonnet 24.
[13] *Mahbarot*, ed. Yarden, 277.
[14] *Tzror Zehuvim*, ed. Bregman, sonnet 3.

feminine figure in the poem sheds a poetic inspiration that ennobles the man and brings him closer to perfection. But here she is the poet's wife, and not the unobtainable beloved of courtly convention. Indeed, nowhere in the sonnet does this lady conform with the feminine stereotypes. As a woman of intellectual refinement she is scarcely the typical beloved in Spanish Hebrew poetry, remarkable only for her beauty, nor is she a traditional "Woman of Valor" as in Proverbs 31:10–31, since it is not her diligence and bustling activity which elicit praise, but her spiritual strength. This is an original and complex figure, one that draws from different styles without being subordinated to any one of them in particular.

The sonnet *Lu qomemiyut halkha ha-yaʿalah* ("If the doe walked upright")[15] also shows the conventions of the *dolce stil nuovo* in a unique light. Here the beloved's "stars" (a necessary appurtenance in the "sweet style") exert a powerful attraction on both the celestial beings above and the corpses who "dwell in the dust" in their graves. So powerful is her attraction that she turns into a veritable public menace. She wisely hides her attractions by walking bent over, thus concealing her face from observation. In this image Immanuel takes *ad absurdum* the motif of the attraction exerted by the beloved and jeers at the vision of angels ("the heavenly troops") by mentioning them in the same breath as those who "dwell in the dust," i.e., the bodies of the dead. This is, apparently, a parody of the "sweet new style," and perhaps even of Dante's vision of heaven and hell.

Love as Sin

In total contrast to the refined love sonnet of the *dolce stil nuovo*, the low sonnet of the "realistici" poets describes sensual, sinful love in a tone of jovial vulgarity. Unlike the sublime lovers and exalted circumstances in the high sonnet, the low sonnet features a variety of sensual, earthy characters who, in situations that are fresh and filled with vitality, eagerly indulge in a life of joyous promiscuity. This is a poem that revolts against the values hallowed by society and by the major trend of poetry.

Absorbing this nonconformist style was obviously a bold thing to do. Because of its realistic character and patent desire to irritate, its earthy sensuality could not be masqueraded as allegory or a poetic falsehood unconnected to reality, as Hebrew poets had often done in the past. Of course, Immanuel was able to employ a device accepted by writers of *maqamas* from the very beginning. As a mere "narrator" he could always put the most outrageous speech into the mouths of his characters, and then disclaim responsibility for them through pious speeches of his own. Yet Immanuel used this option only once, when he attributed a preference for hell over heaven to one of his poetic rivals: "My soul within me thinks it wise / to spurn heaven and desire hell . . . there one finds

---

[15] *Tzror Zehuvim*, ed. Bregman, sonnet 23.

every seductive lady and graceful gazelle." Here Immanuel reserved the right to respond to the poem himself, and in the rhymed prose that comes after the poem he rebukes the "saucy poet" for his impudence. Elsewhere he made sure not to blunt the sharp edge of his burlesque sonnets, for this was the true source of their power. Immanuel was a true poet of the burlesque school. His Italian poems rank among the best of this trend.[16] Clearly, he was aware that in this field there was no room for compromise.

Indeed, Immanuel's realistic love sonnets constitute some of the most erotic poems in all Hebrew poetry. Though women rarely have a voice in medieval Hebrew poetry, the heroine in *Shadai nekhonim* ("My breasts are ready")[17] has an entire monologue to herself: "My breasts are ready, my hair is grown / And here I sit all alone and lonely." She is forthright about her desires and her right to sexual fulfillment: "I am an experienced heifer and love to plow." She complains about her impotent spouse in no uncertain terms: "My husband is unable to satisfy the needs of my house."[18] In short, she is one big transgression against the norms of feminine modesty and the conventions of society and poetry.

Love in these sonnets is founded on sin; its stolen pleasures are enjoyed by poetic characters and readers alike. In order to emphasize its sinful nature, Immanuel wrote about love forbidden beyond all doubt: adultery. The married woman openly desires "to taste something different"[19] and hopes that her husband will come to a speedy end so that she can enjoy her lovers.[20] The narrator encourages beautiful married women to "frolic in the rooms of young men," since it was for this reason, he philosophizes, that fate gave them to rich stupid husbands.[21] He joins ranks with the adulterous lovers and gives them encouragement. Indeed, even the unfaithful beloved, shown in a negative light (from the betrayed man's point of view), is called *ra'ayah*, that is, a "wife," and may perhaps be a married woman, and even the primordial matter of Creation, which changed into different forms, is compared to an adulterous wife and not to a prostitute, as was customary.[22]

---

[16] His Italian poems were included in A. F. Massera, *Sonetti burleschi e realistici dei primi due secoli* (Bari, 1920).
[17] *Tzror Zehuvim*, ed. Bregman, sonnet 26.
[18] *Tzror Zehuvim*, ed. Bregman, sonnets 26 and 18.
[19] *Tzror Zehuvim*, ed. Bregman, sonnet 27.
[20] *Tzror Zehuvim*, ed. Bregman, sonnet 18.
[21] *Tzror Zehuvim*, ed. Bregman, sonnet 17.
[22] *Tzror Zehuvim*, ed. Bregman, sonnets 19 and 28. And see Maimonides, in his preface to *Moreh Nevukhim*, ed. Y.Qafech (Jerusalem, 1984), 11, and Part 3, Chap. 8, 286.

In these sonnets, established values are put to shame — no matter how sacred their source. Thus virginity — a Christian value — is mocked together with Rabbinic laws ("Any woman who dies a virgin / has no part in the world of spirits!");[23] saintly figures such as Abraham, Aaron and Esther are replaced by the negative figures of Terah, Korah and Zeresh; paradise is rejected in favor of hell; and the angel of God's creative power (*ha-sekhel ha-metzayer*) is depicted as a drunken artisan of shoddy workmanship.[24] The adulteress brazenly swears by "God on high, who hung the heavens like a curtain" (Psalm 104:2; Isaiah 40:22) in order to quell suspicion, and, in an original twist, demands the "food, raiment, and sexual relations" allotted to wives by biblical decree, with her husband supplying the first two of these, and her lovers the last.[25]

The heroes of Immanuel's realistic sonnets run the usual gamut of stock characters: husbands, in-laws, neighboring women, all of them busy with everyday matters that have no place in poems of more exalted nature: marriage, adultery, money, ridicule, gossip. The sonnet *Sefer ḥaqaqto* "("The letter you inscribed")[26] stands out in this group of sonnets. As in many realistic poems, love is conceived here in terms of sin and desire, and we find earthy characters with well-defined social positions: a nun and her acolytes. Here too a woman speaks out freely on the subject of love, yet in this case the lady's ideas are not licentious, but ascetic and chaste. This sonnet is a rarity: realistic, but not burlesque. It expresses the tension between desire and the dictates of religion in a way that is reminiscent of Petrarch, who gave this tension its most sublime expression.

The realistic style was more suited to Immanuel's poetic temperament than the "sweet" one, and he adopted it wholeheartedly in sonnets on a variety of topics. His realistic love sonnets are vibrant and full of color, with clear signs of the liberal atmosphere that was according to some views eventually to characterize the Italian Renaissance.[27] When writing in this style, Immanuel forgot the values espoused by the *dolce stil nuovo* and ridiculed it without hesitation, as though he himself had never used it at all. Writing in the realistic style was particularly demanding from the linguistic side of things. Italian sonnets of the realistic school were written in the colloquial language of everyday life, for which Hebrew had no equivalent. Impressive indeed, therefore, is Immanuel's success in making the high-flown rhetoric more flexible, and in giving it the spice of a vernacular in daily use. One could find Italian parallels for various motifs in these poems. For instance, Giacomo da Lentino also disdained heaven in one of his poems

---

[23] *Tzror Zehuvim*, ed. Bregman, sonnet 26.
[24] *Tzror Zehuvim*, ed. Bregman, sonnet 5.
[25] *Tzror Zehuvim*, ed. Bregman, sonnets 19 and 17.
[26] *Tzror Zehuvim*, ed. Bregman, sonnet 7.
[27] See Burckhardt, *Civilization of the Renaissance*, 185–88.

since his beloved, for some reason or other, had no place there. But he noted in the body of the poem: "I am not trying to offend anything sacred."[28] Immanuel, on the other hand, relegated apologetics of this kind to the surrounding prose, as we have already seen — if he bothered to offer them at all.

Social Implications

In his love sonnets Immanuel copied attitudes typical to Italian poetry and abandoned the ones characteristic of Hebrew love poetry in Spain, even though these played an important role in the other parts of his *Maḥbarot*. Immanuel's love sonnet is in no way the traditional love poem of the Spanish Hebrew poets. When composed in the *dolce stil nuovo* it deals with spiritual love; when realistic it deals with sensual desire that finds gratification despite all prohibitions to the contrary. One way or other there is no room in his sonnets for the cruel beloved of the old Hebrew love poem. His love sonnet is a new poem with new kinds of pitfalls: Christian connotations on one hand, social and religious challenges on the other. These aspects were neither blurred in most sonnets nor justified with apologetics in the surrounding text.

The lack of social precaution in Immanuel's love sonnet is something unique. Immanuel, who was not without a poetic-historical consciousness, perhaps relied on the liberal atmosphere that prevailed in his day in certain Jewish circles. But such liberality, if it existed at all, certainly had its limits, and we have already seen that the rabbis criticized his poetry and accused both him and his friend Menahem of straying into foreign territory. The sonnet form was new in Hebrew poetry. It needed to be given a firm social footing, but Immanuel's love sonnets were bound to irritate, even though many must have listened to them with enjoyment. Love sonnets form the largest and most conspicuous part of Immanuel's corpus. We can confidently assume that they stigmatized the entire corpus (especially since that corpus, as we shall see, was not overly pious in several other matters as well) and the Hebrew sonnet in general, which long remained connected with the figure of Immanuel and his *Maḥbarot*. Immanuel's love sonnets — both the sweet and the spicy — were apparently responsible in no small measure for the hesitant acceptance of the genre after Immanuel, and even for its poetic eclipse during the next two hundred years.[29]

---

[28] Langley, *The Early Poetry*, 80.
[29] See D. Bregman, "Parashat ha-Hitqablut shel ha-Sonet ha-ʿIvri," *Tarbiz* 56 (1987): 109–23.

3. Religious Rebuke

Immanuel has eight religious sonnets, all of the *sonetto morale* type: that is, the sonnet that preaches and rebukes. Two of these are directed at the community at large;[30] the rest at the poet himself: "O my harsh-spirited soul, should you not be ashamed . . . !"[31]

The mood of these sonnets is gloomy. In them, thoughts of repentance are stirred by the fear of punishment, which is spelled out in grim detail. The grave is mentioned repeatedly, and the dead inhabit a hell that is overtly pagan in nature: "I remember many who sank / into its watery depths, each one towards / evil and destruction going / to sip from cups poisoned with hemlock."[32] Harsh concepts from the field of law appear in various places: inquisitions, warnings, unbreakable laws, royal edicts, treachery, and crime. Legal concepts of a milder nature — pardon, advocacy — are conspicuous by their absence ("No advocate or counsel of defense will appear for them").[33] There are descriptions of punishment where the flames of hell "devour evil and mischievous souls,"[34] and of the fiery furnace and the soul burnt at the stake:[35] phenomena not far from the grim reality of medieval life. There are also harsh similes comparing God to an all-knowing judge and investigator, and man to a wandering vagrant, rotting wood, or cattle.

Though all of these gloomy elements had roots in traditional Hebrew poetry, they were usually accompanied by elements of a more optimistic nature: divine mercy for the repentant, memory of God's promises, the merit of the Patriarchs, or hope for personal and national redemption. Immanuel's religious sonnets are also marked by the absence of linguistic features characteristic of liturgical Hebrew poetry and completely accepted by poets of his generation. As a poem that preaches and rebukes, and not a prayer, Immanuel's sonnet is addressed to man, not to heaven, and this emphasizes its distance from God and His mercy. In light of all the above, it would appear that Immanuel was influenced by the preachers and religious poets in the Italian environment,[36] and by the spirit of popular ascetic movements that flourished in Italy during his day. While liturgical Hebrew poetry in Provence did absorb such Christian elements as macabre scenes from

---

[30] *Tzror Zehuvim*, ed. Bregman, sonnets 11 and 35.
[31] *Tzror Zehuvim*, ed. Bregman, sonnet 14.
[32] *Tzror Zehuvim*, ed. Bregman, sonnet 11.
[33] *Tzror Zehuvim*, ed. Bregman, sonnet 16.
[34] *Tzror Zehuvim*, ed. Bregman, sonnet 16.
[35] *Tzror Zehuvim*, ed. Bregman, sonnets 13 and 35.
[36] Such as that of Jacopone da Todi. See, for example, Petrocchi, *Scrittori religiosi del Duecento* (Florence, 1974), ix, 133–60 and esp. 156–58.

the grave and the terrors of Judgment Day, it also included traditional optimistic elements as well.[37] Immanuel's sonnets return to ideas, images and claims from Jewish ethical literature, especially from *Ḥovot ha-Levavot*, or "Duties of the Hearts", by Bahya ibn Paquda. Thus, for example, the soul separated from the body was compared to a traveler sailing across the sea; the good deeds which the traveler performed in his lifetime to the provisions for his journey.[38]

4. Complaint

The poem of complaint, a traditional genre in Hebrew poetry in Spain, was adopted in four of Immanuel's sonnets, but it underwent a significant change. In the traditional poems of complaint the aim of the poet is of course to lament his sorrows: separation, sickness, wandering, old age. At the center of the genre stands the concept of "Time" (*zeman*), an evil and capricious fate on whom the poet blames all his troubles. The source of Time's malicious power is not clear. Sometimes it seems to be a messenger of God, more often an independent entity beyond control.[39] Such vagary allows the poet to pour out his heart without seeming to reproach God, and without tangling himself in questions of free will and divine justice. Philosophizing is foreign to this genre, which maintains a lyrical tone, personal and low-key.

In his sonnets of complaint Immanuel blames the "children of Time," as is customary in the Hebrew poetry of Spain,[40] but what is not customary is that he argues with them about reward and punishment. The confrontation with Time turns into a confrontation with himself, and in the end he decides to change his behavior and attitudes. On this point the group of sonnets is divided.

In two of the sonnets Immanuel pleads guilty to sinning.[41] He decides to repent in the spirit of Psalms 119:71: "It is good that I have been afflicted, that I might learn thy statutes." Such humility fits the story in which the sonnets are embedded, and lends the poems a high moral tone. But in the remaining two sonnets, Immanuel sees himself as a suffering innocent and revolts against his plight. His decision to rebel against law and morality spurs him to challenge all

---

[37] Schirmann, *Ha-Shirah ha-ʿIvrit*, 3: 276.
[38] See I. Sonne, "Sifrut ha-Musar ve-ha-Filosofia be-Shirei Immanuel ha-Romi," *Tarbiz* 5 (1934): 324–40.
[39] See D. Pagis, *Shirat ha-Ḥol ve-Torat ha-Shir le-Moshe ibn Ezra u-Venei Doro* (Jerusalem, 1970), 240, 241, 328.
[40] *Tzror Zehuvim*, ed. Bregman, sonnets 29, 30, 1 and 2.
[41] *Tzror Zehuvim*, ed. Bregman, sonnets 29, 30.

men of valor to do the same. Here we recognize the spirit of the realistic poems written in Italian since the days of Immanuel, as in the famous lines by Cecco Angiolieri:

> If I were fire — I'd burn the whole world;
> If I were wind — I'd storm it.[42]

Such shifts in attitude are not rare in Immanuel's poetry; we have seen them, for example, in his love sonnets. Immanuel saw nothing wrong with this. Indeed, just the contrary, since reversals of this kind allowed him to demonstrate his versatility and his ability to express any idea he chose.

Immanuel's fifth sonnet of complaint, about old age,[43] ostensibly conforms to the rules of tradition since he makes no reckoning with either his soul or the world, and expresses only sorrow. Here, however, the Time which "rises up like a murderer" is no longer capricious Fate but old age, whose symptoms are dictated by the laws of nature.

We should also mention in this connection Immanuel's burlesque love sonnet, in which women complain about sexual abstinence, boredom in married life, and impotent husbands, a far cry from the old poem of complaint. Though the main goal in these sonnets is to flaunt a daring cast of characters in piquant situations, we cannot ignore their audacity and innovativeness. It is doubtful whether images of women like these can be found anywhere else in Hebrew poetry up to our own day.

5. Panegyric

The panegyric, the central and most important genre in Hebrew poetry in Spain, plays an important role in Immanuel's *Mahbarot*. But only one of those panegyrics is constructed as a sonnet.[44] This is, in effect, a poem of friendship and apparently part of a *tenzone*.

The element of praise is dominant in Immanuel's love sonnets. The phenomenon is common to Italian poems in the *dolce stil nuovo*, as is evident for example in Dante's preface to the sonnet quoted earlier in this chapter: "I felt a desire to say some words also in praise of this most gentle one, by which I might show how through her this Love awakens . . ."[45]

---

[42] See Italian text with English translation in Kay George ed. and trans., *The Penguin Book of Italian Verse* (Harmondsworth, 1965), 70.
[43] *Tzror Zehuvim*, ed. Bregman, sonnet 10.
[44] *Tzror Zehuvim*, ed. Bregman, sonnet 36.
[45] Dante, *Vita Nuova*, trans. Cervigni and Vasta, 89.

6. Boasting, Criticism, and Debate

Immanuel's sonnets of boasting, criticism and debate are remarkable for their sharp Italian wit and broad range of themes. The poet's boasts about his poetry — a standard theme from Spain — find expression in one sonnet where he challenges the biblical poets Asaph and Jeduthun.[46] While there is nothing new in this, his threat comes straight from the Italian burlesque: "I'll screech and shriek and throw my shoes / at any poet who spouts poetry."

Ḥusha levavi ("Be quick, my heart")[47] is a sonnet criticizing doctors. While we find similar criticism in the *maqamas* of Zabara and Alharizi, Immanuel could also have found his motifs in Italian poetry as well. The satirical sonnet *At bein ʿatzei yaʿar* ("You are amongst the trees of the forest"),[48] which criticizes the poet Joab, may be connected to the traditions of Hebrew poetry in Spain, where poets flung insults and criticism at each other from the very start. We need only mention, for example, the harsh accusations traded in the poems between the followers of Dunash ben Labrat and those of Menahem ibn Saruq. But Immanuel's sonnet has sexual allusions, and these are the main thrust of his barbs. Here he comes close to his Italian colleagues and moves away from Hebrew tradition. To the ranks of the poet who is not a poet, and the doctor who is not a doctor, Immanuel admits the matchmaker who is not a matchmaker.[49] Matchmaking is a low subject by nature; the sonnet which deals with it is thus more vulgar in tone than its two predecessors. Its colloquial flavor mixes Hebrew and Italian elements together. The heroes' names and nicknames are biblical, but the spirit of bravado is purely Italian: you may have one Satan to help you, the speaker boasts, but I have eighty thousand! A pungent burlesque sonnet *Ḥusha meshiaḥ-el* ("Hurry, Messiah")[50] challenges the messiah himself, ridicules the traditions connected with him, and jeers at the sacred idea of redemption.

Elements of debate also characterize Immanuel's burlesque love sonnet. *Yom ererah ʿofra* ("The day the gazelle cursed") attacks the adulteress; *Sekhel metzayer* ("Creative intelligence") attacks the creator of ugly women.[51]

---

[46] *Tzror Zehuvim*, ed. Bregman, sonnet 21.
[47] *Tzror Zehuvim*, ed. Bregman, sonnet 37.
[48] *Tzror Zehuvim*, ed. Bregman, sonnet 20.
[49] *Tzror Zehuvim*, ed. Bregman, sonnet 33 (and the matchmaker is the bride's father!)
[50] *Tzror Zehuvim*, ed. Bregman, sonnet 22.
[51] *Tzror Zehuvim*, ed. Bregman, sonnets 19 and 5.

7. Gluttony

Gluttony is a typically low subject. The lover in classic poetry characteristically disdains to eat and drink. In describing the way he fell in love, Dante relates: "At that point, the natural spirit, which dwells in that part that ministers to our nourishment, began to weep, and weeping said these words: '*Heu miser, quia frequenter impeditus ero deinceps!*'" ["Wretched me, for often hereafter shall I be impeded!"].[52] The high style regarded eating as too trivial for poetry; the realistic poets gave it a value and saw it as a subject worthy of their pen. Immanuel accepted their approach.

An taḥanot libakh ("Where is your heart encamped?")[53] describes a feast in the town of Camerino with concrete details and a tone of longing. *Ereh ani haman* ("I see the manna"),[54] which deals with this same feast, praises the garlic and the onion — common vegetables, spicy to the point of being symbolic — and openly pokes fun at the gourmets too fastidious to eat them. In the context of the *maqama*, the sonnet lends a poetic touch to the narrator's claim that the food in Camerino is tasteless since it lacks the spice of garlic and onion. This sonnet, in its narrative context, was the source of inspiration for Hayyim Nachman Bialik's *Knight of Onions and Knight of Garlic*, which was also written in the form of a *maqama*.[55]

Written in the spirit of Immanuel's poems of gluttony is a long wedding poem from the seventeenth century by Jacob Frances, in which the poet prefers gluttony to love. He illustrates this by a grotesque realization of the traditional images of Hebrew poetry, where the beloved is depicted as a doe or gazelle:

> My stomach is my beloved, my innards my dear ones; I'd love a
>   gazelle — but not in bed;
> On a table, grilled, I desire it! And yearn for a doe's breast, so long
>   as it's dead.[56]

---

[52] Dante, *Vita Nuova*, trans. Cervigni and Vasta, 48.
[53] *Tzror Zehuvim*, ed. Bregman, sonnet 31.
[54] *Tzror Zehuvim*, ed. Bregman, sonnet 32.
[55] D. Bregman, "Yihus Avot shel Aluf Batzlut ve-Aluf Shum," in *Sefer Yitzhaq Baqun*, ed. A. Komem (Beer-Sheva, 1992), 73–90.
[56] Jacob Frances, *Kol Shirei Ya‛aqov Frances*, ed. P. Naveh (Jerusalem, 1969), 244.

Part Two:

The Revived Hebrew Sonnet

VIII. The Flowering of the Italian Sonnet

1. In the Poetry of Petrarch

In Italy, the poets of the *dolce stil nuovo* were followed by Francesco Petrarca, the first humanist and the founder of a new European lyricism. His collection of Italian poems, the *Canzoniere*,[1] includes 366 poems, of which 317 are sonnets. This book, as is well known, became the model for hundreds of poets in Italy and throughout Europe, causing the sonnet to become enormously popular. The writing of poetry in the manner of Petrarch began towards the end of the fifteenth century and continues, in various ways, into our own day. While the following information may appear redundant to the knowledgeable reader, let us take a moment to situate the Hebrew sonnet within the context of contemporary Italian poetry.

Petrarch ostensibly regarded his Italian poems as being less important than any of his other writings in Italian and Latin. In a letter written two years before his death, Petrarch dismissed the poems as "trifles" and hoped they would be forgotten. But from the many annotations and corrections he made in the margins of his poems, we learn that he actually worked hard to polish and revise them. This is especially conspicuous in the sonnets. To quote Tusiani, "it was Petrarch who made [the sonnet-form] live by crystallizing its fluid levity and brittle essence."[2] In the previous chapters we looked at the crystallization of the sonnet primarily in terms of its prosodic elements; let us now examine it in terms of the poem's internal structure.

Petrarch addressed the poems of his *Canzoniere* almost exclusively to "Laura," the great love of his life and the inexhaustible source of his creative imagination. Laura, like Dante's Beatrice, became the central figure in the poet's life, and, also like Beatrice, died prematurely, leaving the poet with a lifelong grief. Like Dante's *Vita Nuova*, the first part of Petrarch's *Canzoniere* deals with his lady during her lifetime and the second part with her after her death. Petrarch learned a great deal from the poets of the *dolce stil nuovo*, but he also went far beyond them. Though his beloved, like that of Dante and his circle, is crowned with every attribute and inner beauty, Petrarch's love was not altogether Platonic. To quote Forster:

---

[1] He himself called it *Rerum vulgarium fragmenta*.
[2] J. Tusiani, *Italian Poets of the Renaissance* (New York, 1971), Introduction, 32.

The beloved Laura remains for him a real woman, whose beauty intoxicates him, and whose physical presence excites him. Hence he can hymn her various physical attributes — eyes, hair, skin, etc. — and do so with a better conscience in that she represents physical and spiritual perfection. Nonetheless, love is not a virtue in itself, for he realizes that his love is a passion and that passion is sinful.[3]

Thus the Petrarchan hero is no longer the Platonic lover of the dolce stil nuovo, but a believing Christian struggling against sin. Erotic elements of troubadour poetry that were either assimilated into the *dolce stil nuovo* or abandoned altogether re-emerge in the poetry of Petrarch, though no longer in their original form. The Petrarchan lady, like that of the troubadours, throws her lover into despair through her steadfast refusal, but this derives from the nobility of her soul and her desire to keep him from sin. The Petrarchan lover thus becomes both a rejected lover who craves the presence of his lady and a devout Christian who recognizes his sin. His suffering is rooted not only in the refusal of his lady but also in his own inner conflict: during her lifetime he struggles between a desire for both sensual fulfillment and the purification of his soul, and after she dies between his oscillating desire for life and death.

The Petrarchan lover is tortured by an ethical dilemma which he is unable to resolve; he is captivated by the paradox that "the root of all bitterness is so very sweet."[4] He looks at his dilemma with an introspective eye, but never manages to reconcile the conflicting demands. He can never be confident, or completely sure of his path. Though he tries to reconcile himself to his fate, his complaints have a note of sadness and melancholy.

The resulting poetry is a balance between opposing elements: sweetness and bitterness, pleasure and pain, happiness and despair. The antithesis so characteristic to Petrarch's style is not merely a poetic device, but also the necessary, almost obligatory result of the paradox at the core of the situation.

In its ability to express the emotional turmoil of the Petrarchan lover, the sonnet-form has no rival. The duality of its structural logic matches the essential paradox at the core of this turmoil. The factors which lend both tension and harmony to the form essentially echo the poem's dramatic situation. Petrarch thus had no need to create a structural correspondence between the wording of a sonnet and its prosody. As already noted, Petrarch did not develop the subject of his sonnets according to an established pattern, and felt no obligation to interrupt

---

[3] Forster, *The Icy Fire*, 3.

[4] See for example Petrarch's "*Cantai or piango*," no. 229 in his *Rime*, ed. G. Bezzola (Milan, 1976), and translated into English in R. Durling, *Petrarch's Lyric Poems* (Cambridge, MA, 1976), 385. Forster, *The Icy Fire*, 13, discusses the "bitter–sweet nature of love" in Petrarch's poetry.

the flow between octave and sestet, or to switch directions at given prosodic intervals. His sonnets flow freely, often in an even tone that makes use of flexible patterns and a syntax that sometimes skips over the division between the stanzas.[5] The sonnet acts according to an inner dynamic of its own, with or without a basic correspondence between the external form and its verbal content.

Petrarch's sonnets won the heart of his readers with the complexity of his dramatic characters, introspective tone, musicality, and the wonderful harmony between form and content. Throughout Europe, his followers adhered faithfully to the sonnet-form, and turned it into one of the most popular literary genres for centuries.

2. After Petrarch

Petrarchism: Major Traits

The admirers of Petrarch created an international idiom on a scale reminiscent of the courtly poetry of the Middle Ages or the Romanticism of the eighteenth and nineteenth centuries.[6] In the effort to duplicate Petrarch's achievements, these poets proceeded to imitate his poems down to their smallest details, openly borrowing his structures, terminology, ideas, metaphors, even entire lines of poetry. Thus the lady of whom they sing has hair of gold, cheeks of lilies, and eyes like stars. Her teeth are pearls, and her teardrops crystal. Then there is the abject servitude in everything connected with the beloved, from the place in which she was seen, to the objects which she owns. The lady is commonly portrayed as a hard-hearted tyrant, the lover as a suffering hero. The Petrarchists exhausted a number of elements common to Petrarch's poetry: expressions of bitterness, similes of torture and death; paradoxes, antitheses, oxymorons. One of Petrarch's most famous oxymorons, the "icy fire" with which he described love, became the motto for a whole generation of Petrarchists.[7]

Among the Petrarchists were some of the finest poets of the Renaissance; poets who used the sonnet as a vessel for casting their own personal poetry. But there were many other, far less talented poets, and these caused the entire school to be branded for its frozen cliches, blind devotion to the venerated model, and a veritable "cult of the sonnet."[8]

---

[5] S. Zandbank was right in criticizing the rigid syntax of Leah Goldberg's translations of Petrarch. See "Leah Goldberg ve–ha–Sonet ha–Petrarqi," *Ha-Sifrut* 6 (1975): 19–31, here 22–25.

[6] Forster, *The Icy Fire*, 2.

[7] See K. K. Ruthven, *The Conceit* (London, 1969); Forster, *The Icy Fire*, 6–10.

[8] Tusiani, *Italian Poets of the Renaissance*, xxvi.

Early Petrarchism

The veneration of Petrarch began early. Already in 1341 Petrarch was crowned poet laureate on the steps of the Capitol in Rome.[9] It was around this time that poets in Italy and elsewhere began writing like Petrarch, and even at this early date their writing was closely identified with the sonnet-form. Boccaccio, the author of the *Decameron* and a friend of Petrarch, composed two sonnets in his style. Chaucer adapted a sonnet by Petrarch into English around 1385, and in Spain, around the year 1440, the Marquis of Santillana wrote his sonnets in the spirit of Petrarch. In 1470 the *Canzoniere* was printed for the first time, and after that there was no stopping Petrarchism.

After a few minor poets, some Petrarchists of real stature began to emerge. The most important of these are Matteo Maria Boiardo, author of *Orlando innamorato*, and Lorenzo de' Medici (*Il Magnifico*), ruler of Florence, famed humanist and patron of the arts. Boiardo, a superb lyric poet, wrote one hundred and eighty poems and sonnets that constitute the finest examples we have of Petrarchan love poetry from the sixteenth century. Lorenzo de' Medici composed, among other things, one hundred and eighty sonnets in the spirit of Petrarch. Some of these he inserted into a prose narrative, in the manner of Dante's *Vita Nuova*. Jacopo Sannazaro, best known for his pastorals (more than fifty editions of his *Arcadia* appeared during the sixteenth century), also wrote dozens of sonnets à la Petrarch. One of his students was Cardinal Pietro Bembo, the major Petrarchist of the sixteenth century.

These writers and their circles created a new sonnet: intellectual, epigrammatic, direct, emotional, highly personal. Their poems emphasized Platonic ideas from Petrarch's poetry, which was being circulated by the Platonic Academy in Florence founded by Cosimo de' Medici. In this Platonic spirit, which was not without a certain hedonism,[10] these poets developed optimistic strains from Petrarch's poetry, creating poems and sonnets that brimmed with light and life. Botticelli's famous *Primavera* was possibly inspired by a sonnet of this kind by Lorenzo de' Medici.[11] But in neglecting the anguished side of Petrarch's poetry, these poets basically denied a major part of the tradition. In their hands, Petrarch's moving confessions became an instrument of literary elegance.

Towards the end of the fifteenth century a new trend emerged in this movement under the leadership of Benedetto Cariteo Gareth of Naples "Il Chariteo," a poet of Catalonian descent who won fame for the collection of sonnets he addressed to his lady, "Luna." His follower, Serafino Aquilano — poet, courtier and musician — wrote one hundred sonnets in the spirit of Petrarch. Serafi-

---

[9] For a description of the ceremony, see Mönch, *Das Sonett*, 76–86.

[10] See J. M. Cohen, *A History of Western Literature* (Harmondsworth, 1956), 95–101; Tusiani, *Italian Poets of the Renaissance*, Introduction, 26.

[11] Mönch, *Das Sonett*, 68–69.

no, who knew every syllable of Petrarch's poetry, made this style his own. He composed melodies for Petrarch's sonnets and performed them in public while accompanying himself on the lute. Several contemporary accounts describe his performances throughout Italy as an unforgettable experience. Serafino's popularity even went beyond Italy, like that of Petrarch himself. Upon his death he was lamented by hundreds of elegies in Greek, Latin, Italian, Spanish,[12] and even Hebrew, as we shall see below. Another of Il Chariteo's followers, Antonio Tebaldeo, dedicated a volume of poems and sonnets to his lady, Flavia. This volume went through eleven editions at the beginning of the sixteenth century. These poets latched onto Petrarch's rhetorical flourishes and exploited them with much talent and a great deal of exaggeration, though without any serious attempt to plumb the depths of his poetry.[13] So, for example, they made exaggerated changes in the dramatic situation of the poem, with the lover's anguish reaching the point of masochism, and the lady's refusal painted as cold-hearted monstrosity. Because of these exaggerations in Petrarch's techniques, the poems sometimes sound almost like parodies. "[Il Chariteo's] cardinal and most infectious sin is the materialization of Petrarchan metaphors, to which he gives an existential literality they were never meant to bear."[14] The superficial approach of these Petrarchists also found expression in a preference for the eight-line *strambotto* over a complete sonnet, and for a sestet of two rather than three rhymes in the sonnet.[15] But this superficiality produced a model that was easy to imitate, and greatly accelerated the dissemination of the style.

Petrarchism in the Sixteenth Century

During the sixteenth century Petrarchism enjoyed a new flowering. Cardinal Pietro Bembo, a humanist and leading poet, rescued Italian poetry from "the flamboyant aberration" of his predecessors. Bembo admired the simplicity of Petrarch's language and the elegance of his style. In such writings as *Gli Asolani* (1505) and *Prose della volgar lingua* (1525) he raised Petrarch to the level of a classic and his own poetry into the model for correct imitation. He emphasized Platonic ideas from Petrarch's poetry and endowed Petrarchism with a sober new respectability.[16] Following Bembo, Petrarchan trends became dominant in literature, art, and music. As Hebrew critic and poet Leah Goldberg remarks:

---

[12] Tusiani, *Italian Poets of the Renaissance*, 108.

[13] Forster, *The Icy Fire*, 24–26.

[14] E. H. Wilkins, *Petrarchism*, "A General Survey of Renaissance Petrarchism," *Comparative Literature* 11 (1950): 327–42, here 330. For more recent research on Il Chariteo, see also *Dictionary of Italian Literature*, 103–4, 399, 474, 500, 509.

[15] Mönch, *Das Sonett*, 69.

[16] Wilkins, "Petrarchism," 330–32; Forster, *The Icy Fire*, 26–30; Mönch, *Das Sonett*, 69–70.

Just how greatly Petrarchan poetry came to symbolize love in sixteenth- and seventeenth-century Italy, we see from the fact that in the theater no lover ever appeared on stage without Petrarch's *Canzoniere* in hand.[17]

Petrarchism made its way into France, England, Spain, Portugal, and the Netherlands, and before the end of the sixteenth century it spread to Poland, Hungary, Bohemia, Croatia and Cyprus. And the sonnet, the main instrument of this movement, spread right along with it.

Bembo made the three-rhyme sestet fashionable again and propelled the genre in its classical form into the center of poetic awareness. In his wake the sonnet found its way into every corner of Europe, and writers of sonnets began to mushroom overnight. Sonnets were written for any and all occasions by anyone with even a pretension to fashion. Indeed, Jacob Burckhardt found himself unable to describe this period without reviewing the history and contribution of "this Procrustean bed, to which [poets] were compelled to make their thoughts and feelings fit."[18] Throughout Europe, the writing of sonnets went beyond literary circles to become the hallmark of education and refinement.[19]

Among the most important sonneteers of the sixteenth century were some of the finest poets of the Italian Renaissance, and many, if not all, of these poets were Petrarchists. All of these adapted the Petrarchan style to their own voice. Below we will list the most important of these poets, in chronological order,[20] and briefly describe their use of the sonnet.

In terms of literary merit, Ludovico Ariosto's *Orlando Furioso* is second only to Dante's *Divine Comedy* as the greatest *poema* of the Italian language. Ariosto's sonnets are among the finest in Italian, and his impact on the genre went as far as Portugal and France.[21] Michelangelo Buonarroti, sculptor, painter, and architect, was also one of the finest lyric poets of the early sixteenth century;[22] most of his poems are sonnets. His reflections on the meaning of beauty, art, love, old age and death have an overtone that is both lyrical and erotic. As an artist and philosopher, Michelangelo used the conflict in Petrarch's poems to examine the relationship between art and the belief in God. Many of his poems were inspired by his literary friendship with Vittoria Colonna, an important poet and deeply religious woman

---

[17] Goldberg, "Petrarcha, Hayav vi–Yetzirato," 126.

[18] Burckhardt, *Civilization of the Renaissance*, 186.

[19] On the diffusion of the sonnet outside Italy see Bregman, *Sharsheret ha–Zahav*, 16–18. For a discussion of the sonnet as a vehicle for other, non–Petrarchist trends (Baroque, Classicism, Romanticism, Symbolism and Modernism), see 24–31.

[20] For a complete list of the sonneteers in Bembo's circle, and his followers, see Mönch, *Das Sonett*, 70.

[21] Mönch, *Das Sonett*, 132.

[22] Wilkins, "Petrarchism," 331.

who also wrote mostly in sonnets. Giovanni della Casa, one of the finest Italian poets of the century, invigorated the sonnet through his keen sense of drama and his sophisticated use of language and syntax. Luigi Tansillo composed Petrarchan sonnets that were both highly philosophical and structurally complex.[23] Gaspara Stampa composed nearly three hundred love poems, most of them sonnets. Her poems, which were compared to those of Sappho, are remarkable for their highly personal tone and their ability to breathe life into the conventions of Petrarchist poetry. They are considered amongst the finest poems written by a woman during the Renaissance.

Giordano Bruno, the renowned philosopher who was burned at the stake for heresy in 1600, was also an important poet. His sonnets, studiously non-lyrical, lent a new tone of philosophical gravity to Petrarchism.[24] This is also true of Tommaso Campanella, a theologian, philosopher, astrologer, and politician who spent long years in prison and wrote poems of deep thought and feeling.

The flowering of original poetry within the stream of Petrarchism did not put an end to the highly mannered style of Il Chariteo. Vestiges of this style can be heard in the poetry of Galeazzo di Tarsia, one of the best known sonneteers of the period. His sonnets usually begin with an allusion to Petrarch, and then continue their own course. Torquato Tasso, the most important lyric poet of the sixteenth century, renowned for his pastoral play *Aminta* and his heroic *Gerusalemme liberata*,[25] wrote more than a thousand poems, among them a large number of sonnets dealing with love, religion, ethics and praise. In these works we see the climax of the Neo-Platonic poetics of the Renaissance, and also the beginning of the new Baroque poetry.

In addition to the mainstream of Petrarchism in the sixteenth century, we also find a few trends that went in different directions. Some Petrarchan poetry was written in Latin, including translations of Petrarch himself.[26] The emphasis here was naturally on the elements of classical mythology from Petrarch's poetry. In Italy, the most important writers in this field were Andrea Navagero, Jacopo Sannazaro, and Giulio Cesare Scaligero. Among them we also find Diogo Pires, a former *converso* who returned to Judaism under the name of Isaiah Cohen.[27] The poems of these poets were important in disseminating Petrarchism throughout Europe, most noticeably — at least for us — in the Netherlands,[28] where the Hebrew sonnet was destined to flourish in the seventeenth century.

---

[23] Mönch, *Das Sonett*, 77.
[24] Mönch, *Das Sonett*, 76.
[25] Forster, *The Icy Fire*, 30.
[26] Forster, *The Icy Fire*, 33.
[27] C. Roth, *The Jews in the Renaissance* (Philadelphia, 1964), 23, 59, 78, 110.
[28] Mönch, *Das Sonett*, 141–42.

Another Petrarchist movement, spiritual in nature and rooted in the Byzantine-Greek traditions of Platonism, emphasized the Christian motifs from the *Canzoniere*. This kind of Petrarchan sonnet first emerged in a volume of poetry by Girolamo Malipiero, *Il Petrarca spirituale* (Venice, 1536). Malipiero rewrote Petrarch's poems, reproducing his rhymes and even his wording in a spirit of religious ecstacy. Malipiero was followed by religious poets, particularly Jesuits from Catholic countries.[29] Under their pens the love of woman was transformed into the love of God, Cupid's arrows into the nails on the Cross, Laura into the Virgin Mary, and so on. Malipiero's book went through ten editions already in the sixteenth century.

So great was the fashion for Petrarchism that some poets decided to spoof it. As we have already seen, the line between Petrarchism and parody could be rather a thin one. There are parodies from the sixteenth century that sound eminently anti-Petrarchist in tone, but are in fact satires aimed against bombastic poets of the Petrarchist school. Giordano Bruno, for example, included in his *Degli eroici furori* a considerable number of sonnets poking fun at the hackneyed style of certain Petrarchists.[30] Well-known Petrarchists outside of Italy also indulged in the same kind of satire: Shakespeare in England, and Joachim du Bellay in France.

Even more extreme were the poets of realism who ridiculed the entire movement. Burchiello, a barber by occupation, and Francesco Berni after him, wrote burlesque sonnets that turned the tradition upside down, describing lice instead of golden tresses, and agonizing over venereal diseases instead of the spiritual sufferings of the lover. Their followers, Teofilo Folengo and Nicolo Franco, continued this tradition. They used the sonnet to ridicule both Petrarchism and the sonnet-form itself, so closely was it identified with this style.

Not Only Love, Not Only Petrarch

Obviously, Italian sonnets in the fifteenth and sixteenth centuries were not limited to the subject of love. Petrarch himself included a few sonnets on other topics in his *Canzoniere*, such as eulogies of various friends and patrons, the pilgrimage to Rome, and his own poetry. Those who came after Petrarch devoted sonnets to public affairs, politics, and metaphysical discussion. One important subject was that of praise. Il Chariteo, for example, wrote sonnets and *canzones* of a political-historical nature praising the royal house of Aragon. Similarly, there were also non-Petrarchan sonneteers who dealt with a number of other subjects, such as the realistic poets Burchiello and his followers, who did so for tendentious reasons.

---

[29] See Mönch, *Das Sonett*, 72; Forster, *The Icy Fire*, 46–48, 54–56.
[30] Mönch, *Das Sonett*, 77.

Luigi Pulci, author of *Il Morgante* (an epic comedy about the reign of Charlemagne, which greatly influenced Rabelais and others), attacked his enemies with sarcastic sonnets. The priest Matteo Franco described his congregation in satirical and folksy sonnets and also used the sonnet to conduct his polemics with Pulci and others. Sonnets were written on the subject of nature and on matters of morality and religion; sonnets served as laments for the dead and as poems for various occasions of all kinds. Poets exchanged sonnets of friendship, in keeping with time-honored traditions. As Walther Mönch reminds us, it was not troubadours who invented the sonnet, but lawyers and jurists. From the very beginning, then, the sonnet was not restricted to the subject of love. Even during the Golden Age of the Petrarchan love poem the sonnet maintained a striking diversity of subject matter.[31]

3. In Baroque Poetry

The middle of the sixteenth century saw the waning of the Renaissance and the beginning of the Baroque. With the Baroque a new poetics came into being, and the sonnet was reshaped accordingly.

Baroque culture flourished during a period of religious wars, political and economic crises, and social unrest following the onset of the Reformation and the schism in the Catholic Church. Some scholars date the beginning of this period to the Council of Trent (1545–1563), which culminated in a general appeal to Catholic artists of all kinds to come to the aid of the beleaguered Catholic Church. With this turmoil in mind, it becomes easier to explain the major characteristics of Baroque poetry.

The poetry of Petrarch and of the best of his followers reflects the spirit of humanism and the effort to synthesize man's spiritual and material needs, both of which were considered worthy and noble in themselves. The people of the Renaissance were confident in the ultimate triumph of truth, in the majesty of nature, in the power of love over death. In this spirit they sought out forgotten texts, founded libraries, and organized literary academies. This confidence, however, began to ebb towards the end of the sixteenth century. Much of Baroque art and literature is infused with a deep sense of religious belief. However, it was not a feeling of vocation that filled the vacuum but rather a sense of despair and crisis, and less than this art calls for repentance it seeks to overwhelm through grandiosity. As in the Middle Ages, religious axioms concerning the vanity of this world began to resound from the pulpit. But many Baroque poets found little comfort in thinking of the next world, and were instead overwhelmed by a sense of fatality

---

[31] Mönch, *Das Sonett*, 47.

and a heightened awareness of death and the Last Judgment. In the words of the German literary critic, Fritz Strich, the Baroque saw the temporal world

> in its fleeting, changeable and transitory aspects. Time as creator and destroyer, passing and overthrowing, is the primary religious experience of the Baroque . . . What is man? Not, as the Renaissance believed, a sovereign, self-governing, harmonious, cosmic entity, a self-reliant independent being, but a shadow, a fading music, a passing wave, a reed tossing in the storm and quickly snapped. A dream, a sport, or as one Baroque poet Andreas Gryphius put it, a fantasy of time. This distinguishes the Baroque so signally from the Renaissance . . .[32]

The world, which appeared to the people of the Renaissance like an open book that revealed its laws to those who diligently studied them, seemed to the Baroque poet transitory and incomprehensible, like a play in the theater complete with props, costumes and scenery. It dazzled, but it was an illusion without reality, "veering between religious sentiments and libertinage, beauty and ugliness, egocentricity and impersonality, temporality and eternity."[33]

The Concept of Meraviglia

"The goal of the poet is to amaze, and whoever is unable to do so is better off grooming horses."[34] This maxim was pronounced by Giambattista Marino, the foremost representative of the Italian Baroque. The concept of *meraviglia*, "wonder," became the goal of Baroque poetics, and for its sake poets frequently sacrificed "decorum": exalted topics, refined expression, perfection of form. Exaggeration, the old way of creating wonder, penetrated Baroque poetics at every level: structure, context, rhetoric. It fed on elliptical and forced syntax, on language that was either brutally direct or obliquely allusive. It found expression in dramatic tones, bold colors, and a macabre atmosphere. It emphasized contrast and opposition, the strange, the bizarre, and the marvelous.

One basic element in this style is "wit": in Italian *acutezza*, in Spanish *agudeza* (literally "sharpness"). It embodies the Baroque aspiration towards verbal conceits, complex syllogisms, and intricacy. It calls to mind the basic paradox of the Petrarchan conceit, only no longer restricted to the poetry of frustrated lovers.

---

[32] Quoted from J. M. Cohen, *The Baroque Lyric* (London, 1963), 15.
[33] L. Nelson, in *The Princeton Encyclopedia of Poetry and Poetics*, ed. A. Preminger (Princeton, 1974), 66–68, here 68. Cf. now idem and H. B. Segel, "Baroque," in *The New Princeton Encyclopedia of Poetry and Poetics*, ed. A. Preminger and T. V. F. Brogan (Princeton, 1993), 121–24, and idem, "Baroque Poetics," 124–26.
[34] "*E del poeta il fin la maraviglia / parlo del eccellente e non del goffo / chi non sa far stupir, vada alla strigllia*": quoted in F. De Sanctis, *Storia della letteratura italiana* (Milan, 1970), 644.

The Baroque style did not renounce Petrarchism; in fact, some consider it to be its direct continuation.[35] Yet the Baroque poets did revolt against the Petrarchist weakness for hackneyed conventions, stereotypes, and frivolity.

In Italy, the major exponent of the new poetics was Giambattista Marino, who belonged in his youth to the Petrarchists of the sixteenth century; and in Spain it was Luis de Góngora. Marino's followers were largely minor poets who testify to the decline of Italian poetry. On the other hand, *gongorismo* became an important element in the work of leading poets during the *siglo de oro* of Spanish literature: Lope de Vega, Francesco de Quevedo y Villegas, Baltasar Gracián, to name only a few. The new poetics were propounded in Spain through Gracián's *Agudeza y Arte de Ingenio*, and in Italy through Emanuele Tesauro's *Il cannochiale aristotelico*, the most important statement on the Baroque metaphor.

Different trends emphasized different aspects of Baroque poetry. *Marinism*, under the inspiration of Giambattista Marino, emphasized the sensual, the musical; *culteranismo*, headed by Góngora and Lope de Vega, rhetorical style and cultural-intellectual dimensions; *conceptismo*, headed by Baltasar Gracián and Quevedo, the primacy of the idea. Marinism and Gongorism found expression in works of great length, such as Marino's *L'Adone* or Góngora's *Fábula di Polifemo y Galatea* and the poems of his *Soledades*, but they also took a more concentrated form of expression in hundreds upon hundreds of sonnets.

This was no coincidence. Once again, the various attributes of the sonnet seemed born to serve the reigning poetic style: the proportions of the unequal symmetry, the complex relations between the different sections and the musical break between them, the tension and compressed musicality of the sestet, the pointed conclusion, the wide range of potential relations between content and form. The Baroque sonnet made the most of the sonnet-form in order to create the effect of wit and *meraviglia*, tantalizing suspense, and illusion and camouflage. It managed to bewilder its audience by subverting the conventions of the sonnet form at various levels of the poetry. The grandiosity and symmetry of Baroque poetry found expression in the sequential organization of dozens and even hundreds of sonnets.

The power of the Baroque began to wane towards the end of the seventeenth century with the emergence of neoclassical trends. The Arcadia Academy, founded in 1690 in Rome, protested the artificiality of the Baroque and demanded a return, not for the first time, to a closer relationship with nature and to a simpler attitude towards life and poetry. A new poetics stood poised on the threshold, and the sonnet was there to receive it.

---

[35]Cohen, *The Baroque Lyric*, 11–14. Concerning the Baroque world–view from the Spanish perspective (relevant to most of the Hebrew poets of the Baroque), see J. A. Maravall, *Culture of the Baroque: Analysis of a Historical Structure*, trans. T. Cochran (Manchester, 1986), and esp. chap. 6.

IX. THE REVIVAL OF THE HEBREW SONNET: THE CORPUS

1. The Decline of the Sonnet after Immanuel of Rome

The fourteenth and fifteenth centuries should have provided a hospitable environment for the Hebrew sonnet.[1] During this period the Jews took considerable part in more than a few branches of the surrounding Italian culture. Kalonymos ben Kalonymos and Shemariah ben Elijah of Crete translated works from the Greek and Latin classics and from Arabic literature in the service of King Robert of Naples. Elijah del Medigo wrote philosophical essays in Hebrew and Latin, translated various works into Hebrew, gave lectures at the University of Padua, and took part in public debates and discussions. Judah Messer Leon showed that Jews could be sympathetic to secular culture in *Sefer Nofet Zufim*, or "The Book of the Honeycomb's Flow" (Mantua, 1478), his great work on Hebrew and classical rhetoric. *Shevet Yehuda*, or "The Staff of Judah," Solomon ibn Verga's theosophical work, reflects trends that were highly characteristic of the Renaissance. Guglielmo da Pesaro composed a treatise on dance that earned him an approving sonnet by Mario Filelfo.[2] Moses da Rieti, who will be discussed below, wrote Hebrew treatises on medicine and philosophy and an Italian treatise defending Judaism, and took part in religious disputations. Johanan ben Isaac Alemanno wrote a commentary on the biblical Song of Solomon, *Hesheq Shelomo*, essentially a philosophical discussion on the nature of love.[3] Obadiah Sforno, the well-known biblical commentator, instructed Johann von Reuchlin in Hebrew. Abraham Farissol, scribe, cantor and biblical commentator, conducted geographical

---

[1] On the subject of Jewish life in Italy see R. Bonfil, *Rabbis and Jewish Communities in Renaissance Italy* (Berkeley, 1994); M. D. Cassuto, *Ha-Yehudim be Firenze bi-Tequfat ha-Renaissance*, trans. M. Hartoum (Jerusalem, 1967); D. Bregman, "Hebrew Literature and Language," in *Encyclopedia of the Renaissance*, ed. Grendler, 3:121–25; J. Melkman, "Amsterdam," in *Encyclopedia Judaica* 2: 895–900; A. Milano, *Storia degli Ebrei in Italia* (Turin, 1992); Roth, *Jews in the Renaissance*; D. Ruderman, *Essential Papers on Jewish Culture in Renaissance and Baroque Italy* (New York, 1992), and idem, *Kabbalah, Magic and Science: The Cultural Universe of a Sixteenth-Century Jewish Physician* (Cambridge, MA, 1988); M. A. Shulvass, *The Jews in the World of the Renaissance* (Leiden, 1973); S. Simonsohn, *History of the Jews in the Duchy of Mantua* (Jerusalem, 1972); W. Van Bekkum, "Judaism in Umbruch," *Jews in Renaissance and Baroque Italy* 1 (2001): 257–66.

[2] Roth, *Jews in the Renaissance*, 276–77.

[3] *Inter alia* Roth, *Jews in the Renaissance*, 119–21.

research that he eventually published as *Iggeret Orḥot ʿOlam*, or "Epistle on the Ways of the World." In a philosophical work that he wrote, we hear echoes of a religious disputation in which Farissol took part, as well as criticism of the Koran. The Portaleone family gave rise to a dynasty of renowned physicians.[4] Ties of friendship grew up between well-known Italian humanists and Jews. So, for example, Lorenzo de' Medici was acquainted with Johanan Alemanno and the Jewish Volterra family,[5] and Pico della Mirandola with Elijah del Medigo. This cultural interaction was fostered by well-to-do Jews such as Jehiel da Pisa, a wealthy banker who patronized Jewish scholars and poets. All this naturally strengthened Jewish absorption of various creative trends at work in the wider cultural milieu, and with the invention of printing and the greater accessibility of Italian literature the process became even easier.

Poetry was no exception to the rule. The Jews were acquainted with Petrarch's *Canzoniere*. David, the son of Judah Messer Leon, did not hesitate to weave a short biography of Petrarch into his commentary on the biblical "Woman of Valor," and to discuss the ever-popular question of whether Petrarch's Laura really existed or not.[6] Hebrew poetry in Italy flourished. J. Schirmann's anthology includes more than twenty Hebrew poets from the fifteenth century, and these are only a selection. These poets were no strangers to secular topics. Shemariah of Crete and Joseph ben Judah Zarko composed poems in praise of Italian nobles; several elegies were written upon the death of Jehiel da Pisa; and Moses Remos, who was executed in Sicily, wrote a lengthy poem lamenting his own early death. Judah Abrabanel described his flight from Spain in a moving poem; Ephraim da Modena protested gambling, licentiousness and greed in a moralistic, satire. Descriptions of daily life and current events also made their way into liturgical poetry. Solomon ben Isaac da Perugia composed prayers begging for an end to the plague, and Mattiahu da Larippa sought divine forgiveness during an earthquake.[7] Hebrew poetry was influenced by the Italian in themes, motifs, meter, and form.

At the forefront of Hebrew poetry we find Moses da Rieti, whose *Miqdash Meʿat* or "A Small Sanctuary" earned him the title *Il Dante Ebreo*, "the Hebrew Dante."[8] The poem describes a mystical journey through Paradise in the manner

---

[4] *Inter alia* Roth, *Jews in the Renaissance*, 202–3.

[5] *Inter alia* Roth, *Jews in the Renaissance*, 30.

[6] A. Neubauer, "Documents inédits," *Revue des études juives* 10 (1885): 79–107, here 94–97.

[7] Most of these works, either in part or in full, can be found in J. Schirmann, *Mivḥar ha-Shirah ha-ʿIvrit bi-Italia* (Berlin, 1934).

[8] See the first two cantos edited by Dvora Bregman, Alessandro Guetta and Raymond Scheindlin with an English translation by Raymond Scheindlin, *Prooftexts* 23 (2003): 1-93.

of Dante's *Divine Comedy*. Rieti composed his poem in *terza rima*, strophes of three lines interlinked by a rhyme scheme of ABA BCB CDC etc., and in a new meter — not quantitative — all under the inspiration of Dante's masterpiece.[9] Both the form and the meter of *Miqdash Me'at* won immediate acceptance in the fifteenth century. We find them, for example, in elegies written upon the death of Jehiel da Pisa and in a series of poems debating the nature of woman, which were composed over the course of the century.[10] Around the same time the *ballata* made its way into Hebrew poetry, after having served the *lauda* of Italian religious poetry. It appears, for example, in a liturgical poem by Elazar bar Menahem Volterra,[11] and in Raphael da Faenza's poem on *Galantina*, a Hebrew adaptation of an Italian song that testifies to the absorption of Italian influences also at the level of popular culture.[12] Another important verse form, the *canzone*, was used by a Hebrew poet from the fifteenth century, whose name appears in the acrostic as "Immanuel."[13]

The sonnet-form was also known to the Jews, some of whom wrote sonnets in Italian. There exists, for example, an exchange of sonnets between one Solomon of Mantua and the Italian poet Giovanni Peregrini. In a collection of poems edited in 1500 upon the death of Serafino Aquilano, the important Petrarchist mentioned earlier, there are three sonnets by Judah ben Solomon (Giuda Hebreo), also from Mantua, and perhaps from the same family as Solomon of Mantua.[14] Italian Jews mention a Jewish poetess from the fourteenth century, Giustina Levi-Perotti, who allegedly sent a sonnet to the Pope and another one to Petrarch himself. According to tradition, the poetess received a reply from Petrarch: the poem which is now the seventh sonnet in the *Canzoniere*.[15] That sonnet is in fact the answering half of a *tenzone*. Critics regard Petrarch's poem as a reply to a friend, although they do not know who this friend was, nor the sonnet which prompted his response.

---

[9] A. Guetta, "Bibliographie", *Revue des études juives* 159 (2000): 501–3; Pagis, *Ḥiddush u-Masoret*, 329–32; idem, "Hamtza'at ha-Iambus," 662–64 [in *Ha-Shir Davur*, 183–186].

[10] D. Pagis, "Ha-Pulmus ha-Shiri ʿal Tiv ha-Nashim," *Meḥqarei Yerushalayim be-Sifrut ʿIvrit* 9 (1986): 259–300 [in *Ha-Shir Davur*, 124–65].

[11] MS. Parma 420, fol. 395r-v.

[12] Schirmann, *Mivḥar*, 203.

[13] Joseph Galiego, *Sefer Imrei Noʿam* (Amsterdam, 1628), 42; and see E. Seroussi and T. Beri, "Rabi Yosef Galiego Baʿal Sefer Imrei Noʿam," *Assufot* 6 (1992): 87-150.

[14] Roth, *Jews in the Renaissance*, 108; Simonsohn, *Toldot ha-Yehudim be-Dukasut Mantova*, 1: 366; and Fabian Alfie, "Giovanni Pellegrino and Salomone", *Prooftexts* 23 (2003): 94 -109; see Appendices I and II in Bregman, *Shevil ha-Zahav*.

[15] M. Soave printed the sonnet in *Sara Coppia Sullam* (Venice, 1726; repr. Trieste, 1864). And see Appendix III in Bregman, *Shevil ha-Zahav*.

Both this sonnet and the sonnet attributed to Levi-Perotti deal with the same subject, use the same rhyme and even some of the same rhyme-words, and appear to relate to each other as question and answer. Of course, none of this means that the sonnet attributed to Giustina might not in fact be a later forgery; and indeed some later critics (such as Cassuto and Roth) are dubious about the whole story. But their predecessors regarded it as fact.[16]

Also worth mentioning are some Italian sonnets written in Hebrew letters which have come down to us from the fifteenth century. These were appended to a Hebrew treatise entitled *Mar'ot ha-Sheten* or "The Treatise on Uroscopy" by the physician Irado Grados,[17] in order to provide, as the good doctor put it, a conclusion that was "brief and in sonnet-form."[18] Cecil Roth reports the existence of women physicians who were active in the Jewish milieu during this period. Jewish ladies, though well educated in other respects, would hardly have understood Hebrew. Perhaps, then, the treatise was written for a woman and the poetic conclusion was an attempt to make the subject under discussion somewhat more elegant.

The vigorous participation in Italian culture; the readiness of Hebrew poets to absorb Italian forms, meters, topics, and trends; the fact that Jews were acquainted with Petrarch's poetry and wrote sonnets in Italian, sometimes even in Hebrew letters: all these are factors that render the absence of the Hebrew sonnet more amazing, especially when we consider its auspicious beginnings. Could the Hebrew poets of the fifteenth century have been unaware of earlier sonnets in Hebrew, and of the striking affinity of those sonnets to the models which they encountered on a daily basis in their Italian surroundings?

The Petrarchan poetics that were so rapidly gaining momentum were admirably, even brilliantly, suited to expressing the conflicts of the Hebrew poet between desire and religion, or between the urge for self-expression and the social norms that discouraged such expression. Why then was the sonnet, the major instrument of the Petrarchists, not used to absorb these poetics immediately upon its diffusion in Italy, even if only to create allegory in the manner of the Petrarchan spiritualists, or parody, like that produced by the Petrarchists themselves? And what about sonnets on topics of social intercourse — sonnets of friendship, praise, polemics? The disappearance of the Hebrew sonnet during the fifteenth century is baffling indeed.

---

[16] Soave relies on "most scholars."

[17] Like that by Joseph ibn Zabara: see his *Sefer Sha'ashu'im*, ed. I. Davidson (Berlin, 1925), 170–73.

[18] MS. Cambridge University Library Dd 1068 (10), fol. 7v, and see Appendix VI in Bregman, *Shevil ha-Zahav*.

[19] The subject is treated at greater length in Bregman, "Parashat ha-Hitqablut."

This surprising phenomenon can perhaps be explained in several ways.[19] One explanation is related to the quantitative-syllabic meter which Immanuel introduced in his sonnets. This complicated meter made exceptional demands on the poet. It required a thorough knowledge of Hebrew grammar and Italian poetry, in addition to considerable linguistic virtuosity. All this was apparently beyond the powers of most Hebrew poets in the fourteenth and fifteenth centuries. There was no poet sufficiently versed in Immanuel's techniques to instruct fledgling poets at this time. The most prominent poet during this period was Moses da Rieti, author of the famous *Miqdash Meʿat*, who followed Dante in his description of Paradise. However, Rieti not only dismissed Immanuel's metrical system but even countered it with a different metrical system of his own. Ostensibly, it should have been possible to write sonnets using Rieti's metrical system, but in reality this was not so easy to do. True, Rieti freed the poet from the constraints of quantitative meter, but he did not create a Hebrew *endecasillabo*, which was necessary for writing a sonnet in Hebrew. The characteristic line in *Miqdash Meʿat* contains ten syllables and has a masculine rhyme, while the regular line of the sonnet has eleven syllables and ends in a feminine rhyme. Moreover, Rieti did not distinguish between feminine and masculine rhymes either in the length of the line or in the stress. According to his method, lines had the same length whether they had masculine or feminine rhyme, and the two could be rhymed together, regardless of stress. Immanuel's method was more successful in this respect.

Theoretically, it should have been possible to create a syllabic meter combining the ideas of both Rieti and Immanuel: one that would renounce quantitative meter, like Rieti's; demand homogenous rhymes, like Immanuel's; present a line of eleven syllables and feminine rhyme, like Immanuel's; and two lines with masculine rhyme: ten syllables like Rieti's, and twelve like Immanuel's.[20] But a fusion of this kind required competency, daring, and talent, and apparently there was no poet ready to take on the task in the fifteenth century.

A second explanation for the disappearance of the Hebrew sonnet might be deduced from the distinctly chaste tone of Hebrew poetry after the death of Immanuel. It appears that during the fifteenth century the literary hegemony passed into the hands of the religious establishment. There were protests against secular content in Hebrew poems, and perhaps against forms not sanctioned by ancient tradition. One of the objectors was Moses ibn Habib, who was born in Lisbon but lived most of his life in Italy.[21] To be sure, ibn Habib's protests fell on deaf ears, but it may be that secular Hebrew poetry during this period was too ambivalent about secular topics to cultivate non-liturgical sonnets, while Hebrew

---

[20] See Bregman, "Shitat Immanuel," 437–39.
[21] See Galiego, *Sefer Imrei Noʿam*, 90r; and see also Schirmann, *Ha-Shirah ha-ʿIvrit*, 4: 663–64.

models for sonnets of religious content were nowhere to be found and adapting Italian models required a certain audacity.

A third explanation, not unrelated to the second, may be rooted in the ambivalent attitude of Italian Jews towards Immanuel himself: an ambivalence which we might call "the Immanuel complex." Italian Jews regarded Immanuel's *Maḥbarot* both as the apogee of Hebrew poetry and as an example of immoral expression. They could not accept his works, but neither could they renounce them. Feelings like these apparently festered over a considerable period of time. As late as the nineteenth century, poet and critic Anania Coen was complaining (in Italian) that: "The Italian poets have many good examples before them: Petrarch, Dante, Ariosto, Tasso and many others. But we have no one but '*the* Immanuel,' who is banned because of his abominations, while the moralistic poems by some of the earlier poets are ill-suited to our modern taste."[22]

The ban to which Coen refers goes back to Rabbi Joseph Caro, who thundered against Immanuel in his *Shulḥan ʿArukh*:

> Licentious words like the book of Immanuel . . . may not be read on the Sabbath, and are forbidden even during the rest of the week . . . and whoever writes them, or copies them, and, it goes without saying, whoever prints them, causes the people to sin.[23]

Caro's ban was published only in 1565, in the first edition of the *Shulḥan ʿArukh*, but in reality the *Maḥbarot* had been banned even before that. The ambivalence which Coen describes apparently divided the Hebrew poets into two camps already during Immanuel's lifetime. One faction embraced Immanuel and the challenge of his poetics, while the other faction wanted nothing to do with Immanuel, either good or bad. This latter camp apparently waxed stronger in the fifteenth century, under the decisive influence of Moses da Rieti. In one of the remarks written in the margins of his *Miqdash Meʿat*, Rieti explains why he did not seat Immanuel in Paradise together with the other great Jews he envisioned in his poem: "And I excluded Rabbi Immanuel from these lines because of his language and because of what he wrote in the licentious *Maḥbarot*."[24] Thus Rieti stigmatized the *Maḥbarot* for their bawdy content, and essentially banned them from the shelves of Hebrew readers.

Indeed, every aspect of Immanuel's poetics was rejected as far back as the fifteenth century. His light-hearted *maqama*s, the dense rhetoric studded with bibli-

---

[22] A. Coen, *Saggio di eloquenza ebrea* (Florence, 1827), 99.

[23] Joseph Caro, *Oraḥ ḥayyim, Hilkhot shabbat*, no. 307 in *Shulḥan ʿArukh* (Venice, 1565).

[24] Moses da Rieti, *Miqdash Meʿat*, ed. J. Goldenthal (Vienna, 1851), fol. 106r.

cal quotations and the sayings of the early rabbis, the quantitative-syllabic meter, the rich rhymes and assorted musical effects: all these had either been rejected or dismissed to make room for other ideas.[25] Such, too, was the fate of the Hebrew sonnet, which Immanuel had made so completely his own.

There is one later and very telling proof for pinning the rejection of the sonnet on Immanuel's negative image. Around 1500, poets began writing Hebrew sonnets once again, but no Hebrew love sonnet was written in Italy until the middle of the seventeenth century. And not because poets refrained from writing erotic love poems. They did indeed write them, only they used other forms for that purpose.[26] Apparently this was a deliberate decision on their part. It seems that would-be sonneteers hoped to rehabilitate the genre by giving it a new image, one that would obscure its dubious past and ease its way into Jewish society.

These three explanations suggest that powerful obstacles stood in the path of the Hebrew sonnet following the death of Immanuel, and perhaps even during his lifetime. But if we weigh the obstacles facing the Hebrew sonnet against the reasons that it had to flourish, it seems unlikely that the former could have swung the pendulum so decisively. The obstacles might be able to explain the waning of the genre but not its complete disappearance for so long a period. And, in fact, there is no reason to assume that not a single Hebrew sonnet was written during this period. As we shall see below, the corpus which formed after 1500 indeed alludes to the existence of Hebrew sonnets before this time. Additional research may well bring the remains of these sonnets to light one day, filling in the missing links in the history of the Hebrew sonnet and establishing the tradition in its entirety.

2. The Renewal of the Hebrew Sonnet

Continuing Participation in Italian Culture

Despite the harsh measures against the Jewish community during the sixteenth century — the public burning of the Talmud and other Hebrew books, the dwindling sources of livelihood, and the rising phenomenon of Jewish ghettoes — the entire sixteenth century, and even later, found Jews involved in every field of creative endeavor: literature, theater, translation, preaching, historiography, science,

---

[25] See D. Bregman, "Megamot Mithalfot be-Signon ha-Shirah ha-ʿIvrit be-Italia," *Tarbiz* 61 (1992): 505–25.

[26] See poems by Joseph Tzarfati and Moses ben Joab Rieti in Schirmann, *Mivḥar*, 223–29, and see below, Chap. 15, Part 2. Tzarfati's sonnets are printed in *Tzror Zehuvim*, ed. Bregman, sonnets 39–43; Moses ben Joab's sonnets are printed as., sonnets 44–48. See love poems by Yosef Tzarfati, ed. Dan Almagor, *Teʿuda* 19 (2003): 329-40.

medicine, music, and dance.[27] In all of these, the Jews of the sixteenth century inspired, and were inspired by, their Italian environment. To mention only a few prominent cases: Abraham Farissol, author of *Iggeret Orḥot ʿOlam* or "Epistle on the Ways of the World" (completed in 1524), a comprehensive and innovative geography; Azariah de' Rossi, author of *Me'or ʿEynayim* or "Light of the Eyes" (completed in 1572), a review of Jewish history in classical literature;[28] or his relative Salamone de' Rossi, who composed music for both Jews and Italians, and is considered the precursor of modern Jewish music (his polyphonic setting for *Ha-Shirim asher li-Shlomo*, or "The Songs of Solomon," a collection of poems by his contemporaries, was intended for use in the synagogue);[29] Abraham Portaleone, author of *Shiltei ha-Gibborim* or "Shields of the Mighty" (completed in 1607), a study of the Temple and various disciplines; Daniel da Rossena, who adapted the Italian romance *Bernabo e Luciana* into Hebrew; Elijah Bahur Levita, grammarian and author of dictionaries; Judah de' Sommi Portaleone, author of the first Hebrew play *Tzaḥut Bediḥuta de-Qiddushin* or "A Comedy of Betrothal", a noted director in the Italian theater and member of the literary academy founded by Cesare Gonzaga, the *Academy of the Lovesick*. Portaleone, who tried to establish a Hebrew theater in Mantua, is also the author of the famous *Dialogues on the Art of the Stage*, as well as various plays in Italian.[30] We should also consider Johanan Judah Alatrini, who wrote a drama[31] in Italian and also translated Hebrew poems for Yom Kippur in his *L'Angelica Tromba*; and Judah Moscato, a rabbi, intellectual, and poet famed for his Italian-style sermons (*Nefutzot Yehuda* [Venice, 1589]). One other especially interesting figure is Judah Abrabanel, author of the most famous work on Neo-Platonic love, *Dialoghi d'Amore* (Rome, 1535). This

---

[27] See Roth, *Jews in the Renaissance*; idem, *History of the Jews of Italy* (Philadelphia, 1946); Shulvass, *Jews in the World of the Renaissance*; Schirmann, *Le-Toldot*, 2: 44; I. Adler, *La pratique musicale savante dans quelques communautés juives en Europe aux xviiᵉ and xviiiᵉ siécles* (Paris and the Hague, 1966); idem, *Musical Life and Traditions of the Portuguese Jewish Community of Amsterdam in the XVIII Century* (Jerusalem, 1974); idem, "Musical Life in the 17th and 18th Centuries," in *Encyclopedia Judaica* 2: 904–5.

[28] Azariah de' Rossi, *Light of the Eyes*, trans. Joanna Weinberg (New Haven, 2001).

[29] See I. Fenlon, "Salamone Rossi," in *The New Grove Dictionary of Music and Musicians*, 2nd ed. (London and New York, 2001), 2: 731–34. The *Shirim asher li-Shlomo* were published by F. Rikko, ed. (New York, 1967–1973.) The entire work was recently published with introduction and notes by Don Harrán, *Corpus Mensurabilis Musicae* 100 Part III Volume 13a (New York, 2004).

[30] See Judah de' Sommi Portaleone, *Tzaḥut be-Diḥuta de-Qidushin*, ed. J. Schirmann (Jerusalem, 1946), Introduction. Portaleone's play has been translated into English by A. S. Golding, *A Comedy of Betrothal* (Ottawa, 1988). See bibiography on Sommo by Yona David, (Tel Aviv, 1988).

[31] I Trionfi, *Favola Pastorale di Angelo Alatini Hebreo*, (Venice, 1611).

book, which may have been written originally in Hebrew, was translated into various languages and became the basis for love poetry in Italy and beyond.[32] Hebrew poets such as Moses ben Joab of Florence studied philosophy; others, such as Samuel Archivolti of Padua, taught Hebrew to Italian intellectuals and exchanged poems with them. Leone da Modena translated passages from Ariosto's *Orlando Furioso* into Hebrew while still a youth;[33] Joseph Tzarfati,[34] for his part, was the Pope's personal physician.

The Jews of Italy were also connected to Spanish culture. The connection grew stronger after the expulsion of the Jews from Spain, for it brought waves of Jewish refugees to Italy, and was further reinforced by the arrival of the *conversos*, who returned to Judaism in Italy and elsewhere. It was in this manner that Judah Abrabanel, author of the *Dialoghi d'Amore* mentioned above, reached Italy. The same is true of the *converso* Samuel Usque, whose *Consolacam as Tribulacoens de Israel* is considered a classic of Portuguese literature, and of Solomon Usque, Samuel's relative, whose Spanish translations of Petrarch are still considered the finest of their kind,[35] Joseph Tzarfati, one of the two poets who revived the Hebrew sonnet, was also the Hebrew translator of the famed tragicomedy *Calisto y Melibea* by Fernando de Rojas. Tzarfati made his translation sometime around 1500, close to the time it was written. Of this translation nothing remains except the opening poem.[36]

Reviving Immanuel's Poetics

Against this background of receptivity to Italian and classical culture, Hebrew poets began writing sonnets again at the beginning of the sixteenth century. This cultural openness, however, was not the only factor in reviving the sonnet. The same kind of openness had also flourished in the fifteenth century, yet it had not kept the genre from waning. Apparently the Hebrew sonnet owed its revival to the change of guard which took place in Hebrew literature during the sixteenth century. Several poets at this time — Joseph Tzarfati, Moses ben Joab, Samuel Anav, Samuel Archivolti, Joseph Carmi, Jacob Segrè and others — left a wide range of secular Hebrew poetry behind them. The first three of these com-

---

[32] See Mönch, *Das Sonett*, 105, 118, 125 concerning his influence on the sonnet in Europe. And see Leon Abrabanel, *Dialoghi d'Amore* (Venice, 1541), 98–99.

[33] Simon Bernstein, *Diwan le-Rabbi Yehuda Aryeh Modena* (Philadelphia, 1932), 33-50.

[34] See Dan Almagor, "Annotated Bibliography" *Italia* 12 (1997): 53-113.

[35] *De Los Sonetos, Cansiones, Mandrigales Y sextinas del gran poeta y Orador Francisco Petrarca.*, (Venice, 1567).

[36] See M. D. Cassuto, "Mi-Shirei Yosef Shmuel Tzarfati: Ha-Qomedia ha-Rishonah be-ʿIvrit," in *Jewish Studies in Memory of George A. Kohut*, ed. S. W. Baron and A. Marx (New York, 1935), 121–28.

posed love poetry. Other poets who generally composed liturgical poetry, such as Mordechai Dato[37] and Abraham Provenzale,[38] also tried their hand at love poetry. The first sign that new winds were beginning to blow came in 1492, when the *Maḥbarot* were printed in their entirety in Brescia. The changes can apparently be credited to the Jewish émigrés who left Spain for Italy prior to the expulsion. These Jews, nurtured on the classics of Hebrew poetry in Spain, sparked a nostalgia for the tradition that culminated in the printing of the *Maḥbarot*, the major exponent of the Spanish-Hebrew poetics in Italy. This is not to say that alongside those who welcomed Immanuel's poetics, more or less, in the sixteenth century, there was not a camp that completely rejected them. Indeed it was precisely at this time that the *Maḥbarot* were so emphatically banned. However, this official ban, like any law, was only a sign of the times. It had been unnecessary so long as the ban of the *Maḥbarot* was an accepted social norm. The very fact that the ban became official testifies to the dwindling impact of this norm.

Since the publication of the Maḥbarot naturally facilitated the dissemination of Immanuel's "dangerous" poetics, it is hardly coincidence that the ban was directed so pointedly against printers. Joseph Caro enjoyed enormous prestige, and upon its publication the *Shulḥan ʿArukh* became the most popular code of Jewish law. Following the ban against the *Maḥbarot*, publication of the entire work came to an end for almost two hundred years.[39] But its influence could no longer be stopped. With two complete editions of the *Maḥbarot* and copies in manuscript made both before and after the advent of printing, the *Maḥbarot* became accessible, in one degree or another, to anyone who wanted to read them. Immanuel's style penetrated Hebrew writing at every level; it was no longer possible to ignore the sonnet.

The Poets who Renewed the Hebrew Sonnet

As mentioned above, Joseph Tzarfati and Moses ben Joab were the poets who revived the Hebrew sonnet. Tzarfati was a renowned physician, well trained in classical languages, philosophy, and literature. He learned the octave-form from the Italian,[40] and introduced drama into Hebrew literature, albeit in translation, as mentioned above. Moses ben Joab, Tzarfati's friend, belonged to the prominent Rieti family. He was an intellectual, a student of philosophy and a noted preacher. Both men apparently belonged to a circle of Hebrew poets in Florence.

Tzarfati and Ben Joab did not represent themselves as pioneers, nor did they lay claim to reviving the sonnet. They did not attach boasting rubrics to their

---

[37] Schirmann, *Mivḥar*, 246.
[38] Schirmann, *Mivḥar*, 247.
[39] *Maḥbarot*, ed. Yarden, 20–22.
[40] See Schirmann, *Mivḥar*, 223–27.

sonnets or make any allusions to their innovation. The silence can perhaps be interpreted as a deliberate attempt to defend the Hebrew sonnet from a disreputable past that had not been forgotten. This interpretation is strengthened by the fact that the two poets refrained from writing anything even remotely erotic in their sonnets, though they did not hesitate to do so in other genres of poetry.[41] A similar kind of caution attended the drama.[42] The play Calisto y Melibea, which was translated by Joseph Tzarfati, fell under the ancient Jewish ban against "theaters and circuses." Even worse, perhaps, the play had as its central character a prostitute, Celestina.[43] In the poem which opens his translation, Tzarfati describes the moral to be derived from the play:

> And my people will veer from the fiery path of desire / They will flee from all of its flames . . . / the community of survivors will rejoice with me . . . / 'Tis the truth that my tongue has copied . . . / assign this to my credit, O pious multitudes . . .[44]

Tzarfati's "apology" sounds almost ludicrous in view of the spirit dominating the original play, but it may be that he radically adapted the Hebrew version. Judah de' Sommi Portaleone attached a similar preamble to his Hebrew play *The Comedy of Betrothal* (*Tzaḥut Bediḥuta de-Qiddushin*).[45] In the sonnet which opens this play Portaleone boasts about his innovations even as he apologizes for them:

> Behold, O generation, the new with which I fill
> The old, like fine oil inside a container.
> A genre in which mouths and hearts will find content
> To rejoice in the riddle of love, which I invent.

Clearly, these Hebrew writers knew their public and the problems they were likely to face. If Tzarfati and Ben Joab did not write a similar defense on behalf of their Hebrew sonnets — and indeed none has come down to us — perhaps this was because they did not regard themselves as the poets who revived the genre.

---

[41] Schirmann, *Mivḥar*, 223–29 and in other places.

[42] On the history of this issue throughout the course of Hebrew drama in Italy see Dvora Bregman, *Tiferet Sinai, Sefer ha-Maḥazot shel Matityah Nissim Terni* (Jerusalem, 2003), Introduction. See also eadem, "Their Rose in Our Garden: Romance Elements in Hebrew Italian Poetry," in *Renewing the Past, Reconfiguring Jewish Culture, From Al Andalus to Haskala* ed. Ross Bran and Adam Sutcliff (Philadelphia, 2003), 50-59.

[43] In Hebrew, this name replaced the original name of the play.

[44] Cassuto, "Mi-Shirei Yosef Shmuel Tzarfati."

[45] Judah de' Sommi Portaleone, sonnet 51, in *Tzror Zehuvim*, ed. Bregman. The sonnet is not found in the English translation of the play cited above in note 28.

Perhaps they knew of Hebrew sonnets written before theirs, either during their own lifetime or somewhat before, as we suggested earlier in this chapter.

Tzarfati left only five Hebrew sonnets, and the same is true of Moses ben Joab.[46] These are lyrical, personal poems — friendship poems — that they wrote to each other and to other poets. Apparently these sonnets were known to only a small circle of friends. A wider circulation of the genre would have depended on the approval of some authoritative public figure, but apparently it was not until after their time that such a person came forth.

The Work of Samuel Archivolti

Samuel Archivolti — rabbi, poet, linguist, proofreader, and teacher of poetics — was the first, after Immanuel of Rome, to write more than ten Hebrew sonnets.[47] Most of these saw publication already in the sixteenth century, during his lifetime. As a professional proofreader for the Hebrew press and a known authority in Jewish law, he appended, as was customary in those times, poems of rabbinic approbation and recommendation to the frontispiece of a number of books. Some of these poems were sonnets. The poems were naturally suited to their distinguished task and generally dealt with subjects of a pious nature. Thus it happens that the poems which were used to recommend some book or other also made a good recommendation of themselves and their genre. Thanks to these books the sonnets reached a wide audience, making people familiar with the Hebrew version of the genre wherever these books circulated.

Archivolti's contribution to the revival of the genre was not limited to the writing and circulation of Hebrew sonnets. In his grammar entitled *Arugat ha-Bosem* or "A Bed of Spices" (Venice, 1602), he included a chapter on poetics, together with a passage instructing potential students in the art of writing Hebrew sonnets, using a Hebrew sonnet of his own as an example:[48]

> From the day that Jubal went down to the springs
> with his harp, like a poet-madman,
> glorious music remained in Heaven:
> Here, too, like the clapping of hammers it rings.

---

[46] The sonnets of both Ben Joab and Tzarfati have recently been published for the first time in Bregman, *Tzror Zehuvim*, 69–80.

[47] The sonnets are printed in *Tzror Zehuvim*, ed. Bregman, sonnets 59–71. And see D. Bregman, "Shelosha ʿAsar Sonetim le-Rabbi Shmuel Archivolti," *Italia* 7 (1988): 29–65. Concerning Archivolti's manifold activities in Italy, see Bonfil, *Rabbis and Jewish Communities*, esp. 92–94, 124–26, 129–33.

[48] Samuel Archivolti, sonnet 59 in *Tzror Zehuvim*, ed. Bregman.

> Until the King of Israel untied a harp with seven strings,
> shining like two-days' light upon
> the sons of the Levites — whereupon
> two more conductors it did then bring:
>
> The godly Messiah will devise music of glorious strains
> upon his eight-string harp, and the gate that was closed
> will open again, all glorious.
>
> God will raise the dead and scatter good grain;
> the hour of grace will find thanks full composed
> upon a harp with ten strings melodious.

This sonnet describes the music of the spheres, to which Greek philosophy attributed the existence of the world (Aristotle, *De Caelo*, Book 2), on the basis of Hebrew traditions. Archivolti thus presented the sonnet as a vehicle for conveying foreign ideas adapted to Jewish sensibilities, and, because this was so potentially attractive to Jews in Italy and elsewhere, it helped facilitate public acceptance of the Hebrew sonnet and its further cultivation in Jewish society.

Widening the Circle: Hebrew Sonnets in the East

No Hebrew poet of the sixteenth century rivaled the output of Immanuel, but whereas Immanuel is apparently the only poet whose sonnets have come down to us from his generation, the sixteenth century could boast of quite a few writers of Hebrew sonnets. Apart from Tzarfati, Ben Joab, Portaleone, and Archivolti, some of the writers listed above also wrote sonnets: Azariah de' Rossi, Judah Moscato, Johanan Alemanno, and Jacob Segrè. Other writers of sonnets were perhaps less well-known: Rabbi Menahem Azariah da Fano, one of the greatest rabbis and Kabbalists of his generation; Abraham Jagel, author of *Lekakh Tov*, the first Hebrew catechism (Venice, 1595), and of *Gai Ḥizayyon* or "Valley of Vision" (Alexandria, 1897), a collection of Hebrew novellas describing a journey through the heavens that shows the influence of Dante;[49] Judah da Saltares, a rabbi and poet; Moses Franchetta Harari, a rabbi and businessman in Mantua; Juliani Cases, also a rabbi in Mantua and a physician; Isaac Levy; and Daniel Foa. There are a few sonnets attributed to anonymous poets in Ferrara. Leone da Modena, who was later to reinvigorate the genre in the seventeenth century, began by writing sonnets in his youth, still in this century.

---

[49] See David Ruderman, *Valley of Vision: The Heavenly Journey of Abraham ben Ḥananiah Yagel* (Philadelphia, 1990).

The Hebrew sonnet went east during the sixteenth century. From the remains that have come down to us we learn that Saadia Longo wrote a Hebrew sonnet in Salonika. David Onkeneira, who lived in Constantinople and Salonika, wrote five sonnets, one of them in Damascus. Isaac Uziel wrote at least two sonnets in Fez. An anonymous sonnet, possibly by Israel Najara, was published in Safed and perhaps written there.[50] The poets relied heavily on Immanuel's *Maḥbarot*, the second edition of which was published in Constantinople in 1535. But it was not only the older models that stood before the eyes of the poets in the east. As mentioned above, there were also newly composed sonnets which reached them in print on the frontispieces of published books, or in letters that contained poems of friendship. A vestige of this last-mentioned channel of transmission has come down to us in letters containing a three-way correspondence in sonnets, unlike the usual *tenzone*, which consisted of only two poems rather than three.[51] This three-way *tenzone* is unusual both in the distance that it traveled and in the manner in which it came into being.

The challenge sonnet was composed by Isaac Uziel in Fez, the city of his birth. The addressee, Saadia Longo in Salonika, was already famous for his poetry, and it was he who instigated the correspondence. Longo recounts the meeting with Isaac Uziel in a prose passage of great rhetorical flourish, relating the way in which he requested the visitor from Fez to "weave a poem on anything he wished," and that the latter agreed to do so "with great humility."[52] Uziel ultimately sent Saadia not one but three poems, all of them "weighed in the holy *sheqel*"[53] — i.e., composed in the hallowed meters of Hebrew poetry in Spain.

The *tenzone* begins with Uziel's sonnet *Et nitzvu ba-shir* ("Upon standing in song").[54] His other two poems are composed in classical Arabic form, with acrostics spelling out the poets' names: the first poem yielding "Saadia," the second one "Uziel Isaac."

Longo responded with the sonnet beginning *Mi-qol zemirakh* ("From the sound of your song"),[55] and his remarks preceding the sonnet are particularly instructive.

---

[50] Israel Najara (?), sonnet 80 in *Tzror Zehuvim*, ed. Bregman.

[51] Sonnets 82–84 in *Tzror Zehuvim*, ed. Bregman. The three sonnets are found in a single manuscript, though not adjacent to each other. See D. Yarden, "Niqbatzot mi-Shirei Rabbi Saʿadia Longo be-Darqei ha-Shir ve-ha-Melitzah," *Sefunot* 12 (1971–1978): 81–122, here 95; MS. Oxford Bodleian Library 2000, fols. 42r, 103r, 104v. And cf. Z. Malakhi, "Saʿadia Longo ve-Yitzhaq Uziel - Vikuah Meshorerim odot ha-Shirah," in *Sefer Yitzhaq Baqun*, ed. Komem, 63–71.

[52] Yarden, "Niqbatzot mi-Shirei Rabbi Saʿadia Longo," 95.

[53] This is a pun based on the Hebrew word for meter: *mishqal*.

[54] *Tzror Zehuvim*, ed. Bregman, sonnet 82.

[55] *Tzror Zehuvim*, ed. Bregman, sonnet 83.

I have been a poet for forty years, thanks be to God. So how will people know that the poems sent to him [the addressee] were written especially for him? In order to prevent this suspicion, I decided to construct my stanzas according to the framework of his poems, even though it took a great effort and few others would have done so . . .[56]

The "framework" to which Longo refers is the prosodic structure of the sonnet that he received from Isaac Uziel, the model for his poem in response. Thus Longo wrote a sonnet without knowing anything about the genre, a fact which is borne out by yet another circumstance. From the letters which include the *tenzone* we learn that there was a long and highly emotional argument between Longo and Uziel. But it was not the sonnet they were arguing about. Both of them saw it as a "rhymeful" poem: i.e., a sort of classic poem in which the first hemistich in the line (the *delet*) also took part in the rhyme scheme, and they made do with this definition. That the two poets discussed the sonnet using the terminology of the classical models from Spain is in no way unusual; Hebrew theorists in Italy did so for hundreds of years.

But in Italy they called the sonnet by name: a "golden poem" or a "*sonetto*." The Hebrew poets in the east did not do so. They apparently regarded it as a variation of the traditional structure from Spain. For them it was a challenge poem, to be used as the model for an answering poem of their own, according to the time-honored rules of the *tenzone*. In this manner the genre apparently reached Isaac Uziel in Fez, who then transferred it to Saadia Longo. Isaac Uziel, who immigrated to Amsterdam at the beginning of the century, is probably the person who introduced the sonnet to that location as well.

The Corpus

To date I have located some eighty Hebrew sonnets from the sixteenth century. But there is no doubt that other sonnets were written. This assumption, logical enough in itself, is reinforced by some tantalizing hints found in several sonnets written over the course of the century. Of the five sonnets written by Joseph Tzarfati, four are addressed to friends, with the names of two of his correspondents appearing in the body of the sonnets themselves: Isaac, a poet who wins Tzarfati's lavish praise, and Solomon of Poggibonzi, a member of the local intelligentsia from whose hand we have several compositions in manuscript. Similarly, four of the five sonnets by Moses ben Joab are also friendship poems. Two of these were addressed to this same Solomon, one to relatives in mourning, and one to some unnamed friends who apparently expressed their amazement that Ben Joab had stopped sending them poems. The poems to Isaac and Solomon led Cassuto to

---

[56] MS. Oxford Bodleian Library 2000, fol. 40v.

the reasonable conclusion that Florence, the city in which Ben Joab was born and in which Tzarfati also lived for a time, had once boasted a circle of Hebrew poets.[57] We can probably assume, therefore, that these friendship poems in sonnet form are the remains of *tenzones* carried on between members of this literary circle. The answering poems were not preserved in the notebooks of Tzarfati and Ben Joab, which included only the poems which they themselves wrote, and were thus lost. Evidence for such a lost sonnet is found in the rubric of an anonymous sonnet written during the seventeenth century in Ferrara: "A response poem to some rhymes sent to me by Abraham ben Daniel Modena." The "rhymes" of this Abraham, a known poet, have not come down to us, but obviously they were a sonnet, just like the "response poem" written by our anonymous poet.

3. Expanding the Corpus

The Flowering of Poetry in Italy

During the sixteenth and seventeenth centuries, the Jews of Italy were subject to harsh decrees that forced them to retreat from their surroundings and from their intimate dialogue with Italian culture. But there were also a number of endeavors in which Jews continued and even increased their activities. Various scholars[58] have compiled long lists of Jews who completed their medical studies at Padua and other Italian universities during this period, and these are only a portion of them. Jews still participated in the arts — music, dance, theater.[59] Nor was there a decline in Hebrew poetry at this time, despite claims to the contrary.[60] The Jews of seventeenth-century Italy read literature in Hebrew and other languages, mastered Hebrew grammar, and studied poetics. The circle of poetry-lovers

---

[57] Cassuto, *Ha-Yehudim be-Firenze*, 265–72.

[58] See for example A. Modena and E. Morpurgo, *Medici e chirurghi ebrei dottorati e licenziati nell'Università di Padova dal 1617 al 1816* (Bologna, 1967); H. Friedenwald, *The Jews and Medicine*, 2 vols. (Baltimore, 1944); D. Carpi, "Yehudim Ba'alei Toar Doqtor Li-rfuah mi-Ta'am Universitat Padova ba-Meah ha-Tet Zayin u-ve-Reshit ha-Meah ha-Yud Zayin," in *Sefer Zikaron le-Natan ben Moshe David Cassuto*, ed. S. Toaff (Jerusalem, 1987), 62–91; D. Ruderman, *Jewish Thought and Scientific Discovery in Early Modern Europe* (Princeton, 1995), 100–17.

[59] Leone da Modena writes that his son-in-law, Jacob Levi, taught dancing and music: see *Hayyei Yehuda*, ed. D. Carpi (Tel Aviv, 1985), 62. And see Schirmann, *Le-Toldot*, 2: 44–94; Simonson, *Toldot ha-Yehudim*, chaps. 7–8.

[60] See, for example, the comments of S. Bernstein in the introduction to his edition of Immanuel Frances's poems: *Diwan le-Rabbi Immanuel ben David Frances* (Tel Aviv, 1932), 18-19.

widened, and many composed poems not only in Hebrew but also in Italian, Spanish, or Portuguese. Poetry commanded respect in society. It was used in polemics against the Kabbalah and the Shabbatean movement, and also in controversies within the local community.[61] Literary works accompanied public events of all kinds: funerals of prominent community members, the inauguration of new synagogues, the completion of a tractate of the Talmud, and, of course, various Purim festivities. The custom of writing poems for wedding ceremonies was particularly widespread. The poet enjoyed enormous prestige and his activity stood at the center of public consciousness. Poets argued over matters of poetry, sometimes to the point of violence. Devotees of poetry and culture gathered in various "Academies" for poetry readings and dramatic performances, or to solve the kind of literary riddles that were so much in vogue. In his *Anthology (Mivḥar) of Hebrew Poetry in Italy*, Schirmann includes the work of more than twenty-five poets who were active during the seventeenth century, most of them highly prolific and well-known, but there were many others as well.

Against this backdrop, four important poets stand out as the major sonneteers of this century: Leone da Modena, Moses Zacuto, Jacob Frances, and Jacob's brother Immanuel. These four left a considerable body of poetry after them, including dozens of sonnets.

Leone da Modena is the most prominent of these four, and though already living in the ghetto, he was still a Renaissance man in the fullest sense of the term. His extensive learning embraced the Bible and Jewish law, philosophy, Jewish and non-Jewish literature, linguistics, poetry, and drama.[62] He was on good terms with Christian intellectuals, who were acquainted with his sermons or learned Hebrew under his tutelage. One of them even compiled a Hebrew dictionary.[63] Several panegyrics in Hebrew were printed on the frontispiece of this dictionary, among them a sonnet by Leone da Modena.[64] Modena was a prolific and innovative poet. He studied poetics with Samuel Archivolti and, like his teacher, wrote a new chapter in the history of the Hebrew sonnet. Modena was

---

[61] D. Bregman, "Polemica Religiosa," in *Appartenenza e differenza: ebrei d'Italia e la letteratura*, ed. J. Hassine, J. Mishan-Montefiore, and S. Debenedetti Stow (Ramat-Gan, 1998): 23–32.

[62] See M. R. Cohen, trans., *The Autobiography of a Seventeenth-Century Venetian Rabbi* (Princeton, 1988); on the subject of Modena's rabbinic activities, see Bonfil, *Rabbis and Jewish Communities*, 112–13, 190–92. See *And the Lion Shall Roar: Leon Modena and his World, Italia*, Conference Supplement Series 1 (Jerusalem, 2003). His poems were printed by S. Bernstein, as mentioned above.

[63] Jean de la Pause Plantavit, *Planta Vitis* (Lodovae, 1645). See Dvora Bregman, "Christians, Jews and Hebrew Sonnets," in *L'interculturalità dell'Ebraismo*, ed. Mauro Perani (Ravenna 2003), 223-28.

[64] Leone da Modena, in *Tzror Zehuvim*, ed. Bregman, sonnet 129.

the first poet after Immanuel of Rome to compose more than thirty Hebrew sonnets, and he deserves the credit for a number of innovations in matters of structure, meter, subject matter, and opening devices. He was especially important in advancing the cause of the occasional sonnet. The occasional poem was the most popular and sought-after kind of poetry in the seventeenth century. By recruiting the sonnet to the ranks of occasional poetry, Modena was able to increase the number of topics it dealt with and to encourage many others to try their hand at composition. If Archivolti placed the Hebrew sonnet on a firm religious and ideological footing, it was Modena who propelled it into the heart of community life.

Unlike Leone da Modena, whose works are infused with the spirit of the High Renaissance, the other three are poets of the Baroque in every respect.[65] Their cultural milieu was also very different from that of Modena. All three were of Portuguese descent and highly knowledgeable in, and deeply influenced by, Spanish and Portuguese literature. Moses Zacuto — rabbi, Kabbalist, playwright, and poet — grew up in the Portuguese community of Amsterdam, settling in Italy only during his later years when he served as rabbi first in Venice, and later in Mantua. Zacuto was deeply rooted in his cultural past. He modeled his play *Yesod ʿOlam* or "The Foundation of the World" on the religious plays of Spain, and his second play *Tofteh ʿArukh* or "Hell Prepared" on Dante, though in Spanish *quintillias* rather than Dante's *terza rima*. His writings can be divided into three different areas: Jewish law, Kabbalah, and poetry.[66] Zacuto wrote both religious and secular poetry, using a wide spectrum of the forms available to him from the rich Jewish heritage as well as from the Italian and Spanish traditions. As recently shown by Dan Pagis, Zacuto was also the inventor of the Hebrew emblem-riddle, which became a popular genre in the seventeenth and eighteenth centuries.[67] His sonnets, over sixty in number, reflect the spirit of the Baroque in their intricate structures, enigmatic language, and deep religious feeling.

Jacob and Immanuel Frances, men of broad learning and outstanding figures in the Jewish community, were known first and foremost as poets. The sons

---

[65] On *Tofteh ʿArukh* as a Baroque drama see Dvora Bregman, "ʿAmimut u-vehirut be-Tofteh ʿArukh le-Rabbi Moshe Zacut", *Peʿamim* 96 (2003): 35-53.

[66] From Zacuto's poetry, most of which is unpublished, see Dvora Bregman, "Ḥamisha Shirei Ḥatuna me'et Moshe Zacut," *Teʿudah* 19 (2002): 341 - 58; "Shirei Ḥatuna me'et Moshe Zacut," *Peʿamim* 96 (2003): 143 - 62. I intend to publish all of Zacuto's poems in the near future. The volume is scheduled for publication by Yad Ben-Zvi Institute, Jerusalem.

[67] See D. Pagis, *ʿAl Sod Ḥatum: Le-Toldot ha-Ḥidah ha-ʿIvrit bi-Italia u-be-Holand* (Jerusalem, 1986), with a substantial summary in English. See also Dvora Bregman, "Al ha-Sod: Zug Ḥidot le-Ḥatuna me'et Moshe Zacut," in *Shefaʿ Tal: Studies in Jewish Thought and Culture Presented to Bracha Zak* (Beer Sheva, 2004): 379 - 96.

of David Frances, the brothers were linked even closer through the bonds of poetry. They took turns praising each other's poetry, and Immanuel even completed a sonnet that his brother Jacob had left unfinished. Though Immanuel had hoped to publish a joint collection of their poems, his plan never materialized. The two brothers wrote in a similar style. The authorship of some of their poems is uncertain, with some critics attributing a given poem to Immanuel, others to Jacob; and indeed it is difficult to be certain. Within the corpus of their diversified writings the sonnet commands an important place. Immanuel wrote over thirty sonnets and Jacob over fifty.

Towards old age, Immanuel Frances wrote his *ars poetica*, *Meteq Sefatayim* or "The Lips' Sweetness." Unlike earlier works in Hebrew, this was no grammar in which one or two chapters were allotted to the subject of poetics, but a work devoted entirely to matters of Hebrew poetry. It is written in dialogue form, with the "teacher" explaining to his "student" poetic terminology and the rules of prosody and poetics as he sees them. There is a special discussion devoted to Italian forms, which are listed one after the other using original Hebrew names that the author made up. At the top of the list is the sonnet, which Immanuel, using the biblical list of place-names from Deuteronomy 1:1, calls *di zahav*, or "golden".[68] The meters of the sonnet are discussed at length and illustrated with examples. They serve as a basis on which the rest of the forms are explained later on. At the end of the discussion on prosody the teacher concludes:

> Behold, I have placed the ways of poetry before you. Know, however, that the glory of the poem does not rest solely on meter and rhyme. If the language and content have no conceits, and if the poet cares for nothing but meter and rhyme, his poem will be like a body without a soul.[69]

Here, in a nutshell, is the entire concept of Baroque poetry.

Jacob and Immanuel Frances put practice to theory, primarily in the form of the sonnet. Their sonnets are striking for a dramatic tension that derives from the power of perfectly crafted and antithetical structures, realistic touches, biting satire, and an obsession with death.

There is a thematic variety in all the brothers' work. They wrote sonnets on a number of different themes: friendship, marriage, praise, boasting, and lamentation. And most important, Jacob and Immanuel Frances were the first after Immanuel of Rome to write Hebrew love sonnets. They cultivated the polemic

---

[68] Each of these two Hebrew words equals the number fourteen, reckoned according to the gematric value of the letters in Hebrew: Immanuel Frances, *Meteq Sefatayim*, ed. H. Brody (Cracow, 1892), 48.

[69] *Meteq Sefatayim*, ed. Brody, 53.

sonnet and pointed its barbs at overweening members of the Jewish community, at people who were recklessly spreading Kabbalah, and, most importantly, against Shabbetai Zevi and his movement, then violently shaking world Jewry. Their fiery and warlike spirit gave the sonnet a new look. Their love sonnets, in which they reached the peak of Baroque perfection, are particularly bold and innovative. Love poetry is the very heart of the sonnet-form. No nation or tongue that has adopted the sonnet has ever failed to use it for writing love poems. Only the Hebrew sonnet shied away from this crucial topic for over a hundred years! The brothers Jacob and Immanuel Frances filled this important gap, and thus brought to completion at long last the rehabilitation of the Hebrew sonnet.

Minor Poets

Jewish men of letters learned poetic theory and tried their hand from time to time at writing poetry, not necessarily because they considered themselves great poets, but because they liked poetry and recognized its value. These active consumers of poetry wrote Hebrew sonnets already in the sixteenth century, but it was only in the seventeenth century that they reached their peak. At least sixty minor writers of Hebrew sonnets flourished during the seventeenth century, along with numerous anonymous and semi-anonymous poets who signed their work using acrostics and nicknames that are difficult to identify. The minor poets flourished increasingly once the occasional poem came into prominence, since such poems were often composed by friends or members of the family rather than by professional poets. By making the Hebrew sonnet such a familiar phenomenon, these poets played an important role in establishing the genre. Nor, in general, did they lower poetic standards, for they were competent in the Hebrew language and poetics and knew how to "turn" a sonnet. The strict rules of the sonnet-form left little room for gushing expression, and led the poet to develop his theme with taste and restraint. Indeed, it is no coincidence that a stern critic like Schirmann speaks of "these elegant sonnets" and does not include them among the other occasional poems of the period that in his opinion deserve to be discreetly hidden away.[70] Among the minor writers of sonnets during the seventeenth century we find poets who were known in their own day, but whose poems have, for the most part, not come down to us. These include Leone da Modena's grandson, Isaac Levi, the well-known bibliophile Abraham Graziano, and Rabbi Judah Briel of Mantua.

---

[70] Schirmann, *Le-Toldot*, 2: 80–81.

The Hebrew Sonnet in Holland

During the seventeenth century the writing of Hebrew sonnets spread to Holland. The Portuguese community of Amsterdam was founded only at the end of the sixteenth century, yet already at the beginning of the seventeenth century it became a hotbed of Hebrew culture, literature and poetry, closely connected to the Spanish culture that was flourishing there. Jewish creativity in seventeenth-century Amsterdam was represented by a broad spectrum of personalities:[71] the known printer Menasseh ben Israel; Rabbi Isaac Aboab; the poet Jacob Sasportas; the Kabbalist Abraham Coen Herrera; the dramatist Antonio Enriques Gomez; the physician and thinker Baltazar Orobio de Castro; the poet and military man Daniel Levi Miguel de Barrios; and the philosophers Uriel da Costa and Barukh Spinoza. Well-educated Jews from different origins came into contact with each other in Amsterdam, and the link between this Jewish community and the communities of Italy became especially strong.[72]

The central figure in Hebrew poetry in seventeenth-century Holland is that of Solomon Oliveyra, a prolific poet well-known in his own day. He wrote a pastoral novel called *Ayyelet Ahavim*[73] or "Gazelle of Love" (Amsterdam, 1665), a prose work interspersed with poetry that includes a Petrarchan love sonnet, the only Hebrew poem of its kind from Holland. Oliveyra also included a chapter about poetics in his rhyme-dictionary, *Sharshot Gavlut* (Amsterdam, 1665).[74] One passage there is devoted to Italian forms, among them the sonnet. In terms of actually writing sonnets, Oliveyra was preceded by a poet whom we have already mentioned, Isaac Uziel of Fez, now the head of the Amsterdam Yeshivah and the author of an impressive collection of poems. Uziel translated the novel *The Proverbs of Iresto* into Hebrew, and included a Hebrew sonnet in his translation. This work was apparently written in Amsterdam.

Let us also mention Joseph Penso, who is no less famous for his Spanish writings[75] than for his Hebrew play *Asirei ha-Tiqvah* or "Prisoners of Hope," which the Amsterdam community mistakenly regarded as the first Hebrew play. The publication of this play was celebrated in a number of poems which were printed on the frontispiece of the book, among them a great many sonnets. The play itself is written in several different poetic forms, including three sonnets.

---

[71] Melkman, "Amsterdam," 895–97.

[72] Anania Coen, for example, does not distinguish between them in his *Saggio di eloquenza ebrea* (Florence, 1827).

[73] Pagis, *ʿAl Sod Ḥatum*, 89.

[74] The title of this book derives from the "wreathen gold chains" on the High Priest's vestments (Exodus 28:22).

[75] Among them the first book about the Stock Exchange, the Hebrew title of which is *Mehumat ha-Mehumot*. See Schirmann, *Le-Toldot*, 2: 132–33.

The Hebrew sonnet also came under poetic scrutiny in Spanish when Moses ben Gideon Abudiente of Amsterdam discussed it in his *Gramatica Hebraica* (Hamburg, 1633), and then illustrated it with a moral sonnet of his own. Another prominent figure in the Netherlands is Jacob Sasportas, for though he served as a rabbi in Amsterdam for only a short time, he maintained continual links with the community. His several sonnets provide outstanding examples of Baroque style.

The Extent of the Corpus

In light of all the above, it is not astonishing to find some three hundred Hebrew sonnets from the seventeenth century. Moreover, it seems highly probable that the actual number was indeed far greater. This number does not include the many sonnets the time period of which cannot be precisely determined, such as the sonnets written by Sabato Vita Marini, who lived at the end of the seventeenth century and the beginning of the eighteenth, and left a considerable collection of poems and sonnets. Similarly, this number does not include the sonnets of minor poets who have not been identified.

The seventeenth century, like the sixteenth before it, has also left us more than a few fragments of once-complete tenzones, among them sonnets by Jacob Frances,[76] Immanuel Frances,[77] and Moses Zacuto.[78] These sonnets testify to writers of lost sonnets, such as Rabbi Joseph Fermo and Abraham Kokhav, the latter a student of Leone da Modena whom the great rabbi reports as having written, in Italian, "one hundred sonnets about the tears of a beautiful, weeping woman."[79] As already noted, there is also explicit evidence of poems and sonnets from this period that are apparently no longer extant. All together, we have some four hundred Hebrew sonnets that belong without doubt to the sixteenth and seventeenth centuries, and it is towards this corpus that we now turn our attention.

---

[76] Jacob Frances, in *Tzror Zehuvim*, ed. Bregman, sonnet 253.
[77] Immanuel Frances, in *Tzror Zehuvim*, ed. Bregman, sonnet 319.
[78] Moses Zacuto, in *Tzror Zehuvim*, ed. Bregman, sonnet 223.
[79] Leone da Modena, Poems, ed. S. Bernstein (Philadelphia, 1932), 116.

X. GENERAL STRUCTURE AND RHYME SCHEME

1. The Classical Model

Acceptance of the Model

The classical model dominates the Hebrew sonnet of the sixteenth and seventeenth centuries: fourteen lines of eleven syllables, more or less, with a general rhyme-scheme of ABBA ABBA CDE CDE. When the Hebrew sonnet was revived at the beginning of the sixteenth century, this was the model which served it, and this model continued to serve Hebrew sonnets for the next hundred years or so almost without exception. Only in the seventeenth century, when Hebrew sonnets became more popular, did variations of the classic model come into being, but even then they were relatively infrequent.

The prosodic conservatism of the Hebrew corpus is all the more striking when compared with sonnets in the Italian language, where there was a longstanding tradition of an open octave, numerous variations in the sestet, and also various combinations of sonnet sequences, not to mention many other variant forms on the margins of poetic creativity. The conservatism of the Hebrew corpus in the sixteenth century is even conspicuous in comparison with Immanuel of Rome, who allowed a few simple structures to suffice, but made numerous variations in the sestet. The tighter the poetic structure, the more constraints for the poet. The revivers of the Hebrew sonnet, untrained in the art of sonnetry and without a firm tradition to rely on, found this unyielding framework especially trying. Even so, they did not deviate from it. During the course of the seventeenth century writing sonnets became easier since there were more examples to follow, and more teachers and manuals for instructing novice poets. There is evidence of a growing temptation to experiment with the sonnet-form. Nevertheless, most poets continued to adhere to the simple, more limited model.

Adhering to the Closed Octave

The structures of the newly-revived Hebrew sonnet are reminiscent of those written by Immanuel of Rome, particularly in the octave: ABBA ABBA. The closed octave was, as we have seen, one of Immanuel's most impressive achievements in creating the Hebrew sonnet, and perhaps the most impressive of all. And indeed, the poets of the new Hebrew sonnet accepted the model enthusiastically, preserving it without change for a hundred years. Only in the seventeenth century did the open octave find its way into the corpus, yet even then it remained rare.

In fact, it was even rarer than the variant structures that began wandering into the Hebrew corpus every now and then, once this began to expand.

Adhering to the closed octave demanded a special effort. We see traces of this in a manuscript from the hand of Jacob Frances, in which he made notes to himself in Portuguese. Apparently he wrote a few sonnets using an open octave that he later transformed into a closed octave. One of these belongs to the sonnet beginning *Anshei emuna ve-emet avadu* ("Men of faith and truth have perished"),[1] which laments the death of certain rabbis. From a comment by the poet, we gather that the third line of the second quatrain originally ended with the words "when they rebelled" and that the poet changed them to "with energetic words," in order to create the preferred closed structure. A similar correction also occurs in the polemic sonnet *ʿAl mi tarḥivu peh*[2] ("Who are you mouthing about?").[3]

This poet's first impulse towards the open octave is easily understood. The quick and uninterrupted flow of the sonnet was by far the most important consideration for Baroque sonneteers. The closed octave, however, disrupts the flow of the poem and slows the pace of development. Jacob Frances, a poet of exemplary Baroque sonnets, forced his poem to stop at the end of the lines in the octave in order to make it conform with tradition. We find him making another poetic sacrifice for the same reason in the sonnet *Im qol havarati* ("If the sound of my poem"),[4] which was apparently the third round in an exchange of sonnets, and the only part that remains of it. From this one remnant, however, we can deduce several facts. It appears that it was Jacob Frances who initiated the correspondence. His sonnet was answered by Abraham Kokhav, who described the impression which the challenge sonnet made on him: with the power of the poet's expression, which was like thunder, it awakened Kokhav from poetic sleep and aroused him to creativity.[5] The third sonnet, in which Jacob Frances made his response, ended the correspondence. Once again, the first quatrain of the sonnet[6] originally had an open octave:

If the sound of my poem, like unto thunder (A)
Wakened your song yesterday from its sleep (B)
The sound of your melody, full of good taste (A)
And sweetness, suddenly lulled me to sleep (B)

---

[1] Jacob Frances, in *Tzror Zehuvim*, ed. Bregman, sonnet 255.

[2] Idem, in *Tzror Zehuvim*, ed. Bregman, sonnet 272.

[3] In Naveh's edition these changes were not taken into account, and the octave was printed according to the first version.

[4] Jacob Frances, in *Tzror Zehuvim*, ed. Bregman, sonnet 253.

[5] This motif also appears in a sonnet by Leone da Modena, *Yashen be-mizmor shir* (in *Tzror Zehuvim*, ed. Bregman, sonnet 127).

In the margins of the text there is a note in which the poet reminds himself to switch the order of the last two lines. The same thing happens again in the second quatrain. These changes were not without a price. In the first version of the above-cited quatrain the syllogism is clearly formulated and strengthened by parallel syntax. There the subject appears first ("my poem"; your song"); then the description ("like unto thunder"; "full of good taste"); and finally the result ("awakened me"; "lulled me to sleep"). Switching the order of the last two lines spoils the symmetry and interrupts the logical flow of ideas.

Immanuel Frances, Jacob Frances's brother, ran into similar difficulties on more than a few occasions. In one sonnet,[7] for example, the first quatrain reads:

> When I recall the days of childhood, and their miraculous glow (A)
> And when I remember adolescence I blush (B)
> Upon seeing old age I grow silent (B)
> For all have fled from me like a shadow! (A)

It would have been better, of course, to reverse the order of the third and fourth lines. That would clarify the meaning: childhood and adolescence have fled from the poet, whereas he flees from old age! As it stands now, the main idea is completely muddled. And similarly, in another sonnet:[8]

> When I see Hannah like a radiant light, (A)
> When I recall Naomi, the crown of glory, (B)
> My soul for Hannah begins to blaze (B)
> And for Naomi my soul is like burning fire! (A)

Far better, though, the following arrangement:

> When I see Hannah like a radiant light (A)
> My soul for Hannah begins to blaze (B)
> And for Naomi my soul is like burning fire (A)
> When I recall Naomi, the crown of glory! (B)

Things get even worse, of course, with poets of lesser talent. Such is the case, for example, in a sonnet by Solomon Conegliano describing the Temple in Jerusalem.[9] There the poet is further hampered by the brevity of the sonnet-form and

---

[6] Jacob Frances, in *Tzror Zehuvim*, ed. Bregman, sonnet 253.
[7] Immanuel Frances, in *Tzror Zehuvim*, ed. Bregman, sonnet 335.
[8] Idem, in *Tzror Zehuvim*, ed. Bregman, sonnet 312.
[9] Solomon Conegliano, in *Tzror Zehuvim*, ed. Bregman, sonnet 396.

the restrictions of meter, but there can be no doubt that by reversing the first two lines, the poet would have greatly clarified his meaning.[10]

Poets who adhered to the closed octave often had to compromise on principles of logical progression and nuance, but they were fully aware of their decision. There can be no doubt that the model of Immanuel of Rome stood before their eyes. In structuring the octave they expressed the unique traits of the form and preserved the characteristic flavor of the Hebrew sonnet. It is worth mentioning that in the Spanish sonnet, which was created during the middle of the sixteenth century, it was in fact the closed octave that gained acceptance. To be sure, this sonnet became known only in the middle of the sixteenth century, and the poets who revived the Hebrew sonnet could not possibly have known of it. But over the course of time Hebrew poets who adhered to this model found support in the Spanish and Portuguese sonnet, as must have been the case with Jacob Frances, Immanuel Frances, Moses Zacuto, and Hebrew poets in Amsterdam.

Restraint in Structuring the Sestet

The renewed Hebrew sonnet also tended towards simplicity in the sestet. During the sixteenth century a sestet of three rhymes was the favored form. Only in the seventeenth century did there begin to be a real use of the two-rhyme model CDC DCD, which was considered almost on a par with the three-rhyme version in the Italian sonnet, even in Immanuel of Rome. This conservatism is especially instructive since the sestet, according to all opinions, had always permitted variation. It seems that the poets of the sixteenth century strove to establish the dominance of the three-rhyme sestet, and indeed succeeded in doing so. The extreme conservatism of the sestet was renounced only after it became clear to everyone that this was the best and most important model. In the seventeenth century the sestet became a matter of personal choice. Immanuel Frances, for example, preferred the two-rhyme sestet. Likewise, some variations from Immanuel of Rome's model also begin to appear, though only infrequently. From then on, it appears that Immanuel's recommendations concerning the sestet were fully understood: the three-rhyme scheme is optimal, but for the sake of surprise other schemes should be used too, though only rarely.[11]

---

[10] A sonnet by Modena would also have benefited by similar changes. See Bregman, *Shevil ha-Zahav*, 101, no. 4, and eadem, *Tzror Zehuvim*, sonnet 110.

[11] On a sonnet by Modena that would also have benefited by similar changes, see Bregman, *Sharsheret ha-Zahav*, 84–95.

In Critical Theory

> *"Accept my poem, whose weight is gold"*
> —Samuel Archivolti

With these words, and a witty pun on the word *mishqal* (which means both "weight" and "meter" in Hebrew, as explained earlier), Samuel Archivolti introduced in 1602 the first Hebrew sonnet to appear in critical theory.[12] His opening remarks indicate the prestige of the form in the eyes of the author, as well as the basic characteristic of the sonnet: its length of fourteen lines (the Hebrew word for gold, *zahav*, has the numerical value of fourteen). Archivolti returned to the typology of the sonnet in yet two other short introductions to sonnets. One sonnet is preceded by the words "a poem arranged *be-ḥezqat ha-yad*";[13] and a second sonnet by the words "In praise of the author I opened my mouth to sing a pleasant song upon *"shileshim* and *ribeʿim"*.[14] This latter expression, which in its biblical setting refers to third and fourth generations, becomes here part of a nickname for the sonnet, hinting at its structure: tercets "upon" quatrains. By means of such nicknames, Archivolti gave the sonnet an indelible stamp of fourteen lines.

Defining the sonnet as a poem of fourteen lines would not have been possible in Italian poetry, since Italian sonnets made use of longer models from the very beginning. But in Hebrew poetry the definition was fully justified. At the time when Archivolti so definitively attributed fourteen lines to the Hebrew sonnet, it would have been difficult indeed to find a Hebrew sonnet that did not fit this definition.

In the seventeenth century, Solomon Oliveyra also spoke about the sonnet in his poetic treatise *Sharshot Gavlut* ("Wreathen Chains of Gold"), calling it a fourteen-line poem "worthy of the name 'golden poem', founded on thirds and fourths."[15] This "golden poem" was the name that stuck to the Hebrew sonnet. Immanuel Frances repeated the idea yet a third time in his *Meteq Sefatayim*, but in greater detail and with a slightly different nickname: "The sonnet," he wrote, "has fourteen lines and I have therefore called it golden [*di zahav*, which is twice

---

[12] Samuel Archivolti, *ʿArugat ha-Bosem* (Venice, 1603), fol. 119r; in *Tzror Zehuvim*, ed. Bregman, sonnet 59.

[13] *Be-ḥezqat ha-yad* ("with a strong hand"), from Isaiah 8:11. The word *yad* ("hand") has the numerical value of fourteen. See Archivolti's *Sadeh le-or ḥamah* ("A sun-lit field"), in honor of *Sefer Ohev Mishpat* by Shimon ben Tzemah Duran and Ovadia Sforno.

[14] *Shileshim* and *ribeʿim* ("upon thirds and fourths") derives from Exodus 20:5 and Deuteronomy 5:9. See *Tzror Zehuvim*, ed. Bregman, sonnet 66, in honor of Isaac Abravanel's commentary on the Bible.

[15] Solomon Oliveyra, *Sharshot Gavlut* (Amsterdam, 1665), fol. 39r. See note 14.

the number fourteen; cf. Deuteronomy 1:1]. It is divided into four parts; the first two each have four lines, and the last two each have three lines."[16]

Seventeenth-century Hebrew writings on the art of poetry gave the sonnet various nicknames but did not go into detail about rhyme-schemes. In this matter they made do with examples of sonnets on the assumption that poets would learn from them. Precise instructions on this point first appear in Moses Hayyim Luzzatto's *Sefer Leshon Limmudim* (1728).[17] Luzzatto gave critical expression to every development in Hebrew sonnetry up to his time. Thus he mentions the fourteen lines of the sonnet, prescribes a closed octave, and insists that there are only three possible rhyme-schemes for the sestet: one with three rhymes, and two with two rhymes. But Luzzatto no longer speaks of a "golden poem," only of the *sonetto*. By his day the Hebrew sonnet no longer required a nickname to justify its existence. It was common and self-evident; just a run-of-the-mill poem,[18] so to speak, as in Italian.

2. Expansion and Change

The Sonetto Caudato

One vestige of the older trends at work in the Italian sonnet is the lengthening of the sonnet beyond fourteen lines.[19] In the thirteenth century the *sonetto ritornello* was popular. After the fourteenth line came an addition (*ritornello*) of varying lengths and rhyme-schemes. This kind of sonnet went out of fashion during the fourteenth century and was replaced by the *sonetto caudato*, which also lengthens the end of the poem and is still used today. The first of the *sonetti caudati* in Italian was a lament for Dante, *O Spirito gentilo, o vero Dante*, by Mucchio Da Lucca. In this type of sonnet the addition, or *coda* ("tail"), generally consists of three lines. A sonnet can have more than one *coda*; a sonnet with more than three is called a *sonettessa*. Every *coda* begins with a *settenario*, a line of seven syllables that is basically just the first part of an *endecasillabo* up to the caesura. It rhymes with the line before it. The two lines which come after it rhyme together, couplet-style. If the sestet is rhymed CDE CDE, the first *coda* will be EFF, then FGG and so on.

---

[16] Immanuel Frances, *Meteq Sefatayim*, ed. Brody, 48.

[17] Moses Hayyim Luzzatto, *Sefer Leshon Limmudim*, ed. A. M. Habermann (Jerusalem, 1945), chap. 9, 57.

[18] Luzzatto, *Sefer Leshon Limmudim*, ed. Habermann, 57.

[19] See for example Biadene, *Morfologia del sonetto*, 75–77.

The *coda* is a sophisticated addition to the body of the sonnet. It is distinct from, yet also linked to, the body of fourteen lines. Through its rhyme it is both a new beginning and a throwback to the sonnet proper. The last two lines of the *coda* are distinguished from the sonnet by their rhyme, but are equal to it in terms of line length. The *sonetto caudato* is very different from the elongated sonnets of former times. Whereas those sonnets included extraneous elements within the basic structure, the *sonetto caudato* absorbs the additions only at the completion of the basic sonnet structure. Yet the *coda* does have an impact on the basic structure. It expands the last part of the sonnet, robbing the sestet of its usual culminating power and blunting its pointed edge. Because of it the proportions of the form change; and the more codas there are, the more distorted the poem becomes. The effect can be comic, or grotesque.

Indeed, the *sonetto caudato* was accepted in Italian poetry only for humorous or burlesque purposes and is found largely in the works of poets who specialized in this field: Cino da Pistoia, Antonio Pucci, Burchiello, and Berni. The last of these turned the *sonetto caudato* into his trademark, composing numerous *sonetti caudati* and multiplying the number of codas. In one sonnet (which deals with the wiles of a physician), Berni reached twenty-one codas.[20] But this was not the record. Diego de Mendoza of Spain managed twenty-seven codas in a single sonnet, and Burchiello forty-four.[21]

Defining the sonnet as a "golden poem" made it hard to ignore the fourteen-line limit. And indeed, no Hebrew *sonetto caudato* was written until the end of the sixteenth century. The first of the Hebrew sonneteers to do so was Leone da Modena. He wrote *sonetti caudati* for weddings, such as *Yair zemir shirai* ("Let my song give light") and *Pitḥu sheʿarim* ("Open the gates"). He also composed a sonnet with two codas: *Yashen be-mizmor shir* ("Asleep in the melody of song"), which he dedicated to Israel Najara and published in the latter's volume of poetry *Shirat Yisrael* (Venice, 1599).[22] Poets of the seventeenth century took note of Modena's innovations and followed his example. However, the *sonetto caudato* remained somewhat the exception in Hebrew, just as it was in Italian, and, like the Italian, was limited by tacit consent to a specific area. But unlike the Italian it was not reserved for humor or burlesque. Rather, it was generally used for such festive events as weddings,[23] Simḥat Torah,[24] or the publication of a book, which

---

[20] F. Berni, *Rime*, ed. D. Romei (Milan, 1985), 126–28.

[21] Mönch, *Das Sonett*, 269.

[22] Leone da Modena, in *Tzror Zehuvim*, ed. Bregman, sonnets 108, 111, and 127.

[23] For example: Leone da Modena, in *Tzror Zehuvim*, ed. Bregman, sonnets 108 and 111; Solomon Conegliano, sonnet 352.

[24] Solomon Oliveyra, in *Tzror Zehuvim*, ed. Bregman, sonnets 343 and 344; and by an anonymous poet, sonnets 422 and 423. See also Bregman, "Sonetim Te'omim le-Simḥat Torah," *Yediʿot Aḥronot*, 2 October 1988.

was an important event.²⁵ Most of these sonnets were written according to the rules mentioned above. A few of them rhymed the first line of the *coda* with any line of the sestet, and not necessarily the fourteenth line.²⁶

Prominent sonneteers generally refrained from writing a *sonetto caudato*, though there are two interesting exceptions. Solomon Oliveyra, who formally defined the sonnet as a poem of fourteen lines, composed two *sonetti caudati* for Simḥat Torah.²⁷ Perhaps this was the reason he made his codas so independent as to be almost separate poems. They begin with great fanfare and move on to independent topics not mentioned in the body of the sonnets. Oliveyra called the *coda* a *mikhtam*,²⁸ a Hebrew word that means "a short poem" and also a "vessel of gold." Under the present circumstances, of course, it means a "short golden poem." The name did not catch on, either because no one noticed it or because it made the coda look too independent. The second case is a sonnet by Jacob Frances. In a wedding pamphlet that ends in two sonnets,²⁹ he added a poetic afterword that, in terms of rhyme and number of lines, might be perceived as a double *coda* to the sonnets preceding it. But it is separated from them by a special rubric, and opens with two *settenari* rather than the usual one. In structure's terms, therefore, it can also stand as an independent poem. In content it is linked to the context before it; not necessarily to the sonnets, but to the general composition as a whole. Though it may be difficult to find a name for this *rara avis*, we can conclude by saying it presents a typical example of Baroque extravagance.

The *sonetto caudato*, a rarity, was perceived as an exciting departure from the norm. Its greater length endowed it with certain grandeur. The sheer size of it was impressive, and it was more challenging to write than a regular sonnet, or at least to fill with meaningful content. Since it was written for show, the Hebrew *sonetto caudato* was sometimes ornamented with other novelties. And since it did not aim for comic effect, unlike its Italian counterpart, it never reached an exaggerated number of codas. Either because of its rarity or because people tended to look somewhat askance when it appeared, the *sonetto caudato* never received critical approval during this period. Only after it expanded and became more varied during the eighteenth century were the rules finally set down, including a typical instruction to keep in mind the ultimate stress characteristic of the Hebrew sonnet. Anania Coen wrote that:

---

²⁵ Leone da Modena, in *Tzror Zehuvim*, ed. Bregman, sonnet 27; Abraham Pimentel, sonnet 167; David Tzarfati, sonnet 376; Solomon Oliveyra, sonnet 340.

²⁶ Joseph Penso, sonnet 366 in *Tzror Zehuvim*, ed. Bregman; Solomon Oliveyra, sonnets 343 and 344.

²⁷ Oliveyra, in *Tzror Zehuvim*, ed. Bregman, sonnets 343 and 344.

²⁸ In *Tzror Zehuvim*, ed. Bregman, sonnet 343.

²⁹ Jacob Frances, in *Tzror Zehuvim*, ed. Bregman, sonnets 248 and 249.

the golden poem, called a *sonetto*, is constructed of thirds and fourths, two versus two, one with a *coda* after it . . . Take care that the *coda* consists of seven syllables when the rhyme is feminine, and six when it is masculine, and that it rhymes with the last line of the second sestet.³⁰

Coen does not distinguish between the last lines of the coda and its first line, but he does point out the need to give the first line only six syllables (and not seven) when the fourteenth line of the sonnet ends in a masculine rhyme. Thus a trait that distinguished the Hebrew sonnet from the beginning was not only preserved, but in fact strongly emphasized.³¹

Expanding the Octave

In his survey of the sonnet structure Tchernikhowsky noted that "the poets were not satisfied till they invented the double sonnet: four stanzas of four lines, four stanzas of three lines, and two rhymes for all of them."³² This form is in fact an old one, known in Italian as the *sonetto raddoppiato*.³³ It grew out of the *sonetto doppio*,³⁴ which was invented by Guittone d'Arezzo.³⁵

Our Hebrew corpus also has examples of the *sonetto doppio*, or "double golden poems" as they were called by their author, Jacob Sasportas,³⁶ though in this case only the octave was doubled. A similar kind of expansion can be found in an early Italian sonnet,³⁷ but the source of Sasportas's inspiration was apparently Spanish. Sasportas was always close to Amsterdam's community of Jewish scholars and poets. One of the most prominent of these, Daniel Levi de Barrios, a former *converso*, achieved renown in Spanish poetry during this period. Among De Barrios's poems we find double sonnets, with a rubric that pronounces them to be just that: "*sonetos dobles*."³⁸ De Barrios and Sasportas were friends. In his letters Sasportas mentions having shown his writings to De Barrios and asking his

---

³⁰ Anania Coen, *Sefer Ruaḥ Ḥadashah* (Reggio, 1822), 54.
³¹ Compare the attitude of Hebrew poets on this subject during the modern period in Bregman, *Sharsheret ha-Zahav*, 121.
³² Tchernikhowsky, *Maḥberet ha-sonetot*, 15.
³³ P. G. Beltrami, *La Metrica italiana* (Bologna, 1991), 361.
³⁴ Biadene, *Morfologia del sonetto*, 57–58.
³⁵ V. Moleta, *The Early Poetry of Guittone d'Arezzo* (London, 1976), 8.
³⁶ Jacob Sasportas, in *Tzror Zehuvim*, ed. Bregman, sonnets 367–371. See D. Bregman, "Shirei Zahav Kefulim le-Rabbi Yaʿaqov Sasportas," *Peʿamim* 49 (1992): 68–83; and also Appendix V in eadem, *Shevil ha-Zahav*.
³⁷ Mönch, *Das Sonett*, 268.
³⁸ See T. Oelman, *Marrano Poets of the Seventeenth Century* (London, 1982); and also Appendix V in Bregman, *Shevil ha-Zahav*.

opinion about them.³⁹ Sasportas helped De Barrios to publish his writings and also assisted him in other matters; surely he was acquainted with De Barrios's poetry.

Sasportas did not use De Barrios's model. The latter's sonnets are indeed "*dobles.*" Each of them combines two regular sonnets, one after the other, with a single coda for the two of them, whereas Sasportas's sonnet is written with a double octave and a regular sestet. It appears that the two poets responded to the challenge of some Spanish source or other, and that each of them met the challenge in his own particular way, De Barrios in Spanish, Sasportas in Hebrew.

Five of Sasportas's sonnets have come down to us, each of them with a double octave. Four were written for Joseph Penso's *Asirei ha-Tiqvah* or "Prisoners of Hope";⁴⁰ but unlike the rest of the panegyrics, which were printed on the frontispiece of Penso's published work, Sasportas's sonnets remained in manuscript. The fifth sonnet was included in a letter to Isaac Aboab,⁴¹ one of the rabbis of the Amsterdam community, congratulating him on the birth of his son. In all these cases, there is a clear desire to create a powerful impression.

The double octave makes for a strange sonnet. It changes the characteristic proportions of the form and blurs the dichotomy between its two parts. The octave becomes gigantic, while the sestet is dwarfed in comparison, losing its usual power and looking somewhat tacked on. Moreover, new dynamics come into play between the double octaves and the sestet. The former becomes the primary part of the poem. It is pompous and self-important; the sestet seems frivolous in comparison. Sasportas's cumbersome and enigmatic language weighs the form down even further, and, as if this were not enough, the four sonnets for Penso are linked together by various prosodic traits that transform them into two pairs of sonnets, a quartet, and also into a single and continuous unit. Such defiance of conventions, complicated structures, and grandiose symmetries all combine to create a real *meraviglia* in the best of Baroque style.

An attempt to expand the sonnet occurred even before this when the poet Solomon Ezobi created a sonnet with five quatrains, all of them in the same rhymes and rhyme-scheme (the usual ABBA). But these efforts were not very successful.⁴² The sonnet's verbal content, rhymes, and opening devices are similar to Sasportas's sonnet,⁴³ and may even have provided him with the model.

---

[39] J. Sasportas, *Tzitzat Novel Tzevi*, ed. Y. Tishbi (Jerusalem, 1954), 363–64.
[40] In *Tzror Zehuvim*, ed. Bregman, sonnets 367, 368, 369, and 370.
[41] In *Tzror Zehuvim*, ed. Bregman, sonnet 371.
[42] In *Tzror Zehuvim*, ed. Bregman, sonnet 162.
[43] In *Tzror Zehuvim*, ed. Bregman, sonnet 371.

Unusual Rhyme-Schemes

Variations in rhyme-schemes that did not penetrate the Hebrew corpus until the seventeenth century now began to appear in the sonnet, though they remained a rarity. Some of these variations from the standard models arose out of a certain poetic ineptitude, as was only natural given the great popularity of the sonnet and the vigorous activity of amateur poets. None of them makes much sense. The rhyme-scheme of one sonnet, for example, is ABBA BAAB ACA DED.[44] Sometimes a rhyme-scheme went wrong due to poetic pretensions in another area. For example, a poet might have taken on the challenge of writing an entire sonnet in words of one syllable, without using any of the words in the same meaning twice.[45] This challenge complicated the rhyme, especially in the octave,[46] which requires four rhyme words of different meaning. But such variants were relatively few.

There are also variants which relied on precedents found in the poetry of Immanuel of Rome, and especially on *Mi he'emin ʿofra* ("Who would believe that the gazelle"),[47] Immanuel's Hebrew version of the Italian *sonetto continuo*, that takes some of the rhyme words from the octave and repeats them in the sestet. These variations must either create a uniform rhyme,[48] or fall back on repeating rhyme words.[49]

Other variants sought to convey a certain festivity, and in doing so created a new kind of symmetry. Since the sestet had always permitted variation in any case, the variants came in the octave. For example: ABBA CDDC;[50] ABBA BAAB;[51] ABAB BABA.[52] Elijah Recanati combined different patterns in one of his sonnets: the lines of the octave have alternating rhyme, as though they were hemistichs in the classic Spanish model, with a single rhyme at the end of each line: AAAA. These are followed by a sestet of BCC BCC.[53] Nathan Jedidiah da Orvieto rhymed one of his octaves ABBA ACCA, and in another sonnet wrote the octave in the classic form of the *ottava rima*: ABABABCC.[54]

---

[44] Joseph Carmi, in *Tzror Zehuvim*, ed. Bregman, sonnet 142.
[45] Moses Zacuto, in *Tzror Zehuvim*, ed. Bregman, sonnet 219.
[46] As noted by Anania Coen in *Saggio di eloquenza ebrea*, 66–67.
[47] Immanuel of Rome, in *Tzror Zehuvim*, ed. Bregman, sonnet 24.
[48] Samuel Abendana, in *Tzror Zehuvim*, ed. Bregman, sonnet 161.
[49] Azariah Figo, in *Tzror Zehuvim*, ed. Bregman, sonnet 138.
[50] Raphael Calleo (Calgi), in *Tzror Zehuvim*, ed. Bregman, sonnet 150.
[51] Samuel Shalom, in *Tzror Zehuvim*, ed. Bregman, sonnet 299; Jacob Shalom, sonnet 159.
[52] Anonymous, in *Tzror Zehuvim*, ed. Bregman, sonnet 394.
[53] Elijah Recanati, in *Tzror Zehuvim*, ed. Bregman, sonnet 158.
[54] Nathan Jedidiah da Orvieto, in *Tzror Zehuvim*, ed. Bregman, sonnets 146 and 148.

The variants used by Moses Zacuto are a matter for special study. Zacuto was a master in the art of the sonnet, and most of his sonnets are models of grace and originality. But some of them are simply overdone and the forms seem ready to burst at the seams. One sonnet, which features an acrostic created from the beginning of each line and from the beginning of each word, has a flawed octave: ABAB BAAB.[55] Another sonnet, made up of only one-syllable words, and precisely scanned in an iambic *endecasillabo*, has the rhyme-scheme ABAB CDCD EFE AGA.[56] Still a third sonnet begins each line with a homonym and a sequence of conjunctions repeated at specific intervals that unify the quatrains and also create a kind of buried quatrain in the sestet. The octave has the usual rhyme, but the rhyme in the sestet is harsh and grating to the ear.[57] This kind of overt flaw in the basic pattern of the sonnet is striking in a series of seven sonnets by Zacuto: these form a cycle which is apparently the first *corona* in Hebrew poetry. The rhyme-scheme in all seven sonnets is ABCA ACBC DBD EBE. There are those who explain the term "Baroque" as a highly polished but flawed jewel. If so, these seven sonnets surely support that interpretation.

The Question of the Sonnet's Boundaries

Variations in the accepted model raise questions concerning the boundaries of the sonnet-form. Do variations mar the basic essence of the sonnet? What kind of boundaries should a sonnet actually have? Are sonnets in unusual patterns or rhyme-schemes still sonnets?

C. Scott suggests that, more than any other poetic form, the sonnet is capable of reinventing itself and of absorbing new poetic and cognitive elements without changing its fundamental character. To support this view, he cites the different models of the Italian, French, and English sonnet, which in spite of their differences can still be grouped into a single genre. For this reason Scott accords the poet complete freedom, thus refraining from any formal definition of the genre and accepting for the purpose of research and observation the kind of classification made by Antonio da Tempo in the fourteenth century.[58] The extreme liberality of this approach overlooks the anarchy that reigned during that period in the composition of Italian sonnets. Yet this approach is indeed justified for a period of several hundred years after Petrarch. Scott relies, and rightly so,

---

[55] Moses Zacuto, in *Tzror Zehuvim*, ed. Bregman, sonnet 218.
[56] Idem, in *Tzror Zehuvim*, ed. Bregman, sonnet 219.
[57] Idem, in *Tzror Zehuvim*, ed. Bregman, sonnet 214.
[58] See C. Scott, "The Limits of the Sonnet," *Review of Literature and Culture* 50 (1976): 237–50. On deviations from the classic models in world languages and their significances, see Bregman, *Sharsheret ha-Zahav*, 37–41. On the boundaries of the genre in modern Hebrew poetry, see 117–20.

on a basic instinct about the genre which eventually became the working reality. Using this same instinct, one could claim that any poem which represents itself as a sonnet is, in fact, a sonnet.

Hebrew poetic theory perceived the sonnet as a poem made up of "thirds and fourths", that is, of quatrains and sestets. It relied on what was accepted and common in the corpus of Hebrew poetry. In talking about the Hebrew sonnet, therefore, it seems that only a poem which is convincingly made up of "thirds and fourths" can be considered a sonnet. The unusual rhyming which was described above does not blur the fact that the sonnet consists of "thirds and fourths." This is stamped on the sonnet in everything from layout and syntax to rhetoric and the logical scheme by which the argument develops. If there is anything definite that can be said to define the Hebrew sonnet, then surely this is it.

XI. Meter

1. Acceptance of the Quantitative-Syllabic System

The adherence of the renewed Hebrew sonnet to Immanuel's old model is especially evident in terms of meter. Apparently Immanuel's metrical system did not catch on in his own time. It was meant first and foremost for sonnets, but if any Hebrew sonnets were written after him, it seems that they were either lost or preserved for only a short period of time, and in a quantity so negligible as to be without influence. In the fifteenth century the system was rejected in favor of the one used by Moses da Rieti, as mentioned earlier, and apparently forgotten. But as already noted, it made a comeback with the re-emergence of the Hebrew sonnet. Rieti's system did not supply the syllabic meter necessary to the composition of any sonnet: the *endecasillabo*, for which Immanuel provided such a successful Hebrew equivalent. His *Maḥbarot* held examples ripe for imitation, and the Hebrew poets who now turned their hands to writing sonnets adhered to these models along with their meter.

Immanuel's meters remained the norm of the Hebrew sonnet up to the last days of the Italian school.[1] The preservation of this system, which gradually became outdated, was aided by a variety of options — veritable safety valves — that gave the poet a certain freedom within its constraints, and that adapted it more and more to Italian cadences. Thus Immanuel's system was perfected, even strengthened, and increasingly disseminated. These safety valves consisted *inter alia* of new options, namely new metrical schemes that were both syllabic and quantitative, as shown in the Table of Metrical Schemes. Even a quick glance at this table shows the impressive development of a system that started with only two different metrical schemes, and ended with thirty.

From the sonnet, Immanuel's metrical system found its way into other Italian forms of poetry absorbed into Hebrew, and already in the sixteenth century was even used for the *terza rima*, the foundation of Rieti's metrical system. The principles of Immanuel's system were also used for many Hebrew poems composed in the older forms. The Hebrew sonnet is apparently responsible for the disappearance of Rieti's system from Hebrew poetry even though it ostensibly

---

[1] On the changes in these meters in Italy after 1700 and in Hebrew poetry of the Enlightenment, see Bregman, *Sharsheret ha-Zahav*, 64–69. On the meters of the sonnet in modern Hebrew poetry, see 69–82.

supplied a way out of the burdensome quantitative tradition, and had been used for over a hundred years: a phenomenon that has mystified scholars.[2]

Immanuel's metrical system was accepted, analyzed and explained in poetic theory, but not expressly attributed to him. Poets clearly believed that the Hebrew sonnet used the same old quantitative meters. Dividing the quantitative line into two separate hemistichs and using each one as an independent line in a strophic poem was accepted practice for different Italian forms, and over time did not seem like an innovation. The same goes for the typical syllabic line, masculine or feminine, and also for the stressed rhyme. Poets regarded the syllabic factors as a "natural" musical requirement and mistakenly attributed them to the old quantitative system.[3] They accepted the system used in Immanuel's sonnets in actual practice but did not distinguish in theory between it and the purely quantitative one used throughout the poems in the rest of the *Maḥbarot*.

2. Old and New in the Quantitative-Syllabic System

An Exact Endecasillabo

The most frequent line in the renewed Hebrew sonnet is the line common to most of Immanuel's sonnets, namely, a feminine line of eleven syllables (*11-mileil*) scanned according to the second hemistich of the meter *ha-shalem*:

mi	Yom	a	sher	ha	ya	ke	mish	ta	ge	ʿha
1	2	3	4	5	6	7	8	9	10	11

(Scheme 1)[4]

This line became very common in Hebrew poetry. Its traditional counterpart, a masculine line of twelve syllables (*12-milraʿ*) and scanned according to the first hemistich of the *ha-shalem*, also became accepted:

im	Mi	qe	naf	E	retz	ze	mi	rot	nish	me	ʿu
1	2	3	4	5	6	7	8	9	10	11	12

(Scheme 2)[5]

---

[2] See Bregman, "Shitat Immanuel," 437–38.
[3] See Bregman, "Shitat Immanuel," 443–50.
[4] Samuel Archivolti, sonnet 59 in *Tzror Zehuvim*, ed. Bregman.
[5] Immanuel Frances, sonnet 327 in *Tzror Zehuvim*, ed. Bregman.

As might be expected, this longish meter was far less popular in the renewed Hebrew sonnet. True, this is the only masculine line in the sonnets of Tzarfati and Ben Joab, who used it for sonnets of both uniform and mixed stress. Soon after them, however, a short line of ten syllables (*10-milraʿ*) appeared, scanned like the twelve-syllable line but without the final *yated:*

qam	ti	a	ni	niv	hal	be	hit	a	sef
1	2	3	4	5	6	7	8	9	10

(Scheme 3)[6]

This line, which Immanuel avoided using, as we have seen, is the exact counterpart of the *endecasillabo tronco*, i.e., shorter than the regular *endecasillabo* by one syllable. Together, the feminine line of eleven syllables (Scheme 1) and the masculine line of ten syllables (Scheme 2) form a complete Hebrew *endecasillabo*.

This endecasillabo won approval already in Archivolti's ʿArugat ha-Bosem, where the author presents it in both its masculine and feminine forms. After describing fifteen quantitative meters, Archivolti introduces it as "the sixteenth kind, composed of two *tenuʿot* and a *yated*, and two *tenuʿot* and a *yated*, and three *tenuʿot*" (Scheme 1). He further notes that "if the end of this line is masculine, then it will close with two *tenuʿot* alone" (Scheme 3).[7] The sonnet *Mi-yom asher haya* ("From the day that he was")[8] illustrates the eleven-syllable feminine line, and another poem, not a sonnet, illustrates the ten-syllable masculine line. Already here the system was accepted for poetry in general and not necessarily just for the sonnet. Immanuel Frances's *Meteq Sefatayim*, composed in 1678, also describes this *endecasillabo* in the masculine and feminine forms, but begins with the ten-syllable masculine line and exemplifies both this and its feminine counterpart in sonnets.[9] These theoretical descriptions gave "official" sanction to a system that, in actual practice, had long existed in Hebrew poetry.

---

[6] Judah da Fano, sonnet 77 in *Tzror Zehuvim*, ed. Bregman.
[7] Samuel Archivolti, *Arugat ha-Bosem*, fol. 110r.
[8] Samuel Archivolti, sonnet 59 in *Tzror Zehuvim*, ed. Bregman.
[9] *Meteq Sefatayim*, ed. Brody, 48–52. His sonnet *Zot qomatekh* ("This, thy stature"), intended to illustrate the ten-syllable masculine line was printed (on p. 49) with errors: lines 1 and 2 both have nine syllables, and line 3 has eleven! For the corrected text see *Tzror Zehuvim*, ed Bregman, sonnet 313.

Two Masculine Lines

The ten-syllable masculine line (Scheme 3) was accepted in the Hebrew sonnet in the middle of the sixteenth century,[10] and it appeared around the same time already in the east as well, in a sonnet written by David Onkineira.[11] Towards the turn of the century Leone da Modena used it in twenty-one sonnets. By the beginning of the seventeenth century, the days of the twelve-syllable masculine line (Scheme 2) seemed to be over. Archivolti did not mention it in his *'Arugat ha-Bosem*, even though this was the masculine line he almost always used in his own sonnets. The book was written after the ten-syllable masculine line had become generally accepted, and the author, who was approaching old age, no longer saw any reason to mention the old twelve-syllable line. Even so, it did not disappear. Despite the antiquity of this line and its obvious drawbacks, and despite the existence of a short masculine line that was pleasing to the ear, poets continued to use the twelve-syllable masculine line throughout the entire period. Moreover, the number of sonnets in our corpus with twelve-syllable masculine lines does not fall short of those with ten-syllable masculine lines. Nor did poetic theory continue to deny the old twelve-syllable line. *Meteq Sefatayim*, from 1678, again mentions it as a legitimate option and even illustrates it with a sonnet.[12]

New Syllabic Lines

The exact Hebrew parallel of the Italian *endecasillabo* was the basis for creating an entire set of syllabic meters that come in pairs, *piano* and *tronco*, *piano* and *tronco*. These meters, which resemble their Italian counterparts in addition to being quantitative, evolved slowly in the Hebrew poetry of the period. The poems of Jacob Frances, for example, provide good examples of these meters, just as they also represent an impressive variety of Italian forms.

Some of the new syllabic meters also found their way into sonnets, even though these were supposed to use the meter of the *endecasillabo*.[13] The phenomenon is not unique to the Hebrew sonnet. Poets in Italian, Spanish, and other languages also experimented with different line lengths for the sonnet, and some

---

[10] Azariah de' Rossi, sonnet 50 in *Tzror Zehuvim*, ed. Bregman; Judah Saltares da Fano, sonnet 77, anonymous, sonnet 74. For a few lines in this meter, see Samuel Archivolti, sonnet 67.

[11] *Tzror Zehuvim*, ed. Bregman, sonnet 85

[12] *Tzror Zehuvim*, ed. Bregman, sonnet 334. See Immanuel Frances, *Meteq Sefatayim*, ed. Brody, 52.

[13] See Appendix VI in Bregman, *Shevil ha-Zahav*. See Table of Metrical Schemes appended to this book.

of their sonnets even merited a special name. Hence the *sonetto minore*,[14] a sonnet with unusually short lines. Here is a Hebrew example in lines of nine syllables (Scheme 25):

> Ha-lo ʿof yetzaftzef renanah
> be-ʿozvo yequsho u-faho
>
> Will a bird not chirp with joy
> Upon leaving its snare and trap?[15]

Lines of unusual length are rare in the Hebrew sonnet. When they do occur it is usually due to the use of quotations from the sacred texts,[16] which then determined the sonnet's meter. Alternatively, they represent attempts by the poet to convey strong emotion. This was Zacuto's method. One particularly rare line is the eleven-syllable masculine line, which is highly dissonant (Scheme 26). The roots of this line go back to the sonnets of Joseph Tzarfati,[17] who also used an eleven-syllable masculine line in his octaves.[18] It may be that both his sonnets and his octaves represent an early and unsuccessful attempt to create an eleven-syllable feminine line, or perhaps a first attempt, which also did not succeed, to create a short masculine meter.

New Quantitative Structures

The meters of the Hebrew sonnet also underwent important innovations in terms of their quantitative metrical schemes. The lines which created the Hebrew *endecasillabo* in the sixteenth century, whether of eleven, twelve, or ten syllables, used meters derived not only from the meter of *ha-shalem*, but from a variety of other meters as well: meters with *tenuʿot* alone (not with the traditional eight *tenuʿot*, but naturally with twelve, eleven, or ten *tenuʿot*: Schemes 13, 15, and 18); *tenuʿot* with only one *yated* (Schemes 5, 6, 7, 8, 9, 11, 16, and 17); *yetedot* without any *tenuʿot* (Scheme 20); and different combinations of *yetedot* and *tenuʿot* (Schemes 9, 10, 21, 22, and 23). We find a wide variety of such metrical schemes in the corpus of sonnets, where they were also used for non-*endecasillabo* lines (Schemes 24–30).[19]

---

[14] Biadene, *Morfologia del sonetto*, 26; Ruschioni, *Il sonetto italiano*, 21.
[15] Moses Zacuto, sonnet 227 in *Tzror Zehuvim*, ed. Bregman.
[16] See further Bregman, *Shevil ha-Zahav*, 132–33.
[17] Joseph Tzarfati, sonnet 42 in *Tzror Zehuvim*, ed. Bregman.
[18] The meter in these poems is scanned according to the *merubeh*.
[19] See Appendix VI in Bregman, *Shevil ha-Zahav*. See Table of Metrical Schemes appended to this book.

These innovations in the quantitative metrical schemes clashed with Abraham ibn Ezra's time-honored demand that poets adhere to the accepted quantitative meters. But in the poetic theory of this later period, the process received the official stamp of approval. In the preface to his sonnet *Mi-yom asher haya*[20] Archivolti allows poets to versify as they wish, so long as they preserve the "order and value" of their meters. And we find similar statements in other works of poetic theory.[21] In the Hebrew sonnet and in Hebrew poetry in Italy in general, the quantitative system gradually lost its old characteristics as it moved closer and closer to the syllabic system.

The new quantitative metrical schemes could have proved a blessing for the Hebrew sonnet. They made the line more flexible, expanded its linguistic potential, and improved the poem's flow. If we look at the notes which Jacob Frances made alongside the text of one of his sonnets, we can see just how much these new metrical schemes helped the poet to express his meaning. Let us take two of his sonnets as examples: *Ma ze yetzurai* ("Why, O my limbs?") and *Ma ze emas hayai* ("Why do I disdain my life?").[22] Both sonnets use the meter of the eleven-syllable feminine line, but while the former is scanned according to the old meter of the *ha-shalem* (Scheme 1), the latter is scanned according to the new metrical scheme of eleven *tenuʿot* (Scheme 4). The former is interrupted by various exclamations in the middle of the lines, and its language is forced. That the poet struggled to find the right words is evident from all the crossed-out phrases and notes in the manuscript. The latter sonnet, on the other hand, does not have interruptions in the middle of the line, and the language flows easily. Here we find an impressive harmony between content and syntax, especially in the first quatrain. While poets less gifted than Jacob Frances obviously found these new metrical schemes even more attractive, they were used only infrequently nevertheless. Generally speaking, the *endecasillabo* of the Hebrew sonnet from this period corresponds to one of the three quantitative schemes that stem from the *ha-shalem* meter (Schemes 1–3).

Sets of Mixed Stress

We have already mentioned that Immanuel's sonnets often mix feminine and masculine lines. The poets who renewed the Hebrew sonnet, Joseph Tzarfati and Moses ben Joab, adopted this practice in most of their sonnets. Gradually, however, mixed metrical schemes became less and less common, while sonnets with a single stress, either masculine or feminine, became more the norm.

---

[20] Samuel Archivolti, sonnet 59 in *Tzror Zehuvim*, ed. Bregman.

[21] See Archivolti, *ʿArugat ha-Bosem*, fols. 118r–119r; Joseph Carmi, *Kenaf Renanim* (Vence, 1627), fol. 3r of the preface; Solomon Oliveyra, *Sharshot Gavlut*, fol. 37.

[22] Jacob Frances, sonnets 285 and 290 in *Tzror Zehuvim*, ed. Bregman .

The trend towards musical uniformity received strong support in poetic theory. Immanuel Frances, who opposed the mixed metrical schemes, subjects the sonnets of Immanuel of Rome to surprisingly harsh criticism:

> Rabbi Immanuel bar Solomon [of Rome] . . . was the first to bring them in the Holy Tongue: most of them are not right in my eyes for he wrote them with a heavy hand. And indeed, their rhymes should be all masculine or [all] feminine, whether simple [i.e., composed of only *tenuʿot* or *yetedot*] or complex [*tenuʿot* and *yetedot* together].[23]

This is an instructive passage. It embodies an important poetic ideal of the seventeenth century: a quick-moving poem that flows without interruption. Likewise, it also shows that in the poetic consciousness sonnets of mixed stress were associated with Immanuel of Rome and indeed regarded as one of the hallmarks of his style.

Metrical uniformity characterizes most Hebrew sonnets of the seventeenth century, and especially those composed by the Frances brothers. These are remarkable for their easy flow. But other poets nevertheless preserved the tradition of alternating stresses. Throughout the period we find mixed metrical schemes in the Hebrew sonnet, both those that were fixed by Immanuel of Rome and new ones that were added over the years. To be sure, their number is not great, and no poet ever achieved the rich variety of alternating structures that characterizes Immanuel's sonnets. An impressive set of mixed stresses was employed in Zacuto's *Yesod ʿOlam* ("Foundation of the World") as a way of increasing dramatic effect and as a prosodic basis for linking sonnets into sequences.[24] Immanuel's tradition therefore remained in use despite the reigning taste of the era, and despite the recommendations of poetic theory.

The permission to create new metrical schemes encouraged some poets to alternate different quantitative schemes in a single sonnet. When used in sonnets with lines of equal syllables, such alternations created a compromise between the desire for musical uniformity and the tendency towards variation and improvisation. Through them, the affinity between twin sonnets[25] or sonnet sequences[26] could be heightened. Immanuel Frances, who objected to new quantitative metrical schemes in principle, ruled against these as well. He demanded that the meters be either "simple" or "complex" throughout the entire poem,[27] and that poets

---

[23] Immanuel Frances, *Meteq Sefatayim*, ed. Brody, 42–43.
[24] Below, Chap. 16, Part 4.
[25] Solomon Oliveyra, sonnets 343 and 344 in *Tzror Zehuvim*, ed. Bregman.
[26] E.g. those of Menasseh Hayyim Padua: see below, Chap. 16, Part 2.
[27] See passage quoted above.

not alternate meters composed only of *tenuʿot* or *yetedot* with meters composed of both elements. This demand he also illustrated with sonnets.[28]

The Caesura

We find the caesura in most sonnets from this period. That it is absent in some sonnets from the period (or, to be more precise, in some lines of sonnets from the period) is understandable in view of the fact, already noted, that the caesura was not an absolute requirement in the *endecasillabo*. The renewal of the ten-syllable masculine line also affected the caesura. Unlike the old twelve-syllable masculine line which divides into two equal parts of six syllables each, like the French Alexandrine, this line divides into two parts of uneven length (6 + 4), with the caesura falling after the sixth syllable. Thus the Italian musicality increased in this respect as well in the new corpus, at least in sonnets with that masculine ending.

In Hebrew sonnets of the sixteenth and seventeenth centuries, as in the sonnets composed by Immanuel of Rome, the caesura can often be interpreted as both "syntactic" and "musical" at one and the same time. But there are lines that divide more conveniently using the first system, as in:

shal na neʿalekha	*be-ʿovrakh, gever*[29]
Pray remove your shoe	when you pass by, O man
im mi-qenaf eretz	*zemirot nishmeʿu*[30]
If from the earth's ends	melodies can be heard

The caesura in these lines, coming after the customary sixth syllable, does not occur next to the stress.

But sometimes the division is more convenient using a musical caesura:

banot ʿalei shur tzaʿ	*adah va-telekh*[31]
Girls on the wall mar	ched and went forth
ʿal pi adonai ya	*hanu yisaʿu*[32]
According to God will they en	camp [or] leave

---

[28] Immanuel Frances, *Meteq Sefatayim*, ed. Brody, 48–52.
[29] Leone da Modena, sonnet 135 in *Tzror Zehuvim*, ed. Bregman.
[30] Immanuel Frances, sonnet 327 in *Tzror Zehuvim*, ed. Bregman.
[31] Elijah Mazal-Tov Modena, sonnet 157 in *Tzror Zehuvim*, ed. Bregman.
[32] Anonymous, sonnet 143 in *Tzror Zehuvim*, ed. Bregman.

If the syntactical caesura in these lines were to come at the end of a word it would fall not after the sixth syllable, but after the eighth. This is legitimate, but it seems that the poets preferred to locate it after sixth even if it split a word.

Beginning with the seventeenth century, poets began giving metrical indications using graphic and typographic signs: abbreviation marks (*tagim*) denoted the stress,[33] and blank spaces the *yetedot* and caesuras. The space after the sixth syllable ostensibly signifies the existence of a *yated*, which falls on syllables 7–8. But often the *yated* falls on syllable 3–4 as well (as in Schemes 1, 2, and others), yet the blank space appears only after the sixth syllable. It is therefore clear that a blank space like this marks the caesura. The same is true of the space that appears in a line composed entirely of *tenuʿot*. Indications like these are found in great quantity in sonnets from the period, in both printed versions and manuscripts. We find many of them, for example, in the manuscript containing the poems of Leone da Modena.

Archivolti marked the caesura with a blank space in the exemplary sonnet *Mi-yom asher haya*,[34] and also did the same for poems not in the form of sonnets which he quoted in *ʿArugat ha-Bosem*. Interestingly, in those poems the caesura comes in the middle of a word, as for example, in:

shahri be-terem yi	*hiyeh zoreʾah*[35]
My dawn before	it rises

while in the sonnet *Mi-yom asher haya* the caesura comes only after the entire word:

heʾir zemir shevaʿ	*ke-or yomayim*
illuminated the song of the seven-string harp	like the light of days

Since it occurs after a complete word and not next to the stress, this is undoubtedly a syntactic caesura. It seems that for the typical Italian poem, Archivolti chose the typical Italian system. Very likely he understood the sonnets by Immanuel of Rome in the same way. The caesura signs of other sonneteers, on the other hand, do not indicate syntactic caesuras, unless they are syntactic and musical at one and the same time.[36] When this does not occur, the notation indicates a musical caesura (sometimes it determines two caesuras) by dividing a word in two.[37]

---

[33] Pagis, "Hamtzaʾat ha-Iambus," 671–74; 696–701 [in *Ha-Shir Davur*, 195–200; 241–46].

[34] Sonnet 59 in *Tzror Zehuvim*, ed. Bregman; Pagis, "Hamtzaʾat ha-Iambus", 671.

[35] Archivolti, *Arugat ha-Bosem*, fol. 106r.

[36] For example, see sonnet 142, lines 1–2 in *Tzror Zehuvim*, ed. Bregman.

[37] For examples see: Azariah Fano, sonnet 73 in *Tzror Zehuvim*, ed. Bregman; Mordechai Modena, sonnet 140; Moses Merrari, sonnet 347; Israel Conegliano, sonnet 395.

From all the above we can see that the standard caesura was indeed syntactical; Archivolti marked it to serve as an example, and over time the practice became self-evident. But poets deviated from the standard caesura and then felt forced to explain their intentions through graphic notation. Their blank spaces therefore denote musical caesuras, precisely because these were not recommended in the poetic theory.

The extensive use of caesuras did not prevent enjambement in the sonnets, in the manner of Immanuel of Rome.[38] "Broken lines" like this appeared in the Italian sonnet from the beginning,[39] and also in Spanish poetry in the seventeenth century.[40]

Tonal Regularity

Let us recall that in the sonnets of Immanuel of Rome the internal rhythm inclines towards the iambic: a tendency explained through the pressure of the quantitative-syllabic system. Theoretically speaking, these pressures now dwindled to a great extent. Because the quantitative schemes multiplied and changed, it became easier to create various internal rhythms, not necessarily iambic, but, for example, anapaestic:

aromem ve-odeh le-yoshev qeruvim
be-mo pi ve-libi azamer le-yotzri [41]
I will exalt and thank He who is enthroned on cherubim:
With my own mouth and heart I will sing to my Creator

Ha-lo ʿof yetzaftzef renanah
be-ozvo yequsho u-faḥo [42]
Will a bird not chirp with joy
Upon leaving its snare and trap?

But the new internal rhythms remained a minority in Hebrew sonnets, which during this period also tend to preserve an iambic rhythm, like the sonnets of Immanuel of Rome. Ostensibly this was because poets made minimal use of the new quantitative meters. But in actual fact the iambic stress is also found in sonnets that use the new meters (such as those made entirely of *tenuʿot*,[43] of *tenuʿot* with

---

[38] For example, Moses Zacuto, sonnet 186 in *Tzror Zehuvim*, ed. Bregman.

[39] Biadene, *Morfologia del sonetto*, 136–39.

[40] Navarro, *Metrica española*, 255–56.

[41] Joshua da Silva, sonnet 303 in *Tzror Zehuvim*, ed. Bregman.

[42] Moses Zacuto, sonnet 27 in *Tzror Zehuvim*, ed. Bregman. See also Menasseh Hayyim Padua, sonnet 357.

[43] See for example Simon Luria, sonnet 383 in *Tzror Zehuvim*, ed. Bregman.

one *yated*,[44] or entirely of *yetedot*[45]), which did not force the creation of iambs. All in all, it appears that the internal musicality of the line was absorbed for itself, and no longer because of any pressure on the part of meter.

Did the poets strive to create tonal regularity in the name of "poetic mellifluity"? Things differ from one poet to another. Poet Nathan Jedidiah of Orvieto made special marks (*tagim*) in his Hebrew translations in *terza rima*[46] in order to draw the reader's attention to their iambic rhythm.[47] Here, as in his sonnets and in other sonnets from this period, the iamb is not exact; in order to stress it, it is sometimes necessary to shift the grammatical stress of a given word. Apparently this is the reason for the marks: regular iambs did not have to be marked. Other poets did not go out of their way to achieve an iambic rhythm. One such poet was Jacob Frances, who unquestionably had a good ear for poetry.[48] A considerable part of his sonnets cannot be read iambically, and indeed there are lines in which he "ruined" the tonal regularity of the iambic rhythm when slight changes in word-order could have preserved it.[49] Italian poetry did not develop exact tonal meters. Some Hebrew poets, like Jacob Frances, were attracted by the striking "Italian-ness" of the sound and did not incline towards tonal regularity, at least in the sonnet. And then there were poets (and these were the ones using *tagim* to mark musical caesuras) who were attracted by the tonal regularity, used it systematically, and prepared the Hebrew poem for syllabic tonal meters.

3. Signs of a Different Path

During this period most Hebrew poetry used the quantitative-syllabic system. Prominent opponents of this system — Moses Hayyim Luzzatto at the beginning of the eighteenth century, and Anania Coen after him — pointed out famous poets from the seventeenth century who composed several poems using syllabic, non-quantitative meter. Luzzatto cited Moses Zacuto as an example of a poet who "did not remember the *yated*,"[50] and Coen mentioned that Solomon Oliveyra composed "a free poem that does not preserve the semblance of [quantitative]

---

[44] Israel Conegliano, sonnet 398 in *Tzror Zehuvim*, ed. Bregman.

[45] For example, Menasseh Hayyim Padua, sonnet 359 in *Tzror Zehuvim*, ed. Bregman.

[46] In his book *Barkhi Nafshi* (Venice, 1628).

[47] Cf. Pagis, "Hamtza'at ha-iambus," 696–710 [in *Ha-Shir Davur*, 235–40].

[48] For example, sonnets 259 (line 10) and 288 (lines 6 and 8) in *Tzror Zehuvim*, ed. Bregman.

[49] For examples see line 10 of sonnet 259, and lines 6 and 8 in sonnet 288, in *Tzror Zehuvim*, ed. Bregman.

[50] Luzzatto, *Sefer Leshon Limmudim*, ed. Habermann, 53.

meter."⁵¹ They could have brought additional examples from even earlier poets, only these were less well-known. The Venetian rabbi Barukh ben Barukh wrote an *ars poetica* in *ottava rima* and one *quartina* free of quantitative elements still in the sixteenth century.⁵² In the first octave he announced his innovation, noting that he created a new poem

> similar to that customary among the gentiles, who do not know about the *yated*. I made a change in my own line in order to distinguish it from their rules (they go in their ways, and we in ours), and I changed it to twelve syllables, in the name of God of spirits for all flesh.

His masculine line of twelve syllables has no quantitative elements. Here, incidentally, we find an explicit declaration of the "national", i.e. Hebraic, nature of the masculine stress and of the twelve-syllable line. None of these poems is a sonnet.

But sonnets also show hints of a new direction at the end of the seventeenth century and the beginning of the eighteenth. Elijah Nahmu, who lived at the turn of the century, appended to his *Aderet Eilyahu* a triplet of sonnets in a syllabic, non-quantitative meter.⁵³ The rhymes in Nahmu's sonnets are not perfect, and the author may have been unable to handle the complicated quantitative-syllabic meter. The poems remained in manuscript; perhaps they were meant from the beginning for his desk drawer alone. More daring is a sonnet by an unknown author from around 1700, also merely syllabic. This sonnet, *Livnat ha-sappir lakh* ("The purity of sapphire is yours")⁵⁴, is a wedding sonnet that was distributed to the guests on a splendid broadsheet. Its rhymes are exact; that the poet was conscious of metrical matters is evident from the caesuras marked by blank spaces.

But these poems are rarities, initial gropings toward a new period in the life of the Hebrew sonnet. Their appearance on the fringe of poetic activity reinforces the impression created by the entire corpus as a whole: from the beginning of the Hebrew sonnet and up till that point, the Hebrew sonnet was quantitative-syllabic.

This hypothesis, however, crumbles under the weight of a single sonnet, *Adina, behira* ("O delicate one, pure one").⁵⁵ This sonnet was published in a poetic afterword to the book *Torah Or* by Joseph ibn Yehiya (Bologna, 1538), and was the first sonnet printed after Immanuel's *Maḥbarot*.

---

⁵¹ Anania Coen, *Sefer Ruaḥ Ḥadashah*, 24–25; and see Oliveyra, *Sharshot Gavlut*, fol. 44r.
⁵² The poem is printed in its entirety in an Appendix at the end of Bregman, "Shitat Immanuel."
⁵³ MS. London, Montefiore 250.1 (5216), fol. 19.
⁵⁴ Anonymous, sonnet 412 in *Tzror Zehuvim*, ed. Bregman.
⁵⁵ Sonnet 49 in *Tzror Zehuvim*, ed. Bregman.

The name "Azariah" appears in the poem's acrostic and may possibly refer to Azariah de' Rossi.[56] But whoever the author, the sonnet was clearly written by a poet of stature. The rhyme is not only exact but also doubled, and, in order to make the first line even more dazzling, doubled and redoubled chiastically. The caesura, after the sixth syllable, is exact and stressed with a mark and a typographic blank space. Apart from the name in the acrostic, the names of both the book (*Torah Or*) and the book's author (Joseph ibn Yahiya) are woven into the body of the poem. Its internal development is consistent. Nor was the meter, with its exact anapaestic rhythms, carelessly determined, or the fruit of a poetic dilettante. Yet with all this, the poem does not have any quantitative traits.

---

[56] As surmised by D. Cassel, who printed the poem at the end of his edition of *Me'or ʿEynayim* (Vilna, 1866).

Given the polished style of this sonnet, its early appearance in print, and the magnificence with which it was printed, this cannot be considered a marginal piece of writing. It is not quantitative, but it has a twelve-syllable masculine line like that of Immanuel of Rome. Evident in both rhythm and language is the neatly camouflaged influence from an echo poem by Immanuel of Rome, *Tzeviya tedameh be-libah* ("The gazelle imagines in her heart").[57]

We can assume that traits like those noted in Adina behira, characterized lost Hebrew sonnets from the fifteenth century and before. The sonnet before us is apparently the last straggler in a camp that has since vanished, providing us with the only remnant of an otherwise lost meter.

---

[57] *Maḥbarot*, ed. Yarden, 61–62.

XII. Rhyme

1. Stressed Rhyme

The Norm

During this period, Hebrew sonnets used stressed rhyme according to the usage established by Immanuel of Rome. Under their influence, stressed rhyme became the norm for Hebrew poetry as a whole. It was discussed in works of poetic theory, and deemed compulsory for poems of all kinds, whether sonnets or not. The clearest and most comprehensive instructions appear in *Meteq Sefatayim* by Immanuel Frances, a known partisan of the sonnet.

Frances distinguishes between masculine and feminine rhymes, demanding that rhymes include every sound from the stress up to and including the end of the rhyme-word:

> Rhyme is the similarity of the sound at the end of a word, as in *shira-bara-tehora*, where *ra* is the final sound. Likewise *dibber-shibber-medabber*, with *ber* as the final sound. All this is obvious in respect to words of ultimate stress. But words of penultimate stress should have a double sound, as in *dibberu-shibberu-heferu*, where *eru* is the final sound. If a *shewa quiescent* comes before the final sound, the rhymes should be *dibbarta-gazarta-sarta*, where *arta* is the [final] sound, and similarly *samti-qamti-hatamti*, where *amti* is the final sound. Therefore one must not rhyme *qiyamta-gazarta-nahta*. I have seen self-declared poets who were not conscientious about this, and they do not know or understand the craft of poetry.[1]

Frances goes on to particularly warn poets about feminine rhymes ending in a closed syllable, emphasizing the need to include all sounds from the final stress on (since the Jews of Italy, who tended to articulate the end of closed syllables, were liable to consider these articulated sounds as independent syllables, and thus be satisfied with rhymes including only that which mistakenly sounded to them like two final syllables):

> If the rhyme is feminine with a final closed sound, as in *tomer-gomer-ʿomer*, [the poet] should also be careful not to rhyme them with *zemer-tzemer*, since the former have the sound of *omer*, and the latter *emer*, and the ear easily discerns the great difference between them.[2]

---

[1] *Meteq Sefatayim*, ed. Brody, 41.
[2] The text of this paragraph is corrupt in Brody's edition.

Last of all, Frances demands homogenous rhyme. He mentions Immanuel of Rome in this context, though not in order to credit him as the founder of stressed rhyme in Hebrew. On the contrary, he denounces him for disregarding the rules!

> Likewise, rhymes should not be made by combining words of ultimate and penultimate stress, such as ᶜ*asiti* and *beyti*, *shoresh* and *yoresh*, even if most of the earlier poets were not meticulous about this. Thus Rabbi Abraham ibn Ezra rhymed *shemesh* and *hamesh*, ᶜ*eser* and *yivaser* . . . and Rabbi Immanuel bar Solomon [of Rome] rhymed *zefet* and *nofet and aderet-qetoret*. But Jacob Frances and Elinoam, his brother, were wary of this, and rightly so.

In point of fact, the flaw in rhyming *zefet-nofet* ("black pitch; flowing honey") has nothing to do with stress, since both these words are penultimately stressed, but with the prohibition against restricting the rhymemes to the last syllable in the penultimate line. Nevertheless, the criticism regarding *zefet-nofet* was justified in principle since this pair of words appears in a sonnet,[3] and in sonnets all the rules of stressed rhyme, including this last one, should be observed. The stringency towards *zefet-nofet* goes back to Immanuel's efforts to emphasize the separation of the quatrains in the sonnet, as already noted. The rhyme *aderet-qetoret*, on the other hand, appears not in a sonnet but in a poem with the classic running rhyme[4] where the short rhyme (composed of the final syllable alone) was normative. Here the criticism directed at Immanuel of Rome is not justified, though indeed it is understandable, and precisely because Immanuel's innovations had become so deeply entrenched among Hebrew poets. Stressed rhyme, now compulsory in poems of all kinds, had come to be the natural order of things. The idea that a different aesthetics might have reigned in Hebrew poetry at some other period simply did not seem possible.

The warning not to rhyme words of different stresses — a prohibition that apparently embraced the entire set of rules governing stressed rhyme — occurs time and again throughout this period. Clearly, stressed rhyme owed its enthusiastic acceptance to Italian poetry, which prompted its creation in the first place. In *Yad Ḥaruzim*, or "The Force of Rhymes" (Venice, 1700), a Hebrew rhyme-lexicon by Gershon Gentili, the author makes particular note of this phenomenon:

> Know that the ancients were careless about this. And that all the later ones criticized them after seeing that all writers of foreign poems did not mix feminine and masculine rhymes (which they call in their language *rime tronchi*). And that they considered and corrected and determined not to combine feminine and masculine rhymes.[5]

---

[3] Sonnet 25 in *Tzror Zehuvim*, ed. Bregman.
[4] *Uri melitzati:* Immanuel, *Maḥbarot*, ed. Yarden, 353.
[5] *Yad Ḥaruzim* (Venice, 1700; repr. 1740), fol. 5r.

Immanuel of Rome, who was "careless" about stressed rhyme in the lion's share of his poetry, was included, in the opinion of Gentili, among the "ancients."

Deviations from the Norm

Naturally enough, there are occasional lapses in the rules of stressed rhyme throughout the corpus, due to the poet's inability or ignorance. But all in all, deviations of this kind are impressively few, or at least open to explanation.[6] So, for example, one anonymous poet rhymed *hishpʿata* ("you influenced") with *konanta* ("you prepared").[7] David Onkineira rhymed *yuladti* with *tzalalti-ḥamadti-baḥanti*. J. Patai, who edited Onkineira's poems, attributed this weakness to the poet's youth,[8] but it could also be due to the fact that Onkineira, who lived in Salonika and composed his sonnets far away from the Italian center, was unaware of the particular rules regarding the sonnet.

Many deviations arose from the practice of shifting the stress for the purpose of rhyme, so that an ultimately stressed word was made to sound penultimate, and vice versa.[9] That this is the case we can see from the metrical equivalence, syllabic and quantitative, between the line with the offending word and the other, normative lines.

Such shifts of grammatical stress are found even in sonnets that do not rhyme ultimate and penultimate stress together. In *Yesod ʿOlam* ("The Foundation of the World"),[10] for example, Moses Zacuto shifted some of his rhyme-words from penultimate to ultimate stress, as we can surmise from their appearance in lines of ten syllables, and from the fact that they rhyme with words in ten-syllable masculine lines. The poet, it seems, simply preferred the pleasant sound to the correct grammatical stress.

The phenomenon is closely analyzed in the above-mentioned *Yad Ḥaruzim* by Gershon Gentili; the author even attributes the custom to Immanuel of Rome, "in addition to every other poet, old and new."[11]

Deviations from stressed rhyme can indeed be explained by the reliance on Immanuel of Rome. Rightly or not, poets looked to Immanuel when they shifted the stress of the rhyme, and sometimes they even borrowed his rhymes verbatim.

---

[6] The overall picture is unfortunately blurred by corrupt texts in the different editions, both new and old.

[7] Anonymous, sonnet 378 in *Tzror Zehuvim*, ed. Bregman.

[8] J. Patai, "David Onkineira ve-Shirato," *Qovetz ʿal-Yad* n.s. 2 (1937): 77–119. The poem is printed in *Tzror Zehuvim*, ed. Bregman, sonnet 87.

[9] For examples, see Bregman, *Shevil ha-Zahav*, 123, with examples in *Tzror Zehuvim*, ed. Bregman, by Joseph Tzarfati, sonnet 39; Leone da Modena, sonnet 109; and Moses Zacuto, sonnets 183 and 186.

[10] Moses Zacuto, sonnets 204 and 206 in *Tzror Zehuvim*, ed. Bregman.

[11] Gentili, *Yad Ḥaruzim*, fol. 5v.

Immanuel Frances, for example, relied on Immanuel in pronouncing *hamaveta* ("death") with the stress on the final syllable.¹² And it was because of a rhyme borrowed from Immanuel of Rome that Jacob Frances pronounced *maḥaq* ("he erased") with the stress on the ultimate syllable, even though the former used the word as a noun.¹³ Thus poets learned from Immanuel of Rome to rhyme a *ḥolam* with a *segol* or a *pataḥ: sheqer-boqer* ("lie; morning");¹⁴ *noʿam-taʿam* ("pleasantness; taste").¹⁵ Immanuel of Rome rhymed *Kamerino-arinu* ("Camerino; we gathered")¹⁶ and Archivolti *arinu-Marino* ("we gathered; Marino").¹⁷

Enriching the Rhyme

The preference for rich rhyme was widely accepted and apparently the first of Immanuel's norms to become entrenched in the theoretical criticism. Solomon Almoli distinguishes in his *Sheqel ha-Qodesh* ("The Holy Sheqel" [Constantinople, 1506]) among the "passable" rhyme, which includes the sounds after the stressed consonant (*barad-neḥmad-gilad*); the "acceptable" rhyme, which also includes the stressed consonant (*yishmor-le'mor-ligmor*); and the "praiseworthy" rhyme, which includes sounds even before the stressed consonant (*devarim-gevarim-qevarim*).¹⁸ Immanuel Frances returned to these categories at the end of the period, adding the necessity of distinguishing between masculine and feminine rhymes. His instructions for enriching the rhyme-word apply to Hebrew poems of all kinds, and not just to sonnets.¹⁹

Like Immanuel of Rome himself, Immanuel's followers also preferred the feminine, rich rhyme. Three-fourths of the entire corpus of Hebrew sonnets uses feminine rhyme alone, while the remaining quarter uses masculine or nixed patterns of both. But the tendency towards feminine rhyme did not work to the advantage of Hebrew poetry. Due to the lack of Hebrew words with penulti-

---

¹² Immanuel Frances, sonnet 334 in *Tzror Zehuvim*, ed. Bregman; Immanuel of Rome, sonnet 9.

¹³ Jacob Frances, sonnet 261 in *Tzror Zehuvim*, ed. Bregman; Immanuel of Rome, sonnet 4. Numerous other examples are found in Bregman, *Shevil ha-Zahav*, 124.

¹⁴ See for example Samuel Archivolti, sonnet 61 in *Tzror Zehuvim*, ed. Bregman.

¹⁵ Elijah Modena, sonnet 154 in *Tzror Zehuvim*, ed. Bregman.

¹⁶ Immanuel of Rome, sonnet 31, in *Tzror Zehuvim*, ed. Bregman.

¹⁷ Samuel Archivolti, sonnet 70 in *Tzror Zehuvim*, ed. Bregman, and see also sonnets 62, 63, and 71.

¹⁸ Solomon Almoli, "Sheqel ha-Qodesh," in *Leshon Limmudim le-David ibn Yahya*, ed. H. Yalon (Jerusalem, 1965), 65. Hrushowsky criticized Almoli for setting a norm which "has no foundation in poetic reality." Indeed, there is probably no such foundation in Hebrew-Spanish poetry, but it is found abundantly in Hebrew-Italian poetry and affiliated schools. See Hrushowsky, *Ha-shitot ha-Rashiot shel he-ḥaruz ha-ʿIvri*, 735 (4.3).

¹⁹ *Meteq Sefatayim*, ed. Brody, 48.

mate stress, poets fell back on the same rhyme-words, and used monotonous morphological rhymes or archaic forms that make their poems sound bombastic.[20] Rhymes such as *zohar-tohar* ("splendor-purity") or *eretz-ᶜeretz-peretz-qeretz* ("land, sky, breach, destruction") as well as morphological rhymes appear in sonnets over and over again.

Critics deplored morphological rhyme. In *Meteq Sefatayim*, for example, Immanuel Frances lamented the work of one poet whose rhymes mostly consisted of such trite combinations as *banekha-ᶜamekha- ḥasidekha* ("your sons, your people, your goodness") or *baneynu- yadeynu* ("our sons, our hands"). In response, the "pupil" Boaz takes his "teacher" to task, pointedly asking: "From what you said before, are his rhymes not correctly done?" To which his teacher replies:

> I know, my lad, I know! But poets ought to run away from the easy and seek that which is hard to attain; this is their glory! The poems **written** by that man: a little child could use them to make poems without number.[21]

The desire for new and rare rhymes was expressed in Italian poetic theory in the concept of the *rima cara*, which stood in contrast to the grammatical *desinenziale* rhyme.[22]

In addition to this, poets also adopted one of Immanuel of Rome's techniques for enriching the rhymeme, whether feminine or masculine. This was to include as many sounds as possible before the stress, even from those located before the rhyme-word. Joseph Tzarfati, for example, wrote *zemirot shorera-qeravot ᶜorera* ("sing songs-raise battles").[23] He reaches his peak of technical perfection in octaves whose rhymes impressed Leah Goldberg.[24] Other poets, such as Leone da Modena, Samuel Shalom, Solomon Oliveyra, Immanuel Frances, Moses Zacuto, and David Onkineira outdid themselves with this kind of rhyme so typical of Immanuel of Rome.[25]

---

[20] See Hrushowsky, "Prosody, Hebrew," 1226, especially in relation to poetry of the Enlightenment. See also D. Landau, "Hebrew Prosody and Poetics," in *The New Princeton Encyclopedia of Poetry and Poetics*, 509-14, here 512-13; and E. Spicehandler, "Hebrew Poetry," 501-9, here 506.

[21] *Meteq Sefatayim*, ed. Brody, 42. The hard to attain was a basic concept in Baroque culture. See Maravall, *Culture of the Baroque*, 220.

[22] Beltrami, *La Metrica italiana*, 352, par. 153 and 353, par. 155.

[23] Joseph Tzarfati, sonnet 43 in *Tzror Zehuvim*, ed. Bregman; for other example see also sonnets 39, 41, and 42.

[24] *Be-ᶜodi ḥai*, in Schirmann, *Mivḥar*, 223: *nehi shavᶜi ve-dimᶜi / ve-tishaᶜmi le-shimᶜi*. See L. Goldberg, *Ḥamishah Peraqim bi-Yesod ha-Shirah* (Jerusalem, 1957), 24-32.

[25] For numerous examples, see Bregman, *Shevil ha-Zahav*, 126.

2. Adorning the Rhymes

Adorning the Rhyme Itself
Some poets created particularly innovative rhymes.[26] Azariah Figo, for example, used the same rhyme words to create a symmetrical effect (e.g. *elef-shever-shever-elef*).[27] In two of his sonnets, Immanuel Frances used rhymes whose vowels shifted according to the Latin sequence of the vowels *a-e-i-o*:[28]

hiLAm-e'aLEm-ekaLEm-kuLAm
uLAm-hitaLEm-hoLEm-tziLAm
miLIm-yigLOm-yahLIm
eiLOm-yaLIm-shaLOm [29]

Echo-rhymes were also a favorite. This kind of rhyme, which repeats part or all of the rhyme word, was called by Moses Hayyim Luzzatto a "wonder of wonders." Echo-rhymes were used by Immanuel of Rome, though not in his sonnets, and in the sonnets of Leone da Modena and Moses Zacuto. The echoes appear in their sonnets at the end of the lines or even in the middle. All these devices are also found in Italian and Spanish poetry from this period.[30]

Rhymed and Metrical Biblical Phrases
The technique of rhyming the Bible and other sacred sources into sonnets, which we saw in Immanuel of Rome, was enthusiastically adopted in the sixteenth and seventeenth centuries.[31] As in Immanuel's sonnets, the sonnets of this period also show great variety in their use of biblical quotations. Once again we find a biblical phrase that contributes only one rhyme member, but takes up the entire line:

ha-ᶜir asher niqra shemakh ᶜaleyha
("the city upon which thy name is called": Daniel 9:18)

---

[26] For a fuller discussion of this subject, see Bregman, *Shevil ha-Zahav*, 127-29.

[27] Azariah Figo, sonnet 138 in *Tzror Zehuvim*, ed. Bregman.

[28] Such rhymes are found in the old Italian sonnets, though not in long and organized sequences. See Biadene, *Morfologia del sonetto*, 162-66.

[29] Immanuel Frances, sonnets 335 and 332 in *Tzror Zehuvim*, ed. Bregman.

[30] See Moshe Hayyim Luzzatto, *Leshon Limuddim*, ed. A.M. Habermann part II and III.59; Dvora Bregman, "Amimut u-vehirut be-Tofteh Arukh le-Moshe Zacut," *Peᶜamim* 96 (2003): 35-52. I intend to publish an extended treatise on the Hebrew echo-poem, whose history stretches from the 13th century to the present. Some seventy Hebrew poems are extant. For examples see Biadene, *Morfologia del sonetto*, 82-91; Navarro, *Métrica española*, 189.

[31] For a detailed study of this, see Bregman, "Ha-Shibbutz ha-Mitḥarez," and also eadem, *Shevil ha-Zehav*, 127-29,

Rhyme

... *tirpah shevareyha ve-hatzileyha*
(... "heal her wounds and save her")[32]

Then there is the rhyme that uses two different biblical phrases and takes up just part of the lines:

... *tanim ve-kivnot ya'ana*
("jackals and like the ostriches": Isaiah 43:20)

... *bi-shfal qol tahana*
("when the sound of grinding is low": Ecclesiastes 12:4)[33]

Once again, poets had to make slight changes in the original biblical phrasing. So, for example, in the citations above *shimkha* became *shemakh* (both mean "thy name"), and *ha-tahana* ("the pestle") became simply *tahana*, without the definite article.

The longer the biblical phrase used for purposes of rhyme, the more the achievement was admired. Moses Zacuto perfected the technique with a rhymed biblical phrase that is also discontinuous:

tzipor, behema, dag ve-hayto ya'ar
("bird, cattle, fish, and beast of the forest")

bi-zman shelosha tzar le-to'altenu
("after three days for our benefit")

az na'aseh amar le-sarfei sha'ar
("Then 'Let us make' he said to the guardian angels")

adam be-tzalmenu ve-khi-dmutenu
("'man in our image and likeness'": Genesis 1:26)[34]

The rhymed and metrical biblical phrase came to be a means for bringing the poem to a grand conclusion. This was achieved in various ways. Thus we find a rhymed conclusion with two rhyme members taken from a single biblical phrase (Psalms 35:5):

... *leshoni tehegeh tzidkekha*
("... my tongue will utter your righteousness")

---

[32] Jacob Segrè, sonnet 90 in *Tzror Zehuvim*, ed. Bregman.
[33] Jacob Segrè, sonnet 97 in *Tzror Zehuvim*, ed. Bregman.
[34] Moses Zacuto, sonnet 171 in *Tzror Zehuvim*, ed. Bregman.

> ... *kol ha-yom tehilatekha*
> ("... your praise all the day long")[35]

The following example has three rhymed biblical phrases, with all four lines (apart from the bracketed words in line 3) coming from Moses' *Song of the Sea* in Exodus 15:

> *uv-rov geonakh taharos qamekha*
> ("And in the greatness of thy excellency thou destroyest thine enemy": Exodus 15:7)
>
> *bigdol zeroakh yidmu ka-aven*
> ("By the greatness of thine arm they are as still as stone": Exodus 15:15)
>
> ʿ*ad yaʿavor ʿam [qorim bi-shmekha]*
> ("Till the people [who call in thy name] pass over": Exodus 15:15)
>
> *mikdash adonai konenu yadekha*
> ("The Temple, O Lord, which thy hands have established": Exodus 15:17)[36]

Moses Zacuto adopted this technique with particular enthusiasm. His sonnets generally conclude with a rhymed biblical phrase, unless they are particularly sophisticated in other ways. One sonnet, for example, consists entirely of one-syllable words;[37] another only of words that take part in an acrostic, and so on.[38]

Zacuto's rhymed biblical conclusions are extremely well-crafted. Often they take up the entire last line of the sonnet, or contribute two rhyme members. For example:

> *rav laqeta gam ki zeman miʿeta*
> ("she gleaned a great deal, even though there was little time")
>
> ʿ*erev, ve-tahbot et asher liqeta*
> ("evening, and she will beat out that which she had gleaned": Ruth 2:17)[39]

Zacuto used variations of a single biblical phrase ("Daughters of Israel, weep over Saul": 2 Samuel 1:24) to conclude each of his seven sonnets lamenting the death

---

[35] Judah Moscato, sonnet 57 in *Tzror Zehuvim*, ed. Bregman.
[36] Jacob Segrè, sonnet 92 in *Tzror Zehuvim*, ed. Bregman.
[37] Zacuto, sonnet 219 in *Tzror Zehuvim*, ed. Bregman.
[38] Idem, sonnet 218 in *Tzror Zehuvim*, ed. Bregman.
[39] Idem, sonnet 226 in *Tzror Zehuvim*, ed. Bregman.

of Rabbi Saul Morteira, and to unify this *corona* of sonnets that we have already had occasion to mention.

The rhymed and metrical biblical phrase helped emphasize prosodic stopping points in the sonnet, and here Moses Zacuto was particularly successful. For example: the first quatrain in one sonnet ends with a quotation from Job 9:5, and the last tercet from Jeremiah 47:6.[40] In another sonnet the octave ends with a quotation from Isaiah 65:11; the sestet from Isaiah 30:33 and Job 3:17.[41]

The need to make the biblical phrase metrical meant that poets fell back time and again on a few old favorites suitable to the major eleven-syllable feminine line (see Scheme 1). For example: *ha-maḥaneh ha-ze asher pagashti* ("this camp that I have met": Genesis 33:8), or *qovei adonai yaḥalifu koaḥ* ("those that hope in the Lord will renew their strength": Isaiah 40:31). Once poets started innovating with meter in their sonnets, the repertoire of standard quotations expanded. So, for example, we find time and again: *adam yelud isha qetzar yamim* ("Man that is born of woman is of few days": Job 14:1), which creates a ten-syllable masculine line (see Scheme 3) or *isha yirat ha-shem hi tithalal* ("The woman who fears God shall be praised": Proverbs 31:30), which creates a ten-syllable masculine line made up entirely of *tenuᶜot*, or "cords" (Scheme 15).

In light of all the above, we might have thought that poets chose rhymed biblical phrases on the basis of their suitability to the metrical scheme, but on further examination this assumption becomes doubtful.

As noted, the new quantitative metrical schemes did not become common in the sonnet, and syllabic meters unsuited to the *endecasillabo* were even more of a rarity. Yet such exceptions as do exist generally have a rhymed biblical phrase. There is, for example, one sonnet in the exceptional eleven-syllable masculine line, and in a new quantitative meter (Scheme 28), that contains two rhymed biblical phrases as well as another, unrhymed one fitting to that meter:

[yaḥad] be-nevel ᶜasor zameru lo
("[together] on the ten-string harp sing unto him": Psalms 33:2)

me-et adonai hayta zot [leḥanen]
("this is the Lord's doing, [to give]": Psalms 118:24)

tifraḥ ve-tagel af gilat ve-ranen
("it shall blossom and rejoice, with joy and singing": Isaiah 35:2)[42]

It is quite clear that the metrical schemes of the poems (both syllabic and quantitative) are determined by the quotations, and not vice-versa.

---

[40] Idem, sonnet 223 in *Tzror Zehuvim*, ed. Bregman.
[41] Idem, sonnet 187 in *Tzror Zehuvim*, ed. Bregman.
[42] Moses Franchetta-Harari, sonnet 99 in *Tzror Zehuvim*, ed. Bregman.

Judging from these and other examples, we can surmise that it was the rhymed biblical phrase that gave rise to unusual meters in sonnets. The assumption that the unusual meter came in the wake of the rhymed biblical phrase, and not vice-versa, is confirmed in the words of Samuel Archivolti. From what we read in his ʿArugat ha-Bosem, it appears that poets willingly sacrificed principles of meter in order to use rhymed biblical phrases.[43] And the same was true of rhyme, according to Immanuel Frances. In *Meteq Sefatayim* the "teacher" no sooner criticizes the morphological rhymes of one poet than his "pupil" points out a poem by Jacob Frances in which the final two rhymes are *lanu* ("to us") and ʿ*imanu* ("with us"). The "teacher" acknowledges the fault and explains: "Jacob Frances allowed himself a certain license [in order] to use two biblical phrases that were almost metrical at the end of the poem."[44] In other words, the poet was prepared to forego fresh rhymes so long as he could rhyme with a biblical phrase.

Borrowing Rhymes from Immanuel of Rome

Considering all the obligations, elaborations, and restrictions, it is no wonder that poets had recourse to dictionaries of rhyme. These were compiled one after the other throughout the period. Solomon da Poggibonsi published his *Mezon ha-Mikhtav* ("Food for Writing") at the beginning of the sixteenth century;[45] Solomon Oliveyra, *Sharshot Gavlut* ("Chains of Gold") in the middle of the seventeenth century; and Gershon Gentili, *Yad Ḥaruzim* ("The Force of Rhymes") at its end. But if a poet was looking for rhymes, Immanuel's *Maḥbarot* proved the most useful repository of all.

Poets took rhymes from every part of the *Maḥbarot*, including the rhymed prose. But the poems, and the sonnets in particular, were the primary source. The sonnets in the *Maḥbarot* supplied a rhyme that was rich, fresh, and eminently serviceable in terms of meter. What could be easier for a beginning sonneteer than to copy them?

Below are some examples of the ways in which poets borrowed Immanuel's rhymes:

1. Immanuel of Rome, on the subject of women, uses the rhymes *daḥaq* ("great haste") and *shaḥaq* ("heaven"):

    bein ha-shemashot ʿal yedei ha-daḥaq
    ("At sunset, in great haste")

---

[43] Archivolti, ʿ*Arugat ha-Bosem*, fol. 119v.
[44] *Meteq Sefatayim*, ed. Brody, 42.
[45] MS. Ferrara, Collection of the Jewish Community, 25.

ʿim kol tzeva-marom ve-elei shaḥaq
("With all the heavenly host and gods in heaven")[46]

Joseph Penso repeats these lines almost verbatim in a sonnet about the soul:

bein ha-shemashot ʿal yedei ha-daḥaq
("At sunset, in great haste")

lirot tzeva-marom ve-elei shaḥaq
("To see the heavenly host and gods in heaven")[47]

2. Immanuel of Rome rhymes *koraʿat* ("bows down") with *tolaʿat* ("worm") in a sonnet about his sins; Moses Zacuto uses these same rhymes in a sonnet about the soul of unbelievers.[48]

3. Immanuel of Rome rhymes *Koraḥ* and *toraḥ* ("a lot of trouble") in a complaint against a crafty father-in-law; Jacob Frances uses these thymes in a sonnet chastising his enemies.[49]

4. Immanuel of Rome, against the father-in-law once again, rhymes *Teresh* (the king's chamberlain in Esther 2:21) with *ḥeresh* ("silently") and *peresh* ("excrement"); Jacob Frances uses these rhymes in a different order in a sonnet against the bridegroom.[50]

5. Immanuel of Rome laments his lady with the rhymes *zevul* ("heaven"), *yevul* ("harvest"), *le-bul* ("to autumn"), *ha-gevul* ("the boundary"); Menasseh Hayyim Padua uses these rhymes with a slight change of order in praise of the bride.[51]

6. Immanuel of Rome longs for the Messiah with the rhymes *ha-zeman* ("Time"), *ne'aman* ("faithful"), and *tzuf u-man* ("the nectar of manna"); Joseph Tzarfati uses these rhymes in a sonnet about playing cards.[52]

---

[46] Immanuel of Rome, sonnet 4 in *Tzror Zehuvim*, ed. Bregman.

[47] Joseph Penso, sonnet 364 in *Tzror Zehuvim*, ed. Bregman.

[48] Immanuel of Rome, sonnet 30 in *Tzror Zehuvim*, ed. Bregman; Moses Zacuto, sonnet 178.

[49] Immanuel of Rome, sonnet 33 in *Tzror Zehuvim*, ed. Bregman; Jacob Frances sonnet 262.

[50] Immanuel of Rome, sonnet 33 in *Tzror Zehuvim*, ed. Bregman; Jacob Frances sonnet 244.

[51] Immanuel of Rome, sonnet 9 in *Tzror Zehuvim*, ed. Bregman; Menasseh Hayyim Padua, sonnet 360.

[52] Immanuel of Rome, sonnet 36 in *Tzror Zehuvim*, ed. Bregman; Joseph Tzarfati, sonnet 41.

7. Immanuel of Rome craves some tasty morsels with the rhymes *halom* ("hither"), *ka-halom* ("like a dream"), *shalom* ("peace"), and *yahalom* ("diamond"); Joseph Tzarfati uses these rhymes in a different order to express his longings for an absent friend.[53]

8. Immanuel of Rome fears death with the rhymes *avadeti* and *ravadeti*:

> ... *avadeti*
> ... ("I am lost")
>
> > ... *ani ravadeti / ᶜarsah*
> > ("... I smoothed / her bed.")

Immanuel Frances uses the same rhymes to express a longing for his bride, while at the same time reworking Immanuel of Rome's original phrasing:

> ... *ani avadeti*
> (... "I am lost")
>
> > ᶜ*arsi, be-marvadim asher ravadeti*
> > ("my bed, with coverlets that I smoothed.")[54]

9. Immanuel of Rome in praise of his wife rhymes *ḥeqer* ("inquiry") with *boker* ("morning"); Samuel Archivolti uses these same rhymes in reverse order to defend the rabbis.[55]

10. Immanuel of Rome in praise of a banquet uses the rhymes ... *be-Kamerino / sham ta'avat nefesh ve-sham arinu* ("in Camerino / There is my soul's delight and there we gathered").

Samuel Archivolti uses the same rhymes to praise a book:

> *sham pri ḥayyim ha-lo arinu*
> ("There we gathered the fruit of life")
>
> *be-niv Don Marco Marino*
> ("through the words of Don Marco Marino")[56]

---

[53] Immanuel of Rome, sonnet 32 in *Tzror Zehuvim*, ed. Bregman; Joseph Tzarfati, sonnet 40.

[54] Immanuel of Rome, sonnet 14 in *Tzror Zehuvim*, ed. Bregman; Immanuel Frances, sonnet 310.

[55] Immanuel of Rome, sonnet 3 in *Tzror Zehuvim*, ed. Bregman; Samuel Archivolti, sonnet 61.

[56] Immanuel of Rome, sonnet 31 in *Tzror Zehuvim*, ed. Bregman; Samuel Archivolti, sonnet 70.

11. Immanuel of Rome complains against women with the rhymes *da'avon* ("grief") and *ra'avon* ("hunger"); Moses ben Joab uses them to bewail the lot of orphans.[57]

These examples are only the tip of the iceberg, for throughout the period under discussion poets borrowed Immanuel's rhymes on a massive scale. Nor were they satisfied with the rhyming syllables alone (which could have been adapted to new rhymes). Indeed, they took complete words (as we see in all the examples above), and sometimes even a considerable part of the entire line (examples 1 and 8). Sometimes they retained the very structure of the poetic line, together with the enjambments so characteristic of Immanuel of Rome (examples 2 and 7), and sometimes even imperfect rhymes (examples 9 and 10). Often they borrowed two or more rhyme members, an entire sequence of rhymes, or even two adjacent sequences (examples 5, 6, and 7). In fact, some sonnets were composed almost entirely with rhymes from Immanuel's sonnets.

This borrowing could not have been a clandestine affair, since the *Mahbarot* were well known in these circles. The borrowing was rather a literary device intended to create significant allusions and new depths of meaning. Sometimes (as in example 2) the original situation and argument were preserved almost intact, thereby infusing the new text with the spirit of the original. Sonnets about morality, religion and death thus benefit by association from the atmosphere of foreboding so characteristic of Immanuel's sonnets on these subjects. In sonnets dealing with the relations between men and women, an apt quotation from Immanuel lends it a certain piquancy (example 4). Sometimes a rhyme planted in a new context invites comparison by alluding to the original source. In this way, for example, Jacob Frances adroitly compares his rivals to a nagging wife (example 3), and Immanuel Frances sings to his far-away bride about love until death (example 8). Other examples of this kind are nos. 4, 6, 7, and 10. The finest poets borrowed from Immanuel, and readers familiar with the *Mahbarot* could enjoy the embedded rhymes just as they enjoyed the embedded biblical quotations. Always fresh due to their new settings, the rhymes borrowed from Immanuel never did lose their charm, even though they were repeatedly used throughout the period.

In order to explain this widespread borrowing from Immanuel, we noted that, among other things, his linguistic weave fit right into the meter common in the Hebrew sonnet of this period. It is therefore interesting to find that not a few of Immanuel's rhymes were borrowed along with unusual prosodic elements, such as rhymes that were less than perfect (examples 9 and 10). Other rhymes were borrowed from the twelve-syllable masculine lines no longer in fashion (examples 6, 7, 11). The practice continued throughout the entire period, from

---

[57] Immanuel of Rome, sonnet 18 in *Tzror Zehuvim*, ed. Bregman; Moses ben Joab, sonnet 46.

Joseph Tzarfati and Moses ben Joab to Menasseh Hayyim Padua. This makes us wonder whether it was not because of these embedded rhymes that the twelve-syllable masculine line survived as long as it did. Perhaps the custom of embedding Immanuel's rhymes began already in the sonnets of Tzarfati and Ben Joab, the renewers of the Hebrew sonnet who established its meters for generations to come. Thus it might also have been their use of Immanuel's rhymes that led them to the meter that became common in the sonnet: the eleven-syllable feminine line. If so, this might be another reason why Immanuel's meters came to be the standard in the Hebrew sonnet and so common in Hebrew poetry as a whole. Immanuel's rhymes were greatly admired. Jacob Frances, no slouch himself when it came to rhyming, dubbed Immanuel the "Emperor of Rhyme-makers"[58] and borrowed his rhymes with a liberal hand in all of his poems, not just his sonnets. It was under the inspiration of Immanuel of Rome that Gershon Gentili compiled his dictionary of rhymes. It seems, therefore, that we have before us an unbroken circle in which meter followed rhymes, and rhymes followed meter. Even with the passage of time, when poets began borrowing Immanuel's rhymes from second- and third-hand sources, the circle remained unbroken. Immanuel's rhymes became accepted in every form of Hebrew poetry, whether sonnets or not. They immediately stand out in even the most cursory glance at poems from this period. Scholars have already noted the importance of the *Mahbarot* in Hebrew literature down to our own times.[59] It seems, therefore, that things went hand in hand, and that the rhymes borrowed from Immanuel acted as a poetic spearhead to disseminate his style to the farthest corners of Hebrew literature.[60] So when Immanuel concluded the Introduction to his *Mahbarot* with the following words:

> Arise, my song, my fair one, and soar; above all the songs be Queen, / Let your doctrine drop, distilled like the dew, and pour your spirit upon all flesh![61]

Our prophet knew what he was saying.

---

[58] In the poem *Matza isha*, printed in Jacob Frances, *Kol Shirei*, ed. Naveh, 355.
[59] See, for example, S. A. Rosanes, *Qorot ha-Yehudim be-Turqiya ve-Artzot ha-Qedem* (Sofia, 1938), 21-23; Y. Ratzhabi, *Yalqut ha-Maqama ha-ᶜIvrit* (Jerusalem, 1974), 41-44.
[60] See Bregman, "Megamot Mithalfot."
[61] *Mahbarot*, ed. Yarden, 6.

XIII. Structures of Syntax and Rhetoric

1. Old Structures of Syntax

Up until the end of the seventeenth century, Hebrew sonnets were structured largely according to the rules of syntax established by Immanuel of Rome: complete separation between octave and sestet, an octave divided into two quatrains, and a sestet in a variety of syntactic divisions. Not only did most sonnets use this structure, but they even took Immanuel of Rome's cue to the extreme. Thus, while Immanuel preferred a syntax dividing the sestet into two tercets, he did not rule out other possibilities, such as uniting the sestet through syntax or dividing it into symmetrical pairs. But most later poets neglected these possibilities and preferred to compose their sonnets in syntax of two tercets.[1]

Because of this general tendency, the sonnets of Moses Zacuto are especially striking, for he was the only poet to divide many of his sestets into syntactic pairs of lines. He also established clear reciprocal relations between syntax and rhyme, creating syntax of three lines in sestets of three rhymes,[2] syntax of two lines in sestets of two rhymes. Let us take in example a sestet of the latter type:

> Why should I abandon my religious determination
> When the truth is there to help me?
> 'Tis not in mankind that I have hope of salvation
>
> For my eye turns towards the Divinity.
> I will hold fast and not let cease my investigation;
> The counsels of the wicked are far from me[3]

2. New Structures of Syntax

From Quatrains to Octave

Together with the traditional trend described above, a new concept of syntax is also evident in the renewed Hebrew sonnet from the beginning. This concept

---

[1] On Tchernikhowsky's viewpoint, which conflicted with that of Immanuel of Rome, and its acceptance in modern Hebrew poetry, see Bregman, Sharsheret ha–Zahav, 96–104.

[2] For an example, see Moses Zacuto, sonnet 192 in *Tzror Zehuvim*, ed. Bregman.

[3] Moses Zacuto, sonnet 186 in *Tzror Zehuvim*, ed. Bregman.

regards the octave not as two units, separate or parallel, as it were, to each other, but an octave of continuous syntax.

Such continuity already appears in the sonnets of Joseph Tzarfati. Each of his sonnets makes the subject explicit in the first line, usually through direct address, while the fifth line relates back to this subject without referring to it explicitly:

1–2: How, Solomon, can you abandon me, the prince of peace /of my soul . . .
5: If only I could see you . . .

1–2: Go quickly, lads, and listen to me . . .
5: Come to my hall . . . [4]

A slight dependence of the second quatrain on the first quatrain is found already in the sonnets of Immanuel of Rome, but Immanuel prefers to open the second quatrain with an explicit mention of the subject, whereas Tzarfati avoids this.

Tighter syntactic links between the quatrains are also evident already in the sixteenth century, surprisingly enough in the east rather than in Italy. David Onkineira united his quatrains into a single flowing sentence:

Blessed be the day wherein I was born
To see the labor of *Hesheq* and to suffer his yoke,
To be the target for the bows of his arrow,
To drown in his sea as I have drowned,

To dwell in his shade as I desired;
   To see his might, to utter his deeds,
   To see his changes, to recognize his treachery,
   To be tested in the furnace of affliction in which I am tested.[5]

This is a considerable deviation from Immanuel of Rome, whose traditions Onkineira knew and respected. Could Onkineira have had access to other, later examples of sonnets? We will discuss this point, and this specific sonnet itself, at greater length further on.[6]

An even tighter connection between quatrains is found in the work of Leone da Modena. He was apparently the first Hebrew poet to compose the quatrains as a complex sentence. In his *Me'az ʿavon avot* ("Since the iniquity of the forefathers"),[7] the octave is so united through the internal logic of syntax that the pause between the quatrains is negligible. In this matter, as in others, Leone da Modena was a path–breaker. Twelve of his sonnets[8] — more than one–third of

---

[4] Joseph Tzarfati, sonnets 40 and 42 in *Tzror Zehuvim*, ed. Bregman.
[5] David Onkineira, sonnet 87 in *Tzror Zehuvim*, ed. Bregman.
[6] See Chapter Fifteen.
[7] Leone da Modena, sonnet 116 in *Tzror Zehuvim*, ed. Bregman.

his entire corpus — have syntax of this kind. Obviously there is no coincidence here, but a system.

The syntactic unity of the octave becomes routine in the seventeenth century, primarily in the work of Baroque poets. Immanuel Frances linked quatrains through a syllogism that begins in the first line of the first quatrain, and continues into the first line of the second quatrain:

> If from the end of the land you hear songs. . . — Do not believe this. . .[9]
> If my hand does not reach . . . — Know . . .[10]
> On the wings of songs . . . fly, my songs . . . — Even if . . .[11]

A Single Sheet of Gold

A much bolder link between the octave and sestet also appears early on. Already Moses ben Joab, in his sonnet against women, *Emas ani ᶜofrot* ("I am sick of gazelles"),[12] writes:

> Line 8: Therefore I will sing a song like the Song of Ascents
> Line 9: To the inhabitants of the world: Let us deal wisely

Such links multiply in the seventeenth century,[13] primarily in the typically Baroque sonnets of Jacob and Immanuel Frances. In these, the syntax linking the octave to the sestet often connects most or even the entire poem into a single sentence. This is usually a complex sentence, beginning with a subordinate clause that is hard to stop in the middle. The poem becomes a single logical unit and must be read in the same breath.

Below are examples from sonnets in which the entire octave is nothing more than a subordinate phrase. The primary sentence begins in the ninth line, and the pause between the sections is negligible:

> When I remember the day that like burning fire / was the face of the gazelle . . . / when I remember the day as she was wringing her hands, / when to separate her . . . / the lovely girls rushed . . .
> — I wished more than anything . . .[14]

---

[8] Sonnets 107, 110, 116, 117, 121, 123, 126, 128, 129, 132, 134 and 137 in *Tzror Zehuvim*, ed. Bregman..

[9] Immanuel Frances, sonnet 327 in *Tzror Zehuvim*, ed. Bregman.

[10] Idem, sonnet 331 in *Tzror Zehuvim*, ed. Bregman.

[11] Idem, sonnet 324 in *Tzror Zehuvim*, ed. Bregman.

[12] Moses ben Joab, sonnet 48 in *Tzror Zehuvim*, ed. Bregman.

[13] See, for example, Mordechai Modena, sonnet 140 in *Tzror Zehuvim*, ed. Bregman; Isaac Nahar, sonnet 300.

[14] Jacob Frances, sonnet 238 in *Tzror Zehuvim*, ed. Bregman.

Did I not know you, love, of old / Did I not feel the work of your hand . . .
/ Did I not feel your flame in my heart . . . / Did I not . . .
— O love, today I'd have thought nothing of you[15]

This linear concept of syntax stands in complete contrast to Immanuel of Rome, who perceived the sonnet as a two-part poem and sought to reinforce this perception at every level of the poem: rhyme, meter, syntax, rhetoric, and subject development. It tightens the poem from within, and transfers its logical center of gravity from the beginning to the end. It creates a new Hebrew sonnet within the traditional prosodic framework.

This linear sonnet is a tense one. The tension that formerly reigned in the sestet of the old sonnet (in rhyme, strophe, and syntax), here dominates the poem as a whole. The message is propelled forward through a tightly woven syntax that stops at nothing, like a race–horse clearing the hurdles. The sonnet loses its simplicity; the meaning of these prosodic stops becomes complicated and a matter for interpretation.

This new type of sonnet existed in Italian and Spanish poetry. Its invention is attributed to Giovanni della Casa, an Italian poet of the sixteenth century already mentioned above as an important exponent of Petrarchism. Among the dozens of sonnets by Della Casa are many with the octave and sestet linked together by syntax. His style was disseminated throughout Europe, and a volume of his poetry had a place in the library of Milton, who composed sonnets of this kind in English.[16] Della Casa was apparently known and appreciated by Hebrew poets both in his own day and at a later period: two of his sonnets were translated into Hebrew by S. D. Luzzatto in his *Kinor Na'im* (Vienna, 1825).[17]

Della Casa expressed his affinity to the poetry of Petrarch through the unified sonnet. As already noted, Petrarch himself leaned towards a flowing syntax, and as a true Petrarchist Della Casa took this tendency to its extreme. Jacob and Immanuel Frances, who learned this Petrarchist motif from Della Casa or his followers, used it to good advantage in poetry of distinctly Baroque trends. It finds expression at various levels of the brothers' sonnets, and especially in the development of the subject, as we shall see below.

---

[15] Jacob Frances, sonnet 236 in *Tzror Zehuvim*, ed. Bregman.

[16] Milton, sonnets 1–15 in *Works*, ed. J. Mitford, 8 vols. (London, 1863), I: 157–66

[17] See Bregman, *Shevil ha–Zahav*, Appendix VII. And see Giovanni della Casa, *Le Rime*, ed. R. Fedi (Rome, 1978): "*Si concente penser*," 4; "*Affliger chi per voi*," 5; "*Cura che di timor*," 10; "*Solea per boschi*," 27; "*L'altero nido*," 39.

In Critical Theory

It is hard to find any explicit reference to the old structures of sonnet syntax in contemporary works of Hebrew critical theory. On the other hand, we do find very clear references to the new structures.[18] Here we have things from the horse's mouth himself, so to speak, for two manuscripts of *Meteq Sefatayim*[19] have a different version from the one published by Brody and quoted earlier.[20] Below is the unpublished version of Immanuel Frances's words:

> The sonnet has fourteen lines and I have therefore called it golden . . . since it is composed of fourteen lines in four parts . . .[21] It is an important poem, relating a single statement from the beginning to the end, with completeness and purity of language. Only, one who is not well–versed in the poems of the Italians will not succeed with them.

In this version of Frances's words, the sonnet turns into a well–crystallized unit, with the syntax uniting the words into a single statement propelled forward through the purity, clarity, and conciseness of its language. *Meteq Sefatayim* further expresses this trend through its demand for a single meter and a single stress the entire length of the poem, as already noted.

This concept of the Hebrew sonnet found a ready audience. Immanuel Frances's words reverberate in the description of the Hebrew sonnet given by Anania Coen at the beginning of the nineteenth century:

> And thus it is indeed a "golden poem": for when it is constructed with purity of language and sublimity of idea, and its ending is bound up with its beginning: nothing exceeds it! But let it be done with taste and good sense.[22]

---

[18] Not that a firm concept concerning this crucial element was lacking, but that it was expressed via demonstration rather than by theoretical explanation. The important *'Arugat ha–Bosem* by Archivolti supplied the first theoretical discussion of the genre in Hebrew, and made most of its regulations by just supplying a sonnet in illustration: *Mi yom asher haya* (sonnet 59 in *Tzror Zehuvim*, ed. Bregman).

[19] MS. Oxford, Bodleian Library 1991, fol. 11; MS. London, British Library 1077 (Add. 27095), fol. 12.

[20] See above, Chap. 10, Part 1.

[21] As already mentioned in Chapter Ten, the numerical value of the Hebrew word for gold, *zahav*, is fourteen. In this paragraph, the author calls the sonnet *di zahav*, which is twice fourteen.

[22] Coen, *Sefer Ruaḥ Ḥidasha*, 17.

3. Rhetorical Structures

The dramatic openings which separate Immanuel of Rome's sonnets into smaller rhetorical units do not make a comeback in the revived Hebrew sonnet, at least not with the same intensity or regularity. Dramatic cries that do sound highly emotional still appear at the beginning of a strophe even in the new Hebrew sonnets. But they are infrequent, and no more than a pale vestige of the old ways. The renewed Hebrew sonnet takes on a lower tone and is less bombastic, and less studded with biblical quotations in comparison with Immanuel of Rome. All this quickens the pace and emphasizes a linear trend also evident in many sonnets through syntactic links, whether strong or loose.

And yet it is precisely the Frances brothers, with their tendency to bring the linear concept to its extreme, who preserve Immanuel of Rome's high–flown rhetoric, along with his dramatic and abrupt kinds of openings. Quite a few of their sonnets open with a perfect storm of emotion:

> Woe is me!
> O doctors, how long will you empty the world of its inhabitants!
> Death, O death!
> What is it, and why is it, you wild boar of the forest![23]

In some of their sonnets the rhetoric emphasizes strophic division, while syntax and other elements work to unify the poem. Thus the opening line separates the quatrains and ostensibly makes the first quatrain (I) parallel to the second quatrain (II), just like the sonnets of Immanuel of Rome:

I: O woe, woe . . .!	II:	Woe![24]
I: What can I do . . . ?	II:	Who would believe . . . ?[25]
I: O, those who link their fate . . .	II:	Woe, all who thirst . . .[26]

Likewise, the first tercet (III) is separated from the second tercet (IV) and made parallel to it by similar openings:

> III: What can there be between me and the gazelle . . . ?
> IV: ʿafar ("dust") and not ʿofera ("a gazelle") will I hug tomorrow![27]

---

[23] Jacob Frances, sonnets 287, 260, 289, and 243 in *Tzror Zehuvim*, ed. Bregman. For other examples, see Bregman, *Shevil ha–Zahav*, 143.
[24] Jacob Frances, sonnet 287 in *Tzror Zehuvim*, ed. Bregman.
[25] Idem, sonnet 239 in *Tzror Zehuvim*, ed. Bregman.
[26] Idem, sonnet 242 in *Tzror Zehuvim*, ed. Bregman.
[27] Idem, sonnet 287 in *Tzror Zehuvim*, ed. Bregman.

III: When I say . . .
IV: My heart responds . . .²⁸

III: Do not believe . . .
IV: If you ask . . .²⁹

The rhetorical structure in the Baroque sonnet is likely to divide the poem in two, as in the trend established by Immanuel of Rome. In such cases, the octave (I) and sestet (II) are clearly separated from each other by the rhetoric, which crystallizes each quatrain unto itself through the use of anaphoras or other words similar to each other:

I: Even if the nations will rage . . . even if the camp of Satan will march . . . even if my skies . . . even if they send arrows . . .
II: I will bring down . . . I will turn them . . . I will make them . . . I will say.³⁰

In contrast to all these, the rhetoric sometimes consolidates the octave (I) and sestet (II) into a single unit, despite the strophic division:

I: Fortified cities . . . I destroyed . . . the heads of camps I scorned . . . hearts . . . I melted . . . crushed . . .
II: Germany and Greece . . . I frightened . . . my thoughts I turned . . . by the hand of an evil doctor I died.³¹

And sometimes the rhetoric serves the interest of both these conflicting trends. On the one hand it links the first three strophes:

I: sun, the lantern of the world . . . sun, the glory of the earth . . .
II: sun, the father of warmth . . . sun, the source of light . . .
III: sun . . .³²

while on the other, it separates the octave and sestet in the very same sonnet:

I: the lantern of the world . . . the glory of the earth . . . the joy of hearts . . . the source of light . . .

---

[28] Idem, sonnet 239 in *Tzror Zehuvim*, ed. Bregman.
[29] Idem, sonnet 242 in *Tzror Zehuvim*, ed. Bregman.
[30] Immanuel Frances, sonnet 309 in *Tzror Zehuvim*, ed. Bregman.
[31] Jacob Frances, sonnet 259 in *Tzror Zehuvim*, ed. Bregman.
[32] Immanuel Frances, sonnet 311 in *Tzror Zehuvim*, ed. Bregman.

II: My tongue . . . was loath . . . to tell . . . I knew . . . I will raise . . . I will say[33]

Both subject and rhetoric undergo a transformation from octave to sestet.

The conflicting goals of rhetorical structures fuel the tension that already exists in the sonnet due to syntax, whether verbal or musical. Yet they also create a clear–cut framework that disguises the tension with a cloak of harmony and poetic virtuosity. The rhetorical structure is a necessary instrument for expressing the Baroque perception of reality, whether it provides a disguise, a catalyst, or an element of confusion and complication.

---

[33] Immanuel Frances, sonnet 311 in *Tzror Zehuvim*, ed. Bregman.

XIV. Developing the Subject

1. A Wealth of Development Models

If we examine the ways in which poets developed the subject in the renewed Hebrew sonnet, we discover a surprising richness. In addition to the model used by Immanuel of Rome, which poets absorbed and refined, we also find ten other clear-cut models for developing the subject, not to mention variations, spin-offs, and one-time solutions for a single sonnet. This wide range stands in stark contrast to Immanuel of Rome's method for developing his theme, since this practically revolves around one standard model. It also contradicts the evident tendency in the new corpus to remain faithful to just a few tried and true techniques, to make minimal use of poetic options, and to pile on restrictions.

Because there were so many ways to develop the theme, the new Hebrew sonnet was constantly undergoing self-regeneration. Strict rules of prosody guarded the sonnet-form like a fortress from "without" and permitted change and flexibility from "within". With its clear-cut outline and relatively high potential for internal flexibility, the Hebrew sonnet of the period amply illustrates the idea that poets best "show their stuff" when challenged by strict verse-forms and tightly limited restrictions.

In developing their themes, poets of the sixteenth and seventeenth centuries realized the unique qualities of the form in a way that Immanuel of Rome almost never did. One reason for this was the fact that in the sixteenth century the Hebrew sonnet absorbed an intellectual trend prevalent in Italian sonnets since Petrarch.[1]

The sonnet-form is unrivaled in its ability to construct an argument, for it unfolds according to the same logic. Following Italian theory of the fourteenth century, we can metaphorically describe the sonnet's musical-prosodic structure as a logical argument: the first strophe presents a thesis, subject, or situation; the second clarifies and emphasizes; the third introduces doubt; the fourth draws the appropriate conclusion.[2] This metaphor is often realized in practice, though it is not an actual requirement of the verse-form. The different structures in which logical discourse unfolds can be adapted to the structures of the sonnet in a variety of ways, as we shall see below. Now, it is often easier for poets to cope with the intellectual, rather than the lyrical side of things. The latter requires introspection

---

[1] See above, Chap. 7, Part 1.
[2] See for example, Fuller, *The Sonnet*, 2.

and a convincing expression of emotion. It easily founders through over-sentimentality or verbosity and runs the risk of "getting stuck." Intellectual development, on the other hand, is less likely to encounter such problems. It proved particularly comfortable for the Hebrew poet, who shied away from expressions of emotion due to social norms. The intellectual side is also relatively easier to formulate, and Hebrew could already boast of appropriate idioms for the sonnet from the language of correspondence, study, and prayer. These idioms were readily available in treatises on rhetoric, philosophical discourse, biblical commentary and Talmudic dialectics, fields in which the educated Hebrew poet felt at home. The greater intellectual element in the Hebrew sonnet did not keep a poet from being lyrical, but it did increase the number of ways he could develop his subject and it opened up the verse-form to any educated Jew.

Independent creativity in the area of thematic development received particular encouragement in the seventeenth century through the criticism directed at Immanuel of Rome. The monotony which we noted in his system of development was now considered a basic poetic weakness, especially from the perspective of the Baroque poet who sought to compress his message and make it flow smoothly. Poets of this period tended to joke about an excess of space, a problem which, in their opinion, confronted the novice writer of sonnets. The joke found expression in a whole sequence of sonnets-on-the-sonnet in various languages.[3] Immanuel Frances wrote a poem in this vein which, in his words, is "like a body without a soul."[4] In his case, however, the criticism came not in a sonnet-on-a-sonnet, but an octave-on-an-octave:

> An octave did my son request
> So I took my pen to write a bit
> But I'd scarce begun at his behest
> When lo! I saw there's half of it.
> With the help of God I'll do the rest
> And make it with his wishes fit
> Two lines remained as yet undone —
> But the poem's already done!

Not for Immanuel Frances to pen fourteen whole lines for nothing! Even when mocking the problem of excess space he preferred things compact.

This attitude explains why, after having accepted most elements of Immanuel of Rome's rhyme and meter, Immanuel Frances criticized the alternating rhyme characteristic of his predecessor's sonnets. Frances saw this kind of rhyme as an obstacle to the smooth flow of the poem's message and a symptom of

---

[3] See Kastner, "Concerning the Sonnet of the Sonnet."
[4] Immanuel Frances, *Meteq Sefatayim*, ed. Brody, 53.

over-stylization. In claiming that Immanuel of Rome wrote his sonnets with a heavy hand, Frances is referring to the interruption of the poem's flow due to alternating rhyme.[5]

All considered, we might have expected poets to shelve Immanuel of Rome's method for developing the theme. But despite the problems of this, and despite the criticism leveled against it and the diffusion of the Hebrew sonnet in many new directions, we find that the old method remains remarkably strong.

Many poets accepted Immanuel's method intact, or made various changes. Others accepted certain elements but combined them in new models. It can be said that Immanuel's technique in fact served as the prototype for most developmental models. Let us now review the different models one by one.

2. Models for Developing the Subject

Immanuel of Rome's Model

Throughout the period we find a not inconsiderable number of sonnets using the basic principle of Immanuel's technique for developing the theme: division between situation and reflection, separation into different parts, and relegation of the reflexive part to the end of the poem.[6] In the first part of these sonnets we find a wide variety of situations already from the beginning of the period; some exalted and "poetic," such as falling in love[7] or the poet's silence;[8] others realistic, such as intestinal sickness,[9] the scandal of a "defrocked rabbi,"[10] and old age.[11] After the situation comes reflection, which expresses emotion, explains things, or evaluates and judges. Whether the sonnet is divided into an octave and a sestet or into some other division, the sonnet remains a two-part poem.

The system also became accepted in the *sonetto caudato*, as we see in *Yashen be-mizmor shir* ("Asleep in the melody of song")[12] by Leone da Modena, which praises Israel Najara's volume of poetry *Shirat Yisrael* ("The Songs of Israel").

---

[5] *Meteq Sefatayim*, ed. Brody, 48.
[6] See examples in *Tzror Zehuvim*, ed. Bregman: Joseph Tzarfati, sonnet 43; Moses ben Joab, sonnet 47; Samuel Archivolti, sonnet 61; Solomon Oliveyra, sonnet 342; David Tzarfati, sonnet 376; Daniel Belilios, sonnet 305; and the sonnets of the Frances brothers, which will be discussed below.
[7] David Onkineira, sonnet 85 in *Tzror Zehuvim*, ed. Bregman.
[8] Moses ben Joab, sonnet 47 in *Tzror Zehuvim*, ed. Bregman.
[9] Idem, sonnet 47 in *Tzror Zehuvim*, ed. Bregman.
[10] Samuel Archivolti, sonnet 61 in *Tzror Zehuvim*, ed. Bregman.
[11] Immanuel Frances, sonnet 335 in *Tzror Zehuvim*, ed. Bregman.
[12] Leone da Modena, sonnet 127 in *Tzror Zehuvim*, ed. Bregman.

The situational part details the strong impression which the volume made on the poet; the reflection explains the phenomenon through the excellence of its content, and the "tail" is an additional reflexive link that continues with a direct challenge to the reader and a recommendation to use the book.

Other characteristics of Immanuel of Rome's technique were sporadically absorbed, especially in sonnets that were developed according to his technique. Such characteristics belong primarily to the typical reflexive part of the sonnet and thus appear in the latter lines, in keeping with his tradition.

The poet addresses himself:

— "If so, adhere to God alone, my heart."[13]
— "My heart, drunk with pride, sober up!"[14]
— "Do not moan, my soul, nor be cast down."[15]

He presents himself as the author of the poem, and speaks about his poetry:

— "About my soul-mate on cymbals or lyre / I shall sing. . . . / how can there be a song in my mouth, with me grown old?"[16]
— "O God, make my hand a pen of lead! / I will write on metals and slabs of marble / in memory of . . ."[17]
— "Therefore in this poem I praise / David Samuel"[18]
— "What can I say about your greatness?"[19]

He expands on a subject already discussed, and rephrases his description:

— "You they will call 'sage' and 'explainer'" [20]
— "I will be judged right for calling you a `star of poetry'." [21]
— "It is not the poor community you should blame." [22]

Verbs of speech call attention to the rhetorical nature of the reflection:

---

[13] Jacob Frances, sonnet 287 in *Tzror Zehuvim*, ed. Bregman.
[14] Jacob Frances, sonnet 285 in *Tzror Zehuvim*, ed. Bregman.
[15] Immanuel Frances, sonnet 334 in *Tzror Zehuvim*, ed. Bregman.
[16] Samuel Archivolti, sonnet 69 in *Tzror Zehuvim*, ed. Bregman.
[17] Leone da Modena, sonnet 128 in *Tzror Zehuvim*, ed. Bregman.
[18] Solomon Lustro, sonnet 409 in *Tzror Zehuvim*, ed. Bregman.
[19] Abraham Tzemah, sonnet 393 in *Tzror Zehuvim*, ed. Bregman.
[20] Isaac Nahar, sonnet 300 in *Tzror Zehuvim*, ed. Bregman.
[21] Jacob Frances, sonnet 253 in *Tzror Zehuvim*, ed. Bregman.
[22] Idem, sonnet 274 in *Tzror Zehuvim*, ed. Bregman.

— "Angels spoke . . ." [23]
— "But what am I to utter your greatness?" [24]
— "I will jeer at them and say . . ." [25]

A figure indirectly presented in the situation (I) is confronted by the poet in the reflection (II), in direct speech:

I: "This Judah, whose eyes opened . . ."
II: "[Who] brings evil to his people, abandon your path!" [26]

I: "A scoundrel, crushed like grain with a pestle"
II: "Take it easy, lad!" [27]

I: "Wisdom and morality the fools mocked"
II: "In vain will you struggle! / amongst the pens of the ox and ass you will sleep." [28]

Immanuel's imprint on the renewed Hebrew sonnet is also evident in the use of idioms characteristic of his reflective sections, such as "Woe is me!" or "What can I say?"[29]

After the model was absorbed, it was often improved in new ways. This is especially striking in sonnets by the brothers Jacob and Immanuel Frances, Immanuel's stern critics, who despite their criticism did not hesitate to make ample use of his method. They took full advantage of various traits of the model in order to emphasize new points.

One of the most fundamental elements in the baroque sonnets of the Frances brothers is the element of suspense. Information vital to understanding the poem is delayed as long as possible in order to excite curiosity and heighten the tension. This technique, when joined to a syntax that unites the poem into a single whole, forces it to be read in one fell swoop. Anania Coen dwelt on this developmental technique, referring to it by its Italian name, *sospenzione*. As an example Coen cited a translated "golden poem" which keeps the reader in suspense till the poem

---

[23] Johanan (Angelo) Alatrini, sonnet 72 in *Tzror Zehuvim*, ed. Bregman.
[24] Abraham Tzemah, sonnet 393 in *Tzror Zehuvim*, ed. Bregman.
[25] Immanuel Frances, sonnet 327 in *Tzror Zehuvim*, ed. Bregman.
[26] Judah Briel, sonnet 388 in *Tzror Zehuvim*, ed. Bregman.
[27] Jacob Frances, sonnet 246 in *Tzror Zehuvim*, ed. Bregman.
[28] Immanuel Frances, sonnet 323 in *Tzror Zehuvim*, ed. Bregman.
[29] For examples see *Tzror Zehuvim*, ed. Bregman: Joseph Penso, sonnet 364; Jacob Frances, sonnet 267; Samuel Bassan, sonnet 151.

reveals itself, at the very end, to be a "lament of a lover over his beloved, since she ignores his desire."[30]

Immanuel's developmental technique limited the suspense of situational information to the boundaries of the first section. But this section, as we have seen, was not restricted to the octave and might well go beyond it. And indeed, the Frances brothers have quite a number of sonnets in which the suspense was created precisely on Immanuel's model. These usually begin with a dramatic cry that begins seemingly out of the blue:

— "My brother, who are these bewailing their sins? . . . "[31]

Only in line 5 does it become clear: the people who considered Shabbetai Zevi the messiah.

— "Desist, fools, desist!"[32]

Only in lines 6-7 is the situation clarified: "No, no man will tempt me to take / a wife."

The moderation and stylization that characterized the situational part in the sonnets of Immanuel of Rome now gave way to dramatic tension and compact, forthright speech.

The static quality of Immanuel's method also faded in sonnets when the reflexive part underwent change in the spirit of the Baroque. Here it developed in unexpected ways, becoming increasingly complex and convoluted: jumping from one situation to another, and making generalizations about all of them;[33] taking a stand, ostensibly retreating from it and then returning to it ironically;[34] explaining and contradicting;[35] explaining and generalizing; posing difficulties and brushing them away; and always, always innovating.[36]

Unlike the old sonnet, the chief part of the Baroque sonnet comes at the end of the poem. It is here that the tangled syntax gets untangled; here that the suspense reaches its end. The main part of the message, therefore, is likely to be delayed to the reflexive part. For example, in the sonnet *Ba ha-tzevi elai* ("There came to me, my friend")[37] by Jacob Frances, we hear about an undesirable

---

[30] Coen, *Sefer Ruaḥ Ḥadashah*, 73-74; and see Appendix VIII in Bregman, *Shevil ha-Zahav*.

[31] Jacob Frances, sonnet 282 in *Tzror Zehuvim*, ed. Bregman.

[32] Idem, sonnet 243 in *Tzror Zehuvim*, ed. Bregman.

[33] Idem, sonnet 247 and 286 in *Tzror Zehuvim*, ed. Bregman.

[34] Idem, sonnet 244 in *Tzror Zehuvim*, ed. Bregman.

[35] Idem, sonnet 269 in *Tzror Zehuvim*, ed. Bregman.

[36] Idem, sonnets 266 and 273 in *Tzror Zehuvim*, ed. Bregman.

[37] Idem, sonnet 244 in *Tzror Zehuvim*, ed. Bregman.

marriage. The reflection predicts a sad ending for the groom and ends on a note of profound sarcasm:

> Let this be a consolation to you, that if you err
> You err in the Law of God, and everlasting Paradise
> Will merit, since you'll already have had enough Hell.[38]

There is nothing before the last tercet to prepare the reader for this sharp conclusion, so while it is still a reflection, it is nevertheless completely new and unexpected.

Thus the kinds of bold matters that commonly come at the beginning of sonnets by Immanuel of Rome, we now find at the end of sonnets by Jacob Frances, even when these were composed according to the old model of development. Thoughts about death, ever present for the Baroque poet, were delayed till the last line, bringing the poem to its pointed, macabre end in a highly elliptical way:

> — "I long for the day of my death like [I long for] the messiah."[39]
> — "Between you and the gallows is like a hair's breadth."[40]

Baroque sonnets used elements characteristic of Immanuel's model for contradictory purposes. The expanded reflection, which sometimes spilled into the octave in the old sonnet and impeded the poem's development, was used by the Baroque sonnet to create a surprise effect. To take one example, let us look at a sonnet by Jacob Frances: "A scoundrel, crushed like grain with a pestle / the body of a graceful gazelle" (*Naval kerifot*).[41] In this sonnet, which describes a case of wife-beating, the description of the beating is crammed into the first quatrain. The reflective part breaks in early, rebuking the wife-beater up till the last line of the poem. There it suddenly turns against the woman, and accusing her of prostitution, suggests that she be killed with a quick knife-thrust. Here and in similar sonnets, the longer the reflective part of the poem, the more powerful the surprise.

Evaluation, a simple reflective element in Immanuel of Rome's method, becomes increasingly complex in the new poem, fostering antithesis and the creation of powerful conclusions:

> — "How can you be the head of these lions? / You're not worth the excretions from their hind parts!"[42]

---

[38] Idem, sonnet 244 in *Tzror Zehuvim*, ed. Bregman.
[39] Idem, sonnet 238 in *Tzror Zehuvim*, ed. Bregman.
[40] Idem, sonnet 271 in *Tzror Zehuvim*, ed. Bregman.
[41] Idem, sonnet 246 in *Tzror Zehuvim*, ed. Bregman.
[42] Idem, sonnet 265 in *Tzror Zehuvim*, ed. Bregman.

— "Though this man is very bad and foolish / he could be your teacher in book knowledge, / but in evil he is not even worthy of being your pupil!"[43]

When the speaker is confronted in the reflection with one of the factors in the situation, this can create a particularly pointed evaluation. In Baroque sonnets it is his own self that the poet confronts, and this gives the sonnet a sense of depth and sincerity:

— "Did I not fear the Living God / . . . before your eyes I'd put a knife to my throat."[44]
— "My heart, drunk with pride, sober up!"[45]
— "Alas, that my iniquities have already passed over / my head."[46]

In order to complicate things even more, the evaluation itself is evaluated and the situation re-evaluated from a contradictory viewpoint:

— "What can I say, my pen, how could my words veer / today from the truth?"[47]
— "Some say they hated you, and that this / fast is so that God will kill you. But they were foolish . . . / Better they feast while you look on / . . . so that you'll die from envy."[48]
— "You were right in saying that I resembled an idol . . . [but] I will be vindicated for calling you / a star . . ."[49]

Reflection and Situation (Leone da Modena's Model)

One easy solution to the weakness of the sestet — a problem in Immanuel's model — was found by switching the order of the different parts. In the model before us, the sonnet opens with the reflection and ends with the situation. This order delays the discovery of the necessary information, so that the beginning of the poem is fraught with a certain tension and the end becomes dynamic. Such a structure is well suited to the argumentative nature of the sonnet.

The model appears incidentally in one of Archivolti's sonnets.[50] In the sonnets of Leone da Modena it appears regularly and more emphatically. Most

---

[43] Idem, sonnet 267 in *Tzror Zehuvim*, ed. Bregman.
[44] Idem, sonnet 289 in *Tzror Zehuvim*, ed. Bregman.
[45] Idem, sonnet 285 in *Tzror Zehuvim*, ed. Bregman.
[46] Idem, sonnet 283 in *Tzror Zehuvim*, ed. Bregman.
[47] Idem, sonnet 267 in *Tzror Zehuvim*, ed. Bregman.
[48] Idem, sonnet 269 in *Tzror Zehuvim*, ed. Bregman.
[49] Idem, sonnet 253 in *Tzror Zehuvim*, ed. Bregman.
[50] Samuel Archivolti, sonnet 68 in *Tzror Zehuvim*, ed. Bregman.

of his sonnets are occasional poems, and in these the situation is paramount. The reflection in this model serves as a festive opening that lends solemnity to the situation. Major elements in these poems are the blessing and the noting of the occasion. In this model, they are situated at the center of the poem: the blessing usually at the end of the first part, and the occasion in the line that begins the second, situational part (the line-number, below, is in parentheses). A sense of actuality is emphasized in the poem through use of the word "today":

— "May the songbird of my poem shine its face upon you . . .
(5) Today, for how comely are thy tents."[51]

— "My heart goes out to the law-makers of Israel . . .
(5) Today, Lord, my heart came across . . ."[52]

— "A majestic thick-branched cedar / the Lord called you . . ."
(9) Today, whose fruit . . ."[53]

As is evident from the examples above, the opening reflection reveals elements of Immanuel's style. The poet appears in person, expresses an opinion, evaluates, addresses himself, mentions a name. Postponing the mention of the occasion to the center of the poem is, on the other hand, one of the stylistic traits characterizing Judah da Leone. It is intentional, even forced, but it serves his purpose.

Generally, Leone da Modena limits the reflection to the octave and the situation to the sestet; but because of its importance the situation sometimes begins in the second strophe, as in the first two examples above. Another basic element in the occasional poem is the name of the addressee or his sobriquet, which in this model always comes in the part containing the situation; in other words, never in the first strophe. This provided another way of filling up the end of the poem. The model described here was primarily used for festive occasions,[54] though we do find it in other sonnets as well.[55]

Situation and Conclusion

The model begins with a situation and leads to a conclusion. The situation, for example, might be that anyone who reads this book recognizes its importance and taste; the conclusion, that everyone should read this book. Or, the sinner will

---

[51] Leone da Modena, sonnet 108 in *Tzror Zehuvim*, ed. Bregman.
[52] Idem, sonnet 125 in *Tzror Zehuvim*, ed. Bregman.
[53] Idem, sonnet 120 in *Tzror Zehuvim*, ed. Bregman.
[54] See examples in *Tzror Zehuvim*, ed. Bregman: Samuel Caceres, sonnet 297; Isaac Nahar, sonnet 301; Moses Zacuto, sonnets 228 and 217.
[55] E.g. Immanuel Frances, sonnet 316 in *Tzror Zehuvim*, ed. Bregman.

get what's coming to him on the Day of Judgment; hence it is better not to sin. A son is born under an auspicious sky; therefore he will enjoy a happy life.[56]

Sometimes the conclusion is a reflection, and then it is reminiscent of the model used by Immanuel of Rome. Poets occasionally played with this model by making hypotheses and then distorting the logic: the situation is not that way but this;[57] the situation is this, but that too, hence the conclusion is not this, but that.[58] Startling conclusions help sharpen the point. Jacob Frances jeers at doctors for diagnosing patients by the look of their urine,[59] and in a sonnet against the disciples of Shabbetai Zevi exchanges an imaginary conclusion for a true one and ends by making a surprising point:[60]

> If your heart fancies a lamb chop
> Take a stick from it to strike your rib
> But not a rib of it for you to eat.

This model is likely to have a passage explaining the situation or the conclusion. The logic goes like this: "thus — because — therefore . . ."; or: "thus — therefore — because . . ." For example, the octave in one sonnet by Immanuel Frances describes "the gazelle's shining hair / hiding the lovers' trap." The first tercet then explains: "Did Cupid not draw his bow like an enemy?" The conclusion in the second tercet is "Therefore, friends, be careful not to approach," and so forth.[61]

This model was used for panegyrics. First the person being honored is described in terms of his work or his special traits, followed by praise and benedictions in conclusion.[62]

Conclusion and Situation

This model is similar to the reflection-situation model except that the first part contains a clear conclusion. We find it, for example, in the opening lines of the sonnet printed in facsimile at the end of Chapter Eleven, where the poet's soul is addressed:

[56] Elijah Mazal-Tov Modena, sonnet 154 in *Tzror Zehuvim*, ed. Bregman; Abraham Ortona (in MS. 1250 of the Jewish Theological Seminary of New York, fol. 29; the sonnet begins: *Im ha-levana*), Moses Abudiente, sonnet 302; Jacob Sasportas, sonnet 371; Moses Zacuto, sonnet 28.

[57] Moses Zacuto, sonnet 228 in *Tzror Zehuvim*, ed. Bregman.

[58] Immanuel Frances, sonnet 313 in *Tzror Zehuvim*, ed. Bregman.

[59] Jacob Frances, sonnet 260 in *Tzror Zehuvim*, ed. Bregman.

[60] Idem, sonnet 277 in *Tzror Zehuvim*, ed. Bregman.

[61] Immanuel Frances, sonnet 306 in *Tzror Zehuvim*, ed. Bregman.

[62] See examples in *Tzror Zehuvim*, ed. Bregman: Anonymous, sonnet 74; Moses Merari, sonnet 348.

O delicate one, pure one, pray take care
To consider my laws and understand my secret.[63]

This request receives added force from the situation described in the continuation of the sonnet.

The model was used to preach morality. The sonnet would open with a moral, as in ʿUra, beni, ʿur mi-tenumatekha ("Awake, my son, waken from your slumber")[64] by Judah Moscato, or, in a sonnet by Menahem Azariah da Fano, in the opening lines:

You whose heart wishes himself counted
Amongst the great ones of the world,
Run and follow the righteous.[65]

This is then followed by a description of the "righteous" and their good deeds.

This model is unrivaled in its ability to delay vital information. The conclusion piques curiosity, and the situation can be stretched out till the very end of the poem. One sonnet by Jacob Frances tells of an unnamed individual more wicked than Ashmedai, king of the demons, whose time has now come to burn in hell. But the poet switches the order of things. First he calls on the demon king to light the flames in order to burn a newcomer to hell. Then he explains who has died, and ends with a warning: "If you take pity on him, O Ashmedai, / tomorrow he'll brazenly steal your crown."[66]

A variation of this model is a conclusion *despite* the situation. In a dramatic monologue someone explains how he became one of the Shabbateans: Shabbetai Zevi is a false prophet; but since his followers are getting rich, I, too, his unbeliever, have joined him. All this is given in reverse order. At first comes the situation and an illogical conclusion: "What can we have in common, Zevi, when I've had nothing but evil to say about you?" At the end of the poem comes the basis for this development: "Whoever puts his hope in you / is saying to wood, 'wake up'; to stone, 'arise!'"[67] This reversal reflects the warped attitude of a speaker who acts against his own belief, and holds the entire Shabbatean movement up to a distorted mirror.

---

[63] Azariah de' Rossi, sonnet 49 in *Tzror Zehuvim*, ed. Bregman.
[64] Judah Moscato, sonnet 55 in *Tzror Zehuvim*, ed. Bregman.
[65] Menahem Azariah da Fano, sonnet 73 in *Tzror Zehuvim*, ed. Bregman.
[66] Jacob Frances, sonnet 270 in *Tzror Zehuvim*, ed. Bregman.
[67] Idem, sonnet 278 in *Tzror Zehuvim*, ed. Bregman.

Problem and Solution

This model describes inner turmoil and offers a solution for it. For example: the speaker complains that he is overcome by desire; desire has taken over his heart and does with him as it pleases. The problem is set forth in the octave. The sestet suggests a solution: fighting against the uninvited guest and annihilating him.[68] Another example: bad luck controls the poet's life. The solution: to fight valiantly for the spiritual values that cannot be put under its control.[69] The Baroque solution is likely to be grim. The miserable wretch anxious to end his life consoles himself: "Death will heal your ills."[70]

Sonnets composed according to this model on the subject of the Jewish people begin with the woes suffered by the Jews and then shift to the idea of redemption.[71] In sonnets of praise, the person being honored is the one who will solve the problem set forth at the beginning of the poem: it is he who glorifies the prestige of the Hebrew language,[72] or cures the sick,[73] or explains conundrums.[74] Here the problem and solution are likely to become purely rhetorical, boiling down to a question — "who is the most esteemed doctor, the most talented craftsman", or whatever — and to an answer that identifies the subject of his panegyric.[75]

Various techniques made the model more sophisticated. Immanuel Frances stretched out one question till the last line, and then answered it only in a riddle.[76] There is something similar in one of Archivolti's sonnets. There the speaker asks: Why am I subjected to a life of abject slavery? The solution: By virtue of my humility, I will bear the messiah on my back. All this is very puzzling, but indeed this is a riddle-sonnet and the reader is supposed to guess who the speaker is.[77] To a typical Baroque problem — love for two women — we are given two possible solutions, neither of them any less Baroque: let an additional heart grow in the lover's chest, or let his heart be torn in two.[78]

The sophistication of the model was achieved by means of an ironic message, as in the following example. The problem: falling in love with a painted picture,

---

[68] Nathan Orvieto, sonnet 148 in *Tzror Zehuvim*, ed. Bregman.
[69] Immanuel Frances, sonnet 333 in *Tzror Zehuvim*, ed. Bregman.
[70] Idem, sonnet 335 in *Tzror Zehuvim*, ed. Bregman.
[71] See examples in *Tzror Zehuvim*, ed. Bregman: Jacob Segrè, sonnet 93; Immanuel Frances, sonnet 329.
[72] E.g. Leone da Modena, sonnet 129 in *Tzror Zehuvim*, ed. Bregman.
[73] E.g. Solomon Lustro, sonnet 407 in *Tzror Zehuvim*, ed. Bregman.
[74] Idem, sonnet 409 in *Tzror Zehuvim*, ed. Bregman.
[75] E.g. in *Tzror Zehuvim*, ed. Bregman: David Luria, sonnet 145; Leone da Modena, sonnet 125.
[76] Immanuel Frances, sonnet 317 in *Tzror Zehuvim*, ed. Bregman.
[77] See Pagis, ʿAl Sod Ḥatum, 58.
[78] Immanuel Frances, sonnet 312 in *Tzror Zehuvim*, ed. Bregman.

an unresponsive plank of wood. The solution: to see the good side of the situation, which is the superiority of a still block of wood over a live and aggravating woman. In order to develop the irony in this sonnet, the problem-and-solution model was woven into a rhetorical model in the manner of Immanuel of Rome. To accomplish this the poet made a rather grating revision in the first draft of the poem. The octave is addressed to "Cupid" and the sestet should thus have carried his response, but in the second draft the words signaling Cupid's answer ("then he answered: 'Woe to you, man . . .'") were erased and replaced with the words: "And my heart answered."[79] The reflexive version that ultimately received preference inverts the rhetorical structure of the poem and transfers the source of the distortion to the soul.

While the Frances brothers wrote a large number of ironic sonnets along this model, they also wrote some that are impressive indeed for their unaffected stance and straightforward logic. In one of these Jacob Frances thinks about death on his wedding day, broods over the final, unavoidable separation and subsequent loneliness, but then says to himself: "Much knowledge is an obstacle before me / . . . On a day for rejoicing, please let yourself rejoice."[80] Immanuel Frances complains: "From the day I wandered from your tent / I've found no rest, my bride, for my soul"; and consoles himself: "I've already found a refuge inside your heart."[81]

Solution and Problem

"Death, Death! O Heavens, do me a favor and let me die!" — This Baroque solution, which usually appears at the end of sonnets,[82] can also come at the beginning, as in this sonnet by Jacob Frances. After praying for release by death, the poem describes suffering, anguish, the desire to die, and a fear of going mad. Similar to this is another sonnet that, parodying the traditional prayer for rain (*Abiaʿ zemirot*), begins "Go, wealth, in peace! Come in peace, poverty!"[83] The opening already provides the solution to the classic paradox: the more money, the more worries.

One variation of the model was to cram both the solution and problem into the octave, and to devote the sestet to reflection, like Immanuel.[84]

---

[79] Jacob Frances, sonnet 239 in *Tzror Zehuvim*, ed. Bregman.
[80] Idem, sonnet 241 in *Tzror Zehuvim*, ed. Bregman.
[81] Immanuel Frances, sonnet 310 in *Tzror Zehuvim*, ed. Bregman.
[82] Idem, sonnets 334 and 289 in *Tzror Zehuvim*, ed. Bregman; see also sonnet 335.
[83] Jacob Frances, sonnet 284 in *Tzror Zehuvim*, ed. Bregman.
[84] Immanuel Frances, sonnet 320 in *Tzror Zehuvim*, ed. Bregman.

Comparing Similarities

Some development models rely on an external matter that is not intrinsically related to the situation under discussion. This model serves to compare similarities. It is likely to come at the beginning of the sonnet, before the subject of the poem is made clear. For example: just as one sees the flowering of spring and is amazed by its beauty, so too the reader of this book is impressed by its special qualities.[85] Or, just as fishermen are patient and hunters courageous, so "the righteous man rebukes / one who deviates from God's ways, and is full of evil."[86] Or, just as someone who deals with the laws of sacrifice is counted as meritorious as though he had actually offered a sacrifice, and just as good thoughts and prayer are as pleasing to God as sacrifice, so too writing a book about the inauguration of the Temple is just as meritorious as actually building it.[87]

In the openings to sonnets of this kind, the words "just as" are often replaced by "if": "If all time looms above our head," "If the orbs of the heavenly stars," "If a man that studies the law of our Rock".[88] The word of comparison, usually *ken* ("so is"), opens the second half of the comparison. Leone da Modena, who emphasizes the day of the event, as noted, includes in this model the transition from the subject of the poem by noting the time: just as the first man was completed by the creation of woman, so is the groom on the day of his wedding.[89]

But sometimes the subject of the poem comes before the comparison. For example, the rabbi who has been summoned to the World of Truth is like the sun, which sets on one side of the globe in order to illuminate the other.[90]

Making Contrasts

This model introduces a non-related subject in order to contrast it with the subject of the poem. For example, of a bridegroom it might be said: "There are many who become wise by studying books, but these are evil-doers. You, however, are not only studious but also righteous like your fathers before you."[91] Or, "Many are those bloated with pride / who brag about their family pedigree, / but in you Torah, priesthood and greatness are combined."[92] Moses Zacuto spelled out this technique in the body of one sonnet, writing: "So with you, too, dear friend, but

---

[85] Mordechai Modena, sonnet 140 in *Tzror Zehuvim*, ed. Bregman.
[86] Moses Hefetz Gentili, sonnet 389 in *Tzror Zehuvim*, ed. Bregman.
[87] Jacob Aboab, sonnet 411 in *Tzror Zehuvim*, ed. Bregman.
[88] Isaac Nahar, sonnet 300; Daniel Belilios, sonnet 304; Jacob Aboab, sonnet 411 in *Tzror Zehuvim*, ed. Bregman.
[89] Leone da Modena, sonnet 110 in *Tzror Zehuvim*, ed. Bregman.
[90] Solomon Oliveyra, sonnet 345 in *Tzror Zehuvim*, ed. Bregman.
[91] Anonymous, sonnet 417 in *Tzror Zehuvim*, ed. Bregman.
[92] Solomon Conegliano, sonnet 395 in *Tzror Zehuvim*, ed. Bregman.

not in the same way!"⁹³ The Baroque sonnet often makes startling comparisons from remote fields, such as the natural sciences. One wedding sonnet compares the nuptial couple to a magnet and iron, mutually attracted to each other, but then makes a distinction: the attraction of the metals is nullified by distance, whereas distance between the couple only makes their hearts grow fonder.⁹⁴

The Baroque sonnet complicates the comparison by means of a negation. In one sonnet the poet uses devious routes to claim that all creation submits to love, apart from one certain woman: did I not suffer from the pain of love myself, and did I not see its impression on the entire world, I would scorn its supposed power, because my beloved certainly remains indifferent to it.⁹⁵ Taking the long way around leaves the poet room to develop imagery and to introduce a moment of poignant lyricism.

Sometimes this model masquerades as another model. The sonnet *Shemesh, penas tevel* ("Sun, the lamp of the world")⁹⁶ by Immanuel Frances, is divided into two parts: the octave describes the subject, the sun; the sestet deals with reflection. Ostensibly, this is a poem about the sun on Immanuel of Rome's model. But in the last line a new element suddenly enters: the bride. It turns out that she is the true subject of the poem and that the comparison has been made only in order to show the contrast: the sun is inferior to the light of the bride's shining beauty.

This model also masquerades as other models, which we shall now see.

Confrontation and Verdict

This model, which describes an allegorical confrontation that ends up with a verdict, is used for sonnets of praise. The rivals are the liberal arts and their representatives; the judge, the lauded individual who is the subject of the poem.

"Today a quarrel broke out amongst the sciences," begins one sonnet,⁹⁷ with natural science, philosophy and medicine each claiming the poem's honoree for itself. But then "the law of the living God" interrupts and informs them all that "you are his maidservants; I am the mistress." Similarly, there is a sonnet noting the "great rivalry" between scholars and soldiers "since the days of Noah's Flood." Thanks to Queen Christina of Sweden, for whose coronation this sonnet was

---

⁹³ Moses Zacuto, sonnet 221 in *Tzror Zehuvim*, ed. Bregman.

⁹⁴ The sonnet was written by Abraham Pacifico, though we are not sure when. According to Moses Soave, it was intended for a wedding that took place in 1683, but the name of the poet and of the wedding couple also fits another wedding, that took place in 1730. See D. Bregman, "Shnei Sonetim le-Ḥatunah," *Moznayim* 61 (1987): 38-39.

⁹⁵ Jacob Frances, sonnet 236 in *Tzror Zehuvim*, ed. Bregman.

⁹⁶ Immanuel Frances, sonnet 311 in *Tzror Zehuvim*, ed. Bregman.

⁹⁷ Abraham Catalano, sonnet 144 in *Tzror Zehuvim*, ed. Bregman.

written, the rivaling parties make peace and she rules over them all — a fitting conclusion indeed for a queen so renowned for her intellectual pursuits.[98] In another sonnet it is the Queen of Sheba who issues the ruling, naturally coming down on the side of the man who is the subject of the poem and who has just been awarded his medical degree.[99] In this model one hears echoes of the debate concerning the hierarchy of the liberal arts which occupied literature during the Latin Middle Ages and during the periods of the Renaissance and Baroque.[100]

A Deteriorating Situation

In his study of the Baroque lyric, J. M. Cohen claims that the Baroque sonnet "will state a mood in the opening and go on to intensify without necessarily resolving it."[101]

And indeed, Hebrew sonnets were content to describe a deteriorating situation, even when they were not Baroque. Judah Moscato dwells in one sonnet on his longings for the synagogue, continues with a description of the winter snow that keeps him from reaching it, and ends by comparing it to the great snowfall recorded in the days of King David.[102] Solomon Oliveyra describes his love-sicknesses in a sonnet that ends with the "fire of desire" still "burning inside" him.[103] No solutions are suggested for the problematic situation.

The model was also used to full advantage in the typical Hebrew sonnet of the Baroque. Moses Zacuto, whose complicated structures express the spirit of the period, combined two sonnets in sequence using this model. In the first of these King Nimrod accuses Abraham: you destroyed the idols, founded a worthless religion, and, worst of all, mocked my glory. Abraham responds: you sin before God, and woe to you on the Day of Judgment.[104] Using the identical model emphasizes the contradictory aims of the two sonnets and reinforces the dramatic effect of the dialogue. Jacob Frances used this model to embody the activity of a demonic hero who destroys everything. A dramatic monologue begins with his threat against the life of an unnamed person and ends in his destroying hell itself.[105] A sonnet criticizing women begins with the mockery of courtship, progresses to the "falsehood" of marriage, and ends with "the joyous day" on which the husband is widowed.[106]

---

[98] Moses Zacuto, sonnet 224 in *Tzror Zehuvim*, ed. Bregman.

[99] Abraham Polako Levi, sonnet 414 in *Tzror Zehuvim*, ed. Bregman.

[100] For example, in *Sefer ha-Mevaqesh*, by Shem Tov Falaqera. And see M. Barash, *Mavo le-Omanut ha-Renaissance* (Jerusalem, 1983), 16-17.

[101] J. M. Cohen, *The Baroque Lyric* (London, 1963), 11.

[102] Judah Moscato, sonnet 56 in *Tzror Zehuvim*, ed. Bregman.

[103] Solomon Oliveyra, sonnet 339 in *Tzror Zehuvim*, ed. Bregman.

[104] Moses Zacuto, sonnets 177 and 178 in *Tzror Zehuvim*, ed. Bregman.

[105] Jacob Frances, sonnet 256 in *Tzror Zehuvim*, ed. Bregman.

[106] Idem, sonnet 242 in *Tzror Zehuvim*, ed. Bregman.

When sonnets of this kind pose a question at the beginning and an answer at the end, they seem to be constructed on the problem-and-solution model. But generally, this is only an illusion. The answer does not solve the problem, but only explains it in greater depth. So, for example, we find the question: if every man dies in the end, why live? The answer is, because death is even harder. It is worse than the illnesses besetting the body and weaker than the illness that clings to the soul. This answer does not solve the problem, but makes it worse by clarifying that the person asking the question is sick, sinful, and cannot even be saved by death.[107] The question might be: how did I fall in love with a picture that is nothing but a painted portrait, and why I am suffering because of it? The answer: some splashes of paint brought me to this foolishness; because of them I am willing to blend into this picture, and serve as *homer* ("matter") for its *tzurah*, even though it is nothing but paint. The term *tzurah* in this sonnet means both "a drawing" and "soul," a play on terms customary in medieval Jewish philosophy. The lover knows that the painting is a "board," that is, gross material, or *homer*. But he is willing to be this *homer*, so that his beloved may become his *tzurah*: his soul. This brief analysis reveals an agonized state of mind. The illusion here of the problem-and-solution model infuses irony into the real model, which describes an unresolvable situation. Jacob Frances wrote only the octave for this sonnet. His brother Immanuel later added the sestet and completed the poem in a manner that was both profound and consistent with his brother's words.[108]

Combining this model with the problem-and-solution model may coincide with Immanuel of Rome's model as well, when the solution comes in the second part of the poem and can be understood as the poet's reflections about the situation he has just described. *ʿEt ezkerah yom* ("When I recall the day")[109] by Jacob Frances sketches a situation that goes from bad to worse: the poet sees a lady refusing to be separated from her dead husband imprinting a kiss on his lips. A desire for this kind of macabre kiss fills his entire being, and in the hope of winning a similar one, he longs for a quick death. The model here is that of the deteriorating situation. But the plot takes up the first part, and the second part is only a meditation in response, as in Immanuel of Rome's model. At the same time, the poem is also a problem and its solution. Life constitutes a problem, and death resolves it.

When this model is combined with other models, it can become impossible to make clear divisions. *Mavet kefui todah be-ʿeinai ata* ("Death, you seem

---

[107] Idem, sonnet 288 in *Tzror Zehuvim*, ed. Bregman.

[108] Idem, sonnet 237 in *Tzror Zehuvim*, ed. Bregman. It is possible, however, that Jacob Frances planned a different kind of ending. Rathaus offers an interesting interpretation of this sonnet in the spirit of the Baroque, especially concerning the motif of falling in love with a picture, a common motif in Baroque poetry: A. Rathaus, "Ahavah le-Diyoqan," *Italia* 2 (1981): 30-47.

[109] Jacob Frances, sonnet 238 in *Tzror Zehuvim*, ed. Bregman.

ungrateful to me")[110] by Jacob Frances, which unfolds the story of a doctor, begins with a macabre situation: the doctor, who is supposed to save people from death, holds a conversation with death, his partner. The poem gradually reveals the doctor to be a murderer who has killed many sick people, almost annihilating the human race in a competition with death itself. This is definitely a deteriorating situation. Yet the sonnet also conforms externally to the conditions of the problem-and-solution model. The problem: why would death take the life of his faithful emissary? The reply: because the emissary threatened to usurp death's role and take its place. In this sonnet one can also see the solution-and-problem model: the doctor's death, with which the poem begins, has saved the world from his evil.

The deteriorating-situation pattern itself serves as an illusionary model. In *Lu ragshu goyim* ("If the nations raged")[111] by Immanuel Frances, the first three strophes join together to create a single sentence describing the growing power of one destructive person. This individual appears to be the hero of the poem; the development model that of the deteriorating situation. But in the last strophe a new figure appears — the beloved, who subdues the hero with a single glance. She, it turns out, is the true subject of the poem. We have before us a comparison of contrasts, the girl proving the stronger. Similar to this is *'Arim betzurot* ("Fortified cities")[112] by Jacob Frances. Here a strong hero is sketched in a dramatic monologue that shows his ascending power, going from the conquest of cities to mastery of the stars. The illusion of the model is broken only in the poem's final words: "One stupid doctor killed me." Thus we learn that the speaker is a dead man, that he was murdered by a doctor, and that his complaint is a comparison of contrasts: the stupidity of the doctor is stronger than any power. This illusory model allows vital information to be delayed till the end of the poem, making the hero's fall more powerful and reinforcing the sonnet's macabre final point.

Disguising one model as another is not just a sophisticated game. It reflects inner turmoil, a distorted situation, and the despair of finding a simple solution.

An Improving Situation

In the model before us, a situation improves till it reaches its peak. One example comes in a sonnet by Samuel Archivolti on the subject of celestial music. It was born with Jubal (Genesis 5:21), who was washed away with his harp by the waters of the Flood, heard again in full strength from the seven-stringed harp of King David, and will be heard with the ten-stringed harp (Psalms 92:4) in the days of the messiah.[113] Other examples: enemies plot against the duke, but he

---

[110] Idem, sonnet 258 in *Tzror Zehuvim*, ed. Bregman.
[111] Immanuel Frances, sonnet 309 in *Tzror Zehuvim*, ed. Bregman.
[112] Jacob Frances, sonnet 259 in *Tzror Zehuvim*, ed. Bregman.
[113] Samuel Archivolti, sonnet 59 in *Tzror Zehuvim*, ed. Bregman.

turns the tables on them, destroys their power, and conquers their subjects;[114] a lover goes from admiring his beloved's beauty to admiring her inner qualities, and in linking his soul with hers grows closer to God.[115]

Contextual Support

In some cases the sonnet is embedded within a specific context. So, for example, the sonnets in the play *Yesod 'Olam*, or "Foundation of the World," by Moses Zacuto. The play consists of poems in various forms. The sonnets, along with the rest of the poems, are the very essence of the play and not just a poetic ornament. They fit smoothly into their context. The first sonnet is clearly linked to the text before it, with Abraham responding to Terah, his father: "If so, dear one, open your eyes, / Understand the decree of truth you [yourself] decreed."[116] The sonnets depend upon the general action in the play and help to create it (in Chapter 16 we will devote a special discussion to the way they are organized). Like the entire play itself, the sonnets are linked to a single world-view, which is in effect its subject and goal.

Asirei ha-Tiqva, or "Prisoners of Hope," an allegorical play by Joseph de la Vega Penso, is also composed of various short poems, with three sonnets scattered among them.[117] The plot of the play is complicated, but the main part consists of the war between "Wisdom" and Satan over the soul of the king, the hero of the drama. The sonnets are dependent upon their context. Only from the context do we realize that "Man born of woman" (the first sonnet in the play) relates to a dream or vision, in which the king is ordered to desist from worldly pursuits; that "Awake, charming friend" (the second sonnet) is addressed to "Wisdom", who has fallen asleep; and that "They hid traps for me" (the third sonnet) is a letter from "Wisdom" to the king, who has been captured by Satan and shut up in prison. Together with this, each sonnet also stands on its own as a complete monologue (one of them expanded at the end to include the necessary information). The influence of Immanuel of Rome is well evident in their language and development.

A sonnet is embedded in a pastoral novel by Solomon Oliveyra, *Ayyelet Ahavim*, or "Gazelle of Love."[118] It can stand on its own as a love poem, but in context it functions as a marriage proposal. Another sonnet, by Jacob Frances, was probably meant to be inserted along with other poems into a work of prose,

---

[114] Jacob Frances, sonnet 251 in *Tzror Zehuvim*, ed. Bregman.

[115] Immanuel Frances, sonnet 314 in *Tzror Zehuvim*, ed. Bregman.

[116] Moses Zacuto, sonnet 169 in *Tzror Zehuvim*, ed. Bregman.

[117] Joseph de la Vega Penso, sonnets 364-366 in *Tzror Zehuvim*, ed. Bregman. Schirmann noted only one of them in his article on *Hamon Hogeg* in *Le-Toldot*, 2: 142. Solomon Oliveyra, sonnet 339 in *Tzror Zehuvim*, ed. Bregman.

[118] Solomon Oliveyra, sonnet 339 in *Tzror Zehuvim*, ed. Bregman.

Shevuel and Naʿama, of which only a few passages were apparently written.[119] The sonnets of Nathan Jedidiah da Orvieto were appended to three long penitential poems in *terza rima*, with one of the sonnets dependent upon context.[120] Isaac Uziel used a sonnet dependent upon context to end the *Parables of Iresto*, a long allegory in prose which he translated into Hebrew.[121]

3. New and Old in Models for Developing the Subject

The Affinity to Immanuel of Rome

The affinity which various development models show to Immanuel of Rome differs from one model to the next. The reflection-situation model resembles his method by separating the description of the situation from its evaluation, dividing the poem into two structural parts in accordance with this, and shifting the narrative perspective. However, reversing the order of the two parts — that is, putting the reflective section before the situational one — testifies to a new tendency to transfer the center of gravity from the beginning of the poem onward, to the center of the poem or the end. The situation-conclusion model preserves the traditional organization of the message in two separate parts and also their order, but shifts the emphasis to the end of the poem by providing it with a trenchant conclusion. The more this model moves away from tradition, the greater the significance of the reflective moment.

The conclusion-situation model comes close to tradition in dividing into two parts, one of them situational, but moves away from it both by foregoing the reflection and by postponing the situation till after the beginning.

The problem-solution model can be included among the options available to the old model: it provides a situation of a certain kind, and a reflection of a certain kind, but not always. The new model was capable of mixing the situation and reflections together, but it was also forced to remove the solution from the situation and to give it its own section further on in the poem.

The solution-problem model is reminiscent of Immanuel of Rome when it breaks down into two basic parts. The same is true of the comparative models and the confrontation-verdict model. Models for situations that either deteriorate or improve were not obliged to separate their message.

---

[119] Jacob Frances, sonnet 210 in *Tzror Zehuvim*, ed. Bregman. See P. Naveh, "Maʿaseh Shevuel ve-Naʿamah le-Yaʿaqov Frances," *Tarbiz* 24 (1955): 88-101, 207-31.

[120] Nathan Jedidiah da Orvieto, sonnet 149 in *Tzror Zehuvim*, ed. Bregman.

[121] Isaac Uziel, sonnet 81 in *Tzror Zehuvim*, ed. Bregman. And see I. Uziel, *Mishlei Iresto*, ed. A. Al-Maliah (Jerusalem, 1945), introduction.

External Influences

The affinity to Immanuel of Rome did not keep outside influences from appearing. The comparative models (like and unlike) and the models of evolving situations (good or bad) were fundamentally removed from the Hebrew tradition. Apparently they were absorbed from Italian and Spanish poetry of the period, where they appear in abundance. Below are a few examples from non-Hebrew poetry:[122]

Vittoria Colonna:

> Like a hungry fledgling, who sees and hears his mother beating her wings about her, when she brings him back nourishment . . . so do I sometimes, when the warm and living ray of the divine sun whence I nourish my heart flashes with more than usual clearness, move my pen urged by inward love, and write his praises without noticing myself what I say.[123]

Michelangelo Buonarroti:

> The best artist has not one idea that a piece of marble, still unworked, does not contain within itself; and that conception is realized only by the hand that obeys the judgment. The evil I fly from, and the good I promise myself are likewise hid in you, gay, proud, divine lady ... and my miserable wit does not know, though burning, how to draw anything from you but death.[124]

Tommaso Campanella:

> As every heavy thing travels from circumference to centre, and as, too, the timorous and playful weasel runs into the mouth of the monster that then devours it, so every lover of great knowledge, who boldly passes from the dead pond to the sea of truth, with which he falls in love, fixes his feet at last in our abode.[125]

---

[122] This may be the right place to mention relevant translations into Hebrew that have appeared lately: *Gizat ha-Zahav,* sonnets from various languages by Reuven Tsur (Tel Aviv, 1988); *Shirat ha-Kochavim,* an anthology of French poetry from the sixteenth century, by Aminadav Dikman (Jerusalem, 1966); *Sonetim min ha-Baroq,* by Avner Perez (Beer Sheva, 2004).

[123] Vittoria Colonna, *Qual digiuno augellin*. English translation from *The Penguin Book of Italian Verse,* ed. Kay, 176.

[124] Michelangelo, *Non ha l'ottimo artista*. English translation from *The Penguin Book of Italian Verse,* ed. Kay, 167.

[125] Tommaso Campanella, *Opere Letterarie,* ed. I. Bolzoni (Turin, 1977), 227: *Come va al centro ogni cosa pesante*. English translation from *The Penguin Book of Italian Verse,* ed. Kay, 206.

Juan Boscán:
> Like one who receives pleasure in dreams, his pleasure proceeding from delirium, so imagination with its figments vainly invents its pleasures in me.[126]

Pedro Espinosa:
> Like the unhappy pilot who, on the inconstant sea, sees himself with troubled eyes . . . so I was ploughing the sea of annoyance and anxieties.[127]

Franceso de Quevedo y Villegas:
> I looked on the walls of my fatherland, so strong once, but now mouldered away. . . I went into my house, and saw that it was the discoloured ruin of an ancient habitation; that my shepherd's crook was more bent and less strong. I felt my sword conquered by the years, and found nothing to look upon that was not a memory of death.[128]

Luis de Góngora:
> Enjoy neck, hair, lip, and forehead, before what was in your golden age gold, lily, pink and lucent crystal not only turns to silver or plucked violet, but you and it together become earth, smoke, dust, shadow, nothing.[129]

The Model as a Symptom of the Concept of Form

The various development models express the two primary concepts of the sonnet verse-form reflected in the corpus.

The model of Immanuel of Rome and the comparative models which divide the sonnet in two perfectly express a concept of the sonnet as a bipartite poem. The models which reworked Immanuel's technique, together with most of the other models, all express an increasingly dynamic tendency within the basic concept of duality. On the other hand, the models for evolving situations express a Baroque concept that contradicts the old concept without compromise, and

---

[126] Juan Boscán, *Poesia*, ed. F. de Herrera (Havana, 1963), 32: *Como acquel que in Soñar*. English translation from *The Penguin Book of Spanish Verse*, ed. J. M. Cohen (Harmondsworth, 1960), 122.

[127] Pedro Espinosa, *Como el triste piloto*. English translation from *The Penguin Book of Spanish Verse*, ed. Cohen, 262.

[128] Franceso de Quevedo y Villegas, *Obra Poetica*, ed. J. M. Blecua (Madrid, 1969), 184: *Miré los muros*. English translation from *The Penguin Book of Spanish Verse*, ed. Cohen, 269.

[129] Luis de Góngora, *Obras Poeticas*, ed. R. Foulche-Delbosc (New York, 1921), 29-30: *Mientras par competir*. English translation from *The Penguin Book of Spanish Verse*, ed. Cohen, 213.

views the sonnet as a single unified poem. Or as Immanuel Frances put it: it is a poem that relates "a single thing from beginning to the end, with completeness and purity of language, and its end is given from the beginning."

The boundaries between the two concepts are not always clear, a fact that is rooted in the nature of Baroque poetics. In disguising different models and casting often complicated states of mind into the simple old forms, Baroque poets created the sense of illusion which they saw as characterizing the universe as a whole. Such tactics were well suited to their treatment of every other element of the sonnet, such as rhyme, syntax, and rhetoric. Moreover, the Baroque poet, it is said, was forced to compete with Petrarch and to prove his own superiority. Hebrew poets of the Baroque also had to compete with a classic model of their own: Immanuel of Rome, whom they tried to outshine using Immanuel's own methods. Applying his model, adapting it to their own taste and diverting it to new goals — all these were fundamental concepts in their *ars poetica*. And finally, for all their proclamations concerning the unity of the sonnet, these poets deep down also accepted the concept of dualism. This contradiction did not bother the Baroque poet, but rather fertilized him and gave him inspiration. He could compose a sonnet that was both bipartite and tightly unified at one and the same time.

The blurring of the boundaries also existed in non-Baroque sectors. Poets gravitated from one pole to the other, wrote a sonnet sometimes this way and sometimes that, or hybridized elements of different models in an attempt to improve the old model, or in response to new challenges. Even poets who disagreed about the unity of the sonnet were not wholly untouched by the new spirit.

In his sermons about the Psalms, John Donne, the great Metaphysical poet, had this to say of the true poem:

> [W]hen it is made, [it] can have nothing, no syllable taken from it, nor added to it . . . in all metrical compositions . . . the force of the whole piece is for the most part left to the shutting up; the whole frame of the poem is a beating out of a piece of gold, but the last clause is as the impression of the stamp, and that is what makes it current.[130]

These words are unrivalled as a description of the Hebrew "golden poem" that is hammered into a single piece, and for many of the Hebrew sonnets of the period. Perhaps they are not all quite worth their weight in gold, but they are, nevertheless, remarkable for their logical construction, tight organization, and trenchant, impressive conclusion.

---

[130] John Donne, *Sermons*, ed. E. M. Simpson and G. R. Potter, 10 vols. (Berkeley, 1953-1962): 6: 41.

XV. Subjects, Approaches, and Attitudes

1. The Love Sonnet

The Renewal of the Hebrew Love Sonnet

The social and poetic factors that kept the Hebrew love sonnet from appearing in sixteenth-century Italy[1] apparently did not obtain in the east. The Kabbalists of Safed composed allegorical-religious love poetry, and the poets of Constantinople and Salonika wrote an impressive range of secular verse. It seems that the acceptance of erotic motifs, albeit in religious garb, together with secular poetry on a variety of subjects, prepared the groundwork there for the acceptance of secular love poetry. Against this backdrop, the *Maḥbarot* of Immanuel of Rome were printed in Constantinople in 1535. It was under the unmistakable influence of the *Maḥbarot* that David Onkineira, the most prominent of the Hebrew poets in Salonika during the sixteenth century, composed Hebrew love poems in various forms,[2] including five sonnets.[3] We will return to these later.

The re-emergence of the Hebrew love sonnet in Italy during the seventeenth century was not the fruit of any particular social toleration. On the contrary, as historians like Roth claim, the openness that characterized Jewish circles in the Renaissance waned. The poems of Jacob and Immanuel Frances remained largely unpublished up until our own times. S. D. Luzzatto attributed this to the biting satire of Jacob Frances,[4] but the eroticism of his poems no doubt played a part as well. His autographs show great caution. He masked risqué expressions in code,[5] crossed out others,[6] and apologized for his love poems with the explanation "I wrote them in my youth."[7] Immanuel Frances wrote a palinode of thirty-one *terzinas* repenting of his "bawdy poems."[8] It seems likely that most of the brothers' love poems remained generally unknown even in their own time.

---

[1] Above, Chap. 9, Part 1.

[2] See J. Patai, "David Onkineira ve-Shirato," *Qovetz ʿal-Yad*, n.s. 2 (1937): 77–119.

[3] See Dvora Bregman, "The Sonnets of David Onkineira," in *The Jewish Communities of Southeastern Europe*, ed. I. K. Hassiotis, (Thessaloniki, 1997): 87-92.

[4] See Luzzatto's preface to Jacob Frances's autograph, MS. Oxford, Bodleian Library 1991.

[5] For example, the word *aḥorayim* ("rear-end"). See the poem *Ho ho ha-zot ʿofra* in Jacob Frances, *Kol Shirei*, ed. Naveh, 317, and the editor's comment there.

[6] See the commentary in *Tzror Zehuvim*, ed. Bregman.

[7] See *Hoḥili toḥelet* in Jacob Frances, *Kol Shirei*, ed. Naveh, 325.

[8] *Shimʿu seḥaqim:* Immanuel Frances, *Meteq Sefatayim*, ed. Brody, 81, and see also the editor's explanation there.

The attitude towards Immanuel of Rome was no less ambivalent. At the end of the century, Immanuel Frances, his disciple *par excellence,* made a list of "poets and renowned men of letters in every generation," from Isaac Khalfun to Judah Alharizi, and added:

> And afterwards rose Rabbi Immanuel ben Solomon, a master of poetry, but one who sullied his path with licentious poems not fit to be heard. May God forgive him and the printers who published everything without pruning the thorns from the vineyard, namely his *Mahbarot,* which have many respectable poems.[9]

Nevertheless, the pendulum swung in favor of love poems. Rather than forbidding poets to write love poems, Immanuel Frances hedged them in with various rules, and in doing so offered a way to keep the practice of love poetry alive. Thus Yakhin, the teacher throughout *Meteq Sefatayim,* directs Boaz, his pupil:

> If the poet intends something adulterous or bawdy in any language, whether the Holy Tongue or not, this is ugly and reprehensible. But if the poet veers not from the path of modesty, and praises his wife or his bride or an unmarried woman whom he intends to take as his wife, he should not be accused of this. And you, Boaz, learn from what our sages of blessed memory said, that people should praise the bride in order to endear her to her husband: how much more so, then, those who are permitted to him! For if the permitted love poems were entirely forbidden they would not come even by way of allegory in the Holy Writings, as they do in the *Song of Songs* — for we should not compare the ugly to the beautiful, or the profane to the sacred. If the poet composes poems in order to include them in some useful composition of moral purpose, as did the author of *The Ancient Parable,* or *The Prince's Son and the Monk,* then this is acceptable so long as they not include the kind of vile things found in the poems of Immanuel bar Solomon [of Rome], even if his work is an ethical treatise. And you, my son, do not do near the entrance to their house, and set my words on your heart like a seal.[10]

Yakhin's advice was illustrated with sonnets for the bride.

These words gave theoretical validation to the tactics already in use, namely the inclusion of love poems, and even erotic ones, within the accepted genre of epithalamium.[11] Such tactics were especially vital for the sonnet form. By the end of the sixteenth century, Hebrew sonnets for weddings began to appear. While these did not usually go beyond poems of blessing and praise, there were

---

[9] Immanuel Frances, *Meteq Sefatayim,* ed. Brody, 34.
[10] *Meteq Sefatayim,* ed. Brody, 48.
[11] Such as the dialogue-poem of Joseph Tzarfati, partly translated below.

also sonnets by the groom to the bride, or of the bride to the groom, and these were love poems in every way. However, poets did not always take advantage of this solution. Quite a few love sonnets by the Frances brothers are completely detached from the context of marriage. This testifies to social independence and courage: qualities which the brothers also demonstrated in poems and sonnets against the followers of Shabbetai Zevi, plagiarists, arrogant community members, and so forth. The group of love poems discussed in this chapter belongs almost entirely to these brother poets.

Below we shall review the different concepts of love embodied in this small corpus of sonnets. The Hebrew love sonnet of the seventeenth century drew from all the various sources mentioned up till this point: the *Maḥbarot*, Petrarch and his followers, and Baroque poetry in Spanish and Italian. Likewise it returned to the Song of Songs and other traditional Jewish sources. Naturally, the various elements were absorbed en masse, without discrimination. Therefore, even when sonnets reveal traces of a particular influence, we will not try to classify them according to these characteristics or attribute them to a specific trend.

Love as a Wound

"Indeed, my lady has greatly emanated her grace / upon me in my vision of her which revived me . . . / I am overwhelmed, and wonder how she enlightened me / and shed light in the heart of darkness." Lines like these could have been written by Dante, but in fact come from a sonnet by Immanuel Frances, *Ḥasdei shenati* ("The grace of my slumber").[12] The sonnet is reminiscent of Immanuel of Rome's *Me ʿarvah shenah* ("How sweet my sleep"),[13] whose "sweet style" embodies the concept of love as divine grace. *Ḥasdei shenati* also features the darkness-banishing beloved as well as the lover who is content merely to gaze upon her. But unlike the sonnet of the *dolce stil nuovo*, the latter sonnet does not focus on the grace emanating from the beloved, but on the suffering of the lover. The dream is not the enchanted meeting between lover and beloved, but the means of escaping her all-too-real image: "And upon wakening, she wearied me." Hardheartedness is the primary feature of the beloved in this sonnet as well as in other Hebrew sonnets of the seventeenth century, and in these, love is perceived as a wound.

In sonnets presenting love as a wound, love is often treated as a shameful matter, the fruit of mischievous *Ḥesheq* — the Hebrew version of Cupid — who sets traps for the unwary and topples them in the "snares of love."[14] Like his counterpart in Greco-Roman mythology, *Ḥesheq* is seen as a capricious child, irresponsible, violent, and enormously powerful: "Cupid caught me from behind

---

[12] Immanuel Frances, sonnet 307 in *Tzror Zehuvim*, ed. Bregman.
[13] Immanuel of Rome, sonnet 34 in *Tzror Zehuvim*, ed. Bregman.
[14] Solomon Oliveyra, sonnet 339 in *Tzror Zehuvim*, ed. Bregman.

and brought me crashing down."[15] The beloved activates him, mechanically, with her glance: "Through her eyes with might of hands / Cupid drew his bow like an enemy."[16] The arrow finds its target: "In my heart I felt your blade";[17] "Your strength and your power I felt in my eye."[18] Now the lover falls ill: "My soul is in flames, my spirit burns like fire."[19] The beloved reigns arrogantly over the lover: "Hannah is my lady today / Naomi reigned over me since yesterday."[20] He is put to shame and forced to creep after his beloved "like a snail."[21] He seeks refuge, but in vain: "What can I do, friend, against love?"[22] He hates Cupid and curses him: "May you be like Sedom, Ḥesheq, and like the tribe of Koraḥ!"[23]

In contrast to the weak lover, the beloved is poised like a mighty hunter: "Friends! the gazelle's hair of shining light / for lovers conceals a snare / the victims fall to oblivion there / trapped, with no hope of flight."[24]

He who values his life will keep away from her: "Therefore, friends, when you approach beware / of the breast, hair, and eyes / for they hold arrows, fire, and a snare."[25] Love is a contest of strength, a duel between two mail-clad warriors armed with bow and arrow.[26] Each of them seeks to escape the trap of love, and to lure the other one into it: "When, my lady, will the time come / that I find peace from the pains of love / and in its fetters see you firmly bound?"[27] The powerful attraction of the beloved stands in inverse relation to her feminine weakness. With a glance from her eye she overpowers the hero who has conquered singlehanded the very forces of nature.[28] But any attempt to woo the beloved leaves her cold and indifferent, and "his arrows fall into her lap like wax on marble."[29]

The creation of *meraviglia* — the "marvelous" — is a basic element in this literary trend, especially in everything concerning the lady's appearance, character, and power. One of the most perennial of Petrarchist motifs, fire and ice, is drafted into the effort to create this effect:

---

[15] Solomon Oliveyra, sonnet 339 in *Tzror Zehuvim*, ed. Bregman.
[16] Immanuel Frances, sonnet 306 in *Tzror Zehuvim*, ed. Bregman.
[17] Jacob Frances, sonnet 236 in *Tzror Zehuvim*, ed. Bregman.
[18] Jacob Frances, sonnet 236 in *Tzror Zehuvim*, ed. Bregman.
[19] Immanuel Frances, sonnet 312 in *Tzror Zehuvim*, ed. Bregman.
[20] Immanuel Frances, sonnet 312 in *Tzror Zehuvim*, ed. Bregman.
[21] Jacob Frances, sonnet 236 in *Tzror Zehuvim*, ed. Bregman.
[22] Jacob Frances, sonnet 239 in *Tzror Zehuvim*, ed. Bregman.
[23] Jacob Frances, sonnet 239 in *Tzror Zehuvim*, ed. Bregman. Koraḥ, of course, was crushed for rebelling against Moses in Exodus 16.
[24] Immanuel Frances, sonnet 306 and 312 in *Tzror Zehuvim*, ed. Bregman.
[25] Immanuel Frances, sonnet 306 in *Tzror Zehuvim*, ed. Bregman.
[26] Jacob Frances, sonnet 236 in *Tzror Zehuvim*, ed. Bregman.
[27] Immanuel Frances, sonnet 315 in *Tzror Zehuvim*, ed. Bregman.
[28] Idem, sonnet 309 in *Tzror Zehuvim*, ed. Bregman.
[29] Jacob Frances, sonnet 236 in *Tzror Zehuvim*, ed. Bregman.

"In her breast snow and burning fire / mingle together and burst into flames. / Who has ever seen ice, with fire below? / Ice and coals — and neither triumphs!"[30]

Baroque motifs give a bizarre twist to the lover's suffering. He falls in love with two women at the same time,[31] and in his delirium seeks to become one with a figure that he realizes is nothing but a painted portrait.[32]

As we saw in *Ḥasdei shenati*, the lover is not without his moments of pleasure. In Oliveyra's *Yom yisruni kilyotai* ("From the day my insides tormented me"),[33] for example, the lover is delighted by the beauty of his beloved even as he agonizes over it, in the way of Petrarchan paradox. The paradox is resolved through the prosaic context of his sonnet, which is a letter of proposal. The prospective groom, it turns out, is Ishmael, son of the Patriarch Abraham; his beloved, as midrash tells us, Fatima. Hardly the typical setting for a Petrarch-like love scene, yet Ishmael's letter is clearly steeped in Petrarchan conventions:

> Fatima, *temima* ("my perfect one"), you have suddenly seduced me, and the beauty of your countenance, O lovely one, has dazed and amazed me. If you desire me at all, then all my steps will go towards serving you! For you will be the wife of my youth and call me 'my husband.' Harken, lady, and see that it was not I who sought to frighten you; the small urchin has felled me: a small and tender lad with arrows at his side. Suddenly, without malice, he struck me unseeing; for he acts with blind madness. His little finger is stronger than my waist and he struggled with me and became my master. He managed to strike me though I was not faint, injured me without my knowing with what weapons. He taunted me, drew his bow like an enemy to undo me for no reason with his malicious arrows; he circled me and lodged them in my heart. And now be gracious and grant my request; fulfill my hope, and sin not against the child, a divine cherub, O thou who art as fair as the moon, as clear as the sun, about whom I wrote this letter of desire, gazelle, in token of my many days of love, and of which I wrote a "golden poem."[34]

Clearly our lover is in distress here!

Few are the moments of pleasure in Hebrew sonnets perceiving love as a wound. Outright despair prevails in some of them, and the situation resolves in tragedy. The Petrarchist motif of the burning love-sickness is sometimes joined

---

[30] Immanuel Frances, sonnet 306 in *Tzror Zehuvim*, ed. Bregman.

[31] Idem, sonnet 312 in *Tzror Zehuvim*, ed. Bregman.

[32] Jacob Frances, sonnet 237 in *Tzror Zehuvim*, ed. Bregman.

[33] Solomon Oliveyra, sonnet 339 in *Tzror Zehuvim*, ed. Bregman.

[34] Solomon Oliveyra, *Ayyelet Ahavim*, fol. 20a. That Fatima was Ishmael's beloved we learn in *Yalqut Shimoni*, Genesis 95.

by the gloomy Baroque motif in which the lover meets his end. This takes expression not only in descriptions of frustrated love, but also in images of love fulfilled. In merging with his beloved the lover is transformed into a painting, or into a monster with two hearts; his heart is torn in two; he loses his sanity.[35] A sonnet by Jacob Frances describes love born in death, a love that can be fulfilled only with the death of the lover: "On my dark day of death / the sun of her kiss will shine on my lips."[36]

The weight of Petrarchist and Baroque conventions in Hebrew sonnets perceiving love as a wound differs from one sonnet to another. Oliveyra's above-mentioned *Yom yisruni kilyotai*,[37] which is Petrarchist to the core, blames the wounds of love on *Ḥesheq*, or Cupid; *ʿEt ezkerah yom* ("When I recall the day"),[38] on the other hand, is far from any mythological association. Its motives are psychological: love is aroused by jealousy, which also causes the wound identified with it. This is a Baroque sonnet, without Petrarchist conventions.

The concept of love as a wound also provided the low sonnet of the seventeenth century with plenty of fodder. Here poetic conventions were turned upside down in order to create a burlesque effect. One satirical sonnet presents a bride and groom who defeated Cupid. It was not he who brought them together, but rather the desire "to drink and get drunk."[39] A similar reversal of the standard love situation provides the barb for various clever low sonnets. These sonnets have a popular appeal that finds expressions in dialogue form, long a convention of popular Italian poetry,[40] rife with vulgar expressions and oaths.[41]

The concept of love as a wound, together with the various motifs accompanying it in the sonnets we have seen, can be found in numerous poems from this period in Italian and Spanish. Below are just a few examples:

Michelangelo yearns for the night:
"O night, O sweet time!"[42]

---

[35] E.g Jacob Frances, sonnets 236, 239 and 238 in *Tzror Zehuvim*, ed. Bregman; Immanuel Frances, sonnet 312.

[36] Jacob Frances, sonnet 238 in *Tzror Zehuvim*, ed. Bregman.

[37] Solomon Oliveyra, sonnet 339 in *Tzror Zehuvim*, ed. Bregman.

[38] Jacob Frances, sonnet 238 in *Tzror Zehuvim*, ed. Bregman.

[39] Idem, sonnet 257 in *Tzror Zehuvim*, ed. Bregman.

[40] Biadene, *Morfologia del sonetto*, 166–69.

[41] See for example Immanuel Frances, sonnets 315, 316, and 321 in *Tzror Zehuvim*, ed. Bregman.

[42] Michelangelo, *Rime*, ed. C. Guasti (Florence, 1863), 205: *O notte, o dolce tempo*. English translation from *The Penguin Book of Italian Verse*, ed. Kay, 165–66.

So too Gaspara Stampa: "O night, more clear and blest for me than the clearest, most blest days."[43]

Campanella complains about Cupid:
"It is now three thousand years since the world first worshipped Love that is blind, with his arrows and wings . . . he does not use golden arrows, since pistols were contrived, but coal, sulphur, flame, thunder and lead . . ."[44]

The motif of love's fulfillment at death appears in the work of Marino: "Or I might crush you together, like Samson, for I would give death a tomb with your sweet fall and death to my grief."[45] Likewise we find the motif of being turned into wood, as in the myth of Apollo and Daphne.[46]

Love for a painting is a common motif in Italian poetry.[47] A sonnet by the Spanish poet Figueroa about a portrait of a woman complains, like that of Jacob Frances, that the woman is stone, the picture — wax.[48]

These examples are but a drop in the ocean.

Ostensibly, there is no point in searching for the roots of this late style in the poems of Immanuel of Rome, and indeed we find no trace of it in his sonnets. However, elsewhere in the *Maḥbarot* we do encounter "Petrarchist" conventions in all their glory. Here are a few examples:

Love is War:
"And lo, I vow to you, by the life of lovers one and all / from the largest unto the small / not to cease my war on you forever."[49]

"And behold, I swear by the life of *Ḥesheq* and his pride . . . / and I place his banner in my right hand and his shield in my left."[50]

---

[43] Gaspara Stampa, *Rime*, ed. G. R. Ceriello (Milan, 1954), 147: *O notte, a me più chiara*. English translation from *The Penguin Book of Italian Verse*, ed. Kay, 180.

[44] Campanella, *Opere Letterarie*, ed. Bolzoni, 147: *Contra Cupido*. English translation from *The Penguin Book of Italian Verse*, ed. Kay, 205.

[45] Marino, English translation from *The Penguin Book of Italian Verse*, ed. Kay, 218: *Donna che si lava le gambe*.

[46] Marino, English translation from *The Penguin Book of Italian Verse*, ed. Kay, 217: *Deh, perche fuggi, o Daphne*.

[47] See Rathaus, "Ahavah le-Diyoqan", *Italia* 2 (1981) 30-47.

[48] Cohen, ed., *The Penguin Book of Spanish Verse*, 303.

[49] Immanuel of Rome, *Maḥbarot*, ed. Yarden, 61, line 362.

[50] *Maḥbarot*, ed. Yarden, 60, line 347.

The cruel beloved shoots arrows with her eyes and preys on souls:

"Oh, cruel-hearted one, of pity bereft / you tear with your right and eat with your left."[51]

"Oh, cruel one, will you not take pity? / You kill pure souls and show no regret."[52]

Love takes ascendancy over the sun:
"[Your luminaries] will mock [your light like] the shining sun / saying, Arise, baldy, arise, bald one!"[53]

Even the famous Petrarchan combination of fire and ice appears in the *Maḥbarot*:
"Desire for you [*ḥishqekh*] within my entrails / resembles the flames of fire and hail." [54]

The Hebrew Petrarchists could even have found *Ḥesheq*, the Hebrew version of Cupid, in this line.

That "Petrarchist" motifs occur in Immanuel's writings is not surprising. He of course received them from the old Hebrew poetry in Spain, the conventions of which overlapped to a great extent those of the Provençal poetry that found new life in the work of Petrarch, Petrarchism, and the Baroque. And it was not only in the poetry of Immanuel that these conventions appear in Hebrew guise. Immanuel's contemporary in northern Spain, Todros Abulafia, also used a number of similar expressions,[55] as did leading poets from the earlier classical period, such as Moses ibn Ezra and Judah Halevi. Why, then, do these motifs not appear in Immanuel's sonnets?

The conventions of Provençal poetry lost their charm for Italian poets at the beginning of the Renaissance. They seemed frozen to them, trivial and barbed. They incorporated them into their poetry only after making adaptations: refining,

---

[51] *Maḥbarot*, ed. Yarden, 60, line 340.

[52] *Maḥbarot*, ed. Yarden, 60, line 342.

[53] *Maḥbarot*, ed. Yarden, 49, line 103 This line makes a witty allusion to 2 Kings 2:23.

[54] *Maḥbarot*, ed. Yarden, 302, line 350. The Hebrew words draw on the dramatic description in Exodus 9:24.

[55] For examples from Todros Abulafia, see his "*ʿEt ha-stav ʿavar*" in *Gan ha-Meshalim ve-ha-Ḥidot*, ed. D. Yellin, 3 vols. (Jerusalem, 1934–1937), 1:100, and in Schirmann, *Ha-Shirah ha-ʿIvrit*, 2: 424; "*Ani melekh*" in *Gan ha-Meshalim*, 1:37, and in Schirmann, *Ha-Shirah ha-ʿIvrit*, 2:426. For other examples, see Bregman, *Shevil ha-Zahav*, 167, notes 53–58.

reinvigorating, and "sweetening" them. Immanuel of Rome had no reason to avoid this tradition, in its Hebrew guise, for the most part. But when he composed his sonnets according to the Italian concept, he either renounced these motifs or adapted them to its spirit. Such distinctions did not trouble the writers of sonnets in the seventeenth century. They found themselves in a very comfortable situation, with a ready-made reservoir of Hebrew idioms suitable to the new trends in poetry and ripe for use in their sonnets. They therefore returned to Immanuel in this as well. But the concept of the sonnet as a love poem had changed from one end to the other, and Hebrew Petrarchists took pains to use in their sonnets the very same elements that Immanuel had taken such care to keep out.

Love as Sin

In some sonnets by Jacob Frances, love is perceived as a sin. These sonnets move away from the conventions of Petrarchism and are strikingly vital and unique.

"O heart, may God will that I stand / my test today and prevail!" The Baroque poet is likely to see the truth with a candid eye, without any poetic mannerisms. This sonnet (*Libi yehi ratzon*) [56] by Jacob Frances conveys a growing storm of passions while using a whole string of synonyms to describe love and desire, nine different words in all. The beloved in this poem seems a living person, neither cold nor haughty. She is an unflinching part of the storm, which reaches its climax at the poem's end. Like the sonnets perceiving love as a wound, here too the situation is one of war. But the field of battle takes place in the poet's heart; the conflict is between the poet and his desire. He does not play innocent, and, taking full responsibility for his plight, blames neither Cupid nor the woman who has rejected him.

In another sonnet, the sins of youth are replaced by the sins of old age. Here it is an old man who despairs over his desires. He too places the responsibility for his feelings squarely on his own shoulders, and laments the "coals of love still smoldering within me."[57]

Both of these unique sonnets emphasize the ethical conflict common in Petrarch's sonnets, but which many Petrarchists tended to ignore. Unlike what happens in the poetry of Petrarch himself, here the vacillations reach an abrupt end. The sonnet *Libi yehi ratzon*, mentioned above, concludes with the triumph of desire ("and pleasure to pleasure cries out"), while the second sonnet mentioned above ends with the triumph of the spirit ("Cling to God alone, my heart / 'tis He we should desire, and for His love yearn").[58]

---

[56] Jacob Frances, sonnet 240 in *Tzror Zehuvim*, ed. Bregman.
[57] Idem, sonnet 287 in *Tzror Zehuvim*, ed. Bregman.
[58] Idem, sonnet 287 in *Tzror Zehuvim*, ed. Bregman.

A third sonnet in this group deals with adultery.[59] It views adultery as a sin, like the sonnets by Immanuel of Rome, but with none of Immanuel's burlesque humor. The poet sides with the husband and not with the adulterous woman: adultery kindles jealousy, and jealousy death. Violence characterizes both the language and the story-line. The sin is uncompromising and absolute, as is the punishment.[60]

While these non-burlesque sonnets might have some affinity to Immanuel of Rome, it would not have been hard to absorb their spirit outside the Hebrew tradition. In a sonnet by Michelangelo, for example, an old man complains that his desire "betrays" him.[61]

As in the past, the concept of love as sin also finds a place in the new Hebrew sonnet. But now it is no longer committed for the sake of pleasure, and there is no general warning for society as a whole. In this poem, the wife has betrayed her husband only to punish him for being parsimonious.[62]

Love as Grace

Love as grace — a far cry from the kinds of love discussed up until now — animates a few Hebrew sonnets in the seventeenth century. In these poems, the beloved woman is described as shedding light, warmth, and happiness on the entire world.[63] Like the beloved in Petrarch's poems, here too she is beautiful. The poet focuses on her physical attractions: "The full moon is in the light of her face / and in her hair the sun is shining."[64] As in the poems of Petrarch, and even more so in those written by Petrarchists of the Platonic stream — Lorenzo de' Medici, Poliziano, and others — her physical beauty is equated with all that is good and pleasant. However, the luminous images in the Hebrew sonnet of the seventeenth century are likely to serve as fodder for a witty Baroque conceit in which, for example, the beloved glows more than the sun and the moon, with the poet invoking both heavenly bodies to sink into the depths of the sea in order to magnify the marvel.[65] But this Baroque conceit by Immanuel Frances does not damage the basic concept of love as grace or the gentle image of the beloved. Her charm, beauty, and radiance shine in every line, and it is these qualities that attract the lover: "I will ignore every light for her light." These things are reminiscent of the "sweet

---

[59] Idem, sonnet 246 in *Tzror Zehuvim*, ed. Bregman.

[60] Jealousy and death are of course important motifs in Spanish love poetry during this period.

[61] Michelangelo, *Rime*, ed. Guasti, 347: *Ohime, ohime, ch'i' son tradito*.

[62] Immanuel Frances, sonnet 321 in *Tzror Zehuvim*, ed. Bregman.

[63] Idem, sonnet 311 in *Tzror Zehuvim*, ed. Bregman.

[64] Idem, sonnet 308 in *Tzror Zehuvim*, ed. Bregman.

[65] Idem, sonnet 308 in *Tzror Zehuvim*, ed. Bregman.

new style," but not identical with it. The beloved of the Italian sweet style is unobtainable, whereas the Hebrew lover can revel in the aura of grace surrounding him precisely because it is bound up with a feeling of confidence. "A refuge have I found in your heart already," the lover says in one Hebrew sonnet,[66] and in another specifically notes that "her halo of light shines for me."[67]

The reason for this confidence is that this kind of gentle, optimistic, and light-filled Hebrew sonnet is a poem for the bridegroom; the love is that of a couple engaged to be married. It uses Petrarchist conventions, but these lose their sting by force of situation and take on a new, positive meaning. Only thus could a bride be described as "devouring men with the burning coals of her eyes"[68] while standing underneath the wedding canopy. Clearly, the metaphors here are not meant to convey the old "cruelty" of the proud lady, but rather the great and shining beauty of the bride.

The bride in the Hebrew sonnet is ostensibly the high-born lady of Italian poetry. In a pair of sonnets by Jacob Frances (inspired by two *contrasti* by Immanuel of Rome, *Yomru sheḥakim lakh*; *Sefer ḥakakto*)[69], the groom finds "the hand of God" in his bride's beauty and marvels at her virtues.[70] This is without doubt the counterpart of the angelic creature of the *dolce stil nuovo,* and indeed, the groom pays his debt to convention when he vows to be her slave. But to this courtly gesture the lady responds with a prototypical "God forbid!" that all at once causes her to descend from her pedestal and become a desirable Jewish bride.[71] The image of the beloved in this type of sonnet is supremely human, and her humanity permits a tone of intimacy.[72] The gap between the lovers' positions, so great in Italian poetry, dwindles in the Hebrew sonnet for the bride and groom, and sometimes disappears altogether. The dialogue framework of the poems reinforces the sense of equality for the bride, who responds to the groom's sonnet with a sonnet of her own. In this unusual poem she refers to him affectionately as "the pride of my soul, the crown of glory," and even makes herself inferior to him: "Compared to your radiance I am like darkness; / I will be your handmaid and the dust of your feet."[73] A Baroque sense of foreboding is likely to descend on the groom's sonnet, but this does not affect the sense of equality between the

---

[66] Idem, sonnet 310 in *Tzror Zehuvim*, ed. Bregman.

[67] Idem, sonnet 308 in *Tzror Zehuvim*, ed. Bregman; and see also Menasseh Hayyim Padua, sonnet 359.

[68] Jacob Frances, sonnet 248 in *Tzror Zehuvim*, ed. Bregman.

[69] Immanuel of Rome, sonnets 6 and 7 in *Tzror Zehuvim*, ed. Bregman.

[70] Jacob Frances, sonnets 248 and 249 in *Tzror Zehuvim*, ed. Bregman.

[71] Idem, sonnet 249 in *Tzror Zehuvim*, ed. Bregman.

[72] Immanuel Frances, sonnet 310 in *Tzror Zehuvim*, ed. Bregman.

[73] Jacob Frances, sonnet 249 in *Tzror Zehuvim*, ed. Bregman; and see also Menasseh Hayyim Padua, sonnet 360.

nuptial couple. Jacob Frances ponders about death on his wedding day, infusing the situation with a sense of the macabre. But he also describes, even if in a negative way, the friendship and companionship that married life affords: "If I bury her, how can I live? / If she buries me, what will she do alone?"[74]

Motifs from the Song of Songs give these sonnets a familiar touch, for despite its elevated language this was a well-known text. *Zot komatekh* ("This thy stature")[75] by Immanuel Frances details the beauty of his beloved's body in the manner of the Petrarchists, but the language is based on the Song of Songs. Taking such familiar phrases as "this thy stature is like unto a palm tree" (Song of Songs 8:8), "thine eyes are doves" (1:16), and "thy lips are like a thread of scarlet and thy mouth is comely" (4:3), the poet weaves them throughout his sonnet to create praise for the bride.

The wedding canopy and concept of sanctification hover in the background of sonnets of this kind; they give religious sanction to erotic desire: "For it is the flame of God!"[76] They elevate the occasion and sanctify the grace which emanates from the beloved. The old concept of grace, Christian at its core, appears in these sonnets in all its religious force, only now with Jewish overtones.

A sonnet unique of its kind by Immanuel Frances takes this process to its peak. Returning to the element of grace from the *dolce stil nuovo* — the kind which radiates from the lady's virtues and not necessarily from her beauty — the poet clothes the poem in the Hebrew convention of old: "I love you not for your surpassing beauty and charm . . . / but because you walk in the awe of God / my soul is bound unto you." In view of the woman's unchanging perfection, the figure of the lover develops and grows more elevated. The emotional bonding with the beloved strengthens his intimacy with God during his lifetime, and allows him to merge with Him after death: "To you / my heart yearns, like the law of Moses and Israel. / Thus will I always stand, and when I am gathered / unto my people, / my passion will finally touch the Infinite."[77] As in Dante, love for a woman does not contradict the love of God, but rather strengthens and merges into it and thus does not end with death.

The Sonnets of David Onkineira

In view of all the above, let us now return to the love sonnets of David Onkineira of Salonika, which were written in the sixteenth century. In some of his sonnets love is perceived as a wound, for he speaks of "thy arrows of light in my

---

[74] Jacob Frances, sonnet 241 in *Tzror Zehuvim*, ed. Bregman.
[75] Immanuel Frances, sonnet 313 in *Tzror Zehuvim*, ed. Bregman.
[76] Menasseh Hayyim Padua, sonnet 359 in *Tzror Zehuvim*, ed. Bregman.
[77] Immanuel Frances, sonnet 314 in *Tzror Zehuvim*, ed. Bregman.

entrails," or "the arrows of love."[78] But his hardhearted lady is also likely to melt and respond to him like a real lover, to the joy of all eager lovers and their ladies: "Her heart, cut like a diamond / hard . . . melts like wax in the face of devouring fire."[79] It seems that Onkineira's sonnets offer a synthesis of the *Maḥbarot*: from the sonnets and from other poems by Immanuel, in which, as we saw, "Petrarchan" motifs could be found. Considering Salonika's distance, both mentally and geographically, from the creative center of the Hebrew sonnet, and the fact that Onkineira was the only Hebrew poet to compose love sonnets in the sixteenth century, this comes as no surprise. But did the *Maḥbarot* indeed supply Onkineira with his only examples? This assumption is doubtful in light of the following sonnet:[80]

> Blessed be the day wherein I was born
> To see the labor of *Ḥesheq* and to suffer his yoke,
> To be the target for the bows of his arrow,
> To drown in his sea as I have drowned;
>
> To dwell in his shade as I desired;
> To see his might, to utter his deeds,
> To see his changes, to recognize his treachery,
> To be tested in the furnace of affliction in which I am tested.
>
> For all I tasted of his bitterness
> Has been sweeter to my palate than honey and nectar!
> In them my spirit lives and my strength is renewed.
>
> But when I was banished from his Eden
> My soul went down to the depths of hell,
> The light of my sun darkened and my light vanished.

This sonnet is reminiscent in argument, structure and tone of the famous sonnet by Petrarch, "Blessed be the day, the month, the year," translated above in Chapter Two. Thus we find ourselves facing not the old conventions of Provençal poetry, but the spirit of Petrarch, unknown to Immanuel of Rome. It seems likely, therefore, that Onkineira had access to a Petrarchan Hebrew sonnet which has not come down to us, written in the sixteenth century or before. Nor can we exclude the possibility that poems and sonnets of Petrarch himself reached Onkineira in translation. Solomon Usque, whom we already mentioned as having authored the classic translations of Petrarch into Spanish (see Chapter Nine), was

---

[78] David Onkineira, sonnets 85 and 86 in *Tzror Zehuvim*, ed. Bregman.
[79] Idem, sonnet 89 in *Tzror Zehuvim*, ed. Bregman.
[80] David Onkineira, *Barukh yehi ha-yom*, sonnet 87 in *Tzror Zehuvim*, ed. Bregman.

born in Portugal during the the 1630s. After spending some time in Ferarra and Venice, Usque arrived in Constantinople, where he most likely wrote the translation published in Venice in 1567.[81] Onkineira, a contemporary of Usque's, was born in Constantinople and lived there and in Salonika, as well as other places in the east. Since he belonged to a family of Spanish descent, he knew the Spanish language. Given all these factors, it seems more than possible that Onkineira saw Usque's book, either before or after its publication. Thus it was through the translations of Petrarch's poems that he learned to write in the great poet's style, just like Petrarchists all across Europe. While Onkineira's poems have not received the scholarly attention they deserve, we can undoubtedly see him as the first composer of Petrarchist sonnets in the annals of Hebrew poetry.

The Debate over Women

A poetic debate over the nature of woman and marriage commenced in the Hebrew *maqama* in Spain and continued until the seventeenth century.[82] Immanuel of Rome took part in this debate, though not in his sonnets;[83] his followers transferred the debate to the sonnet as well. The opening shot in that genre was fired by Moses ben Joab in *Emas ani ʿoferot* ("I am sick of gazelles"),[84] and the debate continued one hundred years later in a group of sonnets by Jacob Frances.[85]

Most of the sonnets in this debate oppose women and relationships with them. Woman is "wicked,"[86] avaricious,[87] overbearing and irritating.[88] The married man has nothing to anticipate but "the joyful day of widowerhood."[89]

---

[81] Concerning the identity of the translator, see C. Roth, "Salusque Lusitano: An Essay in Disentanglement," in idem *Gleanings: Essays in Jewish History, Letters and Art* (New York, 1967): 179–99. Usque printed only part of the translation of the *Canzoniere*, but the sonnet *Benedetto sia il giorno* is included there.

[82] Pagis, "Ha-Pulmus ha-Shiri."

[83] See *Matza isha, matza lo boshet ha-panim*, in Immanuel of Rome, *Maḥbarot*, ed. Yarden, 30–34.

[84] Moses ben Joab, sonnet 48 in *Tzror Zehuvim*, ed. Bregman; and see M. D. Cassuto, "Ein Hebräischer Dichter des 15 [i.e. 16] Jahrhunderts, Mose ben Joab," *Monatsschrift für Geschichte und Wissenschaft des Judentums* 77 (1993): 365–84.

[85] Jacob Frances, sonnets 242, 243, 244, 245, and 247 in *Tzror Zehuvim*, ed. Bregman. On the periphery of this group is the sonnet *Eykh eʿeseh dod* (sonnet 239). It opens with the lyrical complaint of a lover who has fallen in love with a picture, and ends with a cynical reflection along the lines of this debate. (It appears that the poet was not satisfied with it, for in the margins of the poem he noted that "the tercets are weak.")

[86] Jacob Frances, sonnet 245 in *Tzror Zehuvim*, ed. Bregman.

[87] Moses ben Joab, sonnet 48 in *Tzror Zehuvim*, ed. Bregman.

[88] Jacob Frances, sonnet 239 in *Tzror Zehuvim*, ed. Bregman.

[89] Idem, sonnets 242 and 244 in *Tzror Zehuvim*, ed. Bregman.

The sonnets against women are realistic poems of burlesque. Their language is vulgar and blunt: "I am sick of gazelles and the companionship of charming does / and contact with them is like contact with a reptile."[90] They abound with oaths and curses: "May your heart drown in a pit of filth!"[91]

The single sonnet of this kind in defense of woman includes a few high-flown phrases, but primarily is a smutty hymn to the "girl on the bed."[92] True to misogynic tradition, the sonnet recalls feminine figures of mythological proportions: Lilith, Zeresh, Jezebel. Only here, the purpose is not to show the typical woman but to demonstrate her antithesis.

The influence of Immanuel of Rome is evident in this debate. The sonnet *Sikel zeman yadav* ("Time stayed his hands") inspired Moses ben Joab's *Emas ani ʿoferot* ("I am sick of gazelles"),[93] while Jacob Frances's *ʿAl ma teqalel* ("Why are you cursing?") is the antithesis of Immanuel's *Naflah ʿateret ha-zeman* ("The crown of Time has fallen"), in terms of poetic tone and point of view.[94]

2. For Weddings

The Social Aspect

The Hebrew sonnet for weddings appeared, as noted, towards the end of the sixteenth century. It was Leone da Modena, an important innovator in every aspect of the genre in Hebrew, who at the end of the sixteenth century made the breakthrough, starting a process which placed the wedding sonnet at the center of Hebrew sonnetry. It would not be exaggerated to say that thanks to Modena the wedding poem (in all forms) became the hallmark of the Italian-Hebrew school of poetry. As Schirmann comments in his article on the Hebrew theater in Italy during the Baroque period:

> There has not yet been any attempt to list the thousands of occasional poems composed by the Jews of Italy between the sixteenth and nineteenth centuries, but even today we can say that a considerable portion of those

---

[90] Idem, sonnet 244 in *Tzror Zehuvim*, ed. Bregman.
[91] E.g. Moses ben Joab, sonnet 48 in *Tzror Zehuvim*, ed. Bregman; Jacob Frances, sonnet 244.
[92] Jacob Frances, sonnet 247 in *Tzror Zehuvim*, ed. Bregman.
[93] Immanuel of Rome, sonnet 17 in *Tzror Zehuvim*, ed. Bregman; Moses ben Joab, sonnet 48.
[94] Jacob Frances, sonnet 245 in *Tzror Zehuvim*, ed. Bregman; Immanuel of Rome, sonnet 9.

poems were intended for weddings. There are all kinds of poems among them, from refined sonnets containing brief wishes for nuptial joy to entire pamphlets . . .[95]

And in a note he adds, "Only after going through all of them will it be possible to separate the wheat from the chaff."

By the eighteenth century the popularity of the wedding sonnet had reached flood-point. Its authors ranged from famous poets to ordinary householders who wrote because they were related to the bride or groom, or were friends of the families. Over fifty such sonnets have come down to us from the seventeenth century, and there is no doubt that their actual numbers were even greater.

The Hebrew wedding poem goes back to antiquity. The early Hebrew *paytanim* (liturgical poets) composed wedding poems that were meant for inclusion in the synagogue service itself,[96] while Hebrew poets in Spain also wrote secular poems for weddings.[97] Hebrew poets could learn from the epithalamia in Latin — wedding poems which poets of their day were writing in Italy, in memory of the genre's classical roots — or from the Spanish wedding poems then being written in Spain and the Netherlands. Jews, among them the well-known poet Daniel de Barrios, also wrote wedding poems in Spanish.[98]

The wedding poem enjoyed both social and poetic prestige. Let us cite one testimony to this among the many available to us. Moses Zacuto, perhaps finding himself unable to attend the wedding ceremony of his beloved pupil Benjamin Vitale Coen, acted according to the prevailing customs and sent the prospective groom a poem that he composed for the occasion. In a letter to Coen he wrote: "Lo, I anticipate your reply, that I might know when to print the poem I composed for you." To this the groom replied: "For me the poem will be like seeing His Honor's face, and on the day of my rejoicing I shall place it upon my head [like] a great golden crown embedded with rows of precious stones."[99]

The wedding poem was written or even specially printed upon broadsheets that were then distributed to the guests in attendance. It was recited at the wedding festivities, occasionally with musical accompaniment.[100] The broadsheets

---

[95] Schirmann, *Le-Toldot*, 2:80–81.

[96] E. Fleischer, *Shirat ha-Qodesh ha-ʿIvrit bi-Yemei ha-Beynaim* (Jerusalem, 1975), 154; idem, *Ha-Yotzerot* (Jerusalem, 1984), 385, 408, 565.

[97] For example, Moses ibn Ezra, *Shirei ha-Hol*, 159; Judah ha-Levi, in Schirmann, *Ha-Shirah ha-ʿIvrit*, 432.

[98] See Oelman, *Marrano Poets*, 219–21.

[99] Quoted from the letters of Moses ibn Zacuto: A. Appelbaum (Apfelboim), *Moshe Zacut* (Lvov, 1926), 13.

[100] Schirman, *Le-Toldot*, 2:82; Israel Adler, "The Rise of Art Music in the Italian Ghetto," in *Jewish Medieval and Renaissance Studies*, ed. A. Altmann (Cambridge, MA, 1967), 321–64.

were lavishly decorated, sometimes with particular symbols such as the zodiac, or with the heraldic devices used by the families of the nuptial couple, a custom among the Jews of Italy. A sonnet for the wedding of Meir Luzzatto was crammed into a picture of a rooster holding some grain in its claw, with a star-studded sky above it.[101] This is the symbol of the Luzzatto family in memory of the family's German city of origin, Lausitz, also called Freyhan (which sounds like the words for a "free rooster"). A similar picture also served as the device of the Lustro family, whose name indicates shining light. In a sonnet celebrating the doctorate awarded Solomon Lustro, the family device was described allegorically:

> The day the Zarḥi [Lustro] families took as their heraldic device
> A rooster gathering grain by light of the moon,
> The stars of wisdom in their knowing heart
> Shone lustrously out of the windows of truth.[102]

The Lustro family was nicknamed *Zarḥi* because, like the rooster, the family's device, the word *Zarḥi* indicates the rising of the sun. In the sonnet for Meir Lustro's wedding, the name of the groom — Meir ("shining") — reinforced this association.[103]

Wedding poems were recited during the festivities, usually by the poet himself. Leone da Modena noted an exceptional occurrence, signing himself as "[the poet who] brings but does not recite and [who] rejoices in their joy, Leone da Modena." The wedding sonnet could have been included in an entire collection of poems and riddles.[104] A pair of sonnets for the bride and groom by Jacob Frances was included in one such collection.[105]

The reciting of poems at weddings was no marginal event in poetic circles. In a pamphlet of his wedding poems, Jacob Frances added some acute criticism that set off a literary-social scandal. The poet Isaac min-ha-Levi'im grumbled about it in his diary:

---

[101] Moses Hayyim Cantarini, sonnet 404 in *Tzror Zehuvim*, ed. Bregman.

[102] Sabato Marini, sonnet 413 in *Tzror Zehuvim*, ed. Bregman.

[103] On the devices used by Jewish families in Italy, see C. Roth, "Stemmi di famiglie ebraiche italiane," in *Scritti in Memoria di Leone Carpi*, ed. D. Carpi and A. Milano (Jerusalem, 1967), 165–84; on those of the families of Luzzatto and Lustro see 178. See also E. Morpurgo, *Notizie sulle famiglie ebree esistite a Padova nel XVI secolo* (Udine, 1909): 11–12, concerning the device of the Luzzatto family.

[104] Moses Zacuto was renowned for his riddles for weddings. See D. Bregman, "Qesem ha-Ḥidah," *Davar*, 22 August 1986, 20–21.

[105] Jacob Frances, *Kol Shirei*, ed. Naveh, 259–70. The two sonnets are printed in *Tzror Zehuvim*, ed. Bregman, sonnets 248 and 249.

[Frances] states the pitfalls in writing poetry, and that most poets at this time are complete asses who deserve to be struck in the face . . . and that there is no good poet in Venice . . . apart from three: Levi Yozvil, Moses Zacuto, and Yom-Tov Valvasson,[106] but that his brother [i.e. Immanuel Frances] is worth more than all of them. And the wedding poem came after that. This made me sick to death . . . So I wrote him a letter complaining about this in my name and in the name of all the *virtuosi Veneziani*. This sonnet complains about the poems composed . . . and I sent it to him.[107]

The sonnet mentioned by Isaac min-ha-Levi'im has not come down to us. But we do have Immanuel Frances's reply to his letter; an epistle to "so-and-so and his cronies" overflowing with scorn:

Though throughout Israel and Judah I roam / and with a candle search through every home / and each and every corner comb / I will not find anyone as dumb as you / for your mind is like a bedbug, and a mosquito's, too . . .

Frances' letter also contains a poem in running rhyme *Re'u sakhal be-ziknato* ("Behold a fool in old age") and the sonnet *Eykh naʿatzutz yitʾalʿalei tidhar* ("How can a thornbush rise higher than a cedar?").[108]

Actually, Jacob Frances did not merely intend to criticize, for he also included some helpful hints, advising the poet not to "soar like the eagle" or "creep over the ground" lest he "give birth to *nefilim* or *nefalim*": that is, to the giants in Genesis 6:4 who wandered the earth in primordial times, or to aborted infants.[109]

The sonnet ran less danger of such pitfalls since it was restrained by strict considerations of form and meter. When writing wedding poems, poets adhered to a few basic elements: praise of the bride and groom and their respective families, good wishes for the couple and for the Jewish people as a whole, ethical guidance, and ornate descriptions of the occasion. The author of a wedding poem in sonnet-form had either to develop all of these elements in fourteen lines (and to do so according to an accepted, or acceptable, model of thematic development: see Chapter 14), or to develop only some of them. Usually the second option was preferred. Wedding sonnets often limited themselves to the names of the couple

---

[106] The poems of Yozvil have not come down to us; those of Valvasson are known in part.

[107] Isaac min-ha-Levi'im, *Medaber Tahapukhot*, ed. D. Carpi (Tel Aviv, 1985), 110–12; and see the notes of the editor there.

[108] Immanuel Frances, *Diwan*, ed. Bernstein, 31–34, and sonnet 325 in *Tzror Zehuvim*, ed. Bregman.

[109] Jacob Frances, *Kol Shirei*, ed. Naveh, 262.

alone,[110] or to praise of the couple and their families[111] and so forth. Needless to say, such restrictions worked for the best.

The wedding sonnet is a poem of praise, and that praise is fairly standard. Thus the bride is extolled for her beauty, the groom for his learning, and both for their family pedigrees. Levis and Cohens were especially singled out for this purpose. The forebears of the couple are also praised for their learning, charity, and social standing. In order to make up for the generality of such praise, the poet included such details as the names of the bride and groom and the site of the wedding ceremony within the poem itself, either explicitly or through allusion, and generally in a kind of miniature homily of praise. Such concrete details earmarked the poem for a specific occasion, in contrast to the wedding poems in other languages, which went from one wedding to another without change.[112]

The Religious Dimension

The wedding poem accompanied the ceremony under the wedding canopy, and sometimes came right before the afternoon prayer which preceded it.[113] Because it came near to being liturgical poetry, the wedding sonnet often emphasized the religious dimension of the occasion. It would describe the wedding as the work of God — part of his divine plan of Creation[114] — and warn the couple to observe "true charity."[115] It would also include short prayers for the prosperity of the nuptial couple: "Lift your voice now in gladness and song / All ye who strum upon the harp / to God who bears the heavens on high and everything else / for the wedding day of the couple that has now arrived."[116] The blessing wishes the couple children, wealth, and long life, together with hopes for Redemption: "May the rejoicing of Israel yet multiply."[117]

---

[110] Isaac min-ha-Levi'im, sonnet 406 in *Tzror Zehuvim*, ed. Bregman.

[111] Solomon Conegliano, sonnet 395 in *Tzror Zehuvim*, ed. Bregman.

[112] For exceptions in this matter, see D. Pagis, "Piyyutim Me'uharim me-Italia," *Qiryat Sefer* 50 (1975): 288–312, here 304 [rep. in idem, *Ha-Shir Davur ʿal Ofanav*, ed. E. Fleisher (Jerusalem, 1993), 336–60].

[113] See Pagis, "Piyyutim Me'uharim me-Italia."

[114] For examples: Leone da Modena, sonnets 110, 107, and 119 in *Tzror Zehuvim*, ed. Bregman.

[115] Anonymous, sonnet 363 in *Tzror Zehuvim*, ed. Bregman.

[116] Leone da Modena, sonnet 109 in *Tzror Zehuvim*, ed. Bregman.

[117] Idem, sonnet 109 in *Tzror Zehuvim*, ed. Bregman, and see also sonnet 107.

Erotica

Latin and Italian epithalamia are conspicuously erotic in nature. They abound with explicit advice for the wedding night, and do not even shy away from descriptions of the sexual act itself. In Italy and elsewhere, Jewish poets also allowed themselves a certain license in composing wedding poems both in Hebrew[118] and other languages.[119] Here, for example, is a poetic dialogue between the bride and the groom, written by Joseph Tzarfati for the wedding of a groom named Moses (possibly Moses ben Joab).[120] The poem, which is not in sonnet-form, makes witty (and highly erotic) use of several biblical references to Moses, such as the mysterious scene in Exodus 4:25 where Moses' wife calls her husband "a bloody bridegroom," and also Moses' striking of the rock in the wilderness (Exodus 17:6):

> Groom: When I split your belly with the bow of my arrow / I will send the good honey through you / A covenant of salt, my doe / have I prepared to worship you / and a heart purified by salt.
>
> Bride: To you, Moses, prayers within my belly / phylacteries of charm, and sealed drops of nectar. / Strike the closed and sealed rock with the rock / and be unto me a bloody bridegroom.

In the Hebrew sonnet, on the other hand, erotic overtones are generally weak, though not absent altogether. The word *dod*, which in the poetry of this period can refer both to "a friend" or even to someone in a negative sense, means "a lover" in the wedding sonnet.[121] The concept of desire (*Ḥesheq*) crops up now and then. Raphael Cagli (or Calleo) compares the groom to the biblical Boaz, who, according to rabbinic legend, heroically restrained his passion for Ruth that fateful night in the barn.[122] Leone da Modena goes into detail and tells the groom to "Give thanks to God, blessed be his great knowledge / for preparing your lap wherein will lie / the crown of womanhood and grace /... how can snow and cold weather / overpower you when she is a flame?"[123] The name of the bride, Fiammetta, inspired this Petrarchan conceit.

---

[118] See D. Pagis, "Qovetz Piyyutim mi-Provans," in *Sefer Ḥayyim Schirmann*, ed. S. Abramson and A. Mirsky (Jerusalem, 1970), 257–84.

[119] See M. Lazar, "Shirei Ḥatuna Proventzali'im," in *Sefer Ḥayyim Schirmann*, ed. Abramson and Mirsky, 159–77.

[120] As the editor conjectures. See D. Almagor, "Megillah Shelaḥ he-Ḥatan el ha-Kalah," *Yediʿot Aḥronot*, 26 May 1978.

[121] See, for example, Leone da Modena, sonnets 107 and 118 in *Tzror Zehuvim*, ed. Bregman; Jacob Frances, sonnet 257.

[122] Raphael Cagli (Calleo), sonnet 150 in *Tzror Zehuvim*, ed. Bregman.

[123] Leone da Modena, sonnet 117 in *Tzror Zehuvim*, ed. Bregman.

Other sonnets hint at the idea of marital relations through all kinds of "couplings," such as pairs of sonnets.[124] Leone da Modena used echo-rhymes:[125] *kalah-kalah* ("bride-ended"); *ḥushim-ḥushim* ("the senses-hurried"); *rosh-rosh* ("perfume-first").[126]

L. Forster interpreted the bold eroticism of the epithalamium as a sociopoetic safety-valve: Petrarchan convention froze erotic expression, which thus found release in the independent tradition of the wedding poem.[127] This phenomenon is even clearer in Hebrew poetry of the Italian school, where eroticism, though strictly forbidden, was nevertheless granted a certain license in wedding poetry.[128] It is therefore interesting to note that at least in the field of sonnetry, this license was rarely used. Apparently the restraint that guided the writing of sonnets in the sixteenth century did not wane in the seventeenth century either, and certainly not in sonnets meant for public occasions.

Festive Touches

The wedding sonnet was meant to delight the bride and groom, a goal which finds expression in its lighthearted content, words of praise, and descriptions of the occasion: "Behold, the bridegroom with cymbals and lute / now goes forth from his city with a joyful heart / to take a helpmeet, like the moon . . ."[129] The wedding sonnet usually observes the middle ground recommended by Jacob Frances. It is generally simple and can be understood by one and all. But here and there we also find various poetic tricks to amuse the bride and groom, and sometimes these complicate the meaning. This is the case of a sonnet by Moses Zacuto, written entirely in alliterative words of one syllable.[130] Though alliteration dazzles the ear, deciphering it remains a job for scholars. There are numerous word-plays, primarily centering around the names of actual people and places. To a bridegroom whose bride is named Stella ("star"), one sonnet bids the lover to "soar above the constellations."[131] Another sonnet makes an intricate word-play on the name Lucca, the scene of one wedding.[132] The names of the nuptial couple are sometimes strung into acrostics and made the subject of witty

---

[124] Jacob Frances, sonnets 248 and 249 in *Tzror Zehuvim*, ed. Bregman; Moses Zacuto, sonnets 221 and 222.
[125] Leone da Modena, sonnet 112 in *Tzror Zehuvim*, ed. Bregman.
[126] Idem, sonnet 113 in *Tzror Zehuvim*, ed. Bregman.
[127] Forster, *The Icy Fire*, 106–9.
[128] See what Immanuel Frances had to say on the subject, above, Chap. 15, Part 1.
[129] Samuel Bassani, sonnet 151 in *Tzror Zehuvim*, ed. Bregman.
[130] Moses Zacuto, sonnet 219 in *Tzror Zehuvim*, ed. Bregman.
[131] Isaac min-ha-Levi'im, sonnet 352 in *Tzror Zehuvim*, ed. Bregman.
[132] Raphael Cagli (Calleo), sonnet 150 in *Tzror Zehuvim*, ed. Bregman.

homilies.[133] There are allusions to wise sayings of the rabbis,[134] and little riddles in the margins.[135] It was about such devices in wedding sonnets that Jacob Frances complimented Moses Zacuto: "Who is like unto Rabbi Moses Zacuto? / He took nine-tenths of poetry's part. / Not one of his words falls to the ground / and as for word-play, there have been none like him before or since."[136]

The spirit of festivity also nudged the sonnet-form out of its usual routine: poets added "tails"[137] and composed sonnets in unusual forms,[138] though never to excess in either quantity or form.

3. Praise of Books

A Golden Poem of Praise

In a joyful letter to his teacher, Samuel Archivolti, Leone da Modena announced that his *Midbar Yehuda*[139] was now at the publisher's, and "like a son rejoicing his father," Modena asked Archivolti

> to please honor me with one of your poems. Make a "golden poem" for me with joy and delight, as a teacher rejoices over his pupil. For this is my first fruit, and may all the earth know that like a gushing stream I knelt and drank from [your] waters. I will print it at the beginning of the book, God willing.[140]

Having requested Archivolti to write a sonnet for him, Modena went on to detail how he wrote the book, and then entered into a more technical discussion:

> There is an empty space for the poem the length of one sheet, that is, the surface of one square page . . . About half the book is already printed, and the first page, on which I will put the poem, will be printed last, with the help of the Lord, blessed be He. Therefore, make haste and do it twice as quickly as usual, and I shall render you thanks.[141]

---

[133] Moses Zacuto, sonnet 221 in *Tzror Zehuvim*, ed. Bregman.

[134] Leone da Modena, sonnet 108 in *Tzror Zehuvim*, ed. Bregman.

[135] Juliani Cases, sonnet 100 in *Tzror Zehuvim*, ed. Bregman; Leone da Modena, sonnet 106, at the end.

[136] Jacob Frances, sonnet 267 in *Tzror Zehuvim*, ed. Bregman.

[137] Isaac min-ha-Levi'im, sonnet 352 in *Tzror Zehuvim*, ed. Bregman.

[138] Raphael Cagli (Calleo), sonnet 150 in *Tzror Zehuvim*, ed. Bregman.

[139] The title of the book alludes both to a geographical location ("the Judean desert") and to the "speech (*midbar*) of Judah" — this being the Hebrew name of Leone da Modena.

[140] Leone da Modena, *Iggerot*, ed. J. Boksenboim (Tel Aviv, 1989), 83.

[141] Modena, *Iggerot*, 83.

And indeed, *Midbar Yehuda* opens with a "golden poem" by Archivolti, the sonnet *Im ha-zeman yishbor* ("If time destroys").[142]

This episode is instructive in a number of ways. It shows us that a poem of praise served to recommend a book, and to give its blessing to the publication. It shows us that the poem was supposed to deal with the subject of the book, and that a poem in sonnet-form would likely meet with approval. It also shows us that printing a poem of praise at the beginning of a book necessitated special typographic arrangements, and last, that it was considered a worthy enterprise in the eyes of poet and recipient alike.

There was nothing new about a Hebrew poem praising books. Already Abraham ibn Ezra had written poems of this kind back in the twelfth century.[143] But with the invention of printing the genre flourished as never before. It required a great deal of effort to print a book, and the completion of the project was recorded in a festive and often emotional manner on the frontispiece of the book, together with the poem praising and recommending it. Naturally enough, the privilege of expression fell to the proofreader who had seen the work to completion. The proofreader of the 1667 edition of the Bible offers an emotional prayer of thanksgiving in sonnet-form: "I shall exalt and give thanks to Him who sits astride the cherubs /. . . for all His great and good loving-kindness / and for preserving and keeping those who love Him / till the completion of my work, my holiness, my light."[144]

Some books had more than one poem written for them, sonnets included. For example: *Kise'ot le-Veit David* by Judah Asahel del Bene; *Ḥanukat ha-Bayit*, by Moses Gentili; *Asirei ha-Tiqvah*, by Joseph Penso; and *Tzofnat Paʿneah* by Samuel Coen da Pisa. The preface to Moses di Mercado's book, which was published posthumously, has a number of laments, some in sonnet-form.

The Hebrew sonnet of praise was not restricted to Jewish authors of Hebrew books. Samuel Archivolti and Leone da Modena both dedicated sonnets to Christian Hebraists whom they had taught Hebrew, and who published Hebrew dictionaries: Marcus Marinus and Jean de la Pause Plantavit. The poems were printed in Hebrew on the frontispieces of the books.[145]

Sonnets in praise of books are not always praiseworthy in themselves. Their ideas are not always fully crystallized, and their comparisons can be highly exaggerated. The book is likened to honey, light, or refined silver, but the comparisons are not convincing.[146] The style can also be rather bombastic: a sonnet hon-

---

[142] Samuel Archivolti, sonnet 69 in *Tzror Zehuvim*, ed. Bregman.

[143] See *Shirei ha-Ḥol*, ed. D. Kahana, 2 vols. (Warsaw, 1894), 1:65–71.

[144] Joshua da Silva, sonnet 303 in *Tzror Zehuvim*, ed. Bregman.

[145] Jean de la Pause Plantavit, *Planta Vitis* (Lodovae, 1645); Marcus Marinus, *Arca Noe* (Venice, 1581). See Samuel Archivolti, sonnet 70; Leone da Modena, sonnet 128 in *Tzror Zehuvim*, ed. Bregman .

[146] See for example, Daniel Belilios, sonnet 304 in *Tzror Zehuvim*, ed. Bregman.

oring a book by Zecharia da Porto claims that "This Zecharia has conquered by virtue of name and knowledge. / His sun, which shines and never sets, / illuminates the stars of the Hebrew nation."[147] Other sonnets "proclaim [the author's] name to the inhabitants of the entire world,"[148] or declare that even "if the trees of the forest were pens / and the expanse of the heavens parchment, / this would not be enough to sing the splendor of his name."[149] Such high-flown expressions, suitable to liturgical poetry, are liable to sound pretentious in this context. Some sonnets praise books in such a generalized way that they all end up sounding alike. This said, it must be noted that many other sonnets are admirable for simplicity of expression, fully matured ideas, and well-chosen comparisons. Many are strikingly original. The poem in praise of the author served to recommend the book and to express approbation of its content.[150] This function determined the sonnet's choice of subject-matter and made it specific and unique.[151] So, for example, one sonnet praises Isaac Abrabanel's commentary on the Bible for revealing the secrets of Holy Writ.[152] A sonnet dedicated to Israel Najara's poems of prayer notes that these contain "a poem like incense" for every occasion.[153] And a sonnet for Menasseh ben Israel's *Nishmat Ḥayyim* ("The Soul of Life") sees the book as answering "the lying tongue of our enemies."[154] A sonnet by Samuel Archivolti in praise of Bartolomeo di Gandia, who was sent by Philip II, King of Spain, "to remove error from the hearts of the heretics," deals with a book of Catholic theology commissioned by the king. Archivolti extols the author for having proved the immortality of the soul with the help of Greek and Latin philosophy. Nor does he hesitate to offer His Most Catholic Majesty a few words of advice: "No longer will the King order instruments of destruction / against the masses of thirsting people, / for the tongue of wisdom and pen of lead will suffice."[155] Leone da Modena praises the Hebrew thesaurus of his student, the Hebraist Jean de la Pause Plantavit, for having redeemed the Hebrew language from

---

[147] Moses ben Jacob Muggia, sonnet 350 in *Tzror Zehuvim*, ed. Bregman.

[148] Menaḥem d'Ancona, sonnet 168 in *Tzror Zehuvim*, ed. Bregman.

[149] Abraham Pimentel Coen, sonnet 167 in *Tzror Zehuvim*, ed. Bregman.

[150] See M. Benyahu, *Haskama u-Reshut bi-Dfusei Venezia* (Jerusalem,1971), 99.

[151] See Bregman, "Shelosha ʿAsar Sonetim."

[152] Samuel Archivolti, sonnet 66 in *Tzror Zehuvim*, ed. Bregman.

[153] Leone da Modena, sonnet 127 in *Tzror Zehuvim*, ed. Bregman.

[154] Samuel di Mercado, sonnet 294 in *Tzror Zehuvim*, ed. Bregman.

[155] Samuel Archivolti, sonnet 71 in *Tzror Zehuvim*, ed. Bregman. And see S. Bernstein, "Shirim Ḥadashim le-Rabbi Shmuel Archivolti," *Tarbiz* 8 (1937): 55–68. The idea that Catholicism should be propagated by gentle persuasion rather than force was preached by Marsilio Ficino and adopted by early Italian advocates of reform. See D. Cassuto, *Ha-Yehudim be-Firenze bi-Tequfat ha-Renaissance*, trans. M. Hartom (Jerusalem, 1967), 217–20; and in Italian: *Gli ebrei a Firenze* (Florence, 1918. repr. 1966).

anonymity.[156] These and many other sonnets like them do not fall into the trap of over-generalized praise, and deal with their subject in a unique way.

The book determined not only the subject matter of the sonnet of praise but very often the imagery as well, and thus gained a certain unity. So, for example, the sonnet praising *Tiqun soferim* uses images and allusions from the Temple, such as the pillars, ephod, and candelabrum.[157] A sonnet describing the poetic power of drama is based on an almost mythological image of the mighty Nile,[158] and another sonnet, which praises a book of commentary, is based on the parable of a locked house, now opened.[159]

Some sonnets have a more personal tone. A sonnet praising *Midbar Yehuda* mentions the sorrows of its author, Leone da Modena, and offers a comforting thought: if God measures his sins to "a hair's-breadth," He also "repairs the broken fence."[160] In another sonnet for the same book, the poet muses: "How can there be a poem on my lips, when I have grown old?"[161] Despite their generic similarities, these sonnets are completely different from one another.

The Author's Preface

In addition to sonnets of praise and recommendation, there are also sonnets prefacing books written by the authors themselves. Such sonnets usually serve as the author's "apology" and are notable for their self-effacing tone. In the sonnet prefacing *The Comedy of Betrothal*,[162] the first drama ever written in Hebrew, Judah de' Sommi Portaleone apologizes for introducing the genre into the Holy Tongue. He explains that his work is new in form only, and humorously asks his audience to learn a lesson from the play and eat the "good fruit", while disregarding "some of the peel."[163] His defense is mixed with pride over the great novelty of the genre:

> Behold, O generation, the new with which I fill
> The old, like fine oil inside a container.
> A genre in which mouths and hearts will find content
> To rejoice in the riddle of love, which I invent.[164]

---

[156] Leone da Mondena, sonnet 129 in *Tzror Zehuvim*, ed. Bregman.
[157] Solomon Oliveyra, sonnet 341 in *Tzror Zehuvim*, ed. Bregman.
[158] Jacob Sasportas, sonnet 370 in *Tzror Zehuvim*, ed. Bregman.
[159] Solomon Lustro, sonnet 409 in *Tzror Zehuvim*, ed. Bregman.
[160] Azariah Figo, sonnet 138 in *Tzror Zehuvim*, ed. Bregman.
[161] Samuel Archivolti, sonnet 69 in *Tzror Zehuvim*, ed. Bregman.
[162] Judah de' Sommi Portaleone, sonnet 51 in *Tzror Zehuvim*, ed. Bregman.
[163] See Schirmann, *Le-Toldot*, 2: 105–6, 108–11.
[164] Judah de' Sommi Portaleone in his preface to *The Comedy of Betrothal* (sonnet 51 in *Tzror Zehuvim*, ed. Bregman). Schirmann printed this with an error: "indeed" instead of "genre". See Dvora Bregman, *Tiferet Sinai – Sefer Hamaḥazot Shel Matityah Nissim Terni* , introduction.

Moses Gentili included a sonnet which he calls "the author's apology" on the frontispiece of his *Ḥanukat ha-Bayit* ("The Inauguration of the Temple").[165] In the sonnet he apologizes for having written the book in the first place, and for even investigating the subject at all. Like Portaleone, he humorously asks his readers to distinguish between the trivial and the important.[166]

Abraham Jagel dedicated to the well-known patron of letters, Joseph da Fano, a manuscript copy of his *Oraḥ Ḥayyim* ("The Path of Life"),[167] a book which deals with the prevention of the plague. In the sonnet of dedication, Jagel describes his book with a modesty that is mingled with pride: "Here friends will find flowing honey, / medicine for the evil plague abounding with / fragrant salves and ointments."

On the other hand, there is no trace of apology in the sonnet which prefaces Israel Najara's *Zemirot Israel* ("The Songs of Israel"). In the Safed edition we read:

> The hand that carved my poems is superior
> to the carvings of other minstrels in poetry.
> Compared to mine their poems are considered strange,
> And despoiled of beauty, flower and crown.[168]

The self-praise in this sonnet is unusual, especially since it appears in a book of poems for prayer, where expressions of humility might be thought suitable to the opening. But perhaps it was not Najara himself who composed this sonnet, but rather a Jewish friend in Italy, such as Leone da Modena, who wrote a sonnet prefacing the Venice edition of that book. This conjecture is strengthened by the fact that Najara did not otherwise write sonnets, and also by the style of the poem, which includes expressions common to Hebrew poetry in Italy.[169] To be sure, the name Israel appears in the sonnet in a double acrostic, but this might be the name of the poem's recipient, and not of the poet. Though the acrostic was generally reserved in Hebrew poetry for the name of the poet, it sometimes bears the name of the recipient instead, or the name of the person being praised.[170] The

---

[165] Moses Gentili, sonnet 392 in *Tzror Zehuvim*, ed. Bregman.

[166] Moses Gentili, sonnet 392 in *Tzror Zehuvim*, ed. Bregman.

[167] Abraham Jagel, sonnet 79 in *Tzror Zehuvim*, ed. Bregman. The book's title comes from Psalm 16:11.

[168] Israel Najara (?), sonnet 80 in *Tzror Zehuvim*, ed. Bregman.

[169] Cf., for example, with Samuel Archivolti, sonnet 62 in *Tzror Zehuvim*, ed. Bregman; Jacob Frances, sonnets 238 and 254; Leone da Modena, sonnet 136; Joseph Franco-Serrano, sonnet 401.

[170] Fleischer, *Shirat ha-Qodesh*, 129.

acrostic in Jagel's above-mentioned sonnet of dedication spells the name "Joseph," the recipient of the poem, and the sonnet which Isaac Uziel sent to Saʿadia Longo spells the name "Saʿadia."

4. For Various People and Occasions

Panegyrical sonnets were apt to be composed for anyone, and for any occasion. Leone da Modena wrote sonnets for an artisan "as skilled as Bezalel at carving,"[171] and for a Christian preacher whose words "pierce the heart."[172] Joseph Franco-Serrano wrote a sonnet in praise of Amsterdam's famed Torah Academy, *Shaʿarei Tzedek*.[173] Immanuel Frances praised a "great poet by the name of Immanuel" in a reflective sonnet about that person's portrait.[174] The sonnet is a riddle, and the subject of the praise may be none other than the poet himself: a highly Baroque artifice.

Receiving a doctorate for medicine or philosophy, as was customary at the time, was always an excuse to compose poems of praise, and sonnets for the occasion were composed already at the beginning of the seventeenth century. When Joseph Hamitz received his doctorate, Leone da Modena assembled for his favorite student an entire collection of panegyrics, poems, and sonnets composed by various friends under the name *Belil Ḥamitz* (Venice, 1624).[175] He also extolled Moses Uziel, who received his doctorate in 1623. Abraham Ortona wrote and translated sonnets in honor of Benjamin da Forli, who received a doctorate of medicine around 1600.[176] Sonnets of this kind multiplied at the end of the seventeenth century, and even more so in the eighteenth. Among the dozens of Jews who finished their medical studies in the University of Padua, we find a not inconsiderable group of poets who wrote poems and sonnets in honor of the

---

[171] Leone da Modena, sonnet 125 in *Tzror Zehuvim*, ed. Bregman.

[172] Idem, sonnet 126 in *Tzror Zehuvim*, ed. Bregman.

[173] Joseph Franco-Serrano, sonnet 401 in *Tzror Zehuvim*, ed. Bregman. See D. Bregman, "Shirim le-Ḥanukat Batei Knesset," in *Knesset ʿEzra*, ed. S. Elizur (Jerusalem, 1994), 365–71.

[174] Immanuel Frances, sonnet 317 in *Tzror Zehuvim*, ed. Bregman.

[175] The sonnets in this book include: Abraham Catalano, sonnet 144; David Luria, sonnet 145; Elijah Modena, sonnet 153 in *Tzror Zehuvim*, ed. Bregman. The name of the book *Belil Ḥamitz* takes its cue from Isaiah 30:24, where the phrase *belil ḥamitz* refers to a savory mixture of cattle-feed. Hence the book's title might be translated as a "mixture" for Joseph Hamitz, that is, a collection of works from different authors in his honor.

[176] Abraham Ortona, sonnet 141 in *Tzror Zehuvim*, ed. Bregman. And see C. Roth, "Catalogue of the Manuscripts in the Roth Collection," in *Alexander Marx Jubilee Volume* (New York, 1950), 503–35, here 513, item 113.

ceremony. Poems and sonnets of praise were heaped upon Solomon Lustro and Abraham Coen Zante, to name only two.[177] The praise in sonnets of this kind is generally of two kinds. In addition to noting the recipient's mastery of science, sometimes through allegorical motifs and allusions relating to the world of medicine, the poems also mention his knowledge and observance of Jewish law. Poems and sonnets in honor of the doctorate were written and printed on sumptuous broadsheets and distributed amongst the guests during the ceremony itself, like wedding poems.

Some Hebrew sonnets were dedicated to rulers and important public figures, such as the laments written by Azariah de' Rossi and Judah Moscato for Marguerite of Savoy.[178] Sonnets for rulers often include relevant allusions to concrete events. Moses Zacuto devoted a Hebrew sonnet to the coronation of Queen Christina of Sweden,[179] who was in contact with Italian writers and Portuguese Jews. A sonnet by Jacob Frances offered encouragement to Charles II, ruler of Mantua, when his army came under siege there.[180] The sonnet concludes with the words "and you will stand," an allusion to a silver coin minted by that ruler.[181] Sonnets to rulers were not necessarily poems of praise. Another sonnet by Jacob Frances, ostensibly to the Roman emperor Nero, protests against the tyranny of the local prince and advises him to respect his subjects, whether "lord or wayfarer." It threatens anarchy, for "if princes and emperors . . . / break through the barriers, they can anticipate a breakthrough / like this!"[182] This is truly a political statement, and one which testifies to a proud sense of citizenship.

5. Sonnets of Friendship

Between Friends

The sonnet of friendship testifies to the role which the renewed Hebrew sonnet played from the beginning in the daily life of Hebrew poets and men of culture. It often has an intimate tone and alludes to information known to the original addressee, though not necessarily to anyone else.

So, for example, sonnets by Joseph Tzarfati and Moses ben Joab urge a common friend, Solomon da Poggibonsi,[183] the author of a biblical concordance, to

---

[177] M. Benyahu, "Rav Avraham ha-Kohen mi-Zante ve-Lahaqat ha-Rofim ha-Meshorerim be-Padua," *Ha-Sifrut* 26 (1978): 108–10.

[178] Below, in the section on Laments.

[179] Moses Zacuto, sonnet 224 in *Tzror Zehuvim*, ed. Bregman.

[180] Jacob Frances, sonnet 250 in *Tzror Zehuvim*, ed. Bregman.

[181] See Jacob Frances, *Kol Shirei*, ed. Naveh, Appendix V, 576–77.

[182] Idem, sonnet 261 in *Tzror Zehuvim*, ed. Bregman.

[183] Concerning Poggibonsi, see *Tzror Zehuvim*, ed. Bregman, sonnet 69 and 71.

give up his money-changing affairs and return to Florence.[184] They express their longing for him ("When I do not see your face / my heart and mouth both cry out"), invite him to share their bread, and allude to his letter-writing talents in order to suggest another way of making a living, reminding him that "all the treasures of calligraphy open before you." Ben Joab sent a playful sonnet to this same Solomon about his gluttony,[185] as well as another sonnet comforting some friends or relations over the death of their father.[186] Tzarfati taunts friends for not writing poems and playing cards as well as he did.[187] To friends who expressed surprise over his long poetic silence, Ben Joab replies in a way that sounds cryptic today: "How can my heart desire glorious song / when the Rock has punished me, and the whip of his anger lies upon / my spirit, and my soul suffers for ᶜola-li."[188] This Hebrew word means either "my baby" or "my misdeed," and today we have no way of knowing whether Ben Joab was mourning his child, or paying the price for some regrettable act on his part. Leone da Modena reminds his noble friend and pupil, Jean de la Pause Plantavit, who "views the Hebrew tongue with a favorable eye", of the days spent together studying "the Old Faith."[189] Abraham Ortona hopes that his friend rises from his sickbed "healthy and not limping."[190] Immanuel Frances compliments Rabbi Joseph Fermo about a successful verdict, and tells him how this worked to his advantage in a community quarrel.[191] A sonnet by Jacob Frances to Moses Zacuto grumbles about Fate: "Why does the evil hand hurry / to hide the face of the man Moses, great in wisdom, / my soul's beloved and my faithful friend?"[192] Appearances to the contrary, this sonnet is not a lament, but rather a poem in response to Zacuto's sudden exit from Florence.

Poets rebuked each other in sonnets. Samuel Sasportas warns a friend "stretched out asleep on a bed of ivory" against his slothful ways; Jacob Frances rebukes a friend for taking a wife against his advice.[193]

Other sonnets between friends lack the intimate character and realistic details noted above. Since they were attached to letters, the concrete matter at hand — considered too prosaic for poetry — was included in the body of the letter

---

[184] Joseph Tzarfati, sonnet 40; Moses ben Joab: sonnet 44 in *Tzror Zehuvim*, ed. Bregman.

[185] Idem, sonnet 45 in *Tzror Zehuvim*, ed. Bregman.

[186] Idem, sonnet 46 in *Tzror Zehuvim*, ed. Bregman.

[187] Joseph Tzarfati, sonnets 41 and 42 in *Tzror Zehuvim*, ed. Bregman.

[188] Moses ben Joab, sonnet 47 in *Tzror Zehuvim*, ed. Bregman.

[189] Leone da Modena, sonnet 128 in *Tzror Zehuvim*, ed. Bregman.

[190] Abraham Ortona, *Im ha-levana bi-shemei shemayyim*: MS. Jewish Theological Seminary of New York, 1250, fol. 29.

[191] Immanuel Frances, sonnet 319 in *Tzror Zehuvim*, ed. Bregman.

[192] Jacob Frances, sonnet 252 in *Tzror Zehuvim*, ed. Bregman.

[193] Samuel Sasportas, sonnet 379 in *Tzror Zehuvim*, ed. Bregman; Jacob Frances, sonnet 244.

while the sonnet itself made do with general expressions of friendship and exaggerated compliments. Most sonnets by Jacob Segrè, for example, are like this.

Poetic Compliment

Poets expressed feelings of friendship and affection to their friends in sonnets that complimented their poetry. Sometimes the compliment sought to encourage the writer: "Open thy mouth, Isaac, let songs pour forth / . . . / Rise with a joyful song; rouse battles!"[194] Praise of the poem could also be mixed with acute criticism. Jacob Frances devoted a sonnet to his poet brother in which he listed his merits: his poems speak truthfully, use excellent material, and suit their argument to the subject.[195] But most sonnets of this kind make do with generalized and highly exaggerated praise: "From whom, O poet, did you learn the art of poetry, / that the honeycomb of your verse should please more than nectar? / . . . you must have burst into the abode of angels / and tarried there to plunder beauty and splendor."[196] Another poem has "all your contemporaries bowing before you."[197] And so on and so forth.

The compliment involved stylized self-effacement on more than one occasion. In a three-part exchange of sonnets, Jacob Frances competes with a member of the Kokhav family in bestowing compliments. "You were justified in likening me to / a statue," he begins, and then, with a play on his friend's name (*kokhav* = "star"): "I shall be judged right in calling you the star of poetry, the prince of planets."[198] Moses Zacuto extols the poems of Rabbi Jacob Yozvil to the detriment of his own abilities: "The day, my soul, you see and understand the beauties / of Rabbi Yozvil's poetry, fall silent!"[199] Despite the generalizations the expressions remained fresh, never hackneyed.

The compliment was embodied in the very stylization of the poem. Since it was a gift in poetry, the more perfect the poem was the more it was valued as a token of respect and esteem. A *tenzone* between Isaac Uziel of Fez in North Africa and Saʿadia Longo in Salonika offers a striking example of this fact. All three sonnets in this *tenzone* use the same meter, rhyme-scheme, and rhyme-words.[200] They unfold according to the same model (the one used by Immanuel of Rome) and employ similar language. They repeat the same logical constructs, though

---

[194] Joseph Tzarfati, sonnet 43 in *Tzror Zehuvim*, ed. Bregman.

[195] Jacob Frances, sonnet 254 in *Tzror Zehuvim*, ed. Bregman.

[196] Immanuel Frances, sonnet 318 in *Tzror Zehuvim*, ed. Bregman.

[197] Jacob Sasportas, sonnet 368 in *Tzror Zehuvim*, ed. Bregman.

[198] Jacob Frances, sonnet 253 in *Tzror Zehuvim*, ed. Bregman.

[199] Moses Zacuto, sonnet 223 in *Tzror Zehuvim*, ed. Bregman.

[200] The tenzone is made up of sonnet 82 by Isaac Uziel, sonnet 83 by Saʿadia Longo, and sonnet 84 by Isaac Uziel in *Tzror Zehuvim*, ed. Bregman.

with changes of function. So, for example, the poems repeatedly describe the expressive power of poetry.

Uziel likens poetry to the sea and the art of poetry to the splitting asunder of its waters. "When the ancients did wonders with poetry like a wall of waves / the waters of the deep burst out in songs."[201] Longo, in turn, likens poetry to a mountain and the art of poetry to the same elemental forces: "From the sound of your song, poet, mountains of poetry erupted / and rivers burst through the crags of wild gazelles."[202] Uziel repeated these motifs, comparing his own poems to rocks and mountains, and Longo's poetry in criticism of him to an eruption: "The rocks of poetry and the mountains of song were / the bastion of our friendship, but behold! they were burst through!"[203] Thus we see that the sonnet of praise can also contain a strong element of competition. It conveys not only praise for the other poet, but also praise of — if not outright bragging about — the poet's own poetry. This, of course, was one of the conventions of the genre. As Immanuel of Rome himself had put it centuries before, in his own *tenzone* with a rival poet: "Let's have it out and see who's better: / Write a poem in the form of this letter."[204]

6. The Polemic Sonnet

Social Criticism

Tension over the appointment of rabbis, and over the balance of power between the rabbis and the well-to-do, sometimes created a strain in the Jewish communities of Italy. Such tension found expression in sonnets on more than one occasion and indeed from the mid-sixteenth century on the sonnet was drawn into quarrels and polemics of all kinds.[205]

One substantial group of sonnets protests against leaders of the Jewish community, and especially against wealthy individuals whom the poets saw as lording it over the rest of the community. Isaac Levi wrote that "no one grips the staff of truth or honesty," accused the community leaders of "lies and theft . . . beyond measure,"[206] and warned them of divine judgment.[207] Archivolti used the sonnet

---

[201] Isaac Uziel, sonnet 82 in *Tzror Zehuvim*, ed. Bregman.
[202] Sa'adia Longo, sonnet 83 in *Tzror Zehuvim*, ed. Bregman.
[203] Isaac Uziel, sonnet 84 in *Tzror Zehuvim*, ed. Bregman.
[204] See above, Chap. 1.
[205] See D. Bregman, "Polemica Religiosa," in *Appartenenza e differenzia: ebrei d'Italia e letteratura*, ed. Hassine, Mishan-Montefiore, and Debenedetti Stow, 23–32.
[206] Isaac Levi, sonnet 104 in *Tzror Zehuvim*, ed. Bregman.
[207] Idem, sonnet 103 in *Tzror Zehuvim*, ed. Bregman.

to protest the removal of rabbis in exchange for favors;[208] Leone da Modena devoted a sonnet against the rich who regarded the community as their own personal property.[209]

The sonnet of social protest took on new dimensions in the work of the Frances brothers. Sometimes their words thunder convincingly in defense of scholars subjected to disrespectful treatment,[210] or deprived of public office.[211] But other times their attacks are so blatant that we wonder if their words reflect actual reality or just the Baroque tendency towards exaggeration. Their poems are a savage indictment of the rich and powerful, of the rabbis whom they appointed to office,[212] and the members of the Jewish community who supported them.[213] The community leadership appears in these sonnets as a depraved institution characterized by avarice, hypocrisy,[214] ignorance,[215] gluttony and insobriety,[216] a "hunger for power,"[217] "evil and lechery"(!),[218] breach of trust,[219] and contempt for the Torah.[220] All this was said about people well known to the readers, and sometimes their names were inscribed in the body of the poem itself or in the heading above it. Yet despite the storm of passions the sonnets remain highly-focused: "Tis not the impoverished community which is to blame / But its wicked leader that will be cursed from heaven!"[221] The accusation falls entirely on the leaders of the community, and not on the public.

The anti-establishment trend is also found in Italian poetry, and a similarity of motifs is evident. A sonnet by Michelangelo, for example, warns Jesus not to enter sinful Rome, which profits from the death of its Saviour.[222] Similarly, Jacob Frances mournfully addresses the Torah with the words: "Alas, doctrine of God, so full of honesty! / Those who busy themselves with you / do so to fill their coffers with wealth."[223] According to this, the occupation with Torah had become a business and a means for creating ill-gotten gains.

---

[208] Samuel Archivolti, sonnet 61 in *Tzror Zehuvim*, ed. Bregman.
[209] Leone da Modena, sonnet 136 in *Tzror Zehuvim*, ed. Bregman.
[210] Jacob Frances, sonnets 272 and 274 in *Tzror Zehuvim*, ed. Bregman.
[211] Idem, sonnet 263 in *Tzror Zehuvim*, ed. Bregman.
[212] Idem, sonnets 268 and 265 in *Tzror Zehuvim*, ed. Bregman.
[213] Idem, sonnet 267 in *Tzror Zehuvim*, ed. Bregman.
[214] Idem, sonnets 265 and 274 in *Tzror Zehuvim*, ed. Bregman.
[215] Idem, sonnets 264, 265, 267 and 272 in *Tzror Zehuvim*, ed. Bregman.
[216] Idem, sonnet 269 in *Tzror Zehuvim*, ed. Bregman.
[217] Idem, sonnet 266 in *Tzror Zehuvim*, ed. Bregman.
[218] Idem, sonnet 264 in *Tzror Zehuvim*, ed. Bregman.
[219] Idem, sonnet 271 in *Tzror Zehuvim*, ed. Bregman.
[220] Idem, sonnet 268 in *Tzror Zehuvim*, ed. Bregman.
[221] Idem, sonnets 267 and 274 in *Tzror Zehuvim*, ed. Bregman.
[222] Michelangelo, *Rime*, ed. Guasti, 157: *Qua si fa elmi*.
[223] Jacob Frances, sonnet 268 in *Tzror Zehuvim*, ed. Bregman.

In this group of sonnets, Baroque *acutezza* finds expression in vulgar language, bold metaphors, and tight organization. Immanuel Frances begins and ends one sonnet with a single metaphor whose power is reinforced through adept word-play: "How dear you became in my eyes, sir, today, when you passed the razor (*morah*) over that man's face / . . . / since they have no fear (*mora*) of God upon their face / May they face fear (*mora*) and the razor (*morah*)!"[224]

The argument in sonnets like these can be tortuous indeed. In another sonnet by Jacob Frances,[225] the poet jeers at the Jewish community for fasting and praying for the bedridden Rabbi Jehiel Norsi. He tells Rabbi Norsi that God will hear their prayers and not let this illness kill him, but that the day after he will be strung up like Jesus. Moreover, the poet goes on to say, rumor has it that some people hate you and are actually praying for your death. What fools! Why do they fast? Better to eat and drink in front of you, so that you — glutton that you are — will die of envy.

These sonnets have a variety of sharp endings. One sonnet, leaning on the Talmudic injunction that it is better to be the tail of lions than the head of foxes, ends with the following query to one hopeful candidate to the rabbinate: "How can you be the head of these lions? / you're not even worth what they excrete between their tails!"[226]

Against the Followers of Shabbetai Zevi

The brothers Jacob and Immanuel Frances were well-known for their courageous fight against the followers of Shabbetai Zevi, the self-proclaimed messiah.[227] Their weapons were of course poems, many of them sonnets. When historic events eventually proved the brothers right, these poems won public acclaim. Immanuel Frances himself collected them into a single pamphlet and thought about publishing them. Though this did not come about, the poems were published early on, relatively speaking.[228]

Thanks to their concrete nature, the sonnets in this group reflect various stages and details in the course of the ideological struggle in Italy: the activity of Nathan of Gaza and the persecution of Shabbetai's detractors,[229] the vigorous warnings of

---

[224] Idem, sonnet 320 in *Tzror Zehuvim*, ed. Bregman.

[225] Idem, sonnet 269 in *Tzror Zehuvim*, ed. Bregman.

[226] Idem, sonnet 265 in *Tzror Zehuvim*, ed. Bregman.

[227] See G. Scholem, *Sabbatai Sevi: The Mystical Messiah, 1626–1676* (Princeton, 1973).

[228] Jacob Frances, sonnets 276–282; Immanuel Frances, sonnets 326–328 in *Tzror Zehuvim*, ed. Bregman. See Immanuel Frances, *Tzevi Mudah,* ed. M. Morteira, *Qovetz ʿal-Yad* 1 (1885): 99–128; A. M. Habermann, "Le-Toldot ha-Pulmus Neged ha-Shabtaut," *Qovetz ʿal-Yad*, n.s. 3 (1941): 185–216; Scholem, *Sabbatai Sevi*.

[229] Jacob Frances, sonnet 276 in *Tzror Zehuvim*, ed. Bregman.

the brothers ("Don't believe, and don't go crazy! / this is neither our Messiah nor your king");[230] the customs of Shabbetai's followers; their fasts and self-imposed inflictions; and their responses to Shabbetai's conversion to Islam.[231] They describe Shabbetai's rise to power,[232] and in the end rejoice over his fall and that of his followers: "Those who trusted him are ashamed and disgraced."[233]

From the sonnets we understand the problems that Jacob Frances saw in Shabbetian ideology. For one thing, it contradicted the signs traditionally linked with the coming of the messiah. The glad tidings were supposed to be brought by Elijah the Prophet; Shabbetai replaced him with Nathan of Gaza ("Nathan is to you like Elijah!").[234] The city of the messiah is Jerusalem; Shabbetai exchanged it for Gaza ("Gaza and not Jerusalem is his place of power").[235] The messiah was supposed to ride on a donkey; Shabbetai rode on a horse.[236] And most important of all: Shabbetai Zevi urged Jews to go to Jerusalem and rebuild the Temple, whereas the true saviour was not supposed to come until the True Faith triumphed over all others.[237]

The sonnets against the Shabbetians use the technique of dramatic monologue to good effect. Thus Jacob Frances has Shabbetai Zevi delivering a monologue that reveals his worst qualities: his violence and cunning,[238] his arrogance,[239] his materialism and false piety.[240] This strategy can be very confusing to the reader, especially when the poet does not volunteer information about the identity of the speaker. Such a Baroque literary morass created an atmosphere of confusion that worked to the detriment of the Shabbetian movement then dominating the Jewish communities of Italy.

Another way of vilifying the movement was to demonize Shabbetai Zevi. Often this was accomplished by using the very same images that generally refer to the Almighty. So, for example, the Psalmist cries out to the Lord (Psalm 139:7-8):

> Whither shall I go from thy spirit?
> Or whither shall I flee from thy presence?

---

[230] Immanuel Frances, sonnet 327 in *Tzror Zehuvim*, ed. Bregman.
[231] Jacob Frances, sonnet 282 in *Tzror Zehuvim*, ed. Bregman.
[232] Idem, sonnet 279 in *Tzror Zehuvim*, ed. Bregman.
[233] Idem, sonnet 280 in *Tzror Zehuvim*, ed. Bregman.
[234] Idem, sonnet 276 in *Tzror Zehuvim*, ed. Bregman.
[235] Immanuel Frances, sonnet 326 in *Tzror Zehuvim*, ed. Bregman.
[236] Idem, sonnet 328 in *Tzror Zehuvim*, ed. Bregman.
[237] Jacob Frances, sonnet 281 in *Tzror Zehuvim*, ed. Bregman.
[238] Idem, sonnet 276 in *Tzror Zehuvim*, ed. Bregman.
[239] Immanuel Frances, sonnet 326 in *Tzror Zehuvim*, ed. Bregman.
[240] Jacob Frances, sonnets 277 and 278 in *Tzror Zehuvim*, ed. Bregman.

> If I ascend up into heaven, thou art there;
> If I make my bed in the netherworld, behold, thou art there.

Jacob Frances, on the other hand, used the same words to describe the flight from the self-proclaimed messiah:

> Whither shall I flee from you and spread my wings?
> Alas, were I to soar to the skies, thou
> Art there, or plunge to the abyss: lo, thou art there too.[241]

In actual life, Jacob Frances was persecuted because of his opposition to the Shabbatean movement and forced to leave Mantua. The sonnet hints that his persecutors represent a violent force aiming for mastery over the entire world, and encourages the audience to identify with the harassed speaker, unable to evade the evil presence.

Poetic War

Since polemics were conducted in poetry, social criticism was mixed with criticism of poetry that at times eclipsed the actual subject. The protest of the Frances brothers against teaching young students Kabbalah in the Rabbinic academies, and their demand to make conventional teaching of Torah the foundation of study, found expression in poems that were attacked and banned by their opponents. The brothers responded with poems and sonnets of their own; but these already veered towards poetic criticism rather than the topic at hand.[242] The main argument seems to have revolved around the concept of "truth."

From sonnets written by the two brothers we learn that one of Jacob's poems met with disapproval, and that their foes "spread the word that it lacked religion and truth."[243] The brothers naturally denied the charge: "The song of Jacob, recite out loud / For truly it contains the excellent truth."[244] Evidently, a poem that did not serve the accepted values of religion and social justice was considered worthless. This is reminiscent of trends in Italian poetry during the Counter-Reformation, when, in the wake of the Council of Trent, art was linked to the propagation of the True Faith. The old saying that "lies are the best part of poetry," well known to the Hebrew poet in Italy, seems to have been forgotten when

---

[241] Jacob Frances, sonnet 279 in *Tzror Zehuvim*, ed. Bregman.

[242] Immanuel Frances relates the episode in *Vikuah Livni ve-Shim'* in his *Diwan*, ed. Bernstein, 135–46. See Jacob Frances, sonnets 273 and 275; and Immanuel Frances, sonnets 322–325 and commentary in *Tzror Zehuvim*, ed. Bregman.

[243] Immanuel Frances, sonnet 324 in *Tzror Zehuvim*, ed. Bregman.

[244] Idem, sonnet 324 in *Tzror Zehuvim*, ed. Bregman.

caught up in the excitement of polemics. To the charge that "Sir Jacob" was not speaking the truth, the brothers replied that their opponent's poem sounded to them like a barking dog.[245]

The Frances brothers accused their social opponents of plagiarism ("Who placed in your knapsack, you braying ass, / this coin of poetic expression?")[246] and of lacking all literary discernment ("A viper will suck poison from a rose; / an old man whose eyes have dimmed / will fault the light of the sun").[247]

The satire was sharp. As a renowned satirist, Jacob Frances took pride in his ability to cut to the quick: "Behold, I am a devouring lion dressed in sheep-skin: / Those who pursue me I shall rip with my teeth — / beware their bite and great shadow of death: / Neither herb nor ointment will heal them; / the poison of truth I place in the wound, / a poison that kills like a death potion."[248]

In these sonnets the brothers make threats that reverberate both socially and poetically: "He will be a devil to you, if you devil him / and you will be to his raging sea a ship in the storm."[249] The brothers accompany these threats with vigorous name-slinging, variously calling their foes by epithets of all kinds: ignoramuses,[250] barking dogs,[251] wild boars,[252] prickly bushes, pesky insects. Then there are the complimentary names for the poet in which one brother or the other is a lion, a dragon and an eagle,[253] and in one memorable image, a flint-rock that sends sparks of fire in the direction of anyone who dares strike it.[254] The poetic criticism is highly sophistical: since the criticism of their foe makes the sweet bitter, the more his poem criticizes, the sweeter the poem that he criticizes.[255] This casuistry is delayed till the end of the poem in order to give it a sharper point.

The Polemic over Converts

We have from the seventeenth century several Hebrew sonnets which were exchanged between Hebrew poets and converts to Christianity.[256] The Christian side of this debate was represented by an unnamed monk, possibly of Jewish descent,

---

[245] Jacob Frances, sonnet 275 in *Tzror Zehuvim*, ed. Bregman.

[246] Jacob Fances, sonnet 273 in *Tzror Zehuvim*, ed. Bregman.

[247] Immanuel Frances, sonnet 324, and see also sonnet 325 in *Tzror Zehuvim*, ed. Bregman.

[248] Jacob Frances, sonnet 275 in *Tzror Zehuvim*, ed. Bregman.

[249] Immanuel Frances, sonnet 322 in *Tzror Zehuvim*, ed. Bregman.

[250] Idem, sonnet 325 in *Tzror Zehuvim*, ed. Bregman.

[251] Jacob Frances, sonnet 275 in *Tzror Zehuvim*, ed. Bregman.

[252] Immanuel Frances, sonnet 322 in *Tzror Zehuvim*, ed. Bregman.

[253] Idem, sonnet 325 in *Tzror Zehuvim*, ed. Bregman.

[254] Idem, sonnet 322 in *Tzror Zehuvim*, ed. Bregman

[255] Idem, sonnet 325 in *Tzror Zehuvim*, ed. Bregman.

[256] See Bregman, "Christians, Jews and Hebrew Sonnets".

and by Dr. Simon Luria, who was born in 1633 and converted to Christianity in 1680.[257] The Jewish camp was led by Judah Briel, the rabbi of Mantua, who was used to such arguments and found the sonnet an excellent way of conducting the duel. (We also have a sonnet of his praising a book in defense of the Jews.)[258] The *tenzone* was the ideal framework for this theological-poetic debate, and indeed the sonnets are divided into two *tenzones* battling over the soul of two Jews on the verge of conversion: Ezra Fano and Judah Ancona.

The *tenzone* over Ezra Fano was apparently conducted in the following way. The convert Luria wrote the challenge-sonnet,[259] which was then sent to Judah Briel or brought to his attention. Briel responded in the same form;[260] both sonnets were publicly circulated, or at least among the rabbi's pupils, and some of these then wrote their own sonnets,[261] following the patterns set by the challenge-sonnet and the response.

The sonnets in this tenzone use the same rhyme-words, meter, and rhetoric. All the poems begin by addressing Ezra directly by name, and speak to him in the first person. Within this uniform framework, the accusations fly back and forth. Luria's claim runs like this: God is saving Ezra from the Jews who persecute him; his sin will be made as white as snow — as it is written in Psalm 51:7 — by opening his eyes to the True Faith; his soul will be exalted in this world and redeemed from hell in the next; his righteousness will save him at the Resurrection. The poems in response remind Fano that the way of repentance is open before him. They denigrate Christianity, which glorifies a "hanged man" who will not be resurrected "when the graves open,"[262] and predict that any convert who adheres to him will also be lost, body and soul. Central motifs in the challenge-sonnet were also used in all the replies, though of course with a change of meaning: the waters of baptism, for example, were transformed into the waters drawn from the rock by Moses. On the other hand, the sonnets use different development models. Luria's

---

[257] Simon Luria is none other than the son of the well-known Venetian physician David ben Simon Luria (see Modena and Morpurgo, *Medici e chirurghi ebrei*, 11). Leone da Modena, a friend of the family, composed a sonnet (120 in *Tzror Zehuvim*, ed. Bregman) for the circumcision of the infant Simon. Little did he anticipate that the newborn would grow up to become a convert to Christianity. Leone da Modena also composed a sonnet for Simon's grandfather (also named Simon); see sonnets 120 and 134, in *Tzror Zehuvim*, ed. Bregman.

[258] Judah Briel, sonnet 382 in *Tzror Zehuvim* ed. Bregman. The sonnet was dedicated to Yshac Cardoso for his book *Las exelencias de los Hebreos* (Amsterdam, 1679).

[259] Simon Luria, sonnet 383 in *Tzror Zehuvim*, ed. Bregman.

[260] Judah Briel, sonnet 384 in *Tzror Zehuvim*, ed. Bregman.

[261] Among them Abraham Segrè, sonnet 385, and Joseph Barukh Cases, sonnet 386 in *Tzror Zehuvim*, ed. Bregman.

[262] Abraham Segrè, sonnet 385 in *Tzror Zehuvim*, ed. Bregman.

sonnet encouraging the convert develops along the model of the improving situation, whereas the replies develop according to that of the deteriorating situation — all in keeping with the speaker's point of view.

Things are similar in the second *tenzone*. The monk's sonnet begins: "If the People of the Covenant were smart, they would proclaim / that the wisdom of their sages has been lost." Judah Briel's sonnet replies: "Idolaters who scorn the Covenant would proclaim / that the wisdom of their sages is sublime."[263]

The *tenzones* might sound like a literary game, but the topic was too weighty for such an interpretation and there can be no doubt of its serious intent. The term *tenzone*, often viewed in the past as a synonym for a friendship poem, was restored at the height of the Baroque to its plain meaning of "war." And in this war the Hebrew sonnet unsheathed a double-edged sword.

7. Prayer, Ethics, and Religious Thought

Traditional Characteristics

The renewed Hebrew religious sonnet, especially in the sixteenth century, is often personal and contemplative, like the religious sonnet of Immanuel of Rome. Like his predecessor from the fourteenth century, the sixteenth-century poet exhorts his soul in direct terms: "Look, O my soul, and see thy actions!"[264] He confesses: "I am exhausted with life; exhausted! / For the sins of my actions I die."[265] He asks: "Why, my soul, are you distressed and downcast? / Are you tangled in the snare of desire? / Or are you going up in the smoke of frivolity, / caught between two paths?"[266] Preaching also bore an intimate rather than public character in that period: "Awake, my son, awake from your slumber, / . . . for there is a living God who observes."[267]

The renewed Hebrew sonnet of faith saw a return of sermonizing in the style of Immanuel of Rome, with gloomy descriptions of death, macabre scenes from the grave, and the terrors of Judgment Day.[268] The poet predicts that the wicked will end "together in Gehenna in a boiling cauldron."[269] He reminds his

---

[263] Sonnets 387 and 388 in *Tzror Zehuvim*, ed. Bregman.
[264] Joseph Tzarfati, sonnet 39 in *Tzror Zehuvim*, ed. Bregman.
[265] Judah Moscato, sonnet 57 in *Tzror Zehuvim*, ed. Bregman.
[266] Isaac Uziel, sonnet 81 in *Tzror Zehuvim*, ed. Bregman.
[267] Judah Moscato, sonnet 55 in *Tzror Zehuvim*, ed. Bregman.
[268] Joseph Tzarfati, sonnet 39 in *Tzror Zehuvim*, ed. Bregman.
[269] Isaac Levi, sonnet 103 in *Tzror Zehuvim*, ed. Bregman.

soul of the body's decay and frightens it with God's anger.[270] He warns the sinner that there will be "a time to sip hemlock," and that "his flesh will be food for worms."[271]

Baroque sonnets reinforce the macabre tone through a dramatic monologue uttered by Death.[272] The motif of *memento mori*, common in the Middle Ages, suited the Baroque concept of the world as a transitory illusion. These elements, however, are no longer as dominant as they were in the poems of Immanuel of Rome. Their gloom fades, and the harshness of tone is softened by the addition of both new and ancient elements.

The Element of Forgiveness

Thoughts of repentance are based on the fear of punishment in the new religious sonnet, just as they were in the old one. At the same time, however, the element of forgiveness also becomes conspicuous. For example, Immanuel of Rome uses a Platonic note in one sonnet of repentance to evoke pain: "Alas, that though I knew the merits of the soul over the merits of the body, I did not fear." Joseph Tzarfati, on the other hand, uses the same idea to evoke hope: "Look, my soul, and see thy Creator . . . illuminate thyself in the light of wisdom and it will carry thee up to heaven . . . It will redeem and raise you out of hell, It will shed grace upon thee before the face of the Lord."[273] Judah Moscato reminds one addressee that his "pure soul came down, by God's will, from a holy abode to dwell in his living corpse," and urges him to "listen to the words of her voice."[274]

Some morality sonnets could essentially be categorized as penitential hymns, a genre in which the element of forgiveness is dominant. Nathan Jedidiah da Orvieto appended sonnets for repentant sinners to a book adapted from old Hebrew penitential poems, a fact which testifies to the nature of the sonnets.[275] The customary reliance on God's mercy was now largely the function of the religious sonnet. The poet humbly begs God: "Thou who sittest astride the cherubs, O sublime one, appear! / Have mercy, have pity on the work of Thy hands."[276] Or, in another sonnet: "Be not deaf unto me . . . / Straighten Thy path before me and

---

[270] Nathan Orvieto, sonnet 149 in *Tzror Zehuvim*, ed. Bregman.

[271] Moses Abudiente, sonnet 302 in *Tzror Zehuvim*, ed. Bregman.

[272] See for example Jacob Frances, sonnet 291 in *Tzror Zehuvim*, ed. Bregman.

[273] Joseph Tzarfati, sonnet 39 in *Tzror Zehuvim*, ed. Bregman.

[274] Judah Moscato, sonnet 55 in *Tzror Zehuvim*, ed. Bregman.

[275] The book was adapted by Orvieto's grandfather, Johanan Alatrini. The sonnets (146, 147, 148, and 149 in *Tzror Zehuvim*, ed. Bregman) were written in Italian by Alatrini and translated into Hebrew by Orvieto.

[276] Jacob Segrè, sonnet 91 in *Tzror Zehuvim*, ed. Bregman.

guide me."[277] We find images not of an Almighty Judge but of a forgiving deity, and this imbues the religious sonnet of the sixteenth and seventeenth centuries with a gentle optimism, despite the terrifying images. Joseph Tzarfati encourages his soul, which has forgotten God's mercy: "Why hesitate before this [road], and why feel alone?"[278] Judah Moscato tones down his preaching, promising the observant that he will be "like a watered garden, like a source of flowing water; / Princes will bow down before you," and optimistically nudges young men towards good behavior.[279] Moses Zacuto bases his morality on an optimistic philosophical premise: the choice between good and evil is in the hands of man himself.[280] In a sophisticated play of meaning and sound, Zacuto exhorts the soul to prefer the wheat over the chaff, to carefully choose its path, and to build a solid foundation. The belief in free will and in the reward of the righteous lends a conciliatory tone even to the monologue uttered by Death in the sonnet mentioned above by Jacob Frances: "Understand this, God-fearer, for it means / that your soul will enjoy a double portion."[281]

Poetic sensibility softened the gloomier aspects of morality-preaching to the point where poets found it possible to write about submission to God even in wedding sonnets, as we have already seen.

The Communal Dimension

By the end of the sixteenth century, the religious sonnet placed increasing emphasis on the needs of the Jewish community as a whole. The request for redemption becomes common and appears in numerous variations. Jacob Segrè requests: "Guide us in thy righteousness! / Save our remnants, my Lord!"[282] and in another sonnet: "Command the salvation of Jacob, O Father, / from the midst of those who eat insects, / and remove thy servants from prison."[283] Immanuel Frances describes the death of Jews for the sake of their religion, and demands retribution: "For thy own sake rise, unsheathe thy sword! / Let them be a banner, as they bore a banner / inscribed: O Lord, rise, and fight thine own battle!"[284] With the rise of Shabbetai Zevi, a sonnet by Jacob Frances predicts the triumph of Judaism over the rest of the religions: "Awake and rise up, O Jerusalem! / Thy religion will live, the religion of [other] nations will cease."[285] An anonymous sonnet from

---

[277] Judah Moscato, sonnet 57 in *Tzror Zehuvim*, ed. Bregman.
[278] Joseph Tzarfati, sonnet 39 in *Tzror Zehuvim*, ed. Bregman.
[279] Judah Moscato, sonnet 55 in *Tzror Zehuvim*, ed. Bregman.
[280] Moses Zacuto, sonnet 212 in *Tzror Zehuvim*, ed. Bregman.
[281] Jacob Frances, sonnet 291 in *Tzror Zehuvim*, ed. Bregman.
[282] Jacob Segrè, sonnet 90 in *Tzror Zehuvim*, ed. Bregman.
[283] Idem, sonnet 93 in *Tzror Zehuvim*, ed. Bregman.
[284] Immanuel Frances, sonnet 329 in *Tzror Zehuvim*, ed. Bregman.
[285] Jacob Frances, sonnet 281 in *Tzror Zehuvim*, ed. Bregman.

the seventeenth century pleads with God to heal his people, for their hearts "have turned to water."[286] Sonnets ostensibly about other subjects turn out to be poems about the redemption of the Jews. Archivolti slips the subject into a riddle-sonnet about the donkey which will bear the messiah into Jerusalem,[287] in a pointed response to a sonnet by Immanuel of Rome poking fun at the messiah and his donkey. Among his other occupations, Archivolti was a teacher of young children, and he composed the poem in order to amuse the youngsters during Purim. It mentions the story of Cain and Abel, which would have been familiar to children of a young age, and depicts a line of soldiers marching to the sound of trumpets and drums, a sure-fire way of drawing their attention. The pedagogical aim of the poem is clear, but it may also aim at introducing children to the verse-form. In his sonnet concerning the music of the spheres, Archivolti foresees that the secret behind it will be revealed with the coming of the messiah.

Some religious sonnets commemorate events in which local Jews were redeemed from danger. A poet of the sixteenth century, possibly Johanan Alatrini, thanks God for saving his community from expulsion.[288] Likewise, Judah Moscato wrote a sonnet thanking God for having saved the Jews of Ferrara from the earthquake that struck the city in 1571: "The Lord's kindnesses I shall utter day after day: / He has saved his servants, for they have returned to his service."[289]

Popular Idioms and Touches of Realism

The optimistic and communal element evident in Hebrew sonnets of the sixteenth and seventeenth centuries linked them to an accepted tradition and made them seem intimate and well-known. This is also noticeable in the style of these sonnets, which returns to ancient and familiar phrases. In one poem, Nathan Jedidiah da Orvieto borrowed from the Prayer of Moses (Exodus 34:6), which was used for penitential prayers: "The Lord, the Lord God, merciful and gracious, long-suffering," and from Moses's prayer over Miriam (Numbers 12:13), which also became a familiar liturgical phrase. Sonnets fell back on older layers of the liturgical language, and sprinkled phrases from the Bible and midrash with a liberal hand. In one sonnet, for example, Daniel Foa structured his poem according to a rabbinic saying (*Jerusalem Talmud* 3:3). This saying was jotted on the margins of the manuscript poem, divided among the strophes according to content: strophe 1: "three people whose iniquities are forgiven"; strophe 2: "a convert who undergoes conversion"; strophe 3: "he who rises to greatness"; strophe 4: "he who

---

[286] *Im ish be-ʿet yishqot* (and see MS. Jewish Theological Seminary of New York 1250, fol. 31).
[287] Samuel Archivolti, sonnet 60 in *Tzror Zehuvim*, ed. Bregman.
[288] Johanan Alatrini (?), sonnet 72 in *Tzror Zehuvim*, ed. Bregman.
[289] Judah Moscato, sonnet 52 in *Tzror Zehuvim*, ed. Bregman.

marries a woman."[290] Moses Abudiente in Amsterdam composed a sonnet based on a well-known rabbinic saying from *The Wisdom of the Fathers* (3:1), writing: "Remember, therefore, your shame and from whence you came / . . . / and before Whom you are due to render judgment!"[291]

The new religious Hebrew sonnet returned to traditions of the old in matters of imagery and metaphor. Some of Judah Moscato's images, for example, may recall Italian motifs. "Listen to your soul, and harken to it / so that you will ascend the steps of the bridge / till you come face to face with your Maker." But clearly they also return to Hebrew tradition, as in these lines based on a Talmudic source (*BT Pesahim* 112:a): "Run like a gazelle, be as light as an eagle / to do the will of God with all your might."[292]

The Hebrew religious sonnet is striking for its simplicity and for the intimacy of tone that brings the speaker down from the raised pulpit of the preacher. Colloquialisms blend without dissonance into expressions of a more exalted kind: "Those who sanctify thy Name are come amidst fire / Alas, thine enemies rejoice over them."[293] The religious sonnet opened itself to current events, daily affairs and realistic, vibrant descriptions. Judah Moscato expresses regret for not being able to attend synagogue due to the "harsh cold" and winter snows.[294] In another sonnet he describes the earthquake in Ferrara and the churches which collapsed "to the foundations," noting that steeples that formerly "soared / like cedars towards the sky" had all toppled. He does not hide his joy over the fall of these "cedars," or over the rest of the damages incurred by the churches.[295] Joseph Tzarfati adopts a colloquial tone, telling the soul that pleasure-seekers are not even worth a "shoe-lace."[296] A sonnet by Jacob Frances begins by describing a conversation between friends in which a merchant ship, runaway debtors, and "a pack of creditors" are all mentioned. Only in the last tercet do we discover the ethical bent of the poem.[297] Another poet, possibly Johanan Alatrini, celebrates the fall of a tyrannical ruler who plotted to expel the Jews from the city. In order to heighten the communal tone of celebration, he paints the details in vivid colors and compares the ruler to a pig that "stretches forth its hooves to hide his crimes." The comparison alludes to a well-known midrash: "While the pig is wallowing in its filth, it puts forth its hooves as though to say: I am kosher"

---

[290] Daniel Foa, sonnet 101 in *Tzror Zehuvim*, ed. Bregman.
[291] Moses Abudiente, sonnet 302 in *Tzror Zehuvim*, ed. Bregman.
[292] Judah Moscato, sonnet 54 in *Tzror Zehuvim*, ed. Bregman.
[293] Immanuel Frances, sonnet 329 in *Tzror Zehuvim*, ed. Bregman.
[294] Judah Moscato, sonnet 56 in *Tzror Zehuvim*, ed. Bregman.
[295] Idem, sonnet 52 in *Tzror Zehuvim*, ed. Bregman.
[296] Joseph Tzarfati, sonnet 39 in *Tzror Zehuvim*, ed. Bregman.
[297] Jacob Frances, sonnet 283 in *Tzror Zehuvim*, ed. Bregman.

(*Bereshit Rabbah* 65:1). Nor does the poet hesitate further on in the poem to suggest that the laws of this ruler "be shoved up his arse[!]."[298] Here the realistic verges on the burlesque.

The Sonnet as a Semi-Liturgical Poem

The communal dimension evident in the religious sonnets from the end of the sixteenth century sometimes places it on the border of liturgical poetry. This quasi-liturgical nature becomes even more evident during the seventeenth century.

Five sonnets for the festival of Simḥat Torah have come down to us from the seventeenth century, among them: a pair of "twins" — that is, two sonnets with identical prosodic traits and subject matter[299] — by Solomon Oliveyra;[300] another anonymous pair of twins from the end of the seventeenth century;[301] and a single sonnet by Israel Conegliano.[302] Since two men are honored on this holiday — the Ḥatan Torah, who recites the blessings for the last pericope of the Torah, and the Ḥatan Bereshit, who recites the blessings for the first pericope from the beginning of the Torah — the sonnets for them were written in pairs.

The sonnet for "the bridegroom of Torah" is a kind of offshoot of the wedding sonnet in general. Addressing Fate, as it were (since the "bridegroom of the Torah" was apparently chosen by lot), the poet begins with a mock complaint: "*This* is the bridegroom of the Torah?! How could you be such a fool / as to call *him* a bridegroom? You've made a big mistake!" But then he immediately relents and explains that the cyclical nature of the biblical readings is like the cyclical pattern of nature itself: "the earth renews the flowers, vegetation and growth every year / so, too, this is a bridegroom today [but] a husband last night."[303]

The completion of the lectionary cycle was celebrated at a literary gathering of the "Academy" amidst the recitation of poems, songs and riddles, the latter complex affairs for which prizes were awarded. The celebration for which Oliveyra wrote his sonnets was also the occasion for a highly intricate riddle by Daniel de Barrios.[304]

---

[298] Johanan Alatrini (?), sonnet 72 in *Tzror Zehuvim*, ed. Bregman.

[299] See below, Chap. 16, Part 2.

[300] Solomon Oliveyra, sonnets 343 and 344 in *Tzror Zehuvim*, ed. Bregman.

[301] Anonymous, sonnets 422 and 423 in *Tzror Zehuvim*, ed. Bregman.

[302] Israel Conegliano, sonnet 398 in *Tzror Zehuvim*, ed. Bregman.

[303] Idem, sonnet 398 in *Tzror Zehuvim*, ed. Bregman. Using both meanings of the word *baʿal* ("husband" and "owner"), the sonnet reinforces the comparison to nature by adding: "Though he has already acquired a great deal of Torah, / He will renew himself, and do even more."

[304] See Pagis, *ʿAl-Sod Ḥatum*, 84. He mentions only one of Oliveyra's sonnets, and is referring to the sonnet twins.

The sonnets written by Oliveyra and Conegliano were meant to be heard only once. They included the names of the "bridegrooms" and concrete details about them in the body of the text, just like wedding sonnets. While these could not be reused in future ceremonies, this is not the case for the other two sonnets mentioned above by an anonymous poet. These lack concrete details, and the manuscript in which they are written — apparently the diary of a cantor — indicates that the poet indeed meant to use them again and again, just like poems of prayer.[305]

Other sonnets for holidays and religious occasions were intended from the beginning to be heard more than once. We find, for example, a sonnet by Leone da Modena for Sukkot, though not for any particular year.[306] The same is true of another sonnet by da Modena, this one marking a *siyyum*, that is, the occasion in which various study-groups complete their study of a certain Talmudic treatise. Here the poet specifically noted that "Rabbi A. Q. wrote this for a *siyyum* and I changed the language to make it always useful, for it was set to music."[307]

A sonnet by Moses Hayyim ben Isaiah Azriel Katz Cantarini commemorates a miracle that occurred in the town of Rovigo in 1686, when worshippers in the local synagogue escaped the collapse of the building without injury. It was recited in synagogue every year on a specific date.[308] Elijah Recanati dedicated a sonnet to what is, for our purpose, the most impressive of all occasions, calling it "a lovely poem based upon peace and forgiveness, and proper to say on Yom Kippur."[309] Like Leone da Modena, Recanati did not mean to use the poem only once. Whether it was ever sung on Yom Kippur in some community or other is something we do not know; but the fact that it was designated for Yom Kippur is in itself highly revealing and undoubtedly proves that the Jewish community had taken the sonnet-form to its heart.

The Religious Sonnet in "Yesod ʿOlam"

Under the rubric of religious sonnets, we find a special group of sonnets in the play *Yesod ʿOlam* ("The Foundation of the World") by Moses Zacuto. As was customary in religious plays of the period, *Yesod ʿOlam* seeks to describe the triumph of faith, but here it is the Jewish faith that ultimately carries the day. Of the more than forty sonnets included in the play, most deal with matters of religion and faith. Some occur in scenes of religious debate. They summarize

---

[305] Pagis, "Piyyutim Me'uḥarim," 304 [in *Ha-Shir Davur*, 359].

[306] Leone da Modena, sonnet 123 in *Tzror Zehuvim*, ed. Bregman.

[307] Leone da Modena, sonnet 122 in *Tzror Zehuvim*, ed. Bregman. The initials of the Rabbi may stand for Asher Qilirli as S. Bernstein supposed. See in his *Diwan le-Rabbi Yehudah Arieh Modena* 131, where this sonnet appears in distorted form.

[308] Moses Cantarini, sonnet 405 in *Tzror Zehuvim*, ed. Bregman.

[309] Elijah Recanati, sonnet 158 in *Tzror Zehuvim*, ed. Bregman.

briefly and simply basic theological beliefs: the creation of the world *ex nihilo* in six days, the attributes of God, and reward and punishment.[310]

The religious sonnet invests *Yesod ʿOlam* with elements of pathos and drama. It creates brief monologues in which the wise-men of the idolaters explain the principles of their faith, and King Nimrod boasts about his power and wealth. On the opposite side of the drama, the Patriarch Abraham rebukes King Nimrod and the representatives of idolatry, calls for God's help from the fiery furnace, and declares his unwavering faith.

In *Yesod ʿOlam*, the religious sonnet was revitalized, primarily in terms of a broader conception. Here the religious sonnet took its place as an important and comprehensive genre, new and innovative. In everything concerning plot, theological discussion, rhetorical pathos, prosodic structure and allegorical undercurrents, the religious sonnet in *Yesod ʿOlam* expanded the modest parameters in which the genre began at the beginning of the fourteenth century. The communal dimension which developed in the religious Hebrew sonnet during the seventeenth century becomes here the harbinger of a new message for the Jewish nation as a whole.

Yesod ʿOlam ostensibly describes the life of the Patriarch Abraham, persecuted because of his faith, but it allegorically reflects the persecution of the Jews by the Catholic Church during the author's own lifetime. Just as Abraham pleaded his faith in biblical times, so *Yesod ʿOlam* expresses faith in the superiority of Judaism and its eventual triumph, and in the rescue of those who believe in it during his own generation. The devouring fire, a motif of the religious Hebrew sonnet from the beginning, appears once again in *Yesod ʿOlam*. But here it is the wicked gentile who is destined for hell, and not the Jewish sinner. King Nimrod's fiery furnace represents the pyres of the Inquisition, seen by the play as instruments doomed to failure. The optimistic tone characterizing the religious sonnet of this period reverberates powerfully in the sonnets of *Yesod ʿOlam*.

The popular bent common to the religious Hebrew sonnet of the time is well suited to the play's aim in general. The poetic language of Moses Zacuto, often emblematic of Baroque complexity at its best, is simple and comprehensible throughout *Yesod ʿOlam*, and in the religious sonnets no less, despite its philosophical content.

Italian Influence

With a wealth of Jewish sources at its disposal, the religious Hebrew sonnet really had no need to borrow forms of expression from the religious sonnet in Italian. Nevertheless, and despite all the difficulty involved, some poets were indeed ready for the challenge.

---

[310] The sonnets of *Yesod ʿOlam* are discussed below in Chap. 16, Part 4.

A bold adoption of the Petrarchist *spirituale*, unique of its kind, is found in three Italian sonnets by Johanan Alatrini, later translated into Hebrew by his grandson, Nathan Jedidiah da Orvieto.[311] The Petrarchan elements are especially striking in the second of these sonnets: *Qatan ke-khaf yalud* ("One as small as an infant's palm"). It begins by telling about an uninvited guest: "One as small as an infant's palm, young in days, / sleeps at my house, and his actions are wicked!" The "guest," it turns out, is none other than *Ḥesheq*: the Hebrew Cupid that here symbolizes the "evil urge" of rabbinic doctrine. The house — namely, the heart — is urged to slaughter *Ḥesheq* and to offer him up as a sacrifice to God, who will then "hear your cry, and bless your sacrifice."

The other two sonnets also lend themselves to a Petrarchan reading, and this is important since the three sonnets come in sequence and form a single entity.[312] The Italian superscription ("*sonetti spirituali*") testifies to their source of inspiration. Orvieto published his Hebrew version together with this superscription and the Italian original.[313]

While other Hebrew sonnets were apparently also influenced by the Italian example, foreign elements were assimilated in them beyond recognition. This is apparently what happened to the anonymous sonnet below, printed together here with a religious poem by Michelangelo for comparison:[314]

Michelangelo's poem:
Le favole del mondo m'hanno tolto
il tempo dato a contemplare Iddio
nèsol le grazie sue poste in oblio,
ma con lor, piu che senza, a peccar volto.

Quel c'altri saggio, me fa cieco e stolto,
e tardi a riconoscer l'error mio,
Manca la speme, e pur cresce 'l desio,
che da te sia dal proprio amor disciolto.

Ammezzami la strada c'al ciel sale,
Signor mio caro, e a quel mezzo solo
salir m'e di bisogno la tua 'ita

Mettimi in odio quanto 'l mondo vale,
e quante sue belleze onoro e colo,
c'anzi morte caparri eterna vita.

---

[311] Nathan Jedidiah da Orvieto, sonnets 147–149 in *Tzror Zehuvim*, ed. Bregman.

[312] See below, Chapter 15, Part 8.

[313] Angelo Alatrini, *L'Angelica Tromba*, in Nathan Jedidiah da Orvieto, *Barkhi Nafshi* (Venice, 1628).

[314] Michelangelo, *Rime*, ed. Guasti, 72. English translation from *The Penguin Book of Italian Verse*, ed. Kay, 174.

A literal translation:
The idle tales of the world have robbed me of the time I was given to know God, nor have they only thrust his gracious gifts into oblivion, but, with them, rather than without, have turned me to sinning. What makes them wise makes me blind and stupid, and slow to acknowledge my error. Hope fails me, and yet the desire to be freed from self-love by you, God, grows.

Cut by half the road that climbs to heaven, my dear Lord, and for that half alone I shall need your help to climb. Make me hate what has value in the world, and those of its beauties that I honour and serve, so that before death I may have earnest of eternal life.

The Hebrew poem (in a literal translation):
Because of my life, my eye sheds a spring of water
For I expended it on aimless pleasure
Rather than rise like a bird I chose to descend,
Though I had the ability to ascend the heavens.

O God who sees into the heart, not the eyes,
Thy hand is always ready to recompense good;
Take pity on this lost soul of mine
And in thy loving-kindness be patient even more.

Purify and erase the filth of all her sins,
From the bitter, O Lord, make sweet;
That which is pure in her, O Living God, direct.

Be abundant with her in thy abundant splendor
And like the very heavens illuminate her face!
Then like a bride will she shine most radiant.

Several elements are common to both sonnets: sorrow at having wasted the life given man in order "to rise like a bird," the personal appeal to a merciful God, and the desire to be purified in this life as a kind of foretaste of the world to come. In the Hebrew poem there is an emphasis on God's patience and His ability to sweeten that which is bitter, but this does not blur the similarity which it bears to Michelangelo's poem or to the *sonetti spirituali* of the period.

A frequent Christian motif was absorbed in a sonnet by Jacob Frances, *Ayom ve-nora* ("Fearsome and awful").[315] The sonnet deals with a picture typical of the period, "the dance of death," which aimed at making the sinner repent.

---

[315] Jacob Frances, sonnet 291, in *Tzror Zehuvim*, ed. Bregman.

8. The Lament

Expanding the Genre

The lament takes up an entire chapter of Anania Coen's survey of Hebrew literature,[316] and rightly so. The lament is one of the oldest and most conspicuous genres in Hebrew poetry, and extremely common in Italy.[317] In the sonnet, however, it made but a poor beginning. Immanuel of Rome wrote only one sonnet of lament, *Naflah ʿateret ha-zeman* ("The crown of Time has fallen"),[318] but this was not an actual lament for a real person.

With the revival of the Hebrew sonnet, the genre was put to actual use. Already at the outset we find a sonnet of lament by Moses ben Joab,[319] and from approximately the same time, also an anonymous lament from Ferrara for Malakhi ben Joseph.[320] In these laments the tone is personal and intimate. The anonymous poet addresses the deceased, recalls "days gone by / when I saved you from sorrow and failure," and laments that his friend has now fallen "like a stalk of grain." Already in the sixteenth century the genre took on a communal dimension, in laments for well-known figures such as Moses Cordovero,[321] Joseph Caro,[322] and also Marguerite of Savoy, who had dealt kindly with the Jews.[323] Sonnets of lament were printed on the frontispieces of books and thus enjoyed a wide circulation.[324]

During this period it was customary to carve words of poetry on gravestones in the cemetery. The poems were elegantly chiseled along with heraldic devices, signs of family pedigree, and so forth. Such gravestone poems, designed to arouse thoughts of repentance, included sonnets;[325] and this despite the considerable space, relatively speaking, which this verse-form takes up.

---

[316] Coen, *Saggio di eloquenza ebrea*, 102.

[317] On funeral customs among the Jews of Italy, see Bonfil, *Jewish Life in Renaissance Italy*, 265–84.

[318] Immanuel of Rome, sonnet 9 in *Tzror Zehuvim*, ed. Bregman.

[319] Moses ben Joab, sonnet 46 in *Tzror Zehuvim*, ed. Bregman.

[320] Anonymous, sonnet 76 in *Tzror Zehuvim*, ed. Bregman.

[321] Samuel Archivolti, sonnet 62 in *Tzror Zehuvim*, ed. Bregman.

[322] Samuel Archivolti, sonnet 63 in *Tzror Zehuvim*, ed. Bregman; Judah Saltares, sonnets 77 and 78. And see M. Benyahu, "Qinot Hakhamei Italia ʿal Rav Yosef Caro," in *ʿIyyunim u-Meḥqarim* (Jerusalem, 1969): 302–9.

[323] Judah Moscato, sonnet 53 in *Tzror Zehuvim*, ed. Bregman; Azariah de' Rossi, sonnet 50.

[324] Such as Cordovero's *Seder Avodat Yom Kippur* (Venice, 1587), and Mercado's commentary on Ecclesiastes and Psalms: see Moses di Mercado, *Perush Qohelet ve-Tehilim* (Amsterdam, 1653).

[325] Leone da Modena, sonnets 130, 132, 133 and 134 in *Tzror Zehuvim*, ed. Bregman; Moses Zacuto, sonnets 225, 226, and 228. And see A. Berliner, *Hebräische Grabschriften in Italien*, ed. J. Kauffman (Frankfurt, 1881); S. Bernstein, "Luḥot Abanim 2," *Hebrew Union College Annual* 10 (1935): 483–552; Coen, *Saggio di eloquenza ebrea*.

Breaking with Convention

A number of factors conspired to create a highly conventional genre of poetry: the common denomination of situation, the necessarily repeated elements of praise, and the rest of the conventions with which this genre abounds, both because of its hoary antiquity, and because of its proximity to the rituals of mourning. Nevertheless, there was nothing imitative about the sonnet of lament.

One way to break the mold was to focus on concrete details about the deceased, whether personal and intimate or related to his or her activities in public life. In this way the sonnets achieved variation almost of their own accord. One person was described as "a doctor who healed all flesh and performed wonders / [and] served the Queen of France . . ."[326] Another was a "Cohen," i.e., a priest, "of the mighty house of Roman, / a sweet singer of God, overflowing [with song], / a circumciser and teacher."[327] Then there was the "Moses" di Mercado known for his defense of the Jews, whose name apparently inspired the use of imagery from Moses' Song of the Sea (Exodus 15): "The moment you blew with the strength of your wind, / the abysses of false religions congealed."[328] Some people were mourned for their tragic death: "How can the earth cover the source of your blood?/ . . . / Indeed your soul was sacrificed in place of a goat!"[329] All these sonnets have a strong biographical basis that blunts the hyperbole and makes the poem unique. Concreteness of detail flourished in poems of lament far more than in poems for weddings, where the subjects were young and unknown.

For the most part, however, breaking the mold was primarily the result of a conscious poetic effort to stylize, innovate and impress. In order to achieve these goals, poets deviated from the norm, sometimes by means of unusual structural forms which were found in early Italian poetry, but which in Hebrew poetry were new and unique.

Azariah de' Rossi used several methods to achieve these goals in his sonnet lamenting the death of Marguerite, Duchess of Savoy.[330] The classical tongues were considered the most suitable medium for lamenting the departed great in the Renaissance.[331] Accordingly, Azariah's sonnet was written in Aramaic and gathered into a group of poems lamenting the Duchess's death in Hebrew and Latin. His lament takes the form of a sonnet-in-dialogue, an early Italian form of popular origin, constructed as a series of questions and answers in direct speech.[332] In Hebrew it is rare and impressive. Last, but not least, the dialogue in Azariah's sonnet is surprisingly audacious. Echoing Jesus' words on the cross,

---

[326] Leone da Modena, sonnet 132 in *Tzror Zehuvim*, ed. Bregman.
[327] Idem, sonnet 133 in *Tzror Zehuvim*, ed. Bregman.
[328] Samuel Caceres, sonnet 297 in *Tzror Zehuvim*, ed. Bregman.
[329] Jacob Segrè, sonnet 98 in *Tzror Zehuvim*, ed. Bregman.
[330] Azariah de' Rossi, sonnet 50 in *Tzror Zehuvim*, ed. Bregman.
[331] See Coen, *Saggio di eloquenza ebrea*, 76–79, 102–11.
[332] Biadene, *Morfologia del sonetto*, 166–69.

the Duchess complains to God: why did Death come to me so early, and why hast Thou forgotten me? To which God replies: Because you were as full of good qualities as a venerable saint, your days were fulfilled and I called you to Me.[333] A dialogue in direct speech is also used in a sonnet lamenting Joseph Caro,[334] adding drama to the situation.

Another early Italian form, macaronic in nature, was used by Leone da Modena in a sonnet lamenting Rabbi Leib Saravel.[335] The Italians tended to combine Italian with Latin or another Romance tongue, or Latin with other Romance tongues.[336] In the sonnet by Leone da Modena, lines in Italian alternate with lines in Hebrew to create a single unit of syntax and meaning. The Italian words rhyme with the Hebrew. This device recalls a macaronic and well-known poem of lament composed by Leone da Modena in his youth, which is entirely made up of Hebrew-Italian homophones.[337] In (transliterated) Hebrew:

Qina shemor, oy meh, ki pas otzar bo!
("Continue lamenting, alas, for a treasure has gone with him")

And in Italian:

Chi nasce muor; Oime che pass acerbo!
(He who is born will die, alas, what a bitter sorrow!)

A *sonetto minore* — that is, a sonnet with lines shorter than usual — was used in a lament by Moses Zacuto, already mentioned above for its unusual metrical scheme.[338]

Sonnets also used argument and rhetoric to break with convention. Immanuel Frances used a lament to answer the question of why he was unable to compose a lament worthy of its name.[339] Other sonnets create dramatic monologues

---

[333] Azariah de' Rossi, sonnet 50 in *Tzror Zehuvim*, ed. Bregman.

[334] Judah Saltares da Fano, sonnet 77 in *Tzror Zehuvim*, ed. Bregman.

[335] Leone da Modena, sonnet 131 (beginning with the Italian words *Rapito hai*) in *Tzror Zehuvim*, ed. Bregman.

[336] Biadene, *Morfologia del sonetto*, 177–81. In Hebrew a series of macaronic poems in the form of the *ballata* were written in the framework of the debate about women. See D. Pagis, "Ha-Pulmus ha-Shiri ᶜal Tiv ha-Nashim," *Meḥqarei Yerushalayim be-Sifrut ᶜIvrit* 9 (1986): 259–300, here 285-95 [in *Ha-Shir Davur*, ed. Fleischer, 150-55].

[337] Leone da Modena, *Shirim*, ed. Bernstein, 51.

[338] Moses Zacuto, sonnet 227 in *Tzror Zehuvim*, ed. Bregman. And see above, chap. 11, Part 2.

[339] Immanuel Frances, sonnet 331 in *Tzror Zehuvim*, ed. Bregman.

addressed to the deceased[340] or to the grave.[341] Baroque sonnets, fraught with tension, delay the purpose of the poem to the end, together with all clarification of subject and theme.[342]

Some sonnets of lament were written in sequences as "twins" and "triplets."[343] Moses Zacuto's remarkable use of language reached its apogee in a corona of sonnets lamenting the death of Rabbi Saul Morteira, where the seven sonnets correspond with the seven days of mourning.[344] The density of allusions, quotations and word-plays bind these together into a single, riddle-like piece. The text abounds with rare words, rare meanings of standard words, names of books, and a sophisticated use of quotations from the Bible. All these lend grandeur to the situation (as well as a touch of the bizarre) and glorify the reputation of the deceased.

Efforts to perfect poetic technique are more evident in the sonnet of lament than in the wedding sonnet, and the reason for this is clear. While the wedding sonnet was generally limited to family circles, the lament was likely to be heard in an event involving the entire Jewish community, especially when the deceased was a person of importance. It was intended for a large audience and sometimes printed in a book or carved in stone. Unlike the wedding sonnet, which was disseminated in a limited number of broadsheets and had little hope of surviving the ravages of time, the poem of lament was frequently meant to be preserved and used as historic testimony.

Conventions

Despite all these techniques, Hebrew sonnets of lament remained faithful to convention, repeating common motifs time and again. When the subject was a great scholar, we hear that "from the grave, he is still whispering the law of God," in accordance with the rabbinic dictum: "The lips of a [deceased] scholar, in whose name a traditional saying is reported in this world, murmur in the grave."[345] In the wake of another dictum of the sages ("Weep for those who have lost their leader, and not for what was lost. For that which was lost goes towards peace, and we towards sorrow"),[346] the people are described as having been orphaned of

---

[340] Anonymous, sonnet 76 in *Tzror Zehuvim*, ed. Bregman.

[341] Joseph Carmi, sonnet 142 in *Tzror Zehuvim*, ed. Bregman; Moses Zacuto, sonnet 228.

[342] Immanuel Frances, sonnet 330 in *Tzror Zehuvim*, ed. Bregman.

[343] See below, Chap. 16, Part 2.

[344] Moses Zacuto, sonnets 229–235 in *Tzror Zehuvim*, ed. Bregman.

[345] *BT Yebamoth* 97a; and see Leone da Modena, sonnet 132 in *Tzror Zehuvim*, ed. Bregman, and similarly: Samuel Caceres, sonnet 297; Isaac Nahar, sonnet 300; and others.

[346] Samuel Shalom, sonnet 299 in *Tzror Zehuvim*, ed. Bregman.

the religious leader who has passed away: "He will sing when he happily reaches Paradise, but woe to the Palace ruined to its foundation,"[347] the "Palace" being the community or yeshiva. The sonnets distinguish between the joy of the soul ascending to heaven and the sorrows of the mourners: "All those who love him will grovel in the dust . . . / but he will gird himself with splendor in the Mountains of Beauty."[348] (A similar convention appears in a lament by Tasso: "Troubled and compassionate for our sake, happy and sure for your own, you bid the world good-bye, pure soul.") [349]

The poets take consolation in the spiritual heritage left behind by the deceased and often describe their welcome in Paradise, sometimes in direct speech: "A resounding voice calls out before you in Paradise: / . . . / Come sit over here alongside the prophets."[350] Of course, the belief in the immortality of the soul and in the resurrection of the dead was the most common source of consolation.

Convention does not overpower the sonnet of lament, and does not weary the reader. On the contrary, it sometimes provides a welcome relief from the plethora of verbal pyrotechnics and cunning conceits. And it can also be impressive. A striking example of simplicity is provided by none other than Jacob Frances, usually the most sophisticated of poets. One of his sonnets of lament[351] is modeled on a well-known poem from antiquity (*Anshei emunah avadu*), and like its model uses a simple expression — "Their light is extinguished, our eyes are grown dark" — in which the conventional metaphor comes to life through its dual image.

Of all secondary genres of the Hebrew sonnet in this period, the lament is one of the most carefully crafted. It combines the new with the old, the simple with the sophisticated, and succeeds in conveying emotional spontaneity together with respectful restraint.

9. Meditation and Complaint

Though there are few sonnets dealing with the traditional themes of meditation and complaint, these are interesting indeed. Conventions that went back to Hebrew poetry from medieval Spain were used to express new attitudes. Unlike the meditational poem of old, the new meditational sonnet treats topics with wider social implications. In one sonnet, Jacob Frances yearns for the simple life, imagining "the serenity of the poor man, who day and night / eats his crust in

---

[347] Moses Zacuto, sonnet 233 in *Tzror Zehuvim*, ed. Bregman.
[348] *BT Moed Katan* 25b.
[349] Torquato Tasso, *Opere*, ed. Sozzi, 157: *In morte di Margherite*.
[350] Samuel Caceres, sonnet 298 in *Tzror Zehuvim*, ed. Bregman.
[351] Jacob Frances, sonnet 255 in *Tzror Zehuvim*, ed. Bregman.

joy and tranquility." He expresses a willingness to renounce his money, and with this all his cares: "Go out in peace, wealth! Come in peace, poverty!"[352] He also expresses a similar attitude in a pastoral poem not of sonnet-form.[353]

Moses Zacuto also meditated on the comparative merits of poverty and stressed its positive aspects by calling it "a tabernacle of peace."[354] This trend, common in the idyllic Italian sonnet, grew stronger in the Arcadian poetry that flourished towards the end of the century. Christina of Sweden, whose coronation was commemorated in a sonnet by Moses Zacuto,[355] encouraged the establishment of this trend. A yearning for the simple life also forms a motif in Portuguese poetry of the period, as in a poem by Camões which Moses Hayyim Luzzatto translated into Hebrew. Here the speaker ponders the pastoral life and sighs that "if only man's heart was sufficiently humble" to be satisfied with "a stream of water" and milk "taken from the teats of his flock, / how goodly would his portion be!"[356]

Meditation of a personal kind finds expression in a revealing confession of Jacob Frances, where he rebukes himself for desiring a lofty position within the yeshiva and decries the pride that makes him desire the "crown of learning."[357] Unusual here is the self-recrimination based not on the usual religious reasons, but on humanist values of sincerity and humility.

New directions are also evident in the complaint. Complaints about old age return to a traditional topic and to the fatalistic outlook of old.[358] But in complaints about other subjects, the speakers cease blaming Fate and take personal responsibility for their own lives. So, for example, Moses ben Joab complains of his sorrows, but in attributing them to his sins places the blame squarely on himself.[359] Jacob Frances complains about his illness and seeks merciful death, but knows that the choice is not entirely out of his reach: "Did I not fear the Living God / I would put a knife to my throat before your eyes."[360]

---

[352] Idem, sonnet 284 in *Tzror Zehuvim*, ed. Bregman.

[353] *Eyzeh de'ah eyzeh*: Jacob Frances, *Kol Shirei*, ed. Naveh, 167–74. The lines which are missing from this poem in Naveh's edition are completed by Bregman in *Shevil ha-Zahav*, 204–5, note 341.

[354] Moses Zacuto, sonnet 214 in *Tzror Zehuvim*, ed. Bregman.

[355] Idem, sonnet 224 in *Tzror Zehuvim*, ed. Bregman.

[356] Moses Hayyim Luzzatto, *Shirim*, ed. S. Ginzburg and B. Klar (Jerusalem, 1945), 214; and on 215, the Portuguese source.

[357] Jacob Frances, sonnet 285 in *Tzror Zehuvim*, ed. Bregman.

[358] In the Baroque sonnet of complaint these topics provide an excuse for pondering the terrors of death, or for yearning for it. See for example: Jacob Frances, sonnet 286; Immanuel Frances, sonnet 335 in *Tzror Zehuvim*, ed. Bregman.

[359] Moses ben Joab, sonnet 47 in *Tzror Zehuvim*, ed. Bregman.

[360] Jacob Frances, sonnet 289 in *Tzror Zehuvim*, ed. Bregman.

A conventional complaint about the brevity of life is used for purposes of introspective examination in a sonnet by Jacob Frances: "If man's days on earth are a shadow / why moan, my heart, and be cast down? / If all mankind is a guest herein / why cry out, my soul, to He who dwells above?" Such words sound like an echo of a sonnet by Quevedo which argues: "death is the last breath, short and bitter. But if this is the law and not punishment, why should I complain?"[361]

Moses Zacuto complains about Time, which "at times elevates fools / and at times poisons the great." The argument sounds standard enough, but the continuation is unconventional. With a neat use of homonyms, Zacuto bewails the fact that man's soul is a servant (*ama*) to her people (*ʿamah*)[362] and thus transfers the problem to the level of society in general.

Immanuel Frances begins a sonnet with the old complaint about bad luck but ends addressing Fate on a completely new note: "You may rule everything, but you do not rule the spirit!"[363] Thus we find that the Hebrew sonnet, though aware of traditional conventions and observant of them, was also receptive to humanistic trends born in the period of the Renaissance, and remained so into the seventeenth century.

10. Mockery and Laughter

Trivial matters provided subjects for humor and entertainment in the renewed Hebrew sonnet of the sixteenth century. The suffering of a donkey,[364] games of cards,[365] gluttony,[366] even the loftier subject of plagiarism all became an excuse for laughter.[367] Traces of this trend can still be found in the seventeenth century, for example in a sonnet by Jacob Frances about the marriage of two drunkards.[368] But in the Baroque period a certain cynicism begins to set in, intensifying the negative element to the point where the loathsome becomes positively demonic.

The trend appears already in a sonnet by Leone da Modena, where illness takes on the satanic personification of a goat or ram. At this stage things are not too bad, and the sick person manages to take control: "If God heals me within two days . . . / . . . I'll finish you off like Egypt."[369] But Jacob Frances transfers

---

[361] Quevedo, *Obra poetica*, ed. J. M. Blecua (Madrid, 1969), 1:185: *Todo tras si*.
[362] Moses Zacuto, sonnet 213 in *Tzror Zehuvim*, ed. Bregman.
[363] Immanuel Frances, sonnet 333 in *Tzror Zehuvim*, ed. Bregman.
[364] Samuel Archivolti, sonnet 60 in *Tzror Zehuvim*, ed. Bregman.
[365] Joseph Tzarfati, sonnet 41 in *Tzror Zehuvim*, ed. Bregman.
[366] Moses ben Joab, sonnet 45 in *Tzror Zehuvim*, ed. Bregman.
[367] Joseph Tzarfati, sonnet 42 in *Tzror Zehuvim*, ed. Bregman.
[368] Jacob Frances, sonnet 257 in *Tzror Zehuvim*, ed. Bregman.
[369] Leone da Modena, sonnet 137 in *Tzror Zehuvim*, ed. Bregman.

the demonization to a human agent, a doctor who makes a covenant with death and then takes his place: "It's me they will call death, and not you."[370] Moses Zacuto also devoted a sonnet to criticism of physicians.[371] In its gravity of tone this sonnet borders on religious rebuke. The accusation rests on moral grounds: "The responsibility lies on your head; / how can you remove its yoke . . . ?" His charge is indicative of a real doubt in the power of medicine and science. Moses Zacuto developed the criticism in his *Tofteh ʿArukh*, a work dominated by a demonic figure.

Demonization of the subject under attack is found in sonnets by Jacob Frances in every field, from the debate over women[372] to the war against Shabbetai Zevi and his followers.[373] His Baroque sword of demonization flashes in every direction. Sometimes the negative figure himself appears to be chased by demons.[374] In a sonnet dripping with black humor the poet-speaker masquerades as a power of darkness himself: "I will be death in this world / and thrash around like Satan in hell."[375]

---

[370] Jacob Frances, sonnet 258 in *Tzror Zehuvim*, ed. Bregman; see also idem, sonnet 260.

[371] A facsimile of Zacuto's sonnet in manuscript is printed in Bregman, *Shevil ha-Zahav*, 212.

[372] Jacob Frances, sonnet 245 in *Tzror Zehuvim*, ed. Bregman.

[373] Idem, sonnet 279 in *Tzror Zehuvim*, ed. Bregman.

[374] Idem, sonnets 270 and 271 in *Tzror Zehuvim*, ed. Bregman.

[375] Idem, sonnet 256 in *Tzror Zehuvim*, ed. Bregman.

XVI. Sonnet Sequences

1. The Autonomy of the Sonnet

As we have said, the sonnet is not a "little poem" in terms of size. Other Italian forms of poetry are smaller in their basic structure. But these forms can become part of a longer poem. The *quartina*, for example, comes primarily in sequences. This is also true of the *sestina narrativa*, which Immanuel Frances, in a play on the Hebrew homonyms of "linen" and "six," called *shesh moshzar* : the "fine twisted linen" adorning Aaron's priestly garment (Exodus 39:5), since the sestina gravitates towards sequences.[1] The rhyme of the *terza rima* (ABA BCB CDC) links it into a long sequence that Immanuel Frances dubbed *ha-ḥut ha-meshulash*, since, as the saying goes, "the threefold cord is not easily broken" (Ecclesiastes 4:12).[2] These forms lose their independence in sequences. Their basic contours become blurred and turn into strophes of a long poem. Others, such as the *canzone* and the *ballata*, are complex from the start and have repeating elements: the former, strophes; the latter, rhyme.

The sonnet is also linked in sequence. However, the basic dichotomy of its form refuses to be blurred; the distinction between the beginning and end remains intact. If no change is made to the basic forms, sonnets linked together in sequences remain independent, small poems. On the subject of Petrarch's sonnets, which in various ways create a continuous long story, and here and there even link up through prosodic similarity, Carlyle passed some rather querulous criticism: "He might have built a palace and has made some half-a-dozen snuff boxes with invisible lids — very pretty certainly, but useless."[3] This criticism, which derives in large part from the Romantic ambivalence towards the sonnet-form, expresses discomfort with small forms of poetry that insist on staying just that.[4]

Although sonnets tend to be independent, and maybe precisely because of this reason, poets never stopped looking for ways to link them together. Hebrew poets were perhaps less anxious to do so, but they did not reject the trend. We have already noted examples of linkage in the work of Immanuel of Rome. In the renewed Hebrew sonnet they multiply and become increasingly complex and

---

[1] Immanuel Frances, *Meteq Sefatayim*, ed. Brody, 52.
[2] *Meteq Sefatayim*, ed. Brody, 52.
[3] Quoted from Fuller, *The Sonnet*, 7.
[4] On sonnet sequences afer 1700 and in modern Hebrew poetry, see Bregman, *Sharsheret ha-Zahav*, 122–31.

varied, sometimes expressing the Baroque tendency towards complexity, perfection of technique, and the desire to create wonder. Moses Zacuto was especially successful in this respect.

Definitions for the various kinds of sonnet sequences are not clear-cut. Some define a sonnet *corona* as any combination of two or more sonnets on the same topic.[5] Others see the *corona* as a group of sonnets that complies with the conditions established by the Italian poet Giovan Mario Crescimbeni: fifteen sonnets, of which the last is the *sonetto coronale*. The first sonnet begins with the rhyme of the *sonetto coronale*, and ends with the second rhyme of this sonnet. The second sonnet begins with the second rhyme of the *sonetto coronale* and ends with the third rhyme of this sonnet, and so on. The fourteenth sonnet begins with the final rhyme of the *sonetto coronale* and ends with the first. The sonnets thus come full circle, justifying the name *corona*. Between this first liberal definition of the *corona* and the last, we find a host of definitions in various degrees of rigidity.[6] Let us look now into the corpus of Hebrew sonnet-sequences. We will start with a variety of simple and comparatively loosely organized sequences, pass to a more articulated *corona*, and end up with a highly elaborated, complex and symmetrical set of sonnet sequences.

2. Sonnet Series

Pairs

Pairs of sonnets are linked through a common topic, narrative continuity, and other means. Judah Saltares da Fano laments the death of Joseph Caro in two sonnets joined through a heading above the second sonnet: "Another one for the above *Gaon* ("Rabbi").[7] These sonnets could easily have stood on their own, independent of each other. But joined in sequence they take on a chronological order, first telling the news of the disaster, then moving on to express the acceptance of God's will, and finally ending with a lament. In a later pair of lament-sonnets, this kind of linkage is reinforced through joint acrostics that spell out: "To Moses di Mercado [the deceased] by Samuel di Caceres [the poet]."[8] There is also a pair of sonnets by Jacob Schneur in which the first offers the author's apology for daring to consider himself a poet, and the second is a poem of praise.[9]

---

[5] Elwert, *Versificazione italiana*, 133–34, and also see the Index.
[6] See Mönch, *Das Sonett*, 30–31; Coen, *Saggio di eloquenza ebrea*, 66.
[7] Judah Saltares da Fano, sonnets 77 and 78 in *Tzror Zehuvim*, ed. Bregman.
[8] Samuel di Caceres, sonnets 297 and 298 in *Tzror Zehuvim*, ed. Bregman.
[9] Moses Zacuto, sonnets 221 and 222 in *Tzror Zehuvim*, ed. Bregman; Jacob Schneur, sonnets 165 and 166.

A pair of wedding sonnets by Jacob Frances mentioned above is linked together through dialogue: the bridegroom speaks in the first one; the bride responds in the second, forming the known genre of *contrasti*.[10]

Sonnet Twins

We shall call "sonnet twins" pairs of sonnets that are linked *inter alia* by a common rhyme-scheme, and usually by a common meter as well. The linkage formed by meter is especially evident when the meter is not one of the common syllabic-quantitative lines. "Twins" may also have additional common traits. When Abraham of Zante received his medical diploma, Solomon Lustro composed in honor of the occasion twin sonnets that share one rhyme and that develop the theme in a similar way.[11] Similar to this is a pair of twin sonnets for a circumcision by Moses Zacuto. The first sonnet describes the anticipation, while the second prays for his prosperity and begins where the first one leaves off to describe the happy father. Twin sonnets by Samuel di Caceres (additional laments for Moses di Mercado) have, moreover, identical rhymes. They also continue a narrative, the first describing the disaster, the second attempting to console.[12]

S*onetti caudati* create impressive sequences of a kind that we see in the twin sonnets for Simḥat Torah by Solomon Oliveyra and in another pair by an anonymous poet mentioned earlier.[13] Each pair is united by elements of prosody and subject matter. Oliveyra links his sonnets through identical rhyme-words (apart from the lines naming the two honorees) and subjects, namely the two "bridegrooms of the Torah." One sonnet begins with the *Hatan Bereshit* (who, as noted, recites the blessings for the first pericope from Genesis) and continues in the "tail" with the *Ḥatan Torah* (who recites the blessings for the last pericope from Deuteronomy), while the second does just the reverse. The anonymous poet also links his sonnets through rhyme-words and headings that divide each sonnet into three parts, all of which unfold in the same way.

Above we mentioned four "double sonnets" by Jacob Sasportas. These can also be seen as two pairs of twins, with each pair united by rhyme and meter. We will return to these sonnets further on.

---

[10] Jacob Frances, sonnets 248 and 249 in *Tzror Zehuvim*, ed. Bregman.
[11] Solomon Lustro, sonnets 407 and 408 in *Tzror Zehuvim*, ed. Bregman.
[12] Samuel di Caceres, sonnets 295 and 296 in *Tzror Zehuvim*, ed. Bregman.
[13] Solomon Oliveyra, sonnets 343 and 344 in *Tzror Zehuvim*, ed. Bregman; Anonymous, sonnets 422 and 423.

Sequences of Three

One of the *tenzones* described earlier is in fact a sequence of three, namely the exchange of sonnets between Saᶜadia Longo and Isaac Uziel.[14] Three sonnets in Johanan Alatrini's *L'Angelica Tromba*, later translated into Hebrew by Nathan Jedidiah da Orvieto, create a similar sequence:[15] all three sonnets deal with the purification of the heart and describe its different stages in order. Headings before the second and third sonnets point out the connection among all three. These three sonnets are also linked through rhyme: they all have one rhyme in common, and two of them are further linked by yet another rhyme. Each of them has a different rare meter, which is another way to link them together. And last of all, the three sonnets unite to create an epilogue for the three penitential prayers in Alatrini's book, a role to which the third sonnet alludes: "Hurry, my heart, take in support / my three supplications, and turn to supplicate God." This triple epilogue is a particularly fitting way to conclude a book composed entirely in *terza rima*. Emphasizing the number three is certainly a bold thing to do in a Hebrew religious poem, especially when the poem is so markedly Petrarchist in nature, as we already have seen.

Another triplet of sonnets, in honor of the book *Ḥanukat ha-Bayit*, or "Inauguration of the Temple," by Moses Gentili (Amsterdam, 1696), was created through combined poetic activity, as we learn from the preface.[16] The three sonnets are also united by a heading: "A song of praise for the inauguration of the Temple by Moses." This heading is mentioned again at the end of each sonnet, for the first two sonnets conclude with the words "The Lord's Temple you have established," a reference to Exodus 15:17. The third sonnet concludes with a slightly adapted version of this line: "The Lord's Temple your soul has created." Secondary headings create further links between the poems: the words "while this one was speaking" appears above the second sonnet, and "the best for last" appears above the third one.

A Sequence of Three or Four Poems and a Sonnet?

One group of sonnets by Moses Zacuto has an ambiguous structure that can be interpreted in various ways. The poems come in a treatise dedicated to a certain physician named Halevi, as we learn from the manuscript heading, and are linked together by subject, argument, and prosodic elements. They all deal with the criticism of physicians.

---

[14] Sonnets 82–84 in *Tzror Zehuvim*, ed. Bregman.

[15] Nathan Jedidiah da Orvieto, sonnets 147, 148, and 149 in *Tzror Zehuvim*, ed. Bregman.

[16] Jacob Aboab, sonnet 411 in *Tzror Zehuvim*, ed. Bregman; Moses Merrari, sonnet 348; Solomon Conigliano, sonnet 396.

Sonnet Sequences

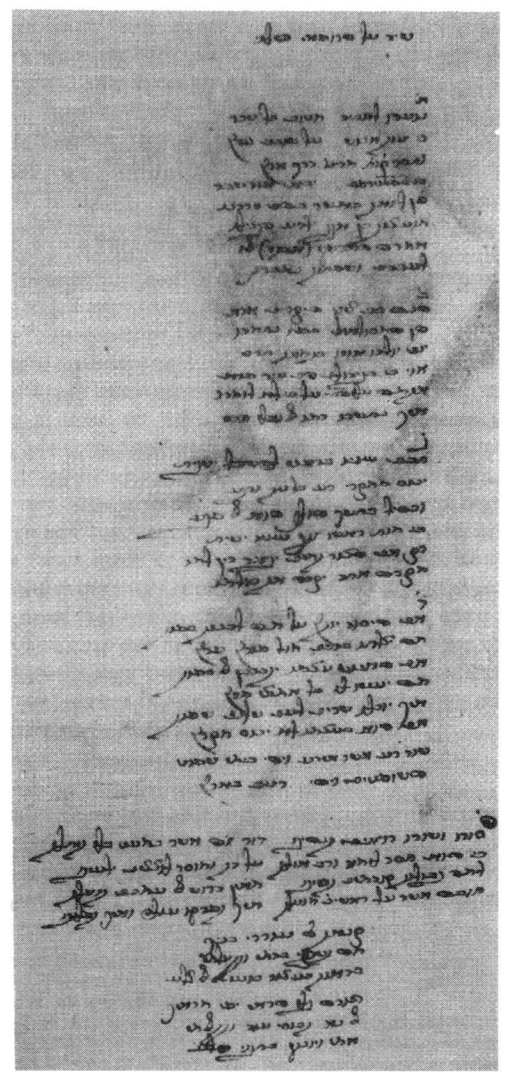

MS. 459, Kaufmann Collection, Budapest, fol. 211

The manuscript divides the text into four numbered poems and a sonnet with the rhyme-scheme of ABBA ABBA CDE CDE. But the poems can also be perceived as three sonnets. The first poem has eight lines; the second, six. When joined together, they form one sonnet with a rhyme-scheme of ABBA CDDC EFG EFG and a feminine line of eleven syllables (Scheme 1). The third poem has six lines; the fourth, eight. Together they create an "upside-down sonnet" with a rhyme-scheme of ABB ACC DEDE DEDE. We find a sonnet like this in Italian poetry. Its creator, Anton Maria Borga, explains in the body of the poem itself why he created an upside-down sonnet. For one thing, he says, innovation is always desirable, and, for another, this is not a masculine *sonetto* but rather a *sonettesa* (that is, a longer or otherwise unusual sonnet) — and women, after all, always turn everything upside down.[17] Zacuto's four "poems" each have different quantitative structures of meter, but this does not keep them from being joined together, since it was possible, as already mentioned, to alternate different quantitative schemes in a single sonnet. The four poems deal with the same subject matter. Why, then, did Zacuto divide these sonnets into separate poems? Perhaps this was yet another Baroque artifice meant to create a veritable wonder of form that lends itself to various interpretations. We can also assume that Moses Zacuto was not familiar with the structure of the upside-down sonnet, and that since he hesitated to be overly ambitious in making innovations in the sonnet-form, he divided the poems as he did.

Sequences of Four

Two pairs of wedding sonnets by Menasseh Hayyim Padua[18] create a sequence of four sonnets through headings which join together to form the biblical verse from Jeremiah 33:11: "The voice of joy / and the voice of delight"; "The voice of the bridegroom / and the voice of the bride." The first two sonnets describe the bridegroom's joy, and the last two consist of a dialogue between the bride and the groom forming *contrasti*. All four have unusual meters (Schemes 22; 29 alternating with 10; 20 alternating with 14; and 18 alternating with 10).

As two pairs of twin sonnets, the four double sonnets of Jacob Sasportas, mentioned above, also create a sequence of four.[19] A heading that reads "a double golden poem" links them together so that they form one sequence. The concluding words of the last sonnet refer to all four sonnets together. This pyramid is indeed a well-crafted example of the Baroque style.

Sequences of Five

Menasseh Hayyim Padua added a fifth sonnet to his sequence of four sonnets, in which the poet-speaker praises the couple and prays for their prosperity. It is united to the previous four by a heading that continues the biblical quotation: "A

---

[17] Mönch, *Das Sonett*, 171, 289.
[18] Menasseh Hayyim Padua, sonnets 357, 358, 359 and 360 in *Tzror Zehuvim*, ed. Bregman.
[19] Jacob Sasportas, sonnets 367, 368, 369, and 370 in *Tzror Zehuvim*, ed. Bregman.

voice that says: give thanks!" Through the addition of this sonnet the sequence of four turns into a sequence of five, though this fifth sonnet functions primarily as a unit unto itself (its meter is the usual feminine line of eleven syllables with the regular quantitative metrical scheme).[20]

Sequences of Six
A sequence of six sonnets was created in the polemic over Jewish converts to Christianity, with the convert Simon Luria ranged on one side of the debate, and Rabbi Judah Briel and others on the opposite side.[21]

Sequences of Seven
Menasseh Hayyim Padua was not satisfied with a sequence of merely four or five sonnets. By adding two other sonnets and a conclusion that unites the group as a whole, he turned the sonnets into a sequence of seven,[22] thereby alluding to the seven blessings over the nuptial couple and the seven days of wedding festivities.

3. The Corona

While Padua's series can be interpreted as two sequences (four and three, five and two), the seven sonnets in which Moses Zacuto laments his teacher, Rabbi Saul Halevi Morteira, are tightly and unmistakably organized into one sequence and may indeed be considered as the first step towards the elaborated crown of sonnets that was later invented by Cresimbeni, and composed in Hebrew for the first time by Saul Tchernikhowsky. (Coincidentally enough, the name "Saul" plays a role in both of the Hebrew examples.) This sequence is included in a letter that is basically a long prose "double" of the sonnets in both its subject and ideas, and especially in its bizarre tone, obscure style, and highly enigmatic language. This prose "preface" creates a sense of disaster and awe that carries over into the sonnets.[23]

The seven sonnets have almost identical endings which form a kind of refrain. Each of them ends in a variation of the famous verse from David's lament for King Saul: "Daughters of Israel, weep over Saul" (2 Samuel 1:24), chosen, of course, because the deceased was also named Saul. The sonnets have the

---

[20] Menasseh Hayyim Padua, sonnet 361 in *Tzror Zehuvim*, ed. Bregman.
[21] Printed in *Tzror Zehuvim*, ed. Bregman: Simon Luria, sonnet 383; Judah Briel, sonnet 384; Abraham Segrè, sonnet 385; and Joseph Cases, sonnet 386. See also MS. 365A in the Ginzburg Collection, Moscow, fols. 1–10.
[22] Menasseh Hayyim Padua, sonnets 362 and 363 in *Tzror Zehuvim*, ed. Bregman.
[23] See D. Kaufmann, "L'elégie de Moise Zacout sur Saul Morteira," *Revue des études juives* 37 (1898): 115–32.

same unusual meter established by this biblical quotation and share the unusual rhyme-scheme: ABCA ACBC DED EDE. The breakdown in the classic structures reflects the calamity of the great man's death.

The sonnets have a continuous development. The *corona* opens with a description of the mourning. The first sonnet describes the grief of the sages and scholars of Torah and the second, the grief of the Levites, the Temple poets to whose tribe the deceased belonged.[24] Here the poet shifts to praise of the dead: the third sonnet praises the work of the deceased in defense of the Jewish faith;[25] and the fourth extols his knowledge of Talmud.[26] The fifth[27] poses the eternal question: "Where is he now?" and in reply compares the death of the saintly rabbi with the removal of the divine presence. The sixth sonnet[28] presents the dismay of the people who are left without a leader, while the seventh[29] consoles the mourners by reminding them of the spiritual legacy that the deceased has left behind, his future role in heaven as the advocate of the Jews, and the coming of the messiah. None of this destroys the sense of loss that prevails throughout the sonnets and is enforced by the biblical refrains in the conclusions. The seven sonnets, which correspond to the seven days of mourning, merge into a single creation. As such it creates the impression that though the death of the leader is so terrible, it is still part of a divine plan in which nothing happens by accident.

4. Sonnet Sequences in "Yesod ʿOlam"
by Moses Zacuto

Scope and Organization

The play *Yesod ʿOlam* ("The Foundation of the World") has come down to us in an incomplete text containing forty-two sonnets, plus half of a forty-third.[30] Even in its incomplete state, *Yesod ʿOlam* contains more sonnets than any other Hebrew work of the period, including *Maḥbarot Immanuel*. While scholars have not overlooked this fact, they also did not consider it to be especially praiseworthy. Schirmann merely remarked that the play contains "a huge number of sonnets."[31] And according to Melkman:

---

[24] Moses Zacuto, sonnets 229 and 230 in *Tzror Zehuvim*, ed. Bregman.
[25] Idem, sonnet 231 in *Tzror Zehuvim*, ed. Bregman (this alludes primarily to his book *Givʿat Shaul*).
[26] Idem, sonnet 232 in *Tzror Zehuvim*, ed. Bregman.
[27] Idem, sonnet 233 in *Tzror Zehuvim*, ed. Bregman.
[28] Idem, sonnet 234 in *Tzror Zehuvim*, ed. Bregman.
[29] Idem, sonnet 235 in *Tzror Zehuvim*, ed. Bregman.
[30] The fragmented state of the last sonnet is due to the condition of the text.
[31] Schirmann, *Le-Toldot*, 2:125–39.

> The boredom that besets the modern reader of the play is increased by the inordinate use of sonnets. This literary form may be suitable for lyrical outpouring, but it is absolutely unsuitable for character description. The principal characters speak in sonnets and its effect is most undesirable.[32]

Granted, there is no arguing with taste, but it is worth noting that the number of sonnets in *Yesod ʿOlam* would not have caused much of a commotion in Zacuto's own time. Those were the days in which the Provençal poet Jean de la Ceppede composed his *Théorèmes Spirituels*, depicting the life of Jesus in no less than five hundred sonnets.[33] The number of sonnets in *Yesod ʿOlam* is certainly impressive against the background of Hebrew poetry, but it is in no way exaggerated in terms of Baroque poetics, of which *Yesod ʿOlam* is a typical product.

No less interesting than the number of sonnets is the way they are woven into the text, which consists of verse in various forms. As it turns out, the sonnets in *Yesod ʿOlam* are all organized into sequences. There is not a single isolated sonnet in the entire play, a fact which has gone unnoticed in previous research.

The plot of *Yesod ʿOlam* is based on the rabbinic *midrash* dealing with Abraham's life prior to leaving the land of his birth for Canaan. Teraḥ, the *midrash* tells us, worshipped idols and also sold them. One day when away from home, he put Abraham to sell them in his place. Abraham smashed all of the idols. When Teraḥ demanded an explanation, Abraham claimed that a woman had brought an offering for the idols, and in the ensuing quarrel between them over their respective portions the largest idol smashed all the rest. Teraḥ handed Abraham over to King Nimrod. An argument between Nimrod and Abraham ended with the king consigning Abraham to the fiery furnace. His brother, Harran, was also thrown into the fire. Abraham was saved by a miracle, but Harran, who wavered in his faith, succumbed to the flames and died.

The entire play is written in poems of various verse-forms. The sonnets, organized, as noted, into sequences, are distributed among the rest of the poems. Below we shall briefly describe them.

> *Sequence 1* : Sonnets 1–5.[34] In Teraḥḥ's house. After smashing the idols Abraham tries to persuade Teraḥ of the vanity of idol-worship. He tells his father about the One God in whom he believes and describes the creation of the world in six days. This God, Abraham claims, watches over all his creatures and defends those who believe in him. He will defend Abraham even against his father. The idols, on the other hand, have no existence at all, and it is better for Teraḥ to abandon them.

---

[32] Y. Melkman, "Moses Zacuto's Play *Yesod ʿOlam*," *Studia Rosenthaliana* 1 (1967): 1–26, here 24.

[33] Cohen, *The Baroque Lyric*, 155.

[34] Sonnets 169–173 in *Tzror Zehuvim*, ed. Bregman.

Sequence 2 : Sonnets 6–10.³⁵ The sequence begins in Teraḥ's house and ends in the palace of King Nimrod. Abraham, alone in the house, surmises that Teraḥ has gone to denounce him. And indeed, Nimrod's emissaries (conversing amongst themselves) appear and after arguing with Abraham, and with the encouragement of Teraḥ who also appears, they arrest him. Nimrod, before whom Abraham is brought, rebukes Abraham for founding a new religion and for not fearing his king. Abraham rebukes the king in turn, and warns him that if he does not abandon idol-worship he will be punished on the Day of Judgment after his death.

Sequence 3 : Sonnets 11–20.³⁶ In the king's palace. A religious debate. Two of Nimrod's wise men try to persuade Abraham to recant. Abraham refutes their arguments, demands that they recognize the One True God, threatens them with God's wrath, and expresses his belief that God will defend him from all harm.

Sequence 4 : Sonnets 21–25.³⁷ In the king's palace. Abraham prays for God's help and is brought to the fiery furnace. Harran, his brother, declares his own doubts and decides to wait and see if Abraham is indeed saved by a miracle. Nimrod is pleased to be rid of Abraham, but admits that his joy is mingled with fear of him.

Sequence 5 : Sonnets 26–32.³⁸ In Nimrod's palace, after Abraham has been saved. Nimrod, in a long monologue, vents his anger on Harran, brags about his power and riches, and consigns Harran to the flames. Harran is brought to the fiery furnace.

Sequence 6 : Sonnets 33–39.³⁹ In the king's palace. Sara rebukes her relations Naḥor and Naḥor's wife, Milka, for not accepting Abraham's faith, as Teraḥ and Lot had done. Abraham, in a brief aside to himself from his place of hiding, praises her intelligence.

Sequence 7 (incomplete): Sonnets 40–42 and the octave of Sonnet 43.⁴⁰ Abraham (emerging from his hiding place) also reproaches Naḥor and Milka, but Naḥor, in the last half of the remaining sonnet, declares his adherence to idol-worship.

---

[35] Sonnets 174–178 in *Tzror Zehuvim*, ed. Bregman.
[36] Sonnets 179–188 in *Tzror Zehuvim*, ed. Bregman.
[37] Sonnets 189–193 in *Tzror Zehuvim*, ed. Bregman.
[38] Sonnets 194–200 in *Tzror Zehuvim*, ed. Bregman.
[39] Sonnets 201–207 in *Tzror Zehuvim*, ed. Bregman.
[40] Sonnets 208–211 in *Tzror Zehuvim*, ed. Bregman.

The Sonnet Sequences of *Yesod ʿOlam*

Sequence	Scene	Speakers	Sestet Rhyme	Syntax	Meter
Sequence 1 (5 sonnets)	Monologue on principles of Judaism	1–5: Abraham	CDE CDE	tercets	Scheme 1
Sequence 2 (5 sonnets)	Abraham brought before Nimrod	6–10: Shift within and between sonnets	CDC DCD	distichs	Scheme 1
Sequence 3 (10 sonnets)	Religious Disputation	Shifting Speaker: 11–12: 1st wise man 13–14: 2nd wise man 15–20: Abraham	Shifting rhyme: 11–12: CDE EDO 13–14: CDD CCD 15–20: CDC DCD	distichs	Scheme 3
Sequence 4 (5 sonnets)	Abraham consigned to the flames	Shifting speaker: 21–23: Abraham 24: Harran 25: Nimrod	Shifting rhyme: 21–23: CDC DCD 24: CDE CDE 25: CDE CDE	Shifting syntax: 21–23: distichs 24: tercets 25: tercets	Shifting meter: 21–23: Scheme 1 24: Scheme 3 25 Scheme 2
Sequence 5 (7 sonnets)	Nimrod's panegyric monologue	26–32: King Nimrod	ABB/AAB	distichs	Scheme 1
Sequence 6 (7 sonnets)	Monologue of Sarah reproving her family	33–39: Sarah, with slight intervention from Abraham	CDE CDE	tercets	Scheme 3
Sequence 7 (3½ sonnets) (fragment)	Family religious disputation	40–42: Abraham 43: Quatrain of last remaining sonnet: Naḥor	3 sonnets: CDC EDE	tercets	Mixed. quatrain of 3: Schemes: 2, 3, 3, 2 tercet of 3: Schemes: 2, 3, 2 quatrain of last remaining octave: Schemes 3, 2, 2, 3

As can be seen from the above synopsis, each of the sequences is unique and independent. At the same time, however, some of them split off into secondary sequences through a change in speakers or through variations in elements of prosody. These elements belong to several categories, as illustrated in the Table, below. In the rubric "Meter," the numbers indicate syllabic-quantitative schemes:

1. 11 syllables with a penultimate stress.

2. 10 syllables with a final stress.

3. 12 syllables with a final stress.

In the rubric "Syntax" we refer to the syntax of the sestet, which is dual or ternary in structure. In the first case the lines are divided by syntax into couplets or into a quatrain and a couplet (distichs). In the second case they are divided into two tercets or united into a single sextain.

Consolidation and Disintegration within Three Sequences

The above description shows the precision with which the sonnet sequences were constructed and the complexity of the relations within it. This was not technical virtuosity for its own sake. The bonds between the sonnets, formed through prosody, syntax, and rhetoric, as shown above, are tightened or loosened in coordination with bonds of other kinds: narrative, scenic, and ideological. They create changes in emphasis, increase or decrease dramatic tension, and help to develop the characters more fully.

Let us see how they function in sequences 3, 2, and 5, which differ greatly from one another. Sequence 3 constructs a single philosophical edifice. It presents first the claims of the idolaters, and then Abraham's refutations. The sonnets are linked through the following arguments:

(11) 1st wise man: Abraham, repent, for man is like a beast
(12) and has no existence after death.
(13) 2nd wise man: It is the stars that determine Fate:
(14) Repent or be punished.
(15) Abraham: Listen to my words:
(16) Do you say that man ceases to exist after death?
(17) If so, how can he possibly be as wise as God?
And is it because man dies like the beast

(18)	you all say that there is no divine guidance? On the contrary, it is universal and regards equally all that live! In sum, the truth is with me, and I shall not renounce my faith.
(19)	And you [idolaters]! Beware of the fires of hell.
(20)	Remember what happened to the generation of the Flood!

In this solid structure, the outlines of the individual sonnet are preserved in terms of subject development. It begins from a clearly specified starting point and ends with a definite conclusion. Together with this, the sonnets are inextricably linked together, so that the end of one sonnet provides the starting point for the next. In Sonnets 17–18, this tight logical connection even translates into syntax:

Sonnet 17 ends with an unfinished sentence:

But since man born of woman
dies in disgrace and is short-lived -

Sonnet 18 begins by completing this sentence:

You say that God in his palace
Hides behind the clouds and does not see?

Sometimes an unwritten conjunction echoes between the sonnets. For example, an unspoken "Therefore" resounds between Sonnets 13 and 14, and Sonnet 15 is nothing but a preamble to Sonnet 16. The structure of the solitary sonnet is therefore used to clarify the argument forming part of the larger thesis, which is itself constructed from the orderly march of the sequence in its entirety.

A glance at the Table shows how the prosodic factors assist the processes of consolidation and disintegration in Sequence 3. The sequence is consolidated through the identical syntax of the sestets. This emphasizes the unity of subject, scene, and event. At the same time, barriers between the speakers are created through the use of different rhyme-schemes in the sestets.

Rhetorical links isolate Abraham's monologue even further from the other speakers and consolidate the monologues of Nimrod's wise men into a separate unit. In Sequence 3 the sonnets of the first wise man (11, 12) open with the question: "Why . . .?" The sonnets of the second wise man (13, 14) are linked by this same question, that also opens the octave in sonnet 13. Their speeches are also linked by the following words of transition, uttered by the second wise man in his opening line:

> Let me answer and add my part
> To complete the words of my friend

Abraham's speech (sonnets 15–20), on the other hand, remains as isolated as his message.

This fosters the impression of one against the many. But because Abraham's monologue consists of six sonnets and that of the wise men only four, and because the last crucial word goes to the patriarch, it is Abraham who carries the day.

Sequence 2 is a narrative, and its function is to advance the plot. Here the play of consolidation and disintegration reaches its peak. On the one hand, the individual sonnet itself is divided among several speakers, but on the other, it still functions as a link in a long sequence. The disintegration of the sonnet illustrates the confrontation between the various characters and intensifies the drama of the situation, whereas the consolidation unifies and advances the plot. The prosodic factors defend the unity of the sequence against the breakdown that is liable to occur through the changes in speakers (see Table).

Sequence 5 describes a static and unchanging situation in which King Nimrod gives a long and thunderous speech. Unlike the philosophers, he has nothing of real substance to say. His speech lacks development and is little more than a boastful inventory of his possessions. Here we must consider the rhyme-scheme as a whole. The seven sonnets have only two rich rhymes: *eret* and *lenu*, and these occur in a single-rhyme scheme, forward (ABBA ABBA ABB AAB) and backward (BAAB BAAB BAA BBA), and then back again throughout the entire series. The whole sequence is thus turned into a solid monolith. As content and sound grow more and more monotonous, the sonnet-form becomes blurred and the individual sonnet essentially turns into a strophe of a long poem — a mere link in the chain. In order to blur the outline of the single sonnet, the author deviates from the ground-rules of the sonnet-form, repeating a rhyme from the octave in the sestet. He also foregoes his custom of ending the sonnet with a verse from the Bible; instead he makes repeated use of anaphora and consolidates the whole speech with a few prosodic elements. The uniform nature of this sequence, which blurs the lines of the individual sonnets, also turns the mighty Nimrod into a pompous windbag and his thundering oration into a pathetic tirade.

Reconstructing the Structure of the Play

The elaborate set of sonnet sequences in *Yesod ʿOlam* is the first and probably the only one of its kind in Hebrew poetry. Its complex symmetry, which could have been examined in even more detail than we have done here, plays a central role in advancing the plot, building the argument, and creating dramatic effect. But apparently this symmetry is even more important to the play in yet another respect.

Though the surviving text of *Yesod ʿOlam* breaks off before the end of the play,[41] the symmetry that dominates its sequences allows us to reconstruct the missing part: first the sestet of the last, fragmented sonnet, then the final sonnet sequence, and finally the missing text in its entirety: all, of course, in the most general way.

Since the meter of the last remaining octave is the reverse of that of the three octaves before it, we can assume that the missing sestet was constructed in the same manner. Thus the tercet would have had a meter of the schemes: 3, 2, 3, in reverse of that from the three sonnets before. We can therefore conjecture that two other sonnets with the same meter were supposed to follow this sonnet, in order to set three sonnets against three sonnets in reverse meter. Since the adjoining sequences contain seven sonnets, we can assume that a seventh sonnet was supposed to appear here as well, with elements that either reconcile or sum up the meter of the six sonnets preceding it.

Having completed the reconstruction of the last sequence, let us take another look at the Table. We can now see that the play as a whole is composed of two major parts: the first constructed of sequences based on the number five, and the second on sequences based on the number seven. The two parts were supposed to be parallel. This assumption is reinforced by the similarity between Sequences 2–3 in Part One and the parallel Sequences 6–7 in Part Two. Each of these pairs links internally into a chain of sonnets, like one big sequence with various subdivisions. All the remaining sequences are separated from one another by poems in various forms. We can assume that Sequences 1 and 2 should have had their parallels as well in the missing part of the play. We can also conjecture that Parts One and Two paralleled each other in the way the sonnets were arranged.

Part One has 5 x 5 sonnets. It seems likely, therefore, that Part Two was supposed to parallel this by containing 7 x 7 sonnets. Of these, only the first two sequences and half of the third are still extant. If indeed the two parts were supposed to be completely parallel, we can assume that Part Two was supposed to begin with a sequence of seven sonnets, just as Part One begins with a sequence of five; and to end with a sequence of seven, just as a sequence of five concludes Part One. In between are the fifteen sonnets in Part One, that is, 5 x 5 minus 5 + 5. To parallel this, 7 x 7 sonnets minus 7 + 7 sonnets were supposed to come in the middle of Part Two. The general structure of the sonnets in the play would thus have been:

---

[41] This was already noted by Melkman and Schirmann. See Melkman, "Zacuto's Play," 1–26, and Schirmann, *Le-Toldot*, 2:125–39. The editor, Maroni (whose text is less corrupt than that of Berliner), divided the text according to the model of the Spanish *comedia*, as though he had a complete text in front of him.

Part One: 5 + 15 + 5
Part Two: 7 + 35 + 7.

According to this, Part Two should contain forty-nine sonnets. But the parallelism might also have taken the form of:

Part One: 5 + (5 x 3) + 5
Part Two: 7 + (7 x 3) + 7

According to this, Part Two was supposed to contain only thirty-five sonnets. If we go by the first conjecture, the entire play was supposed to contain seventy-four sonnets, or by the second conjecture, sixty. The second conjecture gives us a round number, and also, as we shall see, a basis for solving the problem of why the text before us ends where it does.

The author might have attributed a symbolic value to the numbers five and seven, seeing them as symbols of the divine presence: the number five symbolizing the hidden presence of God, and the number seven his revealed presence. And indeed, the transition from the sequences of five to those of seven occurs precisely at the point where Abraham, after being saved from Nimrod's fiery furnace, propagates his belief in the One God. *Yesod ʿOlam* was meant to portray the triumph of faith, like the religious plays in the contemporary Italian and Spanish theater. Describing the dissemination of the True Faith was an important stage in the depiction of its victory. M. Maroni, who edited the play, divided the text into three acts in order to adapt it to the form of the Spanish *comedia*. Of course, such a division makes little sense when the text before us is incomplete. But if we apply this division to the supposed form of the play as a whole, we can conjecture that it was in this transition from sequences of five to sequences of seven that the second act was supposed to begin. We can further suggest that if the play contained no other sonnets in addition to the sequences of five and seven, the transition from Part Two to Part Three probably occurred in the middle of the sequences of seven. And if we accept the conjecture that there were five of these sequences (see above), then the transition to Part Three would have begun after two and a half sequences, that is, exactly in the place where our text breaks off.

Moses Zacuto had no qualms about dividing a sonnet between different characters in the play. Perhaps he did not even hesitate to begin a new part in mid-sonnet. He did not add this third part to his original manuscript, and perhaps never wrote it at all.

From all the above, it seems that we have two acts of the play, and that the third and final act is missing in its entirety. At the top of the various manuscripts of *Yesod ʿOlam* comes the cast of *dramatis personae*, some of whom do not appear in the incomplete text that has come down to us. Among these are Isaac, Rebecca, and Ketura, characters who played a role in Abraham's old age. It seems that the missing Part Three was supposed to present the final years in Abraham's life. Our text ends with his departure from Haran. Judging from the length of the plot remaining up to the death of Abraham, it seems that the missing act was long; and according to the symmetry in this work, we can assume that it was equal in length to the two acts before it. In other words, only one act of the play is missing, but that is half of the text which should have been in the play as a whole.

All this is only conjecture, of course. But while we cannot guarantee its validity, neither can it be dismissed as far-fetched or bizarre. A tendency towards the symbolic is evident in Zacuto's very concentration on the Kabbalah,[42] while his highly complicated structures are evident in his deeply learned and emblematic riddles,[43] and in his poems with their unusual linguistic and prosodic devices.[44] Nor was any of this out of keeping with the trends of his time. It was in Zacuto's days, for example, that the Italian poet Crescimbeni composed his *Corona rinterzata* in honor of the accession of Pope Clement XI, with forty sonnets that can be read backwards and forwards in several ways. This work consists of three sonnet sequences symbolizing, in the words of the poet himself, the Pope's triple tiara.[45] The *Corona Dedicatoria* of the English poet Joshua Sylvester, which was published in 1641, creates, typographically, the image of a column.[46] As for the symbolic, sacred nature of the number seven, this was first used in the field of sonnetry as far back as the fourteenth century, in Fazio degli Uberti's seven sonnets on the Seven Deadly Sins.[47] We could also mention John Donne's *La Corona*,[48] which describes the life of Jesus in seven sonnets, and of course the *corona* of seven sonnets by Moses Zacuto himself.

Was the missing part ever written? Or is it perhaps buried in one of the many unexamined manuscripts from the period? Time and research will tell.

---

[42] For a list of his works on the Kabbalah, see Simonsohn, *Toldot ha-Yehudim*, 2:517–18.
[43] Pagis, *'Al Sod Ḥatum*, passim.
[44] I intend to publish his poems shortly, beginning with those that have remained in manuscript.
[45] Fuller, *The Sonnet*, 45.
[46] Fuller, *The Sonnet*, 42–43.
[47] Fuller, *The Sonnet*, 41.
[48] John Donne, *Poems*, ed. H. J. Grierson (London, 1912), 318–21.

XVII. The Hebrew Sonnet: Continuity and Change

1. Tradition and Change in the Sonnets of Immanuel of Rome

In historical perspective, the first Hebrew sonnets were first of all an innovation: the first wide-scale assimilation of Italian poetry into Hebrew. It embraced an entire and well-defined genre, a genre of first importance in Italian poetry and in world poetry in general. The innovation of the early Hebrew sonnets has ramifications beyond the field of Hebrew poetry, for these were the first non-Italian sonnets in the world. And this is not all: the corpus of early Hebrew sonnets is apparently the first complete corpus composed in the form that subsequently became the classic form of the genre from the days of Petrarch onward.

The new genre gave birth to other "firsts." The earliest sonnets caused Hebrew poetry in Italy to turn in new directions, and helped it to develop a common language with its surroundings. They became an instrument for expressing and absorbing subjects, motifs, and new attitudes and ideas. The first corpus of Hebrew sonnets overflows with poetic innovations, some still used up to this day. Love, which stands at the center of these sonnets, may be a "given" in most of world poetry, but in Hebrew poetry it constitutes a unique phenomenon.

The corpus of early sonnets offers unique and striking Hebrew examples of the famous *dolce stil nuovo*. There we find bold and realistic expressions nourished by the poetic legitimization of daily life at its most mundane. There, too, we hear the voice of the woman, with all the desires, urges, and drives of an independent personality. The sonnets of Immanuel of Rome infused the subjects of old with a new spirit, and emphasized trends that heralded the coming of the Renaissance. His religious sonnets address the individual alone, and stress his individual worth, his ability to choose, and his personal responsibility for the fate of his soul. His sonnets of lament veer away from the older conventions of the genre in a similar direction, in a bold and daring protest against the ways of the world. While this attitude had roots in religion, it was largely based on the recognition of man's spiritual independence. This recognition was also the foundation for Immanuel's humorous sonnets, which he liberated from the strict confines of social and religious attitudes.

The first sonnets renewed and regenerated the Hebrew language. Their innovations in the field of expression required nuanced, vibrant, and finely-tuned instruments. Immanuel was able to use the vocabulary of the past with amazing flexibility and create new structures, expressions, and shades of meaning. His sonnets reflect every possible mood: sadness and joy, gravity and lightheartedness, humor and sarcasm. They betray no lack of words, images, or rhymes, and they cater to every style, from high-flown and refined to low and vulgar.

Saul Tchernikhowsky recognized the importance of this regeneration. He regarded Immanuel's sonnets as the beginning of a new era, the point at which Hebrew poetry began to wrench itself free from the "death-hold" of the Bible, which, in his opinion, prevented lively and original expression, and from the yoke of Arabic poetics which had extinguished, as he claimed, every spark of realistic and straightforward diction:

> Our literature needed powers of regeneration to remove the yoke of ponderous intellectualism, trite versification, and so on. It fell to Italy to accomplish this, for it was Moses Hayyim Luzzatto who first ushered us into Europe, and Immanuel of Rome who breached the walls of Spain and brought European literary forms into our literature. And lo and behold! Immanuel, whose flood of words brooked no resistance, brought into our language the most exacting and refined form in all Europe — the sonnet. Just compare Immanuel's prose to his poems, and his Arabic-style rhymed poems to his "golden poems." Only the perfect form, which admits nothing extraneous, could save the Hebrew poet from spouting the masses of hyperboles and exaggerations common to the people of the East in general, and to the Arabs in particular. Had our literature remained under the influence of Arabic literature, we would not have been able to create a literature worthy of its name.[1]

The first Hebrew sonnets saw the creation of the first defined syllabic meter in Hebrew, the *endecasillabo* — a common meter in Italian poetry, and the prerequisite for adopting Italian forms. Immanuel's Hebrew *endecasillabo* served as a basis for developing and perfecting a Hebrew syllabic method by of which means most of the Italian forms of poetry were absorbed over time. The unique features of the old Hebrew *endecasillabo* allowed it to triumph over its competition — the metrical system subsequently created by Moses Rieti — and to prevail up to the twentieth century. Immanuel's meter established new metrical elements: the phonetic syllable; the stressed, homogenous, and rich rhyme; and the principle of equality between vowels. All these became the foundation for a new Hebrew metrics that continue to be used in our own time.[2]

Maḥbarot Immanuel made its readers aware of poetic musicality, an element to which Hebrew poetry in Italy had not been particularly attuned for quite a long period. Here the sonnets acted as spearheads. Their musicality appealed to the

---

[1] Tchernikhowsky, *Immanuel*, 135–37, and see also 11–13.
[2] See Bregman, "Shitat Immanuel."

Italian-speaking Jews and sparked their interest and affection. The Jews of Italy learned from the sonnets a great deal about the musical function of poetic form, and it was largely thanks to them that they developed a love of poetic form and order, the instruments of musicality and the means by which they were created.

Together with these innovations, the first Hebrew sonnets also kept faith with Hebrew traditions, both linguistic and poetic. They were grafted into the old genre of the *maqama*, but Immanuel inserted innovations that turned the eastern story into an Italian *novella* even before it was developed in Italian by Boccaccio. The sonnet lent beauty and grace to the *maqama*, thereby playing the role of the classic Hebrew poem from Spain customarily inserted into it, but in a new and fresh way. In this, as in other matters, the sonnet took on the appearance of a classic poem, central and important, despite the fact that it was new. Tradition is well evident in Immanuel's sonnets: in the thematic genres already used in the past; in rhetorical motifs; and in a Hebrew diction studded with biblical quotations, like the poetry from Spain. The Hebrew flavor was preserved in the quantitative element of the meter and, in many of his sonnets, in the masculine stress of the rhyme, even though this last element went against the overwhelming preference in Italy for the feminine rhyme.

What is the guiding principle for separating the old from the new in Immanuel's sonnet?

It appears that Immanuel strove to preserve structural elements from the Hebrew tradition in his sonnet, but permitted himself to move away from tradition in terms of content: in ideas, attitudes, and ideological values. On the face of things, this is a most surprising approach. It is also an unusual approach among Hebrew innovators, who always tended to stress the newness of their work in terms of form alone, as Judah de' Sommi Portaleone had been so careful to do in the sixteenth century when he presented the first Hebrew drama:[3]

> Behold, O generation, the new with which I fill
> The old, like fine oil inside a container.

Why did Immanuel not act in a similar way? It is not the social point of view that we question — this has already been discussed — but the very method of adopting the form. The sonnet is a verse-form: in order to absorb it, it was important to accept its prosodic structures. And here there is ostensibly no point in preserving traditional elements. On the other hand, there is no need to accept the original verbal content along with the structures. Just the contrary, for pouring the content and values already existent in the target language into newly acquired structures is in itself an interesting poetic challenge!

---

[3] Judah de' Sommi Portaleone, sonnet 51, in *Tzror Zehuvim*, ed. Bregman

However, things become clear in light of the form's uniqueness, and in light of what Immanuel regarded as its essence. Immanuel saw the sonnet as a bipartite form of poetry combining harmony and tension. These fundamental elements, which should not be renounced or blurred, are embodied according to his way of thinking in structures: in prosodic, syntactical, rhetorical, logical structures. He therefore created simple and clear structures that could be easily imitated and concealed possibilities of nuance in them by means of hints alone. He accordingly poured traditional elements into these basic, unchanging structures. In this way he gave the fixed element of form a Hebrew flavor, and completely and genuinely absorbed it into the soil of Hebrew poetry.

The sonnet's verbal content was, on the other hand, in Immanuel's eyes a variable to be treated according to the fancy of the individual poet. At this level, therefore, he permitted himself to do as he pleased, and gave other poets a free hand as well. Had sonnets written by his contemporaries come down to us, we would presumably see examples of this principle of freedom in actual practice.

2. Tradition and Innovation in the Hebrew Sonnet of the Sixteenth and Seventeenth Centuries

The Hebrew sonnets of the sixteenth and seventeenth centuries are first and foremost tradition. Despite the existence of a rich, convenient, and universally admired model in Italian, and despite the explicit sanction against *Maḥbarot Immanuel* (and the sonnets within them no less), Hebrew poets returned to the model of the old sonnet: to its archaic meters, complicated and less than perfectly adapted to Italian musicality; to the modesty of rhyme-schemes and structures that by the seventeeth century appeared not to make any sense; and to rhymes the norms of which were stricter than both the Italian and the traditional Hebrew poem from Spain. Generally speaking, the bipartite concept of the old sonnet also holds sway in the revived sonnet of all kinds. Often this expresses itself without any deviation from the old ways: in the total separation between octave and sestet; in a harmonious and unified octave versus a variegated sestet; in various differences between the two parts of the poem; and even in the reflexive attitude of the end of the poem towards the beginning.

The revived Hebrew sonnet inherited techniques and expressions from Immanuel of Rome, and borrowed rhymes and entire phrases from him word for word. It exploited the old ideas and arguments, either as given in Immanuel's sonnets or turned upside down.

Of course, not everything was accepted, or accepted with the same degree of stringency. But even the criteria for selecting and adapting were ostensibly determined by Immanuel. His heirs learned what he wanted them to learn, and abandoned what he allowed them to abandon. They clung to him in everything concerning the prosody of form, but the more the poetical content moved away from prosody, the freer they felt to innovate and change. In rhyme-schemes and rhymemes they accepted his tradition as given; in meter they accepted his system but augmented and developed it; in syntax and rhetoric they accepted the old but also added elements that were completely new. They diversified beyond comparison his strategies for unfolding the subject, while in thematics and ideological attitudes they changed his outlook from one end to the other and took only certain disparate elements. The assumption embodied in Immanuel's body of work — that prosody is the fixed element, but that the verbal content deserves change and variety — was understood by his followers and carried out to the full.

Immanuel's sonnets practically offered themselves to this kind of choice between the old and the new. But there were other factors as well.

Roughly speaking, there were three sources for the renewed Hebrew sonnet to use: the traditions of Hebrew literature in general, *Maḥbarot Immanuel*, and the non-Hebrew poetic environment. Drawing from these sources was done in a controlled and even-handed way. They took from each source that which harmonized with the other two. When there could be no harmonizing the sources, Hebrew poetics considered the options and made choices.

The Hebrew sonnet clung to the prosodic example of Immanuel only because their creator had been right on target, composing them according to the model that eventually became the classic in Italian poetry. Otherwise his system would not have been accepted, notwithstanding all its attractive features: a successful metrical system, a ringing rhyme, and rich diction. To be sure, we do not find authors of poetic treatises from the period applauding the invention of this successful early model of the early Hebrew sonnet, but this is not surprising. Hebrew poets did not venture into historical investigations of the form, and they thought it was only natural that Immanuel's sonnets corresponded to the accepted model of their own days. But had Immanuel composed his sonnets according to the formal variations common in his time, these poets would have realized their antiquity and turned their back on them, just as the Italians turned their back on their own outdated models. Thanks to his successful model, Immanuel became for Hebrew poetry not what Guittone d'Arezzo was for Italian poetry, or Santillana for Spanish, but what Petrarch was for Western poetry.

Anania Coen noted that Gershon Gentili, author of the Hebrew rhyme-lexicon *Yad Ḥaruzim*, took Immanuel's *Maḥbarot* as his model since he considered Immanuel to be the Hebrew Petrarch.[4] When Gentili composed his lexicon at the beginning of the eighteenth century, he continued the path taken by the poets and theoreticians from the sixteenth and seventeenth centuries. These took Immanuel

---

[4] Coen, Saggio *di eloquenza ebrea*, 31.

as their example, wrote poems and sonnets according to the *Maḥbarot*, and established rules for the Hebrew sonnet according to his model, for they indeed considered him the Petrarch of Hebrew poetry. The more popular Petrarch's poetry became, the more Immanuel's greatness became clear. The tendency of the Hebrew poet to model himself on Immanuel went hand in hand with the general tendency to write according to the model of Petrarch and his followers. Hebrew writers, like the Italians, went back and sought models from the masterpieces of the fourteenth century.

At the same time that Immanuel's legacy passed the test of Italian Petrarchism it was put to the test of the Jewish system of values, both poetic and religious, and apparently found wanting for two hundred years, before eventually being renewed. In accordance with this system, certain values of Immanuel's poetry were rejected in the sixteenth century as well, even though they conformed admirably to Petrarchan poetics, while other elements in his poetry, undeveloped but considered desirable by the Jewish community, were indeed accepted and developed. Love, social criticism, and various burlesque themes in sonnetry were pushed from the center of poetic consciousness into the margins, and replaced with sonnets of praise and friendship representing values of religion, ethnic pride, and morality. Social criticism also influenced the way Immanuel's sonnet was accepted, so that while its prosody was received favorably, its ideological content was not. But things were not static, and over the course of time this trend changed from top to bottom.

At the time of its renewal, the Hebrew sonnet was a modest poem restricted to only a few particular circles. It dealt with relatively few topics. It kept away from contentious subjects, did not sound the battle cry, and did not seek to make waves. In this sonnet, so newly revived, poets were careful not to deviate structurally from Immanuel's tradition: they did not change anything, they did not add to it, and they hardly developed it at all. During the sixteenth century and the beginning of the seventeenth, the genre became increasingly established and accepted in Hebrew poetry, and by the mid-seventeenth century it took center stage. The more established the sonnet became, the more its creators felt free to try their wings. Thus its subjects expanded in number and grew increasingly varied. The love sonnet made its debut and the social sonnet became bold and warlike. New structures also proliferated. Sonnets appeared with "tails", with unusual rhyme-schemes, and in long sequences. Strategies of development multiplied and grew increasingly sophisticated; unifying structures became accepted in syntax and in rhetoric; here and there we see an open octave. The very concept of the poem changed and evolved: no longer was it necessarily a two-part poem, but also a poem hammered into a single, unbroken whole.

With the expansion of the Hebrew sonnet, the attitude towards Immanuel's tradition underwent a complete change. If, in the sixteenth century, the Hebrew sonnet adhered to Immanuel's structures, in the seventeenth century it allowed itself to augment his rules, and to develop and change them. The sonnet of the sixteenth century was wary of Immanuel's thematics and ideology, and of the very idea of variation. The sonnet of the seventeenth century moved closer to Immanuel in all these respects, including subject matter and occasionally even values.

During this process, the affinity to non-Hebrew poetry also underwent a change. Petrarchism skipped over the Hebrew-Italian sonnet of the sixteenth century. The Hebrew sonnet of the seventeenth century was open to the spirit of Petrarchism and the Baroque, and also absorbed old elements from the *dolce stil nuovo*. Of particular interest is the way these styles were absorbed by the religious Hebrew sonnet.

Social values also came under criticism and regeneration. Like all Hebrew poetry of the period, the Hebrew sonnet of the sixteenth and seventeenth centuries was created under the eyes of the socio-religious establishment. It was through this establishment that the Hebrew sonnet achieved a firm footing, and according to its rules that it was allowed to entrench itself in the Jewish community. This socio-religious control led the sonnet to adhere to time-honored conventions, but by virtue of this also opened it up to society across the board. The Hebrew poet whom we find reflected in the sonnets of the Renaissance and Baroque is not the Hebrew poet of the Middle Ages. He is neither the cantor of the synagogue nor the polished courtier of the local ruler, though he may sometimes fill these functions as well. This poet is an educated, believing Jew. He is a rabbi and a physician, a merchant and theater director, a cantor, a preacher, a scholar. That the sonnet in praise of books flowered in his poetry is no coincidence. It is symptomatic of the intellectual spirit which surrounded the acceptance and the establishment of the genre. This poet absorbed the values of humanism in the sonnets of Immanuel when they were embodied in the surrounding culture, and he did not forget them even during the period of religious and political reaction against the Protestant Reformation, though this threatened to obliterate them from memory. His poetry sees truth, justice, and freedom as values in their own right, separate and distinct from religious righteousness. It addresses common sense and demands that its protagonist and audience judge and decide as free men.

This poet was no innocent. He knew that religious adherence and humanism were all too likely to clash. But he tried with all his strength to fuse them, and preferred to live with the contradictions than to renounce one or the other. Just as he chose his poetic values with the help of filters, one typically Italian, the other typically Jewish and religious, so too he examined his beliefs in the light of an ethical-humanist outlook.

This Hebrew poet served his community in a new kind of way. It was not only the individual which the Renaissance placed at the center of social consciousness, but social organization as well. Social platforms, social criticism, educational programs, political debates: these were all subjects that occupied people's thoughts and feelings during the Renaissance, and the experience was not blotted out of mind even during the Catholic reaction. We see its reflection wherever we find a Hebrew sonnet that opposes political and social tyranny, or creates a dialogue with Italian personalities on the basis of shared human and religious values, or is deeply involved in religious and social polemics. This trend is doubly impressive for poets lacking the normal status of citizenship and who thus might have confined their "political" criticism, as it were, to the boundaries of the Jewish community.

The balance between tradition and change in the renewed Hebrew sonnet did not come about by itself. From the beginning of the sixteenth century till the end of the seventeenth, the guiding hand of poets, critics, and teachers is well evident in the field of Hebrew sonnetry.

The ongoing regeneration of the Hebrew sonnet during the sixteenth and seventeenth centuries gave it a vitality and freshness, but also left it open to certain dangers. The very form of the sonnet is an invitation to experiment. In the sixteenth and seventeenth centuries, there was really no reason why every Hebrew poet should not do as he saw fit with the sonnet-form, just as Italian poets had done with the sonnet during the thirteenth and fourteenth centuries. That this did not occur was the result of responsible poetic leadership.

The major Hebrew poets regarded much of their poetry not as a private matter, but as a building block in a public edifice given to them to cultivate and preserve. They did not hesitate to write wedding poems, even though the field teemed with second-rank poets, and they strove to guide their fellow-poets and to diffuse the art of poetry through every possible means. The minor poets were usually well-educated men, active consumers of poetry who enjoyed reading and producing a well-crafted poem. They had no great poetic pretensions, and proved themselves attentive students. The situation created a never-ending circle: poetic treatises and grammars were written because there was a demand for them, while poetic knowledge and discipline kept the average poet from indulging in tasteless innovations and flights of fancy. It was left to the leading poets to make changes and innovations, and to discover the balance between change and tradition.

Thanks to this remarkable cooperation, the Hebrew sonnet stood by the beginning of the eighteenth century at the center of Hebrew poetic consciousness: a poem with a well-defined nature open to both tradition and change, and a poetic legacy worthy both of preservation, and of continuous and ongoing regeneration.

Appendix:
Table of Quantitative-Syllabic Meters

Used in Hebrew Sonnets from the 16th-17th Centuries

Key:
One cord = −
One peg = ∪ −

Numbers indicate syllables; the apostrophe indicates stress. For example: Scheme 1 contains 2 cords and 1 peg x 2, three cords. It consists of 11 syllables and is stressed on the 10th syllable. The numbers in parentheses represent selected examples of rare schemes in Tzror Zehuvim.

Scheme	1	2	3	4	5	6	7	8	9	10	11	12
Scheme 1	−	−	∪	−	−	−	∪	−	−	−́	−	
Scheme 2	−	−	∪	−	−	−	∪	−	−	−	∪	−́
Scheme 3	−	−	∪	−	−	−	∪	−	−	−́		
Scheme 4	−	−	−	−	−	−	−	−	−	−́	−	
Scheme 5 (108)	−	−	∪	−	−	−	−	−	−	−́	−	
Scheme 6 (151)	−	−	−	−	−	−	∪	−	−	−́	−	
Scheme 7 (173)	−	−	−	−	∪	−	−	−	−	−́	−	
Scheme 8 (229-235)	−	−	−	−	−	−	−	−	∪	−́	−	
Scheme 9 (339)	−	−	∪	−	−	−	−	−	∪	−́	−	
Scheme 10: (358)	−	∪	−	−	−	−	∪	−	−	−́	−	
Scheme 11: (344)	∪	−	−	−	−	−	−	−	−	−́	−	
Scheme 12: (249)	−	−	∪	−	−	−́	−					

Scheme 13: (344)	⏑	—.	—	—	—	–́	—									
	1	2	3	4	5	6	7									
Scheme 14: (359)	—	—	—	—	—	—	—	—	—	—	–́	—				
	1	2	3	4	5	6	7	8	9	10	11	12				
Scheme 15:	—	—	—	—	—	—	—	—	—	–́						
	1	2	3	4	5	6	7	8	9	10						
Scheme 16: (145)	—	—	—	—	—	—	⏑	—	—	–́						
	1	2	3	4	5	6	7	8	9	10						
Scheme 17: (113)	—	—	⏑	—	—	—	—	—	—	–́						
	1	2	3	4	5	6	7	8	9	10						
Scheme 18: (49)	—	—	—	—	—	—	—	—	—	—	—	–́				
	1	2	3	4	5	6	7	8	9	10	11	12				
Scheme 19: (359)	—	—	—	—	—	—	—	—	—	—	—	–́				
	1	2	3	4	5	6	7	8	9	10	11	12				
Scheme 20: (73)	⏑	—	⏑	—	⏑	—	—	⏑	—	—	⏑	–́				
	1	2	3	4	5	6	7	8	9	10	11	12				
Scheme 21: (65)	—	—	⏑	—	—	—	—	⏑	—	—	⏑	–́				
	1	2	3	4	5	6	7	8	9	10	11	12				
Scheme 22: (303)	⏑	—	—	⏑	—	—	⏑	—	—	⏑	—	–́				
	1	2	3	4	5	6	7	8	9	10	11	12				
Scheme 23: (149)	—	—	⏑	—	—	—	⏑	—	—	—	—	–́				
	1	2	3	4	5	6	7	8	9	10	11	12				
Scheme 24: (164)	—	—	—	—	—	—	—	–́								
	1	2	3	4	5	6	7	8								
Scheme 25: (227)	⏑	—	—	⏑	—	—	⏑	—	–́							
	1	2	3	4	5	6	7	8	9							
Scheme 26: (42)	—	—	⏑	—	—	—	⏑	—	—	—	–́					
	1	2	3	4	5	6	7	8	9	10	11					
Scheme 27: (73)	⏑	—	⏑	—	⏑	—	⏑	—	⏑	—	–́					
	1	2	3	4	5	6	7	8	9	10	11					
Scheme 28: (99)	—	—	⏑	—	—	—	—	—	⏑	—	–́					
	1	2	3	4	5	6	7	8	9	10	11					
Scheme 29: (358)	—	⏑	—	—	—	—	⏑	—	—	—	–́					
	1	2	3	4	5	6	7	8	9	10	11					
Scheme 30: (150)	⏑	—	—	—	⏑	—	—	—	⏑	—	—	—	⏑	—	—	–́
	1	2	3	4	5	6	7	8	9	10	11	12	13	14	15	16

Bibliography

Manuscripts

Budapest, Kaufmann Collection, 459.
Cambridge University Library, Dd 1068 (10).
Ferrara, Collection of the Jewish Community, 25.
London, British Library Add. 27095, Cat. Margoliouth 1077.
London, Montefiore Collection, 250.
New York, Jewish Theological Seminary, 1818, 1250.
Oxford, Bodleian Library Opp. Add. Qu. 92, Cat. Neubauer 1991.
Oxford, Bodleian Library, 2000, Poc. 7.
Parma 3003 (De Rossi 420).

1. Primary Sources

Abrabanel, Isaac. *Perush ha-Torah*. Venice, 1579.
Abrabanel, Leon. *Dialoghi d'Amore* .Venice, 1541.
Abudiente, Moses. *Grammatica Hebraica*. Hamburg, 1663.
Abulafia, Todros. *Gan ha-Meshalim ve-ha-Ḥidot*, ed. D. Yellin. 3 vols. Jerusalem, 1932–1937.
Alatini, Angelo. *I Trionfi*. Venice, 1611.
———. *L'Angelica Tromba*. Ferrara, 1589; repr. Venice, 1628.
Alemanno (Alemano) Johanan ben Isaac. *Shaʿar Ha-Ḥesheq*. Leghorn 1790.
Alharizi, Judah. *Taḥqemoni*. Ed. Y. Toporowsky. Tel Aviv, 1952.
———. *The Taḥqemoni*. Trans. David Segal. London, 2001.
Almagor, Dan, ed. "Megillah Shalaḥ he-Ḥatan el ha-Kalah." *Yediʿot Aḥronot*, 26 May 1978.
———. "Yod Daled Shirei Ahavim le-Yossef Tzarfati." *Tĕuda* 19 (2003): 329–40.
Almoli, Solomon. *Sheqel ha-Qodesh*. Constantinople, 1506. In *Leshon limmudim le-David ibn Yiḥye*, ed. H. Yalon. Jerusalem, 1965.
Archivolti, Samuel. *ʿArugat ha-Bosem*. Venice, 1603.
Bar Tikvah, B., ed. *Piyyutei Rabbi Yitzḥaq ha-Seniri*. Ramat-Gan, 1998.
Ben Israel, Menasseh. *Nishmat Ḥayyim*. Amsterdam, 1651.
Berliner, A., ed. "*Luḥot Avanim*." In *Hebräische Grabschriften in Italien*, ed. J. Kauffman, Frankfurt a.M., 1881.
Berni, Francesco. *Rime*. Ed. D. Romei. Milan, 1985.
Bernstein, S., ed. "Luḥot Abanim 2." *Hebrew Union College Annual* 10 (1935): 483–552.

———. *Mi-Shirei Yisrael bi-Italia*. Jerusalem, 1939.
———. "Shirim Ḥadashim le-Rabbi Shmuel Archivolti." *Tarbiz* 8 (1937): 55–68.
Bialik, Hayyim Nachman. "Aluf Batzlut ve-Aluf Shum." In *Kol Kitvei Ḥayyim Naḥman Bialik*, 367–71. Tel Aviv, 1963.
———. *Shirim*. Ed. D. Miron. Tel Aviv, 1983.
Boscán, Juan. *Poesia*, and Garcilaso de la Vega, *Eglogas*. Ed. F. de Herrera. Havana, 1963.
Bregman, D. (ed.) "ʿAl ha-Sod: Zug Ḥidot le-Ḥatuna me'et Moshe Zacut." In *Shefaʿ Tal: Studies in Jewish Thought and Culture Presented to Bracha Zak*, 379–96. Beer Sheva, 2004.
———."Ḥamisha Shirei Ḥatuna me'et Moshe Zacut." *Teʿuda* 19 (2002): 341–58.
———."Shelosha-ʿAsar Sonetim le-Rabbi Shmuel Archivolti." *Italia* 7 (1988): 29–65.
———."Shirei Ḥatuna me'et Moshe Zacut," *Peʿamim* 96 (2003): 143–62.
———. "Shnei Sonetim le-Ḥatuna." *Moznayim* 61 (1987): 38–39.
———. "Sonetim Te'omim le-Simḥat Torah." *Yediʿot Aḥronot*, October 2nd 1988.
———. *Tiferet Sinai: Sefer ha-Maḥazot shel Matityah Nissim Terni*. Jerusalem, 2003.
———. *Tzror Zehuvim: Sonetim ʿIvri'im mi-Tequfat ha-Renasans ve-ha-Baroq* ("A Bundle of Gold: Hebrew Sonnets from the Renaissance and Baroque"). Jerusalem and Beer Sheva, 1997.
Brodo, Abraham. *Birkat Avraham*. Venice, 1696.
Campanella, Tommaso. *Opere Letterarie*. Ed. I. Bolzoni. Turin, 1977.
Cardoso, Yshac. *Los exelencias de los Hebreos*. Amsterdam, 1679.
Carmi, Joseph Yedidya. *Kenaf Renanim*. Venice, 1627.
Caro, Joseph. *Shulḥan ʿArukh*. Venice, 1565.
Cassuto, M. D., ed. "Mi-Shirei Yosef Shmuel Tzarfati: Ha-Qomediah ha-Rishonah be-ʿIvrit." In *Studies in Memory of Rabbi Amram Kohut*, 121–28. New York, 1936.
Cordovero, Moses. *Perush Seder ʿAvodat Yom ha-Kippurim*. Venice, 1587.
Dahlberg, C., trans. and ed. *The Romance of the Rose by Guillaume de Lorris and Jean de Meun*. Hanover and London, 1986.
Della Casa, Giovanni. *Le Rime*. Ed. R. Fedi. Rome, 1978.
Dante Alighieri. *De Vulgari Eloquentia*. Ed. and trans. Steven Botterill. Cambridge, 1996.
———. *Vita Nuova*. Trans. D. S. Cervigni and E. Vasta. London and Notre Dame, 1995.
Duran Shimon Ben Israel Zemah and Ovadia Sforno, *Ohev Mishpat*. Venice, 1589–1590.
Donne, John. *The Poems of John Donne*. Ed. H. J. Grierson. London, 1912.
———. *The Sermons of John Donne*. Ed. E. M. Simpson and G. R. Potter. 10 vols. Berkeley and Los Angeles, 1953–1962. Vol. 6.
———. *The Songs and Sonnets of John Donne*. Ed. T. Redpath. London, 1956.
Durling, R. M., trans. and ed. *Petrarch's Lyric Poems: The Rime Sparse and Other Lyrics*. Cambridge, MA and London, 1976.
Dykman, A., trans. *Shirat ha-Kokhavim*. Jerusalem, 1996.
Farisol, Abraham. *Iggeret Orḥot ʿOlam*. Venice, 1587.
Frances, Immanuel. *Meteq Sefatayim*. Ed. H. Brody. Cracow, 1892.

———. *Diwan le-Rabbi Immanuel ben David Frances.* Ed. S. Bernstein. Tel Aviv, 1932.
———. *Tzevi Mudaḥ.* Ed. M. Morteira. *Qovetz ʿal-Yad* 1 (1885): 99–128.
Frances, Jacob. *Kol Shirei Yaʿaqov Frances.* Ed. P. Naveh. Jerusalem, 1969.
Galino (*sic*) [Galiego], Joseph Shalom. *Sefer Imrei Noʿam.* Amsterdam, 1628–1630. (Author's name misspelled.)
Gentili (Hefetz), Gershon. *Yad Ḥaruzim.* Venice, 1700; repr. 1740.
Gentili (Hefetz), Moses. *Ḥanukat ha-Bayit.* Venice, 1696.
Gillaume de Lorris and Jean de Meun. *Le Roman de la Rose: traduction en francais moderne*, trans. A. V. Lanly. Paris, 1971–1976.
Gongóra y Argote, Luis de. *Obras Poeticas.* Ed. R. Foulche-Delbosc. New York, 1921.
Harrán, D., ed. *Complete Works of Salamone Rossi.* Corpus mensurabilis musicae 100. New York, 1995.
Hazan, E., ed. *Tehilla le-David.* Ramat-Gan, 1999.
Holy Bible. Atthias Press. Amsterdam, 1667.
Ibn Bilia, David. "Derekh Laʿasot Ḥaruzim," ed. N. Allony. *Qovetz ʿal-Yad* n.s. 6 (1966): 225–46.
Ibn Ezra, Abraham. "Sefer Tzaḥut." In *Diqduqim.* Venice, 1546. Ed. Z. Hindheim. Dalheim, 1806.
———. *Shirei ha-Ḥol.* Ed. D. Kahana. 2 vols. Warsaw, 1894.
Ibn Ezra, Moses. *Sefer Shirat Yisrael.* Ed. B. Halper. Leipzig, 1924.
———. *Shirei ha-Ḥol.* Ed. H. Brody and D. Pagis. 3 vols. Berlin, 1935 and Jerusalem, 1978.
Ibn Habib, Moses. "*Darkhei Noʿam*" and "*Marpe Lashon.*" In *Diqduqim.* Venice, 1546. repr. Rodelheim, 1806.
Ibn Yahya, Joseph. *Torah Or.* Bologna, 1538.
Ibn Zabara, Joseph. *Sefer Shaʿashuʿim.* Ed. I. Davidson. Berlin, 1925.
Immanuel of Rome. *Maḥbarot Immanuel ha-Romi.* Ed. D. Yarden. Jerusalem, 1957. (First printed Brescia, 1492.)
Judah Messer Leon. *Nofet Tzufim.* Ed. A. Jellinek. Vienna, 1864.
———. *The Book of the Honeycomb's Flow.* Trans. I. Rabinowitz. Ithaca, 1983.
Kaufmann, D., ed. "L'Elégie de Moise Zacout sur Saul Morteira." *Revue des études juives* 37 (1898): 115–32.
Langley, E. F., ed. *The Early Poetry of Giacomo Da Lentino.* Cambridge, 1915.
Luzzatto, Moses Hayyim. *Sefer Leshon Limmudim.* Ed. A. M. Habermann. Jerusalem, 1945.
———. *Shirim.* Ed. S. Ginzburg and B. Klar. Jerusalem, 1945.
Luzzatto, Samuel David. *Kinnor Naʿim.* Vienna, 1825.
Marinus, Marcus. *Arca Noe.* Venice, 1581.
Masséra, A. F., ed. *Sonetti burleschi e realistici dei primi due secoli.* Bari, 1920.
Mercado, Moses di. *Perush Qohelet u-Tehilim.* Amsterdam, 1653.
Michelangelo Buonarroti. *Le Rime di Michelangello Buonarroti.* Ed. C. Guasti. Florence, 1863.

Milton, John. *The Works of J. Milton in Verse and Prose.* Ed. J. Mitford. 8 vols. London, 1863.
Min ha-ʿAnavim, Benjamin ben Abraham. *Masa Gai Ḥezyon.* Ed. A. Nahon. Tel Aviv, 1967.
Min ha-Levi'im, Isaac. *Medaber Tehapukhot.* Ed. D. Carpi. Tel Aviv, 1985.
Min ha-Tov, Judah Asael. *Sefer Kiseʾot le-Veit David.* Verona. 1669.
Modena, Leone da (Judah). ed. *Belil ḥamitz.* Jerusalem, 1936.
———. *Galut Yehuda.* Venice, 1612.
———. *Ḥayyei Yehuda.* Ed. D. Carpi. Tel Aviv, 1985.
———. *Iggerot.* Ed. J. Boksenboim. Tel Aviv, 1984.
———. *Midbar Yehuda.* Venice, 1602.
———. *Shirim.* Ed. S. Bernstein. Philadelphia, 1932.
Moleta, V., ed. *The Early Poetry of Guittone d'Arezzo.* London, 1976.
Morteira, Saul. *Givaʿt Shaul.* Amsterdam, 1645.
Moscato, Judah. *Nefutzot Yehuda.* Venice, 1589.
Najara, Israel. *Zemirot Yisrael.* Safad, 1587.
———. *Zemirot Yisrael.* Venice, 1600.
Nathan ben Jehiel. *Sefer he-ʿArukh.* Venice, 1553.
Neubauer, A., ed. "Documents inédits." *Revue des études juives* 10 (1885): 79–107.
Oelman, T., ed. and trans. *Marrano Poets of the Seventeenth Century.* London, 1982.
Oliveyra, Solomon. "Ayyelet Ahavim." Amsterdam, 1665. In *Musar Haskel.* Venice, 1688.
———. *Sharshot Gavlut.* Amsterdam, 1665.
Olmo, Jacob Daniel. *ʿEden ʿArukh.* Venice, 1744. Printed together with Moses Zacuto, *Tofteh ʿArukh.*
Orvieto, Nathan Yedidia da. *Barkhi Nafshi.* Venice, 1628.
Pagis, D., ed. "Piyyutim Meuḥarim me-Italia." *Qiryat Sefer* 50 (1975): 288–312.
———. "Qovetz Piyyutim mi-Provans." In *Sefer Ḥayyim Schirmann*, ed. S. Abramson and A. Mirsky, 257–84. Jerusalem, 1970.
Patai, I., ed. "David Onkineira ve-Shirato." *Qovetz ʿal-Yad* n.s. 2 (1937): 77–119.
Penso, Joseph de la Vega. *Asirei ha-Tiqvah.* Amsterdam, 1673.
Perez, A., trans. *87 Sonetim Sefradim min ha-Baroq.* Beer-Sheva, 2004.
Petrarca, Francesco. *Rime.* Ed. G. Bezzola. Milan, 1976.
Plantevit, Jean de la Pause. *Planta vitis.* Lodovae, 1645.
Portaleone, Abraham. *Shiltei ha-Gibburim.* Mantua, 1612.
Porto, Zechariah. *Sefer Asaf ha-Mazkir.* Venice, 1675.
Qafech, Y., ed. *Moreh Nevukhim.* Jerusalem, 1984.
Quevedo Y Villegas, Francisco Gomez de-, *Obra Poetica.* Ed. J. M. Blecua. Madrid. 1969. Vol. 1.
Ratzhabi, Y., ed. *Yalqut ha-Maqama ha-ʿIvrit.* Jerusalem, 1974.
Rieti, Moses da. *Miqdash Meʾʿat.* Ed. J. Goldenthal. Vienna, 1851.
Rossi, Azaria de. *Meʾor ʿEynayim.* Ed. S. Cassel. Vilna, 1866.

———. *The Light of the Eyes.* Trans. J. Weinberg. New Haven, 2001.
Rossi, Solomon de'. *Ha-Shirim asher li-Shlomo.* Venice, 1623.
——— *Ha-Shirim asher li-Shlomo,* ed. F. Rikko. New York, 1967–1973.
———. *Cantiques de Salomon Rossi Hebreo.* Ed. S. Naumbourg. Paris, 1877.
Ruderman, David B., ed. and trans. *A Valley of Vision: The Heavenly Journey of Abraham ben Hananiah Yagel.* Philadelphia, 1990.
Salusque Lusitano. *De los sonetos, canciones, madrigales y sextinas del grande poeta y orador Francesco Petrarcha. Traduzido de Toscano por Salusque Lusitano: Parte Primera.* Venice, 1567.
Samuel ha-Cohen da Pisa. *Tzofnat Pane'ah.* Venice, 1646.
Sasportas, Jacob. *Tzitzat Novel Tzevi.* Ed. Y. Tishbi. Jerusalem, 1954.
Schirmann, J., ed. *Ha-Shirah ha-'Ivrit bi-Sefarad u-bi-Provans.* 4 vols. Jerusalem and Tel Aviv, 1971.
———. *Mivhar ha-Shirah ha-'Ivrit be-Italia.* Berlin, 1934.
Shem-Tov, Falaqera. *Sefer ha-Mevaqesh.* Warsaw, 1924.
Sommo, Judah da (Portaleone). *Tzahut be-Dihuta de-Qidushin.* Ed. H. Schirmann. Jerusalem, 1946.
———. *A Comedy of Betrothal.* Ed. and trans. A. S. Golding. Ottawa, 1988.
Stampa, Gaspara. *Rime.* Ed. G. R. Ceriello. Milano, 1954.
Tchernikhowsky, Saul. *Mahberet ha-Sonetot.* Berlin, 1923.
———. *Shirim.* Jerusalem and Tel Aviv, 1948.
Tasso, Torquato. *Opere.* Ed. B. T. Sozzi. Turin, 1964.
Tesauro, E., ed. *Il cannocchiale aristotelico.* Ed. A. Buck. Berlin, 1968.
Tempo, Antonio da. *Summa artis rithimici.* Venice, 1509..
Tusiani, J., ed. *Italian Poets of the Renaissance.* New York, 1971.
Tsur, R. trans. *Gizat Zahav.* Tel Aviv, 1988.
Usque, Samuel. *Consolaçam as tribulaçoens de Israel.* Ed. M. dos Remedios. Coimbra, 1906. First printed in Ferrara, 1553.
———. *Consolation for the Tribulations of Israel.* Trans. and ed. M. A. Cohen. Philadelphia, 1977.
Usque, Solomon (*see* Salusque Lusitano)
Uziel, Isaac, trans. *Mishlei Iresto.* Ed. A. Al-Maliah. Jerusalem, 1945.
Valvasson, Yom-Tov. *Hed Urim.* Venice, 1662.
Viterbo, Asher. *Minha Hadasha, Shirim Meusharim.* Venice, 1748.
Yarden, D. "Niqbatzot mi-Shirei Rabbi Sa'adia Longo be-Darqei ha-Shir ve-ha-Melitzah." *Sefunot* 12 (1971–1978): 81–122.
Zacuto, Moses. *Tofteh 'Arukh.* Venice, 1715; repr. Venice, 1744 (printed together with Jacob Daniel Olmo, *'Eden 'Arukh*).
———. *Yesod 'Olam.* Ed. A. Berliner. Altona, 1874.
———. *Yesod 'Olam.* Ed. Y. D. Maroni. Leghorn, 1874.

2. Secondary Sources

Adler, I. *La Pratique musicale savante dans quelques communautés juives en Europe aux XVI-Ic et XVIIIc siècles.* Paris and the Hague, 1966.

———. *Musical Life and Traditions of the Portuguese Jewish Community of Amsterdam in the XVIII Century.* Yuval Monograph Series 1. Jerusalem, 1974.

———. "Musical Life in the 17th and 18th Centuries." In *Encyclopaedia Judaica*, 16 vols., 2: 904–5. Jerusalem, 1972.

———. "The Rise of Art Music in the Italian Ghetto." In *Jewish Medieval and Renaissance Studies*, ed. A. Altmann, 321–64. Cambridge, MA, 1967.

Apfelboim, A. *Moshe Zacut.* Lvov, 1926.

———. *Toldot ha-Gaon Rabbi Yehuda Moscato.* Drohobycz, 1900.

Barash, M. *Mavo le-Omanut ha-Renaissance.* Jerusalem, 1983.

Bekkum, W. van. "Jews in Renaissance and Baroque Italy." *Judaism in Umbruch* 1 (2001): 157–66.

———. "What is Hebrew in the Hebrew Sonnet? Hebrew Sonnets in Renaissance and Baroque Italy." *Frankfurter Judaistische Beiträge* 27 (2000): 95–107.

Beltrami, P. G. *La Metrica italiana.* Bologna, 1991.

Benedetto, L. F. *Il Romane de la Rose e la letteratura italiana.* Halle a.S., 1910.

Benayahu, M. *Hasqama u-Reshut bi-Dfusei Venezia.* Jerusalem, 1971.

———. *Qinot Ḥakhmei Italia ʿal Rabbi Yosef Caro.* Jerusalem, 1969.

———. "Rabbi Avraham ha-Kohen mi-Zante ve-Lahaqat ha-Rofim ha-Meshorrerim be-Padua." *Ha-Sifrut* 26 (1978): 108–40.

Berman, S. L. *The Sonnet over Time: A Study in the Sonnets of Petrarch, Shakespeare and Baudelaire.* Chapel Hill and London, 1988.

Biadene, L. *Morfologia del sonetto nei secoli XIII-XIV.* Florence, 1977.

Bondanella, P., and J. Conway Bondanella. *Dictionary of Italian Literature.* Westport, 1979.

Bonfil, R. *Jewish Life in Renaissance Italy.* Berkeley and Los Angeles, 1994.

———. *Rabbis and Jewish Communities in Renaissance Italy.* London and Washington, 1993.

Bregman, D. "Ha-Shibbutz ha-Mitḥarez." *Meḥqarei Yerushalayim be-Sifrut ʿIvrit* 13 (1992): 103–18.

———. "Ha-Sonet ha-ʿIvri ba-Meot Tet-Zayin Yud-Zayin: Hemsheh u-Temurah." Ph.D. diss., Hebrew University of Jerusalem, 1986.

———. "Ha-Sonet ha-Klassi: Imanuel ha-Romi u-Petrarcha." in *Divrei ha-Qongres ha-ʿOlami ha-ʿAsiri le-Madaʿei ha-Yahadut.* 3: 298–302. Jerusalem, 1990.

———. "Hebrew Literature and Language." in Encyclopedia of the Renaissance, ed. P. F. Grendler. 3: 121–25, 6 vols. New York, 1999.

———. "Le-Parashat ha-Hitqablut shel ha-Sonet ha-ʿIvri." *Tarbiz* 56 (1987): 109–23.

———. "Megamot Mitḥalfot ve-Signon ha-Shirah ha-ʿIvrit bi-Italia." *Tarbiz* 61 (1992): 505–25.

———. "Polemica Religiosa." In *Appartenenza e differenza: ebrei d'Italia e la letteratura*, ed. J. Hassine, J. Mishan-Montefiore, and S. Debenedetti Stow, 23–32. Ramat-Gan, 1998.

———. "Qesem ha-Ḥidah." *Davar* 22 August 1986: 21–22.

———. *Sharsheret ha-Zahav: Ha-Sonet ha-ᶜIvri le-Dorotav* ("The Golden Chain — the Hebrew Sonnet Through the Ages"). Tel Aviv, 2000.

———. *Shevil ha-Zahav: Ha-Sonet ha-ᶜIvri bi-Tequfat ha-Renasans ve-ha-Baroq* ("The Golden Way: The Hebrew Sonnet during the Renaissance and Baroque"). Jerusalem and Beer Sheva, 1995.

———. "Shirei Zahav Kefulim le-Rabbi Yaᶜaqov Sasportas." *Peᶜamim* 49 (1992): 68–83.

———. "Shirim le-Ḥanukat Beit ha-Knesset." In *Knesset Ezra*, ed. S. Elizur, 365–71. Jerusalem, 1994.

———. "Shitat Immanuel u-Meqomah be-Toldot ha-Metriqa ha-ᶜIvrit." *Tarbiz* 58 (1989): 413–52.

———. "Tefilah, Hagut ve-Musar ba-Sonet ha-ᶜIvri ha-Qadum." *Assufot* 4 (1990): 189–201.

———. "The Emergence of the Hebrew Sonnet." *Prooftexts* 11 (1991): 231–39.

———. "The Sonnets Of David Onkineira." In *The Jewish Communities of Southeastern Europe*, ed. I. K. Hassiotis, 87–92. Thessaloniki, 1997.

———."Their Rose in Our Garden: Romance Elements in Hebrew Italian Poetry." In *Renewing the Past, Reconfiguring Jewish Culture, From Al-Andalus to Haskala*, ed. R. Brann and A. Sutcliff, 50–59. Philadelphia, 2003.

———. "Yiḥus Avot shel Aluf Batzlut ve-Aluf Shum." In *Sefer Yitzḥaq Baqun*, ed. A. Komem, 73–90. Beer Sheva, 1992.

Brenan, G. *The Literature of the Spanish People from Roman Times to the Present*. New York, 1957.

Burckhardt, J. *The Civilization of the Renaissance in Italy*. New York, 1958.

Carpi. D. "Yehudim Baᶜalei Toar Doqtor bi-Refuah mi-Taᶜam Universitat Padova ba-Meah ha-Tet Zayin u-ve-Reshit ha-Meah ha-Yud Zayin." In *Sefer Zikaron le-Natan Ben Moshed David Cassuto*, ed. S. Y. Toaff, 62–91. Jerusalem, 1987.

Casella, M. "Endecasillabi di dodici sillabi?" *Studi Danteschi* 24 (1939): 79–109.

Cassuto, M. D. *Dante ve-Immanuel ha-Romi*. Ed. M. Dorman. Jerusalem, 1966.

———. "Ein Hebräischer Dichter des 15. (i.e. 16.) Jahrhunderts, Mose ben Joab." *Monatsschrift für Geschichte und Wissenschaft des Judentums* 77 (1933): 365–84.

———. *Ha-Yehudim be-Firenze bi-Tequfat ha-Renaissance*. Trans. M. Hartom. Jerusalem, 1967.

———. "L'elemento italiano nelle Mechaberoth di Immanuelle Romano." *Rivista Israelitica* 2 (1905), 3 (1906).

Castes, F. *Il fiore*. Paris, 1881.

Coen, Anania. *Saggio di eloquenza ebrea*. Florence, 1827.

———. *Sefer Ruaḥ Ḥadashah*. Reggio, 1822.

Cohen, J. M. *A History of Western Literature*. Harmondsworth, 1956.

———. *The Baroque Lyric*. London, 1963.
———, ed. *The Penguin Book of Spanish Verse*. Harmondsworth, 1960.
Contini, G., ed. *Poeti del Duecento*. Milan, 1960.
Davidson, I. *Parody in Jewish Literature*. New York, 1966.
De Sanctis, F. *Storia della letteratura italiana*. Milano, 1970.
Elwert, W. T. *Versificazione italiana dalle origini ai giorni nostri*. Florence, 1973.
Fichman, Y. *Anshei Besorah*. Tel Aviv, 1938.
Fleischer, E. *Ha-Yotzerot*. Jerusalem, 1984.
———. "Mivnim Strofi'im Me͗eyn Eyzori'im bi-Piyyut ha-Qadum." *Ha-Sifrut* 2 (1970): 194–240.
———. *Shirat ha-Qodesh ha-ʿIvrit bi-Yemei ha-Beynaim*. Jerusalem, 1975.
Forster, L. *The Icy Fire: Five Studies in European Petrarchism*. London, 1969.
Friedenwald, H. *The Jews and Medicine: Essays*. 2 vols. Baltimore, 1944.
Fuller, J. *The Sonnet*. The Critical Idiom 26. London, 1972.
Goldberg, L. *Hamishah Peraqim bi-Yesod ha-Shirah*. Jerusalem, 1957.
———. "Petrarcha, Hayav vi-Yetzirato." In *Mi-Dor u-Meʿever*, ed. A. Krauss and S. Penini, 123–99. Tel Aviv, 1977.
———. *Qolot Rehoqim u-Qerovim: Tirgumei Shirah*. Ed. T. Ribner. Ramat-Gan, 1975.
Grendler, P., ed. *Encyclopedia of the Renaissance*. 6 vols. New York, 1999.
Guetta, A. "Bibliographie." *Revue des études juives* 159 (2000): 501–3.
Habermann, A. M. "Le-Toldot ha-Pulmus Neged ha-Shabtaut." *Qovetz ʿal-Yad* n.s. 3 (1941): 185–216.
———. *Toldot ha-Piyyut ve-ha-Shirah*. Vol. 2. Ramat-Gan, 1972.
Hak, M. "Nitzanei ha-Mishqal ha-Toni ba-Shirah ha-ʿIvrit." *Tarbiz* 11 (1940): 91–109.
Harrán, D. "Tradition and Innovation in Jewish Music in the Late Renaissance." *Journal of Musicology* 7 (1989): 107–30.
Hartom, A. S. "Mivta ha-ʿIvrit etzel Yehudei Italia." *Leshonenu* 15 (1947): 52–61.
Hrushowsky, B. "Prosody, Hebrew." In *Encyclopaedia Judaica*, 13: 1195–1240.
———. "Ha-Shitot ha Rashiot shel he-Haruz ha-ʿIvri min ha-Piyyut ʿad Yameinu." *Ha-Sifrut* 2 (1969): 721–49.
Kastner, L. E. "Concerning the Sonnet of the Sonnet." *Modern Language Review* 11 (1916): 205–11.
Kay, G. R., ed. *The Penguin Book of Italian Verse*. Harmondsworth, 1968.
Kleinhenz, C. *The Early Italian Sonnet*. Lecce, 1986.
Lazar, M. "Fin amor." In *A Handbook of the Troubadours*, ed. F. R. P. Akehurst and J. M. Davis, 61–100. Berkeley and Los Angeles, 1995.
———. "Shirei Hatuna Provensalim." In *Sefer Hayyim Schirmann*, ed. S. Abramson and A. Mirsky, 59–77. Jerusalem, 1970.
Malakhi, Z. "Saʿadia Longo ve-Yitzhaq Uziel – Vikuah Meshorerim odot ha-Shirah." In *Sefer Yitzhaq Baqun*, ed. A. Komem, 63–71. Beer Sheva, 1992.
Maravall, J. A. Culture of the Baroque: *Analysis of a Historical Structure*. Trans. T. Cochran. Manchester, 1986.

Marti, M. *Cultura e stile nei poeti giocosi del tempo di Dante*. Pisa, 1953.
Melkman, Y. "Amsterdam." In *Encyclopedia Judaica*, 2: 895–900.
———. "Moshe Zacuto's Play Yesod ᶜOlam." *Studia Rosenthaliana* 1 (1967): 1–26.
Milano, A. *Storia degli Ebrei in Italia*. Turin, 1992.
Mirsky, A. *Maḥtzavatan shel Tzurot ha-Piyyut*. Jerusalem and Tel Aviv, 1969.
Modena, A. and E. Morpurgo. *Medici e chirurghi ebrei dottorati e licenziati nell'Universita di Padova dal 1617 al 1816*. Bologna, 1967.
Mönch, W. *Das Sonett, Gestalt und Geschichte*. Heidelberg, 1955.
Navarro, T. *Mètrica española*. Syracuse, 1956.
Naveh, P. "Maᶜaseh Shevuel ve-Naᶜamah le-Yaᶜaqov Frances." *Tarbiz* 24 (1955): 83–101, 207–31.
Norsa, P. *Una famiglia di banchieri, la famiglia Norsa*. Naples, 1953.
Pagis, D. *ᶜAl Sod Ḥatum: Le-Toldot ha-Ḥidah ha-ᶜIvrit bi-Italia u-be-Holand*. Jerusalem, 1986.
———. "Hamtza'at ha-Iambus ha-ᶜIvri u-Temurot ba-Metriqa ha-ᶜIvrit bi-Italia." *Ha-Sifrut* 4 (1973): 651–712.
———. "Ha-Pulmus ha-Shiri ᶜal Tiv ha-Nashim." *Meḥqarei Yerushalyaim be-Sifrut ᶜIvrit* 9 (1986): 259–300.
———. *Ha-Shir Davur ᶜal Ofanav*. Ed. E. Fleischer. Jerusalem, 1993.
———. *Ḥiddush u-Masoret ba-Shirat ha-Ḥol ha-ᶜIvrit*. Jerusalem, 1976.
———. *Shirat ha-Ḥol ve-Torat ha-Shir le-Moshe ibn Ezra u-Venei Doro*. Jerusalem, 1970.
Perry, H. "Baroque." *Enciclopedia ha-ᶜIvrit* 9, Cols. 569-572.
Petrocchi, G. *Scrittori religiosi del Duecento*. Florence, 1974.
Praz, M. "Sonetto." In *Enciclopedia Italiana*, 32: 141–43. Rome, 1936.
Rathaus, A. "Ahavah le-Diyoqan." *Italia* 2 (1981): 30–47.
Rosanes, S. A. *Qorot ha-Yehudim be-Turqiya ve-Artzot ha-Qedem*. Sofia, 1938.
Roth, C. "Catalogue of Manuscripts in the Roth Collection." In *Alexander Marx Jubilee Volume*, 503–35. New York, 1950.
———."Salusque Lusitano: An Essay in Disentanglement." In idem, *Gleanings: Essays in Jewish History, Letters and Art*, 179–99. New York, 1967.
———. *The History of the Jews of Italy*. Philadelphia, 1946.
———. *The Jews in the Renaissance*. Philadelphia, 1964.
———. "Stemmi di famiglie ebraiche italiane." In *Scritti in Memoria di Leone Carpi*, ed. D. Carpi and A. Milano, 165–84. Milan and Jerusalem, 1967.
Ruderman, D. B., ed. *Essential Papers in Jewish Culture in Renaissance and Baroque Italy*. New York, 1992.
———. *Jewish Thought and Scientific Discovery in Early Modern Europe*. Princeton, 1995.
———. *Kabbalah, Magic, and Science: The Cultural Universe of a Sixteenth-Century Physician*. Cambridge, MA, 1988.
Ruschioni, A. *Il sonetto italiano. Morfologia, profilo storico, antologia*. 2 vols. Milan, 1985.
Ruthven, K. K. *The Conceit. The Critical Idiom* 4. London, 1969.
Schirmann, J. *Le-Toldot ha-Shirah ve-ha-Drama ha-ᶜIvrit*. 2 vols. Jerusalem, 1979.

———. "Zur Geschichte der Hebräischen Poesie in Apulien und Sizilien." *Mitteilungen des Forschungsinstituts für Hebräische Dichtung* 1 (1933): 132–47.

Scholem, G. *Sabbatai Sevi: The Mystical Messiah, 1626–1676*. Princeton, 1973.

Scott, C. "The Limits of the Sonnet." *Review of Literature and Culture* 50 (1976): 237–50.

Seroussi, E. and T. Beri. "Rabbi Yosef Galiego Baʿal Sefer Imrei Noʿam." *Assufot* 6 (1992): 107–50.

Shulvass, M. A. *The Jews in the World of the Renaissance*. Leiden and Chicago, 1973.

Simonsohn, S. *History of the Jews in the Duchy of Mantua*. Jerusalem, 1972.

———. *Toldot ha-Yehudim be-Dukasut Mantova*. 2 vols. Jerusalem, 1963.

Soave, M. *Sara Coppia Sullam*. Trieste, 1864.

Sonne, I. "Sifrut ha-Musar ve-ha-Filosofia be-Shirei Immanuel ha-Romi." *Tarbiz* 5 (1934): 324–40.

Tchernikhowsky, Saul. *Immanuel ha-Romi*. Berlin, 1925.

Tomlinson, C. *The Sonnet: Its Origin and Place in Poetry*. London, 1874; repr. London, 1970.

Wilkins, E. H. "A General Survey of Renaissance Petrarchism." *Comparative Literature* 11 (1950): 327–42.

———. *A History of Italian Literature*. Cambridge, MA, and London, 1954.

———. *The Invention of the Sonnet and Other Studies in Italian Literature*. Rome, 1959.

Yahalom, Y. "Rabbi Yisrael Najara ve-Hithadshut ha-Shirah ha-ʿIvrit ba-Mizrah leʾahar Gerush Sefarad." *Peaʿamim* 13 (1982): 96–124.

———. "Reshita shel ha-Sheqila ha-Meduyeqet ba-Shirah ha-ʿIvrit." *Leshonenu* 47 (1983): 25–61.

Zandbank, S. "Lea Goldberg ve-ha-Sonet ha-Petrarqi." *Ha-Sifrut* 6 (1975): 19–31.

Index of Names

Anonymous monk, 228–230
Aaron, 60, 76, 249
Abendana (Ibn Dana), Samuel (fl. 17th century), 129
Aboab, Isaac ben Mattathias (1631–1707), 117, 128
Aboab, Jacob ben Samuel (1649–ca. 1735), 182, 252
Abrabanel, Isaac ben Judah (1437–1508), 216
Abrabanel, Judah ben Isaac (*see* Leone Ebreo)
Abraham, 76, 184, 187, 197, 237, 257–265
Abraham Abulafia (1240– d. after 1291)
Abraham ibn Ezra (1089–1164), 11, 31, 138, 148, 215
Abudiente, Moses ben Gideon (1610–ca. 1688), 118, 178, 231, 234
Abulafia, Todros (*see* Todros Abulafia)
Ahitub ben Isaac of Palermo (fl. 13th century), 11
Alatrini, Angelo (*see* Alatrini, Johanan Judah ben Solomon)
Alatrini, Johanan Judah ben Solomon (1530–d. before 1611), 104, 173, 231, 233, 234, 235, 238, 252
Alemanno (Alemano), Johanan ben Isaac (1435–1504), 97–98, 109
Alharizi, Judah (*see* Judah Alharizi)
Alighieri, Dante (*see* Dante Alighieri)
Almoli, Solomon ben Jacob (b. before 1490–1542), 44, 150
Ancona, Judah (fl. 17th century), 229
Angiolieri, Cecco (*see* Cecco Angiolieri)
Apollo, 199
Archivolti, Samuel ben Elhanan Jacob (1545–1611), 37, 105, 108–109, 113, 114, 123, 135, 136, 138, 141–142, 150, 156, 158, 176, 180, 186, 214–216, 223, 233
Ariosto, Ludovico (1474–1533), 90, 102, 105
Asaph, 81

Bahya ibn Paquda, 79
Barberino, Francesco da (1264–1348), 24
Barrios, Miguel de (*see* Levi, de Barios Daniel)
Barukh ben Barukh (fl. 16th–17th centuries), 144
Bassani, Samuel Hai ben Mordechai (d. 1640), 213
Beatrice, 70–71, 73, 85
Belilios, Daniel (d. before 1697), 171, 182, 215
Bembo, Pietro (1470–1547), 88–90
Ben Barukh, Barukh (*see* Barukh ben Barukh)
Ben Israel, Menasseh (1604–1657), 117, 216
Ben Joab, Moses (*see* Rieti, Moses ben Joab)
Ben Labrat, Dunash (*see* Dunash ben Labrat)
Berliner, Abraham (1833–1915), 240, 263
Berni, Francesco (1497/98–1535), 92, 125
Bezalel, 219
Bialik, Hayyim Nahman (1873–1934), 20, 46, 82
Boaz, 151, 194
Boaz (biblical), 212
Boccaccio, Giovanni (1313–1375), 88
Boiardo, Matteo Maria (1441–1494), 88
Borga, Anton Maria (fl. 17th century), 254
Boscán, Juan (before 1500–1542), 190
Bosone da Gubbio (d. after 1349), 15
Botticelli, Sandro (1444–1510?), 88
Briel, Judah ben Eliezer (ca. 1643–1722), 116, 173, 229–230, 255
Brody, Hayyim (1868–1932), 165
Bruno, Giordano (1548–1600), 91, 92
Burchiello, Domenico di Giovanni (1404–1449), 92, 125
Burckhardt, Jacob (1818–1897), 19, 90
Cagli (Calleo), Raphael (fl. 17th century), 212, 213, 214

Camões, Luiz de (1524–1580), 245
Campanella, Tommaso (1568–1639), 91, 189, 199
Cantarini, Moses Hayyim ben Isaiah Azriel (1660–1731), 209, 236
Cariteo, Benedetto Gareth (1450–1514), 88–89, 91–92
Carlyle, Thomas (1795–1881), 249
Carmi, Joseph Jedidiah ben Benjamin Jekutiel (b. ca. 1580), 105, 129, 138, 243
Caro, Joseph ben Ephraim (1488–1575), 102, 106, 240, 242, 250
Cases, Joseph Barukh ben Moses (d. 1721), 255
Cases, Juliani Shalom ben Samuel (d. 1630), 109, 214, 229
Cassel, D. (1818–1893), 145
Cassuto, Umberto (Moses David) (1883–1951), 15, 100, 111
Catalano, Abraham (d. 1642), 183, 219
Cavalcanti, Guido (ca. 1240–1300), 10
Cecco Angiolieri (1260–1313), 10, 63, 69, 80
Celestina, 107
Charlemagne (742–814), 93
Chaucer, Geoffrey (1340?–1400), 88
Christina, Queen of Sweden (1626–1689), 183, 220, 245
Cino da Pistoia (ca. 1270–ca. 1336), 10, 15, 63, 125
Clement XI, Pope (1649–1721), 265
Coen, Anania (1751–1834), 102, 117, 126–127, 129, 143–144, 165, 173, 240, 271
Coen, Benjamin (Vitale Coen) (1651–1739), 208
Coen, Samuel da Pisa (Lusitano da Pisa) (1577–1640), 215
Cohen, J. M., 88, 94, 95, 113, 184, 190, 199, 257
Colonna, Vittoria (1492–1547), 90, 189
Conegliano (Conian), Israel ben Joseph (1650–1700?/1717?), 141, 143, 235–236
Conegliano (Conian), Solomon ben Joseph (1639/1640–1719), 121, 125, 182, 211
Cordovero, Moses (1522–1570), 240
Crescimbeni, Giovan Mario (1663–1728), 250, 265

Cupid, 92, 178, 181, 195, 196, 198–201, 238
Da Costa, Uriel (1585–1640), 117
Da Fano, Ippolito (see Fano, Joseph ben Isaac)
Da Fano, Menahem (see Fano, Menahem Azariah)
Da Gubbio, Bosone (see Bosone da Gubio)
Da Lentino (Lentini), Giacomo (fl. 13th century), 9, 76
Da Pistoia, Cino (see Cino da Pistoia), 216
Da Porto, Zacariah (fl. 17th century), 216
Da Silva, Joshua (d. 1697), 142, 215
Da Tempo, Antonio (fl. 14th century), 24, 130
Da Todi, Jacopone (1236–1306), 78
Da Volterra, Elazar bar Menahem (fl. 15th century), 99
Dante Alighieri (1265–1321), 10, 15, 24, 28–29, 35, 63–65, 69–74, 80, 82, 85, 88, 90, 98–99, 101–102, 109, 114, 124, 195, 204
Daphne, 199
Dato, Angelo (see Dato, Mordechai ben Judah)
Dato, Mordechai ben Judah (1525–1591/1601), 106
David ibn Bilia (fl. 13th–14th century), 47
David, the King, 184, 186
David, Yona, 104
De Castro, Baltazar Orobio Isaac (1620–ca. 1687), 117
De Gandia, Bartholomeo, 216
De la Ceppede, Jean (1550–1622), 257
De Lorris, Guillaume (fl. 13th century), 28
De Meun, Jean (d. 1305), 28
De Rojas, Fernando (1465–ca.1541), 105
De Saltares (Fano) Judah ben Moses (1550–ca. 1629), 135, 136, 242, 250,
De' Medici, Cosimo (1389–1464), 88
De' Medici, Lorenzo (Il Magnifico; see Lorenzo de' Medici)
De' Rossi, Azariah (Bonaiuto) (1511/1514–1578), 104, 109, 136, 145, 179, 220, 240, 241–242
De' Rossi, Salomone (1570–1628), 104
Del Bene, Judah Asahel ben Eliezer David (d. 1678), 215

Della Casa, Giovanni (1503–1556), 91, 164
Della Mirandola, Giovanni Pico (163–1494), 98
Delli Mansi, Benjamin ben Abraham the Physician (fl. 13th century), 11
Di Caceres (Casseres), Samuel (d. 1660), 177, 241, 243, 244, 250, 251
Di Mercado, Moses (d. 1652), 21, 215, 216, 240, 250, 251
Di Mercado, Samuel ben Abraham Jeshurun (fl. 17th century), 216
Di Tarsia, Galeazzo (1520–1553), 91
Donne, John (1573–1631), 191, 265
Du Bellay, Joachim (1522–1560), 20, 92
Dunash ben Labrat (fl. 10th century), 81
Duran, Simon ben Tzemach (1361–1444), 123
Durante (fl. 13th–14th century), 28, 65
Elias Levita (1468/9–1549), 104
Elijah Bahur (*see* Elias Levita)
Elijah, the Prophet, 226
Elisha, the Prophet, 52
Espinosa, Pedro (1578–1650), 190
Esther, 60, 76, 157
Ezobi, Solomon ben Judah (1575–1648), 128
Faenza, Raphael ben Isaac da (fl. 15th century), 99
Falaqera, Shem Tov (*see* Shem Tov ben Joseph Falaqera), 184
Fano, Ezra (fl. 17th century), 229
Fano, Joseph ben Isaac (1548–1620), 218
Fano, Judah ben Moses (*see* De Saltares, Judah ben Moses)
Fano, Menahem Azariah (Immanuel), 109, 179
Farissol, Abraham (ca. 1451–ca. 1525), 97–98, 104
Fatima, wife of Muhamad, 197
Fazio (Bonifazio) degli Uberti (1310–1370), 65, 265
Fermi (Fermo), Joseph (fl. 17th century), 118, 221
Fiammetta, 212
Fichman, Jacob (1881–1958), 38
Figo (Picho), Azariah ben Ephraim (1579–1647), 129, 152, 217,

Figueroa, Francisco de (1536–1620), 199
Filelfo, Mario (fl. 15th century), 97
Flavia, 89
Foa, Daniel ben Solomon (d. after 1622), 233
Folengo, Teofilo (1491–1544), 92
Folgore da San Gimignano (*see* San Gimignano, Folgore da)
Forli, Benjamin da (16th–17th century), 219
Frances, Immanuel ben David (1618–1710), 15, 19, 113, 114–116, 118, 121–123, 135, 139, 147, 150–152, 156, 159, 163–165, 170, 173, 178, 180–181, 183, 186, 191, 193–195, 202, 204, 210, 219, 221, 225, 242, 246, 249
Frances, Jacob ben David (1615–1667), 82, 113–116, 118, 120–122, 126, 138, 143, 148, 150, 156–157, 159, 160, 163, 164, 173, 174–175, 178, 179, 181, 184, 185–187, 193, 198, 199, 201, 203, 204, 205, 206, 207, 209, 210, 213, 214, 220, 221, 222, 224–228, 232, 234, 239, 244–247, 251
Franchetta–Harari, Moses (ben Abraham?) (fl. 16th century), 109, 155
Francisco Gomez de Quevedo y villegas (1580–1645), 95, 190, 246
Franco, Matteo (1447–1494), 93
Franco, Nicolo (1515–1570), 92
Franco–Serrano, Joseph (1652– d. after 1695), 218, 219
Frederick II (Hohenstaufen) (1194–1250), 9
Gallo, Giuseppe (*see* Tzarfati, Joseph ben Samuel)
Gentili, Gershon ben Moses (1683–1700), 148–149, 156, 160, 271
Gentili, Moses ben Gershon (1663–1711), 182, 215, 218, 252
Giuda di Salomone, Hebreo (fl. 16th–17th century), 99
Goldberg, Lea (1911–1970), 35, 87, 89–90, 151
Gomez, Antonio Enriquez (fl. 17th century), 117
Góngora, Luis da (1561–1627), 95, 190
Gonzaga, Cesare (d. 1575), 104
Gracián, Baltasar (1601–1658), 95

Grados, Irado (fl. 15th century), 100
Graziano, Abraham Joseph Solomon ben Mordechai Gallico (1620–1684), 116
Guinizzelli, Guido (1240–ca. 1276), 10, 71
Guittone d'Arezzo (1230–ca. 1294), 10, 24, 65, 69, 127, 271
Hak, Moshe 38
Halevi, the physician, 252
Harran, 257, 258
Hefetz, Gershon ben Moses (*see* Gentili, Gershon ben Moses)
Hefetz, Moses ben Gershon (*see* Gentili, Moses ben Gershon)
Herrera, Abraham Kohen (1570–ca. 1639), 117
Hrushowsky, Benjamin, 38, 43–47, 151
Ibn Bilia, David (*see* David ibn Bilia)
Ibn Ezra, Abraham (*see* Abraham ibn Ezra)
Ibn Ezra, Moses (*see* Moses ibn Ezra)
Ibn Habib, Moses (fl. 15th century), 101
Ibn Khalfun, Isaac (*see* Isaac ibn Khalfun)
Ibn Paquda, Bahya (*see* Bahya ibn Paquda)
Ibn Verga, Solomon (1460–1554), 97
Ibn Yahya, Joseph ben David (*see* Joseph ibn Yahya)
Ibn Zabara, Joseph ben Meir (*see* Joseph ben Meir Zabara)
Immanuel ben Solomon of Rome (ca. 1261–ca. 1335), 11–17, 19, 21, 25–29, 31–41, 43–49, 51, 55, 57–65, 67–82, 97, 99, 101–103, 105–106, 108–110, 114, 119, 122, 129, 133–135, 138, 139–142, 144–145, 147–152, 156–160, 161, 166–167, 169–175, 178, 181, 183, 185, 187, 188–191, 193–195, 199–203, 205–207, 222, 223, 230–231, 233, 240, 249, 267–273
Isaac ibn Khalfun (fl. end of 10th century), 194
Ishmael, 197
Jagel, Abraham ben Hananiah (1553–1623), 109, 218, 219
Jeduthun, 81
Jesus, 224, 225, 241, 257, 265
Jezebel, 60, 207
Joab, poet (fl. 14th century), 13, 17, 27, 66, 81

Joseph ben David ibn Yahya (1494–1534), 150
Joseph ben Meir Zabara (fl. second half of 12th century), 100
Joseph ha-Nahtom (fl. 14th century), 13
Jubal, 108, 186
Judah Alharizi (1170–1235), 15, 16, 65, 81, 194
Judah ben Moses Romano (b. 1292), 17
Judah ben Solomon (*see* Giuda di Salomone, Hebreo)
Judah de' Sommi Portaleone (*see* Leone Ebreo de' Sommi Portaleone)
Judah Halevi (1075–1141), 200
Judah Messer Leon (*see* Messer Leon, Judah)
Kalonymus ben Kalonymus (fl. 13th–14th century), 11, 12, 97
Keturah, 264
King Saul, 255
Kokhav, Abraham (*see* Stella, Abraham)
Korah, 60, 76, 157, 196
Laura, 85, 86, 92, 98
Leone Ebreo (1460/1470–1521/1535), 98, 104–105
Leone Ebreo de' Sommi Portaleone (ca. 1527–1592), 104, 107, 217, 269
Leone da Modena (*see* Modena, Leone da)
Levi, de Barrios Daniel (1635–1701), 117, 127–128, 208, 235
Levi, Isaac ben Moses Hezekiah (fl. 16th century), 223
Levi, Jacob (fl. 17th century), 112
Levi, Polako Abraham Jehiel (fl. 17th century), 184
Levi, Yozvil Jacob (fl. 17th century), 210, 222
Levi–Perotti, Giustina (fl. 14th century?), 99–100
Lilith, 207
Longo, Saadia ben Abraham (1520?– d. after 1597), 110–111, 219, 222–223, 252
Lope, Felix de Vega Carpio (1562–1635), 95
Lorenzo de' Medici (1449–1492), 88, 98, 202
Luna, 88
Luria, David Hayyim ben Simon (d. 1660), 180, 219, 229

Index of Names 291

Luria, Simon ben David (1633–d. after 1680), 229, 255
Luria, Simon ben Hayyim (d. 1624), 142
Lusitano da Pisa (*see* Coen, Samuel da Pisa)
Lustro, family, 209
Lustro, Solomon ben Isaac (1671–1750), 172, 180, 209, 217, 220, 251
Luzzatto, family, 209, 209
Luzzatto, Meir ben Abraham (fl. 17th century), 209
Luzzatto, Moses Hayyim ben Jacob (1707–1747), 35, 124, 143, 152, 245, 268
Luzzatto, Samuel David (1800–1865), 164, 193
Maestro Calo (*see* Kalonymus ben Kalonymus)
Malakhi ben Joseph (fl. 16th century), 240
Malipiero, Girolamo (16th century), 92
Manoah, 27
Marguerite of Savoy (d. 1574), 220, 240–241, 244
Marini, Sabato Vita Marini (1662–1748), 118, 209
Marino, Giambattista (1569–1625), 94, 95, 199
Maroni, D. (1810–1888), 263, 264
Mattiahu da Larippa (fl. 14th century), 98
Melkman, J., 117, 257, 263
Menahem (fl. 14th century), 14, 17, 77
Mendoza, Diego Hurtado de (1503–1575), 125
Merari, Moses (d. 1699), 178
Messer Leone David ben Judah (b. 1470), 98
Messer Leone, Judah ben Jehiel (d. after 1492), 97, 98
Michelangelo Buonarroti (1475–1564), 90, 98, 189, 202, 224, 238, 239
Milton, John (1608–1674), 164
Min ha–Levi'im, Isaac ben Jacob (1621–1670/1684), 209–210
Min ha–Tov, David Hayyim ben Judah Asael (*see* Del Bene, David Hayyim ben Judah Asael)
Min ha–Tov, Judah Asael ben Eliezer David (*see* Del Bene, Judah Asael ben Eliezer David)
Miriam, sister of Moses, 233

Modena, Elijah Mazal Tov ben Benjamin David Elisha (d. 1648), 140, 150, 178, 219
Modena, Ephraim ben Joab (fl. 15th century), 98
Modena, Judah Arieh ben Isaac (*see* Modena, Leone da)
Modena, Leone da (1571–1648), 105, 109, 113–114, 116, 118, 125, 136, 141, 151, 152, 162, 171, 176–177, 182, 207, 209, 212–219, 221, 224, 236, 242, 246
Modena, Mordechai ben Judah Arieh (1591–1618), 141, 163, 182
Morteira, Saul Levi ben Mordechai (1596–1660), 155, 243, 255
Moscato, Judah ben Joseph (1540?– no later than 1591), 104, 109, 179, 184, 220, 230, 231–234, 240
Moses ibn Ezra (1055?–1135?), 200
Muggia, Moses Levi ben Jacob (d. 1707), 216
Nahar, Isaac (1633–d. before 1680), 163, 172, 177, 182, 243
Najara, Israel ben Moses (1555–ca. 1625), 110, 125, 171, 216, 218
Nathan of Gaza (Abraham Nathan ben Elisha Hayyim Ashkenazi) (1643/4–1680), 225–226
Navagero, Andrea (1483–1529), 91
Nero, Emperor of Rome, 220
Nimrod, 184, 237, 257–259, 261–262
Og, King of Bashan, 27, 54
Oliveyra, Solomon ben David Israel (1635–ca. 1708), 117, 123, 125, 126, 138, 139, 143–144, 151, 156, 171, 182, 184, 187, 195, 196–198, 235–236, 251
Onkeneira, David ben Isaac (b. ca. 1550), 110, 136, 149, 151, 162, 171, 193, 204–206
Ortona, Abraham Hai ben David (d. 1664), 178, 219, 221
Orvieto, Nathan Jedidiah ben Eliezer (b. 1610), 129, 143, 180, 188, 231, 233, 238, 252
Pacifico, Abraham Isaac (fl. 17th–18th century), 183
Padua, Menasseh Hayyim (fl. 17th century), 139, 142, 143, 157, 160, 203, 204, 220 254–255,

Pagis, Dan (1931–1986), 37, 38, 61, 114
Penso de la Vega, Joseph ben Isaac (Felix) (1650–1692), 187
Peregrini, Giovanni (fl. 15th century), 99
Pesaro, Guiglielmo da (ca. 1420– ca. 1481), 97
Petrarca, Francesco (1304–1374), 10, 24–29, 34, 63, 85–88, 91, 98, 99, 102, 164, 191, 195, 200–202, 249, 267, 271, 272
Philip II of Spain (1527–1598), 216
Pilling, Christopher (fl. 20th century), 63
Pimentel, Abraham Cohen (d. after 1684), 126, 216
Plantavit, Jean de la Pause (fl. 17th century), 113, 215, 216, 221
Poliziano, Angelo (1454–1494), 202
Portaleone, Abraham ben David (1542–1612), 104
Portaleone, family, 98
Provenzal, Abraham ben David (fl. 16th century), 106
Pucci, Antonio (1310– ca. 1388), 125
Pulci, Luigi (1432–1484), 93
Quevedo, Francisco (*see* Francisco Gomez de Quevedo y Villegas)
Rabelais, Francois (1494? –ca. 1553), 93
Rathaus, A., 185, 199
Rebecca, 264
Recanati, Elijah (d. 1642), 129, 236
Remos, Moses (1406–1430), 98
Reuchlin, Johannes (1455–1522), 97
Rieti, Moses ben Isaac (1388– d. after 1460), 97–99, 101–102, 133, 268
Rieti, Moses ben Joab (d. after 1530), 41, 103, 105, 106–109, 111–112, 135, 138, 159, 160, 163, 171, 206–207, 212, 220–221, 240, 245, 246
Robert, King of Naples (1275–1343), 97
Romano, Judah (*see* Judah ben Moses Romano)
Rossena, Daniel, da (fl. 15th–16th century), 104
Roth, Cecil (1899–1970), 91, 100, 206, 209, 219
Rustico di Filippo (ca. 1240–ca. 1300), 10, 69
Samson, 199

Samuel Anav (ca. 1500–1560), 105
San Gimignano, Folgore da (fl. 13th–14th century), 10
Sannazaro, Jacopo (1458?–1530), 88, 91
Santillana, Inigo Lopez de Mendosa Marques de (1398–1458), 88, 271
Sappho (b. 612 B.C.E.), 91
Sarah, 259
Saraval, Judah Loeb (d. 1617), 242
Sasportas, Jacob ben Aaron (ca. 1610–1698), 117, 118, 127–128, 178, 217, 222, 251, 254
Sasportas, Samuel (fl. 17th century), 221
Scaligero, Giulio Cesare (1484–1558), 91
Schirmann Jefim (Hayyim) (1904–1981), 98, 113, 116, 207, 256
Schneur, Jacob ben Moses, 250
Scott, C., 130
Segrè, Abraham ben Judah (d. after 1740), 229, 255
Segrè, Jacob ben Isaac (d. after 1629), 105, 109, 153, 154, 180, 222, 231, 232, 241
Serafino Aquilano (1466–1500), 88, 89, 99
Sforno, Ovadia ben Jacob (ca. 1470–ca. 1550), 97, 123
Shabbetai Zevi (1626–1676), 116, 174, 178, 179, 195, 225–227, 232, 247
Shakespeare, William (1564–1616), 20, 92
Shalom, Jacob ben Abraham (fl. 17th century), 129
Shalom, Samuel (fl. 17th century), 129, 151, 243
Shem Tov ben Joseph Falaqera (fl. 13th century), 184
Shemaria ben Elijah of Crete (fl. 14th century), 97, 98
Siciliano, Judah (fl. 14th century), 12–14, 17
Sihon, 27, 54
Soave, M. (1820–1882), 99, 100, 183
Solomon ben Isaac da Perugia (fl. 14th century), 98
Solomon da Mantova (fl. 15th–16th century), 99
Solomon da Poggibonsi (fl. 16th century), 111, 156, 220
Sommo, Judah da (*see* Leone Ebreo de' Sommi Portaleone)

Index of Names

Spinoza, Barukh (1632–1677), 117
Stampa, Gaspara (1523–1554), 91, 199
Stella , 213
Stella, Abraham (fl. 17th century), 118, 120
Sylvester, Joshua (1563–1618), 265
Tansillo, Luigi (1510–1568), 91
Tasso, Torquato (1544–1595), 91, 102, 244
Tchernichowsky, Saul (1875–1943), 19–22, 127, 161, 255, 268
Tebaldeo, Antonio (1463–1537), 89
Terah, 76, 87, 257, 258, 76, 187, 257–258
Teresh 60, 157
Tesauro, Emanuele (1592–1675), 95
Todros Abulafia (ca. 1247–1306), 16, 200
Tomlinson, Charles, 20, 63–64
Tzarfati, David ben Aaron da Pina (1657– d. after 1693), 126, 171
Tzarfati, Joseph ben Samuel (d. 1527), 105–112, 135, 137, 138, 151, 157, 158, 160, 162, 212, 220, 221, 231, 232, 234
Tzemach, Abraham Levi (d. 1698), 172, 173
Usque, Samuel (fl. early 16th century), 105
Usque, Solomon (Salusque) ben Abraham (1530–1596), 105, 205–206

Uziel, Isaac ben Abraham (d. 1620), 110–111, 117, 188, 219, 222–223, 252
Valvasson, Yom Tov (Bondi) (1616–1690), 210
Virgin Mary, 70, 92
Vitale (Jehiel) da Pisa (d. 1492), 98, 99
Vitale Coen (*see* Coen, Benjamin)
Wilkins, E. H., 9, 23, 85, 89, 90
Yahalom, Yosef, 47
Yakhin, 194
Yarden, Dov, 44
Yozvil, Jacob (*see* Levi, Yozvil Jacob)
Zacuto, Moses ben Moṛdechai (b. after 1610–1697), 113, 114, 118, 122, 130, 137, 139, 143, 149, 151–157, 161, 182, 184, 187, 208, 210, 213–214, 220–222, 232, 236, 237, 242–243, 245–247, 250–265
Zandbank, S., 87
Zante, Abraham ben Sabbetai Ha-Cohen (1670–1729), 220, 251
Zarko, Joseph ben Judah (d. after 1457), 98
Zeresh, 60, 76, 207

General Index

Academy, 88, 95, 104, 113, 219, 235
acrostic, 99, 110, 116, 130, 145, 154, 213, 218, 219, 250
acutezza, 94, 225
Alexandria, 109, 140, 219
allegory, allegorical, 11, 28, 69, 74, 100, 183, 187–188, 193, 194, 209, 220, 237
Amsterdam, 111, 114, 117–118, 122, 127, 128, 219, 234, 252
anaphora, 21, 27, 167, 262
anonymous, 109, 110, 112, 116, 125, 129, 136, 140, 144, 149, 178, 182, 211, 217, 232, 235, 236, 238, 240, 243, 251
Arab, Arabic, 16, 97, 110, 268
Aramaic 241
Arcadia, Arcadian, 88, 95, 245
Arragon, 92
ars poetica—*see also*: critical theory, 19, 115, 144, 191
'Arugat ha-Bosem, 108, 123, 135, 136, 138, 141, 156, 165
Avignon, 28
ballata, 99, 242, 249
Baroque, 91–95, 114–116, 118, 120, 126, 128, 130, 163, 164, 167, 168, 173–176, 180, 183–184, 190, 191, 195, 197, 200–203, 207, 219, 224–225, 226, 230–231, 237, 243–247, 250, 254, 273
beginning the sonnet, 55–56, 60, 62, 63, 73, 166
Bible, the Torah, 11, 15, 19, 25, 46–49, 113, 152, 182, 215, 216, 224, 227, 233, 235, 243, 251, 262, 268
biblical phrases as rhymes, 46–49, 152–156
Bohemia, 90
Brescia, 106
burlesque, 10, 66, 74–77, 80–82, 92, 125, 198, 202, 207, 235, 272
caesura, 36–38, 124, 140–143, 144, 145
Camerino, 82, 150, 158
camouflage, 95, 146

canzone, 10, 22, 92, 99, 249
Canzoniere, 24, 25, 29, 34, 65, 85, 88, 90, 92, 98, 99, 206
caudato, 124, 125–126, 171, 251
comedy, 93, 104, 107, 217
conceit, *concetto*, 94, 115, 202, 212, 244
conceptismo, 95
conclusion and situation (development model), 178–179
confrontation and verdict (development model), 183–184
Constantinople, 110, 150, 193, 206
contrasti—*see also*: tenzone, 65, 66, 203, 251
corona, sonnet-corona, 130, 155, 243, 250, 255–256, 265
corpus, 10, 14, 23, 27, 40, 51, 69, 70, 77, 97, 103, 111–112, 115, 118–120, 127, 129, 131, 144, 150, 195, 250, 267
critical theory, 123–124, 131, 134–136, 138–139, 142, 147–151, 165, 169
criticism, 13, 19, 20, 27, 64, 66, 67, 81, 87, 94, 98, 99, 100, 102, 115, 116, 123, 126, 139, 148, 150, 151, 156, 165
Croatia, 90
culteranismo, 95
Cupid, 92, 178, 181, 195, 196–201, 238
Cyprus, 90
dactyl, 38
Damascus, 110
dance of death, 239
decorum, 94
delaying information—*see also*: suspense, 173–176, 179, 186, 228, 243
deteriorating situation, (development model) 184–186
developing the subject, 57–63, 169–191
    conclusion and situation, 178–179
    confrontation and verdict, 183–184
    deteriorating situation, 184–186
    improving situation, 186–187
    making contrasts, 182–183

problem and solution, 180–181
  reflection and situation , 176–177
  situation and conclusion, 177–178
  situation and reflection , 57–63,
    171–176
  solution and problem, 181–182
dictionary, 113, 117, 160, 148, 220, 271
Divine Comedy, 15, 29, 70, 90, 99
dolce stil nuovo, 10, 69, 70–78, 80, 85–86,
  195, 203, 204, 267, 273
drama, dramatic effect, 55, 56, 66, 71, 86,
  87, 89, 91, 94, 115, 139, 166, 174, 184,
  237, 242, 260, 262
dramatic monologue, 179, 184, 186, 226,
  231, 242
Egypt, 16, 73, 246
endecasillabo, 31–34, 36, 38, 43, 101, 124,
  130, 133–138, 140, 155, 268
England, English, 37, 63, 88, 90, 92, 130,
  164, 265
enjambement, 34–35, 142, 159
epistle—*see also*: *tenzone*, 210
epithalamium, wedding poem, 82, 144,
  183, 194, 207–214, 220, 232, 235, 243,
  251, 254, 274,
erotic, eroticism 11, 14, 75, 86, 90, 103,
  107, 193–194, 204, 212–213
Europe, 9, 11, 85, 87, 90–91, 164, 206, 268
Expulsion (from Spain), 105, 106, 233
Ferrara, 206, 233, 234, 240
Fez, 110, 111, 117, 222
Florence, 88, 105, 106, 112, 221
food, eating, gluttony, 82, 221, 224, 246
fourteen lines, 20–25, 51, 119, 123–126,
  165, 210
France, French, 9, 28, 43, 130, 140, 240
Freyhan, 209
Gaza, 225, 226
« golden poem », 19–20, 111, 123–127, 165,
  173, 191, 197, 214, 215, 254, 268
Gongorism, 95
Greece, Greek, 14, 89, 92, 97, 109, 167, 216
Haran, 265
ha-shalem (Hebrew meter), 33–35, 41, 134,
  137–138
Ḥatan Torah, 235, 251

Holland, Dutch—*see also*: Netherlands, 117
Humanism, Humanists, 85, 88, 89, 93, 98,
  245, 246, 273
humor, 45, 69, 125, 202, 217, 218, 246,
  247, 267, 268
Hungary, 90
iamb, iambic, 38, 130, 142–143
Il Fiore, 28–29, 65
illusion, 94, 95, 185–186, 191, 231
improving situation (development model),
  186–187
Italy, Italian, 9–13, 28, 31, 38, 44, 46,
  71, 78, 85, 88–92, 95, 98, 100–106,
  109, 112–116, 117, 138, 147, 162, 193,
  207–209, 212, 218, 223, 225–227, 240,
  267–269
Jerusalem, 121, 226, 232, 233
Kabbalah, kabbalistic, 109, 113, 114, 116,
  117, 193, 227, 265
Koran, 98
lament—*see also*: sonnet, 13, 66, 79, 89, 93,
  98, 115, 120, 124, 154, 157, 174, 215,
  220, 240–244, 250, 251, 255, 267
language, linguistic, 9, 19, 26, 29, 31, 36,
  44, 46, 72, 76, 89, 91, 102, 105, 106,
  112, 116, 128, 136, 138, 165, 180, 194,
  204, 207, 211, 222, 225, 237, 255, 267
Latin, 9, 21, 85, 89, 91, 97, 152, 208, 212,
  216, 241, 242
Lausitz, 209
Lisbon, 101
love, lovers, beloved, etc., 9, 11, 14, 28, 36,
  63–77, 80–82, 85–93, 103–105, 159,
  164, 180, 183–185, 187, 193–206, 272
Lucca, 213
macaronic poetry, 242
madrigal, 22
Maḥbarot Immanuel, Maḥbarot, 11–17, 25,
  29, 34, 35, 41, 64–66, 68, 71, 77, 80,
  102–103, 106, 110, 133, 134, 156, 159,
  160, 193, 194, 199, 200, 205, 256, 268,
  270, 271, 272
making contrasts (development model),
  182–183
Mantua, 99, 104, 109, 114, 116, 220, 227,
  229
maqama, 15, 16, 64, 65–68, 74, 81, 82, 102,
  206, 269

Marinism, 95
Marranos, *conversos*, 91, 105, 127
meditation, meditative , 244–245
meraviglia, 94–95, 128, 196
Messiah, 55, 61, 66, 81, 109, 157, 174, 175, 180, 186, 225, 226, 227, 233, 256
Meteq Sefatayim, 15, 19, 115, 123–124, 135, 136, 139–140, 147, 151, 156, 165, 170– 171, 193–194, 249
meter, metrical, 12, 21, 23, 24, 25, 31–41, 47, 98–102, 110, 114, 115, 122, 123, 133–146, 155–156, 159, 160, 164, 165, 170, 210, 222, 229, 251, 252, 254, 255, 256, 259, 260, 263, 268, 269, 270, 271
    feminine 11-syllable, 32–34, 101, 134–135, 137, 138, 253, 255
    masculine 10-syllable, 31, 101, 135–137, 149
    masculine 11-syllable, 137
    masculine 12-syllable, 33–35, 134, 136, 144
    mixed stress, 40–41, 135, 138–139
    quantitative, 31–38, 41, 99, 101, 133–136, 139, 143, 144, 155, 254–255, 269
    quantitative-syllabic, 32, 33–38, 101, 103, 133–136, 138, 142–146, 149, 251, 260
    "simple", 139–140, 143
    tonal, 38, 142–143
    with one *yated*, 137, 143
minnesinger, 9
minor poet, 88, 95, 116, 118, 274
morality, 78–79, 93, 98, 102, 107, 118, 159, 173, 179, 194, 231–232, 247, 272
mythology, mythological, 91, 195, 198, 199, 207, 217
Naples, 83, 97
Netherlands—*see also*: Holland, 90, 91, 118, 208
octave, *ottava*, 21–29, 39–40, 43, 48, 51, 53, 55, 57, 59–60, 120, 129, 144
octet, 63
oxymoron, 87
Padua, 97, 105, 112, 157, 219
Palermo, 9, 11
parody, 11, 74, 89, 92, 100, 181
pastorale, 88, 91, 117, 187, 245

penitential poems, 188, 231
Petrarchism, Petrarchist, 93, 94, 95, 98, 99, 100, 105, 117, 130, 164, 169, 191, 195–206, 212, 213, 238, 249, 252, 267, 271, 272, 273
philosophy, 11, 15, 67, 69, 72, 75, 79, 90, 91, 97, 98, 105, 106, 109, 113, 117, 170, 183, 185, 216, 219, 232, 237, 260
phonetic syllable, 31–34, 37, 38, 268
physician, physicians, etc., 11, 67, 81, 98, 100, 105, 106, 109, 125, 166, 178, 180, 186, 219, 240, 247, 252, 273
Plato, platonic, 15, 69, 72, 85–86, 88, 89, 91, 92, 104, 202, 231
play, drama, theater, 104, 106, 107, 113, 217, 256–265, 269
Poland, 90
polemic, 93, 100, 113, 115, 120, 223–230, 255, 274
politics, 69, 92, 93, 220, 273, 274
Portugal, Portuguese, 90, 105, 113, 114, 117, 120, 122, 206, 220, 245
praise of books, 108, 110, 117, 125, 158, 172, 177, 214–218
prayer, 98, 170, 181, 182, 211, 212, 215, 216, 218, 225, 230–239, 252
preface, 16, 59, 70, 80, 138, 193, 215, 217–218, 252, 255
printing, 98, 106, 215
problem and solution (development model), 180–181
Provençe, Provençal, 9, 10, 11, 12, 16, 34, 78, 200, 205, 257
Purim, 11, 113, 233
quantitative meter, 31–38, 41, 99, 101, 132–136, 139, 143, 144, 155, 254–255, 269
quantitative-syllabic meter , 32, 33–38, 101, 103, 133–136, 138, 142–146, 149, 251, 260
quartet—*see also*: quatrain, 46, 128
quatrain, 21–23, 26, 27, 51, 52–60, 120–121, 123, 128, 130–131, 138, 148, 155, 161–167, 175, 260
rabbi, rabbis, 14, 15, 76, 77, 102, 103, 104, 108, 109, 114, 118, 120, 128, 144, 158, 171, 182, 212, 214, 223–225, 227, 229, 233, 238, 250, 255–256, 273

General Index

realistic, "low" 14, 58, 69, 73–79, 80, 82, 92, 115, 171, 207, 221, 233–235, 267, 268
reflection and situation (developoment model), 176–177
religious rebuke—*see*: religious sonnet
Renaissance, 19, 76, 87, 94–97, 114, 184, 193, 200, 241, 246, 267, 273, 274
rhetoric, rhetorical, 10, 51, 55–56, 59, 60, 61, 63, 76, 89, 94, 97, 110, 131, 161, 166, 168, 170, 181, 229, 237, 242, 261, 269, 270, 271, 272
rhyme, rhyming, rhymeme, 12, 13, 14, 18–29, 43–49, 51, 52, 61, 64, 65, 73, 75, 89, 90, 92, 99, 100, 115, 119–131, 139, 144, 145, 147–160, 161, 164, 170, 222, 229, 249, 250, 251, 252, 253, 254, 259, 268, 269, 271, 272
    alternating, 46, 129, 150, 151, 170, 171
    biblical phrases, 46–49, 152–156
    borrowed 149, 150, 156–160, 270
    broken (*rima rotta*), 35
    classic: *see*: running rhyme
    discontinuous, 45, 153
    echo, 146, 152, 213
    feminine, 34, 44–46, 101, 127, 135, 147, 149, 150, 151, 155, 269
    homogenous, 43, 101, 148, 268
    masculine, 33, 34, 43–46, 101, 127, 135, 147–151, 155, 269
    morphological, 151, 156
    rich, 44–45, 103, 150–152, 262, 268
    running rhyme, 22, 28, 34, 66, 67, 111, 129, 148, 210, 268
    Spanish, classic: *see*: running rhyme
    stressed, 39, 43–44, 45, 49, 134, 147–148, 149, 150, 245, 268
    terminal, 43, 129
    word-rhymes, 27, 129, 152, 251
rhythm, 36–38, 41, 142–146
riddle—*see also*: sonnet-riddle, 113–114, 180, 209, 214, 219, 233, 235, 243, 265
rima rotta, 35
ritornello, *sonetto ritornello*, 124
Roman de la Rose, 28
romance, 104, 242
Rome, Roman, 11, 88, 92, 95, 224
Safed, 110, 193, 218
Salonika, 110, 193, 204, 205, 206, 222

satire, satirical, 11, 66, 81, 92, 93, 98, 115, 193, 198, 228
sestet, 21, 29, 39–40, 43, 46, 51, 52–57, 59, 61–63, 64, 87, 89, 90, 95, 119, 122, 124–131, 155, 161, 163, 164, 167, 171, 176, 177, 180, 181, 183, 185, 260, 261, 262, 263, 270
sestina narrativa, 249
sestina, 22
settenario, 124
Shabbatean movement, 113, 179, 225–227
Sicily, Sicilian, 9, 10, 12, 23, 24, 26, 69, 98
siglo de oro, 95
sirventes, 16
situation and conclusion (development model), 177–178
solution and problem (development model), 181
sonetos dobles, 127, 251, 254
sonettessa, 124
sonetti spirituali, 238–239
sonetto continuo, 27, 129
sonetto doppio, 127
sonetto minore, 137, 242
sonnet, sonnets
    about the sonnet, 19, 63, 170
    bilingual, 242
    blessing, 177, 194, 211, 215, 235, 251, 255
    boasting, 67, 69, 81, 107, 115, 262
    caudato—*see*: *caudato*
    challenge, 17, 65, 81, 110–11, 120, 229
    classic, 21–29, 89, 119–124, 191, 267, 269, 271
    complaint, 69, 79–80, 157, 186, 235, 244–246
    dialogue, 17, 58, 65, 115, 184, 194, 198, 203, 212, 241, 242, 251, 254
    double, *dobles*, 127, 251, 254
    English—*see*: England, English
    ethical, moral, 79, 201, 210, 230–239
    extended 24, 123–127
    for a bridegroom, 182, 203, 213, 251, 254
    for a new synagogue, 113, 252
    for circumcision, 229, 251
    for completing Talmudic study, 113, 236

for publishing a book, 125, 158, 171, 214–217, 273
for receiving a doctorate, 209, 219–220
for royal personages, 92, 183, 186, 220, 234, 241–242, 245
for Simhat Torah, 125, 126, 235, 251
for Sukkot, 236
for weddings—*see*: epithalamium, weddings
for Yom Kippur, 236
friendship 80, 93, 100, 108, 110, 111, 112, 115, 220–222, 272
"high," exalted—*see also*: dolce stil nuovo, 69, 74, 76, 82, 94, 166, 171, 207, 216, 268
lament, 120, 124, 154, 157, 215, 220, 240–244, 250, 251, 255
"low"—*see also*: realistic, "low", 69, 74–77, 81–82, 198, 207, 225, 235, 268
love—*see also*: love, 67, 70–77, 80, 81, 103, 115, 116, 117, 193–207, 272
meditative—*see*: meditation, meditative
occasional , 90, 93, 114, 116, 177, 204, 207, 208, 210–211, 213, 216, 219
one-syllable words, 129, 213
panegyric, 17, 69, 80, 113–115, 123, 128, 178, 180, 183, 211, 219, 222, 250
Petrarchist—*see*: Petrarchism, Petrarchist
poetic compliment, 214, 221, 222–223
polemic, 115–116, 120, 223–225, 228–230, 255, 274
preface, 215, 217–218, 252
read in reverse, 263, 265
rebuke, 12, 66, 69, 75, 78–79, 221, 237, 245, 247, 257, 258
recommendation, 108, 172, 215–217
religious, 66, 69, 73, 78–79, 102, 114, 204, 211, 230–239, 247, 252, 267, 273
riddle—*see also*: riddle, 114, 180, 209, 214, 219, 233, 235
ridicule, mockery, 27, 69, 74, 77, 81, 92, 178, 225, 246–247
spiritual—*see*: religious

tenzone, 17, 65, 80, 81, 99, 110–11, 112, 118, 120, 129, 222, 229–230, 252
triplets, 144, 243, 252
twins, 139, 235, 243, 251, 254
single stressed, 138, 165
sonnet sequence, 119, 139, 249–265
Spain, Spanish, 11, 15, 25, 28, 31, 34, 43, 66, 71, 73, 77, 79, 80, 81, 88, 90, 95, 98, 105, 106, 110, 111, 114, 125, 200, 206, 208, 216, 244, 268, 269, 270
strambotto, 89
suspense—*see also*: delaying information, 95, 173–174
Sweden, 183, 220, 245
symmetry, symmetrical, 21, 38, 39, 46, 53–54, 59, 95, 121, 129, 152, 161, 250, 262–265
syntax, syntactical, 36, 51–54, 55, 56, 60, 62, 63, 87, 91, 94, 121, 131, 138, 161–165, 166, 168, 173, 174, 191, 242, 259, 260–261, 271, 272
teacher, teachers, 10, 11, 13, 108, 113, 115, 119, 151, 156, 176, 194, 214, 227, 233, 240, 255, 274
tenzone, debate-poems, exchange of poems, 12–13, 65–66, 80, 99, 110–112, 118, 222, 223, 229–230, 252
tercet, 21, 23, 25, 51, 53, 54, 56, 61, 64, 123, 155, 161, 166, 175, 178, 206, 234, 259, 263
terza rima, 22, 99, 114, 133, 143, 188, 249, 252
terzina, 193
"threefold cord"—*see also*: terza rima, 249
tradition, 10, 11, 16, 25, 26, 27, 28, 29, 31, 35, 45, 47, 49, 70, 71, 79, 80, 81, 88–90, 92, 93, 103, 106, 109, 114, 119, 120, 139, 161, 172, 188, 189, 195, 201, 202, 229–230, 233, 234, 267–274
tragicomedy, 105
triplets—*see*: sonnet, triplets
trochaic, 38
troubadour, 9, 10, 70, 86, 93
Tuscany, 9, 23
twins—*see*: sonnet, twins
Venice, Venetian, 114, 206, 210
Vita Nuova, 24, 29, 64, 70, 73, 85, 88
Yad Ḥaruzim, 148–149, 156, 271